BOOKS BY PAULA DEEN

The Lady & Sons Savannah Country Cookbook
The Lady & Sons, Too!
The Lady & Sons Just Desserts
Paula Deen & Friends: Living It Up, Southern Style

Paula Deen's
Kitchen
Classics

Paula Deen's Kitchen Classics

THE LADY & SONS
SAVANNAH COUNTRY
COOKBOOK *and*
THE LADY & SONS, TOO!

Introduction by John Berendt

New Foreword by Paula Deen

RANDOM HOUSE / NEW YORK

Published in the United States by Random House,
an imprint of The Random House Publishing Group,
a division of Random House, Inc., New York.

RANDOM HOUSE and colophon are registered trademarks
of Random House, Inc.

The two works contained in this book were published individually
by Random House, an imprint of The Random House Publishing Group,
a division of Random House, Inc.

The Lady & Sons Savannah Country Cookbook was
previously published under the title: *Favorite Recipes
of the Lady & Her Friends.*

Library of Congress Cataloging-in-Publication Data
Deen, Paula H.
Paula Deen's kitchen classics : The lady & sons Savannah country cookbook
and The lady & sons, too! / introduction by John Berendt;
new foreword by Paula Deen.
p. cm.
Includes index.
ISBN 1-4000-6455-4
1. Cookery, American—Southern style. 2. Cookery—Georgia—Savannah.
3. Lady & Sons (Restaurant). I. Deen, Paula H. Lady & sons Savannah country
cookbook. 1998. II. Deen, Paula H. Lady & sons too! 2000. III. Title.
TX715.2.S68D48 2005
641.5975—dc22   2005048958

Printed in the United States of America on acid-free paper

www.atrandom.com

4 6 8 9 7 5

Book design by Victoria Wong

Contents

Perfect Marriage: A New Foreword
by Paula Deen / xi
Introduction by John Berendt / xxiii

The Lady & Sons
Savannah Country Cookbook

A Note from The Lady . . . / 5
. . . And a Tribute from Her Sons / 7

Appetizers / 9

HOT APPETIZERS   11
COLD APPETIZERS   18

Soups and Salads / 25

SOUPS   27
SALADS   34

Main Courses / 43

FISH AND SHELLFISH   47

MEAT   57

POULTRY   68

Vegetables and Side Dishes / 81

Breads / 101

Sauces, Dressings, and Preserves / 113

Desserts / 123

CAKES AND PIES   127

COOKIES AND BROWNIES   151

OTHER CONFECTIONS   159

Cooking Tips from The Lady / 167

Acknowledgments / 169

The Lady & Sons, Too!

The Journey Continues . . . / 175

Helpful Hints from The Lady / 181

Appetizers / 185

HOT APPETIZERS   187

COLD APPETIZERS   193

Soups and Salads / 203

SOUPS   205

SALADS   217

Main Courses / 231

FISH AND SHELLFISH   235

MEAT   248

POULTRY   270

Vegetables and Side Dishes / 281

Breads / 307

Sauces, Dressings, and Marinades / 323

And from My Peers . . . / 335

Desserts / 369

CAKES AND PIES   373

PUDDINGS AND CUSTARDS   401

COOKIES AND BROWNIES   409

Weights and Measures / 417
Acknowledgments / 419
Index / 421

Paula and Michael with friends and family

Perfect Marriage: A New Foreword

A marriage can be a beautiful thing, y'all, especially when the match is just perfect, and I am thrilled to share with you what I think are two perfect marriages.

In the latter part of 2004, I was surprised by a phone call from my friends at Random House that made me squeal with delight! They wanted to combine *The Lady & Sons Savannah Country Cookbook* and *The Lady & Sons, Too!* into one comprehensive, easy-to-use hardcover volume. Talk about a perfect marriage! I couldn't believe that these two fabulous books were gonna become one. Never again would I have to rack my brain to try and remember which recipe is in which book. The wonderful kicker to this new edition is they wanted me to share with y'all another perfect match.

Oh, my goodness, where to begin? My mind automatically flies back to that fateful day in the summer of 2000 when my dogs, Otis and Sam, decided to run away. Little did I know that what they were running to would change the rest of my life.

For those who have already heard my story I will try to make it brief, but I feel compelled to tell it here for those who have not. For three years prior to that fateful day, my business had been thriving but my personal life was empty and at a standstill. I needed help! I was living downtown in Savannah, Georgia, and when I wasn't working I was as miserable as any person could be. It may sound corny, but one day it dawned on me that I was going to have to turn this one over to God. Bear in mind that I had not one activity outside of work. I had no way to meet anybody. So as I lay in bed at night saying my prayers, I added one last sentence: "Lord, please send me a neighbor."

One day I got up and had a wild hair that I wanted to live on the water. I drove out to Wilmington Island and bought the first water-front place that I saw. I loaded up the truck and we moved to Bev-er-lee . . . Wilmington Island, that is. The animals and I all settled in to our wonderful new life on the water. Unfortunately, I couldn't help but notice that all my neighbors were married. I continued praying for a neighbor.

Before long, I was on hiatus from the restaurant life, devoting all of my time to the writing of my next cookbook. It was just great working from my new home. I think the dogs especially loved having me around. We had a regular little routine. I sat at the computer working, and Sam and Otis would come over and put their paws on my leg to let me know they needed to go outside. Our pattern never changed. The gated community we lived in was patterned after the row houses of downtown Savannah; we even had our own square with a beautiful fountain in the center. I always took Otis and Sam out the back door on the water side and then we always took a right and went into the square to do our business. Until that fateful day. Instead of a right, they took a left, pausing long enough to take one look back at me, and then all of a sudden they started running like the very devil himself was chasing them. There I was, running behind them, hollering, "Stop! Stop please, boys!" But by then nothing was going to stop them, so I continued to run after them. We shimmied around the big wall around our compound, trying not to fall into Turner's Creek. As we made our way around the wall, the boys spotted their object of interest: a big, imposing man who resembled Ernest Hemingway. As I continued to follow the dogs, I could see that "Ernest" was propped on his fence, talking on his cell phone. And do I have to tell y'all that Sam and Otis immediately started pooping all over his yard! After gushing apologies, and a couple lines of polite conversation, I scooped Sam and Otis up, and back home we went. I have to be perfectly honest, the thought did run through my head, Could this be my neighbor? Nah! Well, guess what happened two weeks later? The dogs did it again. And can you believe it, it was like "Ernest" had not moved from that position in two weeks. It was just like he was waiting there for us. So this time I wasn't nearly as intimidated; after all, I had made it out alive the first time. I soon found out that "Ernest" was really Michael Groover, a docking pilot who had lived in this spot his whole life. Those were really good signs—maybe he wasn't an ax murderer! With that in mind, I agreed to a date with him for the next day, and a strange feeling inside of me said that life would never be the same again. In the next three years my life went from unhealthy and unbalanced, with nothing but work and solitude, to healthy and balanced, with work, play, and a fabulous companion.

On Christmas morning in 2002, Michael took my breath away with the most romantic proposal a girl could ever hope for. Along with this proposal came the most beautiful engagement ring I had ever seen. I realized then that Michael had made a commitment to be committed. To me that was the most important thing, and so we settled nicely into engagement life.

Days turned into months, still with no talk of a date. Our life together continued to be easy and comfortable. And then, all of a sudden, one phone call changed everything. I was forced to set a date. Not by Michael but, believe it or not, by Food Network. They wanted to be with us and capture our special day forever on film. The executives at Food Network wanted to present a one-hour special titled "Paula Deen's Wedding." And they wanted it to air in June 2004! Before I could give them an answer, my first thoughts were naturally of Michael. If he were to have any reservations at all, then it would be a no-go. When I approached him with the idea, he smiled and said, "Well, yeah, I've never done anything like that before." I just squealed and threw my arms around him. I knew we were both headed for a day we would never forget.

It was now official; the date was set for March 6, 2004. Planning took off at a fast and furious pace. There was so much to do and so many decisions to make. Having it televised involved many more people than a normal wedding. Gordon Elliott, the producer of my TV show, and his crew at Follow Productions immediately went to work planning from their end. After days and days of coordination, we felt that everything was just perfect. But I have to tell y'all that two of my favorite scenes from the show were not planned, they just happened spontaneously. Upon Gordon's arrival, he decided to check in with me at the restaurant. I was just about to leave for a tanning excursion with some of my girlfriends from Albany who were in for the wedding. Hearing this,

Gordon hollered, "Paula, that *has* to be on film." So, dressed to the nines in our matching muumuus, with film crew in tow, we treated the girls to their first spray-on tan! The other unforgettable moment was one with my boys. I have two wonderful sons, Jamie and Bobby, and they crashed my bridal shower dressed in bridesmaids gowns. I have never laughed so hard in my life. In fact, I laughed so much, I was

Paula's surprise bridesmaids: Jamie and Bobby

Paula with Jamie and Bobby

afraid I would not have a voice to say my vows. As a mother, I don't think I've ever been prouder. Just to know that they had enough confidence to do something like that and were that comfortable in their own skin meant the world to me.

The wedding ceremony was held in the chapel at Bethesda, the oldest working orphanage in America. To say the church was breathtaking seems inadequate. I will never forget the moment I entered the chapel on my little brother Bubba's arm; my heart skipped a beat.

I felt like Cinderella as I walked down a canopy-covered aisle that was lush with white hydrangeas, French tulips, garden roses, elaeagnus, and English ivy, which had been designed by my personal assistant, Brandon Branch. The altar was dressed with European stock, southern smilax, our precious children, and my darling Captain Michael. The ceremony, performed by our good friend Judge Tom Edenfield, could not have been sweeter.

Now it was time for the party to begin. The reception was held at The Lady & Sons restaurant. Since the actual wedding ceremony was just for family, all six hundred of our guests were anxiously awaiting our arrival. We dined on shrimp and grits, miniature crab cakes, collard green wontons, mini handle sandwiches, sliced beef tenderloin, oysters on the half shell and other decadent Southern fare. Our first dance was to the sounds of Ben Tucker, a local Savannah favorite. As a special gift

Bubba escorts his sister, Paula, to the church.

from Gordon, Meghan Shanley, an up-and-coming country-western star, serenaded Michael and me with "Here," a beautiful song that was written especially for our wedding. After several hours of dancing and seeing old friends, we left the reception to begin our lives as husband and wife.

Michael and I recently celebrated our first anniversary, and I think I speak for both of us when I say our lives are finally complete. We've been blessed with wonderful children and family, and good jobs. Don't get me wrong though, not every day is a party, nor would I want it to be, because it's the challenging days that teach us life's greatest lessons. So here's the thought I'd like to leave with y'all: For ye of little faith, if it can happen to me, it can happen to you.

Best dishes and love,
From my kitchen to yours,

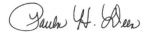

The newly married couple

Recipes from Paula and Michael's Wedding

Shrimp and Grits

SERVES 2

The shrimp and grits station at our wedding was by far the most appreciated by the guests. The grits were ladled into martini glasses and smothered with succulent wild Georgia shrimp in sauce. Our family and friends lapped up glass after glass!

2 cups water
¾ teaspoon salt
1 cup uncooked grits
2 tablespoons olive oil
½ cup diced tasso ham (see Note)
2 tablespoons diced leeks
2 tablespoons diced onion
2 tablespoons diced green bell
    peppers

20 shrimp, medium to large,
    peeled and deveined, with
    tails on
1 to 2 tablespoons white wine
1 cup heavy cream
Salt and pepper
Green onion tops, chopped

Bring the water and salt to a boil. Add the grits, and stir constantly for 1 minute. Cover and cook, stirring occasionally, until the grits are thick and creamy.

Heat the oil in a large skillet over medium-high heat. Add the tasso and sauté until crisp, about 7 to 9 minutes. Add the vegetables and sauté until the onions are translucent. Add the shrimp and sauté for 30 to 45 seconds, or until pink. Remove from the pan and set aside. Deglaze the pan with the white wine. Slowly add the cream and let reduce until thickened. Season with salt and pepper to taste.

Divide the grits between two serving plates. Line the edges of each plate with 10 shrimp. Pour the sauce over the grits. Garnish with green onion tops.

VARIATION: For a make-at-home dish, serve in individual-size bowls.

NOTE: Tasso, a Cajun ham, is often hard to find outside of Louisiana, but it's available at some specialty gourmet shops or by mail order. If not, you can substitute salt pork, pancetta, or prosciutto, but you will have to beef up your seasonings, as tasso is very flavorful.

Mini Handle Sandwiches

SERVES 6

With me being a Southern girl, there was no way I was going to get married without some fried chicken in the house! But how was I going to pull that off and still keep things elegant? In the kitchen at The Lady & Sons, we're constantly on the go and very rarely have time to stop and fix a plate, so we satisfy ourselves quickly and deliciously with what we call a handle sandwich. This is simply a piece of white bread wrapped around a chicken drumette, doused in Texas Pete Hot Sauce. The only thing left when you're done eating is the handle—get it? Well ,we feel like we came up with a new look for an old favorite. I hope y'all will try these and love 'em like we do.

*3 fresh leeks, washed and sliced
  lengthwise*
Peanut oil, for frying
*1 cup Texas Pete Hot Sauce (or
  your favorite brand) plus more
  for dipping*
1 egg, well beaten

6 chicken drumettes
House Seasoning (see page 325)
½ cup self-rising flour
*6 slices white bread, crust
  trimmed*
Mayonnaise, to taste

Prepare the leeks by blanching them in a pot of boiling water for 1 minute. Remove to an ice bath to chill. Set aside. When chilled, drain the leeks.

Place oil in a deep fryer or fill a large, heavy-bottomed pan no more than halfway with the oil; heat it to 350 degrees.

In a shallow bowl, stir together the hot sauce and egg. Season the chicken drumettes with House Seasoning and then dredge in the egg mixture. Coat the chicken in self-rising flour.

When the oil reaches 350 degrees, carefully place the chicken into the oil and deep-fry for 7 to 8 minutes. Remove the chicken with tongs and drain on paper towels. Spread each slice of bread with mayonnaise and place a drumette diagonally in the center. Fold the bread around the drumette and tie with a leek strip. Have extra hot sauce for dipping.

Collard Green Wontons

SERVES 35

Well, here we go again. Leave it to me to dress up a collard green! I put these bad boys inside a beautifully browned blanket, and lo and behold, it was the number one hand-passed appetizer at our reception. Who would have ever thought that collard greens and cream cheese could taste so good!

¼ pound meat (ham hocks, smoked turkey wings, or smoked neck bones)
½ tablespoon House Seasoning (see page 325)
½ tablespoon seasoned salt (see page 180)

½ tablespoon Texas Pete Hot Sauce (or your favorite brand)
½ large bunch collard greens
4 tablespoons butter
32 ounces cream cheese, at room temperature
70 to 80 wonton wrappers

In a large pot, bring 1½ quarts water to a boil and add the meat, House Seasoning, seasoned salt, and hot sauce. Reduce the heat to medium and cook for 1 hour. In the meantime, wash the collard greens thoroughly: remove the thick stem that runs down the center of the greens by holding the leaf in one hand while stripping it down with the other hand. Stack 6 to 8 leaves on top of one another, then roll up and slice into ½- to 1-inch-thick slices. Place the greens into the pot with the cooked meat. Stir in the butter. Cook for 45 to 60 minutes, stirring occasionally. When done, taste and adjust seasoning.

Mix the collard greens and cream cheese in a mixing bowl.

Place 1 tablespoon of the mixture in the center of each wrapper and fold into a triangle. Place the assembled wontons in peanut oil heated to 350 degrees for 2 or 3 minutes, or until golden brown. Drain on paper towels. Best if served immediately.

Banana Nut Cake

SERVES 18–20

Hands down, this is Michael's favorite cake. It's a sweet, scrumptious memory of the days when his mother, Carmel, would bake it for him. In the Groover household, it was a family tradition that on your birthday you chose your favorite cake. Michael remembers this cake becoming his favorite at age five, and his request has not changed to this day. So naturally this just had to be his groom's cake.

CAKE

Butter, for greasing pans
3 cups all-purpose flour, plus more
    for dusting pans
2 cups sugar
1 teaspoon baking soda
1 teaspoon ground cinnamon

½ teaspoon salt
3 eggs, beaten
¾ cup vegetable oil
4 large ripe bananas, mashed
1 cup chopped pecans
1½ teaspoons vanilla extract

FROSTING

8 ounces cream cheese, at room
    temperature
½ cup (1 stick) butter, at room
    temperature

1 pound confectioners' sugar,
    sifted
1 teaspoon vanilla extract
½ cup chopped pecans

Butter and flour three 9-inch round cake pans; set aside. Preheat oven to 350 degrees.

In a mixing bowl, stir together the flour, sugar, baking soda, cinnamon, and salt. Add the eggs and oil and stir just until the dry ingredients are moistened; do not beat. Stir in the banana, pecans, and vanilla. Divide the batter among the prepared pans and bake for 23 to 28 minutes, or until a wooden pick inserted in the center comes out clean. Cool the cake layers in the pans for 10 minutes, and then turn them out onto a rack to cool completely. While the cake cools, make the frosting.

In a bowl, blend together the cream cheese and butter. Gradually add the confectioners' sugar and beat until light and fluffy. Beat in the vanilla. Stir in the pecans, or reserve them to sprinkle over the frosted cake. Fill and frost the cake when it is completely cool.

NOTE: If you are interested in using this recipe for a wedding cake, consult a professional baker, as quantities and bake time will vary based on the number of people you plan to feed.

Almond Sour Cream Cake

SERVES 16–18

A group of us here laughingly call Molly Stone "the Cake Bitch of Savannah, Georgia"! This girl knows what she's doing; her wedding cakes are incredibly divine. They are moist and bursting with flavor. The only thing bigger and better than her cake is her personality. I love you, Molly.

CAKE

1 cup (2 sticks) butter, plus more
   for greasing pan
3 cups sugar
1 cup sour cream
3 cups all-purpose flour, plus more
   for dusting pan

½ teaspoon baking soda
6 eggs
½ teaspoon pure orange extract
½ teaspoon pure almond extract

FROSTING

¾ cup butter (1½ sticks), at room
   temperature

3 to 4 cups confectioners' sugar
1½ teaspoons pure almond extract

Preheat oven to 325 degrees. Butter and flour a tube pan and set aside.

In the bowl of an electric mixer, cream the butter and sugar together and then add the sour cream. Sift the flour and baking soda together and add to the creamed mixture, alternating with eggs, one at a time, beating after each addition. Add the extracts and stir to combine. Pour into the prepared tube pan and bake for 1 hour and 20 minutes. Cool the cake in its pan for about 10 minutes and then unmold and cool completely on a wire rack. Frost the cake when it has completely cooled.

With an electric mixer, cream the butter in a large mixing bowl. Slowly beat in the sugar for about 2 minutes, until smooth and creamy and sweetened to your liking. Add the almond extract and stir to blend. Allow to cool fully, then frost the cake. If you are not using the frosting immediately, cover it and store in the refrigerator. Bring the frosting to room temperature just prior to using.

NOTE: This is the basic recipe for a sour cream pound cake with almond buttercream frosting. To modify this recipe for a larger cake, consult a professional baker for quantities and bake time.

Michael and Paula with their Almond Sour Cream wedding cake

INTRODUCTION BY

John Berendt

AUTHOR OF

Midnight in the Garden of Good and Evil

Friends planning a trip to Savannah usually ask me for travel tips, and I'm always happy to oblige. Naturally, I suggest a walk through the city's twenty-two sumptuous garden squares and a visit to a few of the museum houses. I tell them not to leave Savannah without taking a short excursion to Bonaventure Cemetery, surely one of the most peaceful sanctuaries on earth, with its avenues of live oaks hung with Spanish moss and its romantic statuary set among flowering shrubs and gentle breezes from the meandering inland waterway.

Then I tell them about food.

I tick off a few of my favorite Savannah eating establishments: Williams Seafood, where locals line up for shrimp, oysters, and crabs that are hauled off fishing boats at a dock a mere stone's throw from the table; Johnny Harris, a tradition for special family occasions since the twenties and known for its barbecued lamb sandwiches; Mrs. Wilkes's, one of America's true culinary landmarks, which lists itself in the phone book simply as "Wilkes L H Mrs, 107 W Jones St," and where lunch is still served at big tables for ten in the old boardinghouse style.

I also tell Savannah-bound friends that if they want a short course in the meaning of Southern cooking—the flavors, the ambience, indeed the very *heart* of Southern cooking—they should drop in at The Lady & Sons. The Lady is a hugely popular downtown eatery that serves the whole gamut of Southern dishes and starts serving you steaming, fresh-out-of-the-oven cheese biscuits while you're waiting on line for a table and then keeps a steady flow coming to you all during your meal.

Paula Deen is the gentle force behind the restaurant and the cookbook you now hold in your hands. Lucky you.

Southern cooking is a hand-me-down art, and that's how Paula Deen came into it. Her grandfather drove a dry-cleaning truck, but he knew all along he had a jewel in Paula's grandmother, because she was a fantastic cook. So he bought her a hot-dog stand in Hapeville, Georgia, in the early forties, and put her to work, with Paula's mother waiting on tables. They did so well they moved up to country steak and creamed potatoes. "The reason I can remember they served steak," says Paula, "is because one day a customer got fresh with my mother, and she slapped him with a piece of steak."

Paula spent whole days in the kitchen with her grandmother, learning the techniques as well as the intention of Southern food. "You have to understand," she says, "Southern cooking comes from within. We show our love for someone through the kitchen, through food. We bake a pie or a cake as a welcoming gift or as a show of support in tough times. Southern cooking is comfort food. It's flavorful and filling, and it makes you feel good."

Authentic Southern food is not about pretension. "It does not require a sophisticated palate," says Paula. "It's poor-man's food. Kids don't have to acquire a taste for it. They love it from the start."

And Southern food is distinctly Southern. "Nothing's flown in," she says. "It's all home-grown. There's no quail, no pheasant, no filet mignon, no foie gras, no truffles, no snails, no caviar, and no crêpes. Southern dishes do not require split-second timing. They do not 'fall' in the oven. We don't go in for ornate presentation, either, or sculpted desserts. We just heap food on the plate."

Paula knows that some aspects of Southern cooking are disdained by outsiders. "There are some things we do that would make a French chef sick," she says. "Like, for instance, the way we make red-eye gravy—country ham cooked in a skillet with water and strong coffee. But let the French chef taste it, and he'll get over being sick real quick!"

Southern cooks are proud of their cuisine, and they are not hesitant to tell you that, stacked up against any other cookery, it comes out on top. As Paula says, with a wink to me, "I've never heard anybody say,

'Gee, golly, I can't wait to get up to New York so I can have some of that good Yankee food.' "

The staples of classic Southern food, as laid out in this book, are butter, sugar, salt, pepper, hot sauce, vinegar, ham hocks, and, to lay it on the line: fat. "We can make concessions for the health-conscious," says Paula, "by doing things like using smoked turkey wings instead of ham hocks. But a better approach for weight watchers is to look at Southern food as a treat and just go with it."

Southern food is tied in with the Southern experience, which is a heady combination of good times and bad. Paula has had her share of both. She lived the life of a Southern princess for her first nineteen years—happy, pampered, and carefree. Then her father dropped dead, and four years later her mother died of a broken heart and bone cancer. Paula had to go to work. She was head teller at a bank for a while until a bank robber put a gun to her head and she decided she wasn't cut out for banking.

With her marriage coming to an end and creditors closing in some years ago, Paula got into what she knew best: cooking. She took two hundred dollars and opened a service with her two sons and their girlfriends, wheeling hot lunches through office buildings in downtown Savannah. They called it the Bag Lady. Paula got up every morning at five o'clock and made 250 meals in her own kitchen—grilled chicken, lasagna, trio sandwiches, and custards, banana pudding, and fruit salad for dessert. "If the business hadn't made it, I was looking the Salvation Army square in the face," she says. But it did make it, and Paula's customers insisted she open a restaurant, which she did.

"The day we opened," she recalls, "I was overdrawn at two banks, not just one. I didn't even have enough money for the parking meter. My banker called, and I said to him, 'Just let me open my doors.' He did, and the people came flooding in."

And they still do. Businessmen, housewives, lawyers, students, tourists, and celebrities. The mayor is a regular customer. Paula has had to extend her hours to accommodate all the business.

Ms. Deen is an irresistible example of that extraordinary phenomenon of Southern womanhood, the steel magnolia. She is always appealing and gracious but possessed of an unfailing survival instinct a necessary character trait for a Southern cook to make it.

And make it, she has. If you go to Savannah, you can understand t reason for it by sampling her famous cheese biscuits, her hoe cakes, h sensational gooey butter cakes, and all the rest. However, if you car wait till then, you don't have to. Just follow the Lady's instructions the following pages and you'll know soon enough what all the fuss about.

JOHN BERENI
New York
January 199

The Lady
& Sons
Savannah
Country
Cookbook

The most devoted supporters and confidants of my adult life have been my Aunt Peggy and Uncle George Ort. It is to Aunt Peggy and in fond memory of my Uncle George that this book is most affectionately dedicated.

A Note from The Lady . . .

Growing up in Albany, Georgia, I used to spend hours at a time in my Grandmother Paul's kitchen at River Bend. Grandmother Paul was a wonderful cook, and she handed down her love of cooking to her three daughters. They in turn passed this love on to me. My life has been surrounded by the many wonderful cooks in my family, and I have been blessed by them through their stories and their food.

In 1989, newly divorced and unemployed, I was living in Savannah and was determined to succeed. Using the cooking skills I learned as a child, I invested my last two hundred dollars in a catering business that I started with my two sons, Jamie and Bobby. I had decided to follow in my grandmother's footsteps.

After a few years of local catering, high demand helped my small-scale business evolve into The Lady & Sons Restaurant. My sons and I function as owners, proprietors, chefs, and hosts. We and our staff are dedicated to providing the finest home-cooked meals in an atmosphere of true Southern hospitality.

I hope my story will inspire others to accept the challenges that life offers. My experience proves that whenever one door closes, another one always opens. I hope you will enjoy these favorite recipes of mine. They have been created with love, sweat, and tears.

There are many people in our lives who deserve a great big thank you for helping us produce this book. They include our outstanding staff, the many wonderful customers who have passed through our restaurant doors, the small businesses in the area who have helped support us, and, of course, our dear family and friends.

If you are lucky enough to be in the Savannah area, we would love for you to stop by the restaurant. Please visit us at:

The Lady & Sons
102 West Congress Street
Savannah, GA 31401
(912) 233-2600

If you can't get to Savannah to sample the wonderful food at The Lady & Sons, you can still taste the dishes at home. The recipes in this book that we serve at our restaurant are followed by:

❧ ❧ ❧ *The Lady & Sons*

Additional copies of this book can be ordered by calling **(800) 793-BOOK.**

. . . And a Tribute from Her Sons

Our mother, Paula H. Deen, is a true symbol of strength and perseverance. This book is a product of her twenty-hour workdays. It is her "third child," and she has nourished and cherished this book just as she has cared for her two sons, in a way that only a mother could do. This book spans many years and many jobs; from homemaker to bank teller to caterer to restaurant owner, our mom's dreams for the future have come true.

Thanks to our mother, these are now the best days of our lives. We have more pride in this lady than can possibly be imagined. She has our undying adoration and our commitment to follow in her direction. Mother is a remarkable lady. We hope you enjoy her wonderful cookbook.

We love you, Mom.

Jamie and Bobby

Appetizers

HOT APPETIZERS

Pecan-Stuffed Dates

Georgia Sugared Peanuts

Hot Asparagus Dip

Hot Crab Canapé

Mini Onion Quiches

Sausage Balls

Cheese-Stuffed Mushrooms

Sesame Chicken Strips

Oysters in the Patty Shell

Brie en Croûte #1

Brie en Croûte #2

South of the Border Mason-Dixon Dip

Bacon Wraps

Artichoke and Spinach Dip

COLD APPETIZERS

Shrimp Butter

Italian Roasted Red Peppers

Southwestern Dip

Pickled Okra Sandwiches

Herbed Cream Cheese Round

Quick Guacamole-Spinach Dip

Garlic Cheese Spread

Creamy Roquefort Dip

Strawberry Cheese Ring

Black Bean Salsa

Bobby's Pimento Cheese

Pecan-Stuffed Dates

YIELDS APPROXIMATELY 30

One 8-ounce box pitted dates   *10 to 12 slices bacon*
30 pecan halves

Preheat oven to 400 degrees. Stuff each date with a pecan half. Cut each slice of bacon into 3 pieces. Wrap 1 piece around each stuffed date and secure with a toothpick. Bake until bacon is crisp, 12 to 15 minutes. Drain and serve.

Georgia Sugared Peanuts

YIELDS 2 CUPS

1 cup sugar   *2 cups raw shelled peanuts, skins on*
½ cup water   *¼ teaspoon salt*

Preheat oven to 300 degrees. Dissolve sugar and salt in water in saucepan over medium heat. Add peanuts. Continue to cook, stirring frequently, until peanuts are completely sugared (coated and no syrup left). Pour onto ungreased cookie sheet, spreading so that peanuts are separated as much as possible. Bake for approximately 30 minutes, stirring at 5-minute intervals. Let cool and serve.

Hot Asparagus Dip

YIELDS 3 TO 4 CUPS

Two 12-ounce cans asparagus
   spears
1½ cups mayonnaise
1½ cups freshly grated Parmesan
   cheese, plus additional for
   sprinkling

2 cloves garlic, chopped
Salt and pepper to taste

Preheat oven to 350 degrees. Drain and chop asparagus. Add to remaining ingredients and mix; pour into baking dish. Bake for 20 to 25 minutes until slightly brown and bubbly. Remove from oven and sprinkle with additional Parmesan cheese. Serve hot with lightly toasted French bread rounds.

Hot Crab Canapé

SERVES 6 TO 8

One 8-ounce package cream
   cheese, softened
1 tablespoon milk
⅓ cup mayonnaise
1½ teaspoons horseradish

8 ounces crabmeat, picked free of
   shell
2 tablespoons chopped onion
¼ teaspoon garlic salt

Preheat oven to 350 degrees. With an electric mixer, mix all ingredients in a bowl. Place mixture in a shallow ovenproof casserole dish. Bake for 15 to 20 minutes or microwave until warm (2 to 3 minutes). Serve with crackers. This may be frozen for future use.

Mini Onion Quiches

YIELDS 2 DOZEN

¾ *cup crushed saltine crackers*
4 *tablespoons (½ stick) butter,*
  melted
1 *cup chopped green onion with*
  tops
2 *tablespoons butter*

2 *eggs*
1 *cup milk*
½ *teaspoon salt*
¼ *teaspoon pepper*
1 *cup grated Swiss cheese*

Preheat oven to 300 degrees. Combine cracker crumbs and melted butter. Divide crumbs among mini muffin tins that have been sprayed with no-stick cooking spray. Sauté onion for 10 minutes in 2 tablespoons butter. Cool, then divide evenly on top of cracker crumbs. Beat eggs; add milk, salt, pepper, and Swiss cheese. Pour by spoonfuls on top of onion in tins. Do not fill to top, as they will run over. Bake until set, about 15 to 20 minutes. Do not overbake. May be stored in refrigerator or freezer. Warm in oven before serving.

Sausage Balls

YIELDS APPROXIMATELY 3 DOZEN

3 *cups Bisquick*
2 *cups grated Cheddar cheese*

1 *pound fresh ground sausage*
  (hot or mild)

Preheat oven to 350 degrees. Mix all ingredients together. If not moist enough, add a little water. Form mixture into 1-inch balls. Bake for 15 minutes. Drain on paper towels. Serve warm. This freezes well before or after baking.

Cheese-Stuffed Mushrooms

YIELDS 2 DOZEN

24 fresh mushrooms, stems removed
One 10-ounce package frozen
   chopped spinach
2 ounces cream cheese
4 ounces feta cheese

½ cup finely chopped green onion
   with tops
Salt to taste
1 cup grated Parmesan cheese

Preheat oven to 350 degrees. Wipe mushroom caps clean with a damp paper towel. Thaw spinach in colander; squeeze out as much moisture as possible. In mixing bowl, combine all ingredients except mushrooms and Parmesan cheese. Mix well. Fill mushroom caps with mixture and place on a cookie sheet. Sprinkle Parmesan cheese on top. Bake for 15 to 20 minutes. Serve warm.

Sesame Chicken Strips

SERVES 8 TO 10

6 skinless boneless chicken breast
   halves
1 cup sour cream
1 tablespoon lemon juice, or juice
   of ½ lemon
2 teaspoons celery salt
2 teaspoons Worcestershire sauce

½ teaspoon salt
¼ teaspoon pepper
2 cloves garlic, minced
1 cup dry bread crumbs
⅓ cup sesame seeds
4 tablespoons (½ stick) butter,
   melted

Lightly grease a 15 × 10-inch jelly roll pan. Cut chicken crosswise into ½-inch strips. In a large bowl, combine sour cream, lemon juice, celery salt, Worcestershire sauce, salt, pepper, and garlic. Mix well. Add chicken to mixture, coat well, and cover. Refrigerate at least 8 hours or overnight. Preheat oven to 350 degrees. In medium bowl, combine bread crumbs and sesame seeds. Remove chicken strips from sour cream mixture. Roll in crumb mixture, coating evenly. Arrange in single layer in prepared pan. Spoon butter evenly over chicken. Bake for 40 to 45 minutes or until chicken is tender and golden brown. Serve with honey mustard.

Oysters in the Patty Shell

YIELDS 30 PIECES

½ pound mushrooms, chopped
3 tablespoons butter
3 tablespoons all-purpose flour
1 cup milk
½ teaspoon salt
¼ teaspoon celery salt
Pepper to taste

1 teaspoon lemon juice
1 cup shelled fresh oysters, drained
 and chopped
Eight 1-ounce prebaked mini-
 piecrusts or patty shells (approx-
 imately 3 inches in size)
Fresh parsley, for garnish

Sauté mushrooms in butter until tender. Blend in flour and cook until bubbly. Gradually add milk; cook until smooth and thickened, stirring constantly. Add salt, celery salt, pepper, lemon juice, and oysters. Cook over medium-low heat until oysters start to curl up (about 5 minutes), stirring occasionally. Serve in mini-piecrusts or patty shells. If desired, garnish with parsley.

Brie en Croûte #1

SERVES 8

1 sheet frozen puff pastry (package
 comes with 2 sheets)
1 tablespoon butter
½ cup chopped walnuts

⅛ teaspoon ground cinnamon
1 small wheel of Brie (8 ounces)
¼ cup brown sugar
1 egg, beaten

Preheat oven to 375 degrees. Defrost one sheet of puff pastry for approximately 15 to 20 minutes and unfold (place remaining sheet in freezer for later use). Melt butter in a saucepan over medium heat. Sauté walnuts in butter until golden brown, approximately 5 minutes.

Stir in cinnamon, coating nuts well. Place mixture on top of wheel of Brie. Sprinkle brown sugar over the mixture. Carefully place pastry sheet over wheel of Brie (make sure Brie is centered). Gently pick Brie up with pastry hanging over edge and fold the pastry under Brie. Trim excess pastry with scissors so Brie lies flat, and seal all edges to prevent leakage. To give an extra-special look to the Brie, I like to cut the left-over pastry into heart shapes, flowers, etc., and place them onto the pastry on top of the Brie. Brush beaten egg over top and sides of Brie, then place cutouts on top (the egg will secure them); brush cutouts with egg. Place wrapped Brie on an ungreased cookie sheet and bake for 20 minutes until pastry is golden brown. Serve with top-quality crackers.

Brie en Croûte #2

SERVES 8

1 sheet frozen puff pastry (package comes with 2 sheets)
1 tablespoon butter
¼ cup chopped pecans or walnuts

1 small wheel of Brie (8 ounces)
½ cup raspberry jam
2 eggs, beaten

Preheat oven to 375 degrees. Defrost one sheet of puff pastry for approximately 15 to 20 minutes and unfold (place remaining sheet in freezer for later use). Melt butter in a saucepan over medium heat. Sauté nuts in butter until golden brown, approximately 5 minutes. Place nuts on top of Brie and spread jam on top of nuts. Gently roll pastry with a rolling pin to increase the size of the sheet 1 to 2 inches in each direction. Brush both sides of the sheet with beaten egg. Center the wheel of Brie on top of the pastry sheet. Bring all four corners of the sheet together above Brie and twist slightly to form a "bundle." Tie gathered pastry with kitchen/cooking string (tie string in the form of a bow). Work with pastry until you are satisfied with the "bundle" shape. Place "bundle" on an ungreased cookie sheet and bake for 20 to 25 minutes until pastry is golden brown. Serve with top-quality crackers.

South of the Border Mason-Dixon Dip

YIELDS 4 TO 5 CUPS

One 15-ounce can chili
Two 8-ounce packages cream
cheese, softened

2 cups grated sharp Cheddar
cheese
3 green onion tops, chopped

Preheat oven to 350 degrees. Heat chili in a saucepan over medium heat for 5 minutes (or microwave for 2 to 3 minutes). Press softened cream cheese into the bottom of a 1½-quart casserole dish. Pour heated chili over cream cheese and sprinkle grated cheese over top. Bake for approximately 20 minutes, until mixture is hot and bubbly. Remove from oven and top with chopped green onion tops. Serve immediately with tortilla chips.

Bacon Wraps

YIELDS 2 DOZEN

1 cup grated Parmesan cheese
2 teaspoons garlic salt or powder
12 slices bacon

Twenty-four 4½-inch-long sesame
breadsticks (one package)

Preheat oven to 350 degrees. Mix Parmesan cheese with garlic salt or powder in a shallow bowl and set aside. Cut the slices of bacon in half so that each is approximately 5 inches long. Wrap one piece of bacon around a breadstick, starting at one end of breadstick and finishing at other end (I find that bacon adheres to sesame breadsticks better than plain breadsticks). Place on a cookie sheet lined with parchment paper. Repeat this process, using all of breadsticks. Bake for approximately 15 minutes, or until bacon is browned. Remove from cookie sheet and immediately roll bacon wraps in cheese mixture. Let cool and serve at room temperature.

Artichoke and Spinach Dip

YIELDS 3 CUPS

One half of a 10-ounce package
   frozen chopped spinach, thawed
Two 13¾-ounce cans artichoke
   hearts, drained and mashed

½ cup mayonnaise
½ cup sour cream
1½ cups grated Parmesan cheese
Salt and pepper to taste

Preheat oven to 350 degrees. Drain all water from spinach. Mix all ingredients and bake in greased casserole for 30 to 40 minutes. Serve with butter crackers or bagel chips.   ❦ ❦ ❦   **The Lady & Sons**

Shrimp Butter

YIELDS APPROXIMATELY 4 CUPS

½ pound (2 sticks) butter, at room
   temperature
1 tablespoon sherry
½ teaspoon lemon zest
1 teaspoon House Seasoning
   (see page 325)
Juice of ½ lemon

Cayenne pepper to taste
Two 3-ounce packages cream
   cheese, softened
2 tablespoons chopped onion
1 pound shrimp, shelled, deveined,
   and cooked

Add all ingredients except shrimp to a food processor. Process until well mixed. Drop in shrimp and process until either pureed or chopped to desired consistency. (This recipe can be pureed to the consistency of butter or left with chunky pieces of shrimp.) Serve on crackers as an appetizer. It is also wonderful served on top of hot grits. (If served with grits, sprinkle grated Cheddar cheese over grits and shrimp butter.)

Italian Roasted Red Peppers

SERVES 8

4 large red bell peppers
1 cup olive oil
2 to 3 cloves garlic, minced
1 tablespoon dried basil, or ½
*   bunch fresh snipped, cleaned*
*   basil*

2 teaspoons salt, or to taste
Pinch of sugar
Ground black pepper to taste

Preheat oven to 450 degrees. Wash red bell peppers and bake until skin is charred; turn periodically to ensure that the skin blackens on all sides. Remove peppers from oven and put into a paper sack. Fold the top of the sack over. Allow peppers to steam in the sack for 30 minutes to 1 hour. Peel the skin from the peppers; pull the peppers into strips, allowing the juice to drip into the bowl where the peppers will go. Toss the peppers with olive oil, minced garlic, basil, salt, sugar, and pepper. Let stand for several hours. Serve peppers on slices of Italian bread or as a side dish.

Southwestern Dip

YIELDS 3 TO 4 CUPS

One 16-ounce can refried beans
One 8-ounce package cream cheese
2 large tomatoes, diced
One half of a 1½-ounce package of
*   dried taco seasoning*
One 6-ounce carton prepared
*   avocado dip (see Note next*
*   page)*

One 4-ounce can chopped ripe
*   olives*
1 small onion, chopped
One 4½-ounce can chopped green
*   chilies*

Layer ingredients in a 9 × 13-inch dish in the order given. Chill for several hours. Serve with tortilla chips.

NOTE: In place of the prepared mix, you may substitute 2 medium ripe avocados, mashed and mixed with 2 tablespoons lemon juice, ½ teaspoon salt, and ¼ teaspoon black pepper.

Pickled Okra Sandwiches

YIELDS 20 TO 24 WHOLE SANDWICHES

One 24-ounce loaf sliced white bread
One 8-ounce package cream cheese, softened

One 16-ounce jar pickled okra
1 cup finely chopped fresh parsley

Remove crusts from bread. With a rolling pin, roll slices very thin. Coat each slice with cream cheese and place an okra spear in center; roll up. Spread a light coat of cream cheese on each rolled-up sandwich (I like to use my fingers to spread the cream cheese). Roll sandwich in finely chopped parsley. Cut in half, if desired.

Herbed Cream Cheese Round

YIELDS 4 CUPS

Two 8-ounce packages cream cheese, softened
1 cup chopped fresh parsley
¾ cup grated Parmesan cheese
¼ cup chopped pine nuts
2 cloves garlic, crushed

1 tablespoon dried basil
¼ teaspoon salt
⅛ teaspoon pepper
⅓ cup olive oil
2 tablespoons butter, melted
2 tablespoons boiling water

Shape cream cheese into a 5½-inch circle on serving dish, making a slight well in center of circle; set aside. Combine parsley with rest of ingredients. Mix well. Spoon onto cream cheese round; garnish with fresh basil sprigs if desired. Cover and chill at least 2 hours. Serve with crackers or toasted pita triangles.

Quick Guacamole-Spinach Dip

YIELDS 2 CUPS

1 package dry guacamole dip mix
(found in produce
departments)
One 8-ounce container soft cream
cheese

One 10-ounce package frozen
chopped spinach, thawed
1 large tomato, finely chopped

Combine guacamole mix and cream cheese. Squeeze excess liquid from spinach. Add to cheese mixture. Add tomato. Mix well to combine. Serve with tortilla chips.

Garlic Cheese Spread

YIELDS 2 CUPS

One 8-ounce package cream cheese
One 8-ounce jar Cheez Whiz
¾ teaspoon garlic powder, or to
taste

⅛ teaspoon seasoned salt
⅛ teaspoon pepper

Combine all ingredients and beat with hand mixer for 2 minutes or until smooth. Serve with freshly toasted French bread.

Creamy Roquefort Dip

YIELDS 2 CUPS

This also makes a wonderful dressing for salads.

½ cup crumbled Roquefort cheese
One 3-ounce package cream
   cheese, softened
½ cup mayonnaise

1 tablespoon lemon juice
1 tablespoon wine vinegar
½ cup sour cream

Blend Roquefort and cream cheese until smooth. Mix in remaining ingredients. Beat well. Chill for 2 hours. Serve with vegetable crudité.

Strawberry Cheese Ring

SERVES APPROXIMATELY 20

I've heard this was our governor and later president Jimmy Carter's favorite cheese dish. His First Lady, Rosalynn Carter, has been credited for making this a famous Southern favorite.

16 ounces sharp Cheddar cheese,
   grated
One 3-ounce package cream
   cheese, softened
¾ cup mayonnaise

1 small onion, chopped
1 cup chopped pecans or walnuts
½ teaspoon garlic salt or powder
Cayenne pepper to taste
1 cup strawberry preserves

Combine all ingredients except preserves in a food processor or electric mixer. Mix thoroughly and refrigerate for 2 to 3 hours. Scoop mixture onto a platter. Use your hands to mold mixture into a ring formation (I suggest placing a sheet of wax paper between your hands and the mixture to prevent melting and stickiness). Spread strawberry preserves in center of ring and serve with some good, buttery crackers.

Black Bean Salsa

SERVES 12

Two 15-ounce cans black beans,
  rinsed and drained
One 17-ounce package frozen
  whole-kernel corn, thawed
2 large tomatoes, seeded and
  chopped
1 large avocado, peeled and
  chopped (optional)

1 small onion, chopped
⅛ to ¼ cup chopped fresh cilantro
3 to 4 tablespoons lime juice
1 tablespoon red wine vinegar
Salt and pepper to taste

Mix all ingredients thoroughly in a large bowl. Cover and chill overnight. Taste and add salt, pepper, or more lime juice as necessary. Serve with tortilla chips as an appetizer, or with grilled chicken breast as a meal.

Bobby's Pimento Cheese

YIELDS APPROXIMATELY 2½ TO 3 CUPS

This is my son Bobby's own recipe for pimento cheese. It is a definite favorite.

One 3-ounce package cream cheese,
  softened
1 cup grated sharp Cheddar cheese
1 cup grated Monterey Jack cheese
½ cup mayonnaise

½ teaspoon House Seasoning
  (see page 325)
2 to 3 tablespoons mashed pimentos
1 teaspoon grated onion (optional)
Cracked black pepper to taste

With an electric mixer, beat cream cheese until fluffy. Add remaining ingredients and beat until well blended.

Soups and Salads

SOUPS

She Crab Soup

Roasted Red Pepper Soup

Oyster Stew

White Bean Chili

Shrimp Bisque

Sherried Avocado Bouillon

The Lady's Chicken Noodle Soup

Creamy Cheddar Soup

Sausage and Lentil Soup

Shrimp or Lobster Bisque

Confederate Bean Soup

Cream of Artichoke Soup

Tomato Dill Soup

SALADS

Orange Walnut Salad with Sweet-and-Sour Dressing

Jamie's Chicken Salad

Southern Shrimp Salad

Georgia Cracker Salad

The Lady's Coleslaw

Oriental Chicken Salad

The Lady's Warm Potato Salad

Potato-Egg Salad

Cranberry Salad

Black-Eyed Pea Salad

Esther's Dill Coleslaw

Avocado Chicken Salad

Cornucopia Salad

Broccoli Salad

Roasted Beet Salad

She Crab Soup

This is a traditional favorite down here. We try to use female crabs, but you can use either male or female.

One 2-pound fish head (preferably
   grouper), eyes, gills, and scales
   removed
1 medium onion, peeled
2 ribs celery, including tops
½ teaspoon salt
½ teaspoon white pepper
¾ cup chopped green onion, with
   tops
2 teaspoons minced garlic
4 tablespoons (½ stick) butter

3 tablespoons all-purpose flour
1 cup heavy cream
1 cup milk
1 pound crabmeat, picked free of
   shell
¼ cup sherry
½ teaspoon lemon-pepper seasoning
1 cup freshly grated Parmesan
   cheese
½ cup chopped fresh chives

To make fish stock, combine fish head, whole onion, celery, salt, and white pepper in a large pot. Cover with 4½ cups of water. Bring pot to a boil, reduce heat, cover pot, and cook for 30 minutes. Remove fish from pot and allow to cool. Separate fish into pieces that resemble picked crabmeat and set aside. Discard celery and onion from stock. Sauté chopped green onion and garlic in butter until tender. Stir in flour, stirring until well blended. Slowly add 2 cups of the fish stock, continuing to cook until smooth and bubbly. Slowly add cream and milk. Stir in fish and crabmeat. Add sherry and lemon-pepper seasoning. Simmer until piping hot; adjust seasoning (sherry, garlic, salt, and pepper) to taste. Serve in bowls topped with cheese and chives.

🌸 🌸 🌸   *The Lady & Sons*

NOTE: You may freeze leftover fish stock for future use. If you wish, you may skip preparing the fish stock and substitute 2 cups chicken stock.

Roasted Red Pepper Soup

SERVES 3 TO 4

1 medium onion, chopped
2 tablespoons butter
4 cloves garlic, minced
2 large red bell peppers, roasted
  and chopped

2 tablespoons chopped fresh thyme
Salt and pepper to taste
½ cup white wine
2 cups chicken stock
1 cup heavy cream

Over medium heat, sauté onion in butter until soft. Add garlic, red pepper, thyme, salt, and pepper. Add wine and scald. Lower heat and add chicken stock and cream. Cook 3 to 5 minutes and remove from heat. Put in blender and blend until smooth. Return to saucepan and cook for 5 minutes over medium heat. Serve immediately.

Oyster Stew

SERVES 4 TO 5

2 green onions, chopped
2 tablespoons butter
12 ounces fresh raw oysters,
  undrained
1 quart half-and-half or whole
  milk

¼ teaspoon salt
¼ teaspoon white pepper
⅛ teaspoon cayenne pepper

Sauté onion in butter until tender. Add remaining ingredients. Cook over low heat until edges of oysters begin to curl and mixture is hot but not boiling. Serve stew with crackers.

White Bean Chili

SERVES 10 TO 15

1 pound dried navy beans
6 cups chicken stock
4 tablespoons (½ stick) butter
1 tablespoon minced garlic
¾ cup diced onion
1½ green chilies (fresh or canned), chopped
1 pound skinless boneless chicken breast, finely chopped

1½ tablespoons ground cumin
1 tablespoon dried oregano
1 to 2 teaspoons ground black pepper
¾ teaspoon white pepper
½ bunch cilantro, chopped

Wash beans, cover with water, and soak for 2 hours. Drain. Place beans in large pot with chicken stock. Bring to a boil. In saucepan, heat butter and sauté garlic, onion, and chilies for 5 minutes. Add to bean pot. Add chicken, cumin, oregano, black pepper, white pepper, and cilantro. Lower heat to medium and cook, stirring occasionally, for approximately 1½ hours. Serve with corn bread.

Shrimp Bisque

SERVES 6 TO 8

One 10¾-ounce can condensed cream of mushroom soup
One 10¾-ounce can condensed cream of chicken soup
Two 12-ounce cans evaporated milk

2 tablespoons butter
½ pound cooked shrimp, peeled, deveined, and chopped
Dash of Worcestershire sauce
Dash of Tabasco
¼ cup sherry, or to taste

In top of double boiler, heat soups, milk, and butter over boiling water. Add shrimp, Worcestershire sauce, and Tabasco. Stir in sherry to taste. Continue heating until desired temperature. Great served plain or over steamed rice.

Sherried Avocado Bouillon

SERVES 6

Two 10¾-ounce cans condensed
    beef broth
1⅓ cups water
¼ cup sherry

2 tablespoons chopped fresh parsley
Salt and pepper to taste
1 medium avocado, peeled and
    finely diced

Heat broth and water to boiling. Add sherry and parsley and season to taste with salt and pepper. Remove from heat and stir in avocado. Pour at once into heated bouillon cups. Garnish with avocado slices, if desired.

The Lady's Chicken Noodle Soup

SERVES 8 TO 10

One 2½- to 3-pound fryer, cut up
3½ quarts water
1 onion, peeled
1½ to 2 teaspoons Italian
    seasoning

1 teaspoon lemon-pepper seasoning
3 cloves garlic, minced
4 bay leaves
3 chicken bouillon cubes
Salt and pepper to taste

Add all ingredients to a pot. Cook until chicken is tender, about 35 to 45 minutes. Remove chicken from pot and set aside to cool. Remove and discard bay leaves and onion. You should have approximately 3 quarts of stock. When chicken is cool enough to touch, pick bones clean, discarding bones, skin, and cartilage. Set chicken aside. For the next step, you will need:

2 cups sliced carrots
2 cups sliced celery, with leafy
    green tops
2½ cups uncooked egg noodles
3 tablespoons minced fresh parsley

⅓ cup grated Parmesan cheese
    (optional)
¾ cup heavy cream (optional)
⅓ cup cooking sherry
Salt and pepper to taste

Bring stock back to a boil, add carrots, and cook for 3 minutes. Add celery and continue to cook for 5 to 10 minutes. Add egg noodles and cook according to directions on package. When noodles are done, add chicken, parsley, cheese, cream, and sherry. Cook for another 2 minutes. Adjust seasoning if needed by adding salt and pepper. Enjoy along with a nice hot crusty loaf of French bread. If you are watching calories, you may leave out the cheese and cream.

🌿 🌿 🌿 *The Lady & Sons*

Creamy Cheddar Soup

SERVES 3 TO 4

1 small onion, chopped
2 large pimentos, chopped
3 tablespoons butter
3 tablespoons all-purpose flour
1½ cups chicken stock

1½ cups half-and-half
¾ cup grated sharp Cheddar cheese
Salt and ground black pepper to taste
Dash of cayenne pepper (optional)

In a saucepan, sauté onion and pimentos in butter for 5 to 7 minutes. Blend in flour. Add stock and half-and-half. Cook until thick. Add cheese and stir until melted. Add salt and black pepper to taste, and cayenne if desired.

Sausage and Lentil Soup

SERVES 8 TO 10

2 tablespoons olive oil
1 pound sausage (chorizo, Polish, etc.)
7 ounces smoked ham, shredded
2 large onions, chopped
1 large green bell pepper, chopped
1 medium carrot, diced
2 cloves garlic, minced
½ teaspoon ground cumin

¾ teaspoon dried thyme
1 bay leaf
8 to 9 cups chicken stock
One 16-ounce can peeled tomatoes, crushed
½ pound dried lentils (1¼ cups)
12 large spinach leaves, cut into small pieces
Salt and pepper to taste

Heat olive oil in a large saucepan over medium heat. Add sausage and cook until done. Remove sausage and place on a platter, allowing time to cool. When cool, slice sausage into ⅛-inch slices. Discard all but 2 tablespoons of drippings from pan. Reheat drippings and add ham, onion, green pepper, and carrot to the saucepan. Cover and cook over medium heat for 15 minutes. Stir in garlic, cumin, thyme, and bay leaf. Cover and cook for 5 more minutes. Add chicken stock, sliced sausage, tomatoes, and lentils. Cover and cook over low heat for 2 hours. As soup cooks, skim off fat that rises to the top. After 2 hours turn off heat and discard bay leaf. Add spinach, salt, and pepper and let stand for 2 to 3 minutes before serving.

Shrimp or Lobster Bisque

SERVES 4 TO 5

*8 ounces cooked shrimp or lobster
   meat*
*2 tablespoons sherry, plus
   additional to taste*
Pinch of thyme
*3 to 4 green onions with tops,
   chopped*
2 tablespoons butter

*One 10¾-ounce can condensed
   tomato soup*
1 soup can measure of milk
*One 10¾-ounce can condensed
   cream of mushroom soup*
1 soup can measure of heavy cream
Chopped fresh parsley, for garnish

Finely chop the shrimp or lobster meat and marinate 30 minutes in 2 tablespoons of sherry and the thyme. Sauté onions in butter until soft. Add shrimp or lobster meat and cook over a low heat for 3 to 5 minutes. In a separate bowl, combine tomato soup with milk and blend mushroom soup with cream. Combine the two soup mixtures with the shrimp-lobster sauté. Simmer over low heat for 3 to 5 minutes. Add more sherry to taste. Cool, then mix in blender until thick and smooth. To serve, reheat in a double boiler. Add more sherry to taste and garnish with chopped parsley.

Confederate Bean Soup

SERVES 3 OR 4

This is a great soup to make when you find yourself with leftover baked beans.
If you don't have leftovers, Bush's canned baked beans work wonderfully.

½ pound Hillshire Farms smoked
   sausage, sliced in rounds ¼ inch
   thick
2 slices bacon, diced
1 clove garlic, minced
1 medium onion, diced
½ green bell pepper, diced
   (optional)

2 tablespoons butter
2 cups leftover baked beans, or one
   16-ounce can Bush's Baked
   Beans
1½ cups half-and-half

Sauté sausage, bacon, garlic, onion, and pepper (if desired) in butter until bacon is cooked. Add beans and simmer for a few minutes over medium to low heat. Add half-and-half. Increase or decrease half-and-half for preferred thickness. Serve with piping-hot corn bread.

❦ ❦ ❦   **The Lady & Sons**

Cream of Artichoke Soup

SERVES 6

Two 13¾-ounce cans artichoke
   hearts, chopped
1½ cups chicken stock
1 cup chopped onion
4 tablespoons (½ stick) butter

One 10¾-ounce can condensed
   cream of mushroom soup
⅓ cup heavy cream
Salt and pepper to taste

Bring artichokes and chicken stock to a boil. In a saucepan, sauté onion in butter and add to mixture. Gradually add mushroom soup to desired thickness. Slowly add cream, stirring constantly. Remove from heat. Add salt and pepper.   ❦ ❦ ❦   **The Lady & Sons**

Tomato Dill Soup

SERVES 6

3 cups peeled and diced fresh
   tomatoes (or one 28-ounce can)
1 medium onion, chopped
2 cups chicken stock
1 teaspoon chopped garlic
⅓ to ½ cup white wine
1 teaspoon lemon-pepper seasoning

3 tablespoons chopped fresh dill
¾ cup heavy cream
¼ cup chopped fresh parsley
¼ cup grated Parmesan cheese
Salt and coarsely ground black
   pepper to taste

In a large pot, mix all ingredients together except heavy cream, parsley, Parmesan, and salt and pepper. Cook over medium heat about 30 minutes, until tomatoes are tender. Add cream, parsley, and Parmesan cheese last. Season with salt and pepper to taste. Simmer for about 10 minutes.   ❦ ❦ ❦   **The Lady & Sons**

Orange Walnut Salad with Sweet-and-Sour Dressing

SERVES 10 TO 12

SALAD

3 small heads Bibb lettuce, cleaned
   and torn into bite-size pieces
1½ pounds fresh spinach, cleaned
   and torn into bite-size pieces
3 oranges, peeled, sectioned, and
   seeded

¾ medium red onion, sliced and
   separated into rings
¾ cup coarsely chopped walnuts
3 teaspoons butter

Combine lettuce, spinach, oranges, and onion in a large bowl. In a saucepan, sauté walnuts in butter until lightly browned. Add to lettuce mixture. Toss with Sweet-and-Sour Dressing.

SWEET-AND-SOUR DRESSING

1½ cups vegetable oil	*1½ teaspoons celery seed*
¾ cup vinegar	*1½ teaspoons dry mustard*
¾ cup sugar	*1½ teaspoons paprika*
1½ teaspoons salt	*1½ teaspoons grated onion*

Combine all ingredients in a jar. Chill. Shake and serve over salad.

Jamie's Chicken Salad

SERVES 6 TO 8

This is my son Jamie's recipe. It's the best! For a little variation, try adding walnuts and canned mandarin oranges or grapes for a Hawaiian taste.

One 2½- to 3-pound chicken	*½ cup mayonnaise*
Salt and pepper to taste	*1 teaspoon lemon-pepper seasoning*
1 onion, quartered	*¼ teaspoon pepper*
2 ribs plus 1 cup chopped celery	*2 to 3 tablespoons chicken stock*
4 hard-boiled eggs, chopped	
2 teaspoons Jane's Krazy Mixed-	
Up Salt	

Put the chicken in a large stockpot along with salt, pepper, onion, and celery stalks. Boil chicken until well done. Reserve stock. Remove chicken from pot. Cool; remove skin and bones. Dice the chicken and combine it with chopped celery and eggs in a large bowl. Add remaining ingredients and mix well. ❦ ❦ ❦ **The Lady & Sons**

Southern Shrimp Salad

SERVES 6

2 tablespoons (more or less to taste)
   Old Bay Shrimp Boil
2 pounds shrimp, cleaned, peeled,
   and deveined
1 cup uncooked white rice

½ cup chopped onion
½ cup chopped green olives
Pepper to taste
1 cup mayonnaise

Dissolve shrimp boil in 4 cups water and bring to a boil. Add shrimp and boil 4 minutes; drain, reserving shrimp boil water. Chop shrimp into bite-size chunks and put on paper towels; set aside to cool. In the reserved water, boil rice until tender for 15 to 20 minutes; drain rice in colander. Let cool. Add onion, olives, and pepper to rice; stir in mayonnaise. Add cooled, dry shrimp last.   ❦ ❦ ❦ *The Lady & Sons*

Georgia Cracker Salad

SERVES 6

We serve this salad with most of our seafood dishes at the restaurant. It's also quite good at an outdoor fish fry.

1 sleeve saltine crackers
1 large tomato, finely chopped
3 green onions, finely chopped

1½ cups mayonnaise
1 hard-boiled egg, finely chopped

Crush crackers. Mix all ingredients together and serve immediately.

❦ ❦ ❦ *The Lady & Sons*

The Lady's Coleslaw

SERVES APPROXIMATELY 6

To me, the secret to good slaw is the way you cut your cabbage. I have found that I prefer half of the cabbage coarsely chopped in a food processor and half hand-sliced very thin. Use outside dark green leaves, too, for color.

½ bell pepper, chopped
1 green onion, chopped
½ large carrot, chopped
⅛ cup chopped fresh parsley
½ head cabbage
½ cup mayonnaise
½ teaspoon Jane's Krazy Mixed-
   Up Salt

¼ teaspoon coarsely ground black
   pepper
2 tablespoons sugar
¼ teaspoon lemon-pepper seasoning
1 tablespoon white vinegar

In food processor, gently process bell pepper, onion, carrot, and parsley, being careful not to overprocess (don't let mixture become mushy). Cut up half the cabbage into chunks and place in food processor. Process lightly (once again, don't let cabbage become mushy). Thinly slice remaining cabbage. Mix the cabbage together, adding the processed vegetables. Mix remaining ingredients together and allow to stand for a few minutes. Pour over slaw ingredients and toss. Chill for at least an hour.   ❦ ❦ ❦ **The Lady & Sons**

Oriental Chicken Salad

SERVES 6

4 cooked skinless boneless chicken
   breasts, diced
1½ cups bean sprouts
1½ cups snow peas
¼ cup chopped green onion
¼ cup vegetable oil
5 teaspoons soy sauce

1 teaspoon ground ginger
⅛ teaspoon salt
⅛ teaspoon sugar
½ cup chopped celery
One 8-ounce can sliced water
   chestnuts, drained

Combine chicken, bean sprouts, peas, and scallions. Make dressing using oil, soy sauce, ginger, salt, and sugar. Add to chicken mixture. Add celery and water chestnuts and mix well. Serve chilled.

The Lady's Warm Potato Salad

SERVES 10 TO 12

8 medium red potatoes
¼ cup chopped fresh parsley
¼ cup chopped green onion tops
1 cup chopped celery
3 hard-boiled eggs, chopped
¼ cup chopped bell pepper
¼ cup diced pimento

1 teaspoon lemon-pepper seasoning
2 tablespoons Jane's Krazy Mixed-
    Up Salt
1 tablespoon Dijon mustard
¼ cup mayonnaise
1 cup sour cream

Boil potatoes with skins on for 10 to 15 minutes, until tender. Let cool just to the touch and cut into cubes. In a large bowl, combine remaining ingredients. Add potatoes. Mix gently and serve at room temperature.   ❦ ❦ ❦   *The Lady & Sons*

Potato-Egg Salad

SERVES 8 TO 10

6 cups diced new potatoes
⅓ cup Italian salad dressing
1 teaspoon salt
1 cup diced celery
⅓ cup sliced green onions with tops

4 hard-boiled eggs, chopped
1 cup mayonnaise
½ cup sour cream
1 teaspoon dry mustard
½ teaspoon horseradish

Boil potatoes with skins on for 15 to 20 minutes or until tender. Pour salad dressing over warm potatoes. Chill for about 2 hours. Mix remaining ingredients and fold into potato mixture.

Cranberry Salad

SERVES 7 TO 8

One 4-ounce can crushed pineapple
One 3-ounce package black cherry
  Jell-O

6 ounces raw cranberries, rinsed
1 cup broken pecans
½ cup sugar

Drain pineapple and reserve juice. Add juice to ½ cup hot water and heat to boiling. Soften Jell-O in ¼ cup cold water. Dissolve softened Jell-O in hot water–juice mixture. Let cool until it starts to set; *don't let the Jell-O harden.* Put cranberries through a grinder. Add ground berries, pineapple, nuts, and sugar to cooled Jell-O mixture. Mix well. Pour into a bowl or mold. Refrigerate until completely set.

Black-Eyed Pea Salad

SERVES 8

¾ cup olive oil
¼ cup balsamic vinegar
¼ cup sugar
3 cups black-eyed peas, cooked
1 red bell pepper, seeded and diced
½ cup chopped green onion with
  tops
1 large tomato, diced

1 tablespoon minced fresh thyme
1 tablespoon minced fresh rosemary
4 tablespoons minced fresh parsley
2 tablespoons minced fresh oregano
1 large banana pepper (mild),
  seeded and diced
1 hot green pepper, seeded and
  diced (optional)

Mix olive oil, vinegar, and sugar together and pour over the rest of ingredients. Mix well and chill. Use a slotted spoon to serve.

❧ ❧ ❧ **The Lady & Sons**

Esther's Dill Coleslaw

SERVES 6 TO 8

Esther Shaver owns one of the best bookstores in town. Her store, E. Shaver's, was one of the first places to carry my cookbook. Not only is her store great, but so is her coleslaw!

1 small head cabbage, shredded
½ cup finely chopped Vidalia onion
½ cup Hidden Valley Ranch
    Buttermilk salad dressing
    (made as per directions on the
    dry mix)

½ cup shredded carrots
2 tablespoons chopped fresh dill

Mix all ingredients together except dill. Place slaw in bowl and sprinkle dill on top. Chill and serve.

Avocado Chicken Salad

SERVES 8

For a beautiful presentation, I like to cut the avocado in half, carefully scoop the meat from the shell, and then stuff the shell with the chicken salad. Garnish with dressing and a lemon wedge.

3 cups cooked, diced chicken
3 cups cooked white rice
2 avocados, peeled, diced, and
    tossed with 1 tablespoon lemon
    juice (to prevent browning)

¾ cup chopped onion
1 cup mayonnaise
1 to 2 teaspoons pepper
1 teaspoon salt
¼ cup chopped fresh parsley

Mix all ingredients and chill. Pass with avocado dressing.

AVOCADO DRESSING

YIELDS 2 CUPS

1 large avocado, peeled and
   mashed with 2 tablespoons
   lemon juice
1 cup mayonnaise
½ cup sour cream

½ teaspoon Worcestershire sauce
⅓ cup chopped onion
2 cloves garlic, minced
1 teaspoon salt
Dash of cayenne pepper

Place all ingredients in a food processor and blend until smooth. Chill and serve alongside chicken salad. ❧ ❧ ❧ **The Lady & Sons**

Cornucopia Salad

SERVES 10 TO 12

1 head lettuce (any variety),
   washed, patted dry, and torn
   into pieces
1 cup diced green bell pepper
1 cup diced celery
1 cup frozen green peas (uncooked)
Two 8-ounce cans sliced water
   chestnuts
1 cup fresh chopped mushrooms

3 bananas, sliced and tossed in
   ¼ cup lemon juice
1 cup grated Cheddar cheese
¾ cup raisins
¾ cup chopped nuts (pecans,
   walnuts, or salted peanuts)
¾ cup chopped green onion with
   tops
10 to 12 slices bacon, crisply cooked

DRESSING

2 cups mayonnaise
¼ cup sugar

1 tablespoon white vinegar

In a large rectangular dish, layer salad ingredients in order listed, stopping after bananas. Mix dressing ingredients and let stand for 5 minutes. Frost entire top of salad with dressing, covering it completely. Sprinkle layers of cheese, raisins, and nuts (combined), chopped green onion, and bacon. Chill for 3 to 4 hours before serving.

❧ ❧ ❧ **The Lady & Sons**

Broccoli Salad

SERVES 6 TO 8

1 head broccoli
6 to 8 slices cooked bacon, crumbled
½ cup chopped red onion
½ cup raisins (optional)
8 ounces sharp Cheddar cheese, cut
   into very small chunks

1 cup mayonnaise
2 tablespoons vinegar
¼ cup sugar
1 cup halved cherry tomatoes

Trim off large leaves of broccoli. Remove tough stalks at end and wash broccoli thoroughly. Cut flowerets and stems into bite-size pieces. Place in a large bowl. Add crumbled bacon, onion, raisins, and cheese. In a small bowl, combine remaining ingredients, stirring well. Add to broccoli mixture and toss gently.   ❧ ❧ ❧ **The Lady & Sons**

Roasted Beet Salad

SERVES 6 TO 8

Two 15¼-ounce cans sliced beets,
   rinsed and drained
1½ cups crumbled feta cheese
½ cup pitted ripe olives
¼ cup chopped fresh dill

½ cup olive oil
¼ cup rice wine vinegar
Salt, pepper, and garlic powder
   to taste
Dash of tabasco

Remove broiler tray from oven and coat with nonstick cooking spray. Replace tray and preheat broiler. After beets are drained place on coated broiler tray. Place under hot broiler, turning every 2 to 3 minutes until edges start to brown, approximately 10 to 15 minutes. Remove beets from oven and allow to cool. Mix remaining ingredients with cooled beets. Toss and serve.

Main Courses

FISH AND SHELLFISH

Low Country Boil

Black Pepper Shrimp

Savory Salmon

Savannah Crab Cakes

Spicy Shrimp and Pasta Casserole

Scallops Charleston

Deviled Seafood Casserole

Mushroom-Stuffed Baked Red Snapper

Shrimp and Scallop Fraîche

Fillet of Sole Paprika

Shrimp with Rice

Shrimp Gumbo Casserole

Lemon Mackerel

Shrimp and Mushroom Casserole

Red Snapper Stuffed with Crabmeat

Shrimp and Artichoke Bake

MEAT

Bourbon Beef Tenderloin

Old-Time Beef Stew

Basic Meat Loaf

Barbecue-Style Pork Chops

Pot Roast

Pepper Steak

Burgundy Beef Roast

Sausage-Rice Casserole

Beef Stroganoff

Cheeseburger Meat Loaf and Sauce

Veal and Creamed Spinach

Foolproof Standing Rib Roast

Swiss Steak

Farmer's Pork Chops

Steak and Greens

The Lady's Oven-Roasted Ribs

Sausage and Grits

Piggy Pudding

POULTRY

Southern Fried Chicken

Chicken Pot Pie

Chicken Brunswick Stew

Baked Hen and Dressing

Chicken in Wine Sauce

Chicken Paprika

Chicken Georgia

Herbed Stuffed Chicken Breasts

Honey Game Hens

Pecan Chicken

Chicken and Rice Casserole

Chicken and Dumplings

Marinated Cornish Hens

Herb-Baked Chicken

Chicken Breasts in Sour Cream Sauce

Duck Burgundy

Chicken Casserole

Low Country Boil

This dish is indigenous to Savannah and our lifestyle. Calling up a dozen friends for a cookout is a great casual way to entertain, especially if the food is cooked outside over an open flame (you can also use a portable gas fish cooker). Once the Low Country Boil has been cooked and drained, I like to pour it out on a table covered with newspaper.

Crab boil (2 teaspoons per quart
   of water)
12 small red new potatoes
Six 4-inch pieces good smoked link
   sausage

6 ears fresh corn
3 pounds fresh shrimp (26 to 30
   count per pound), unpeeled

Fill a large pot with enough water to cover all ingredients. Add crab boil and heat until boiling. Adjust crab boil to suit your taste. When boiling, add potatoes and sausage. Cook on medium heat for 20 minutes. Add corn and cook for an additional 10 minutes. Add shrimp and cook for no more than 3 minutes (do not overcook!). Drain and serve with piping-hot bread and ice-cold beer.   ❧ ❧ ❧   **The Lady & Sons**

Black Pepper Shrimp

3 pounds fresh shrimp, unpeeled
8 tablespoons (1 stick) butter
2 to 3 tablespoons chopped garlic

4 tablespoons freshly ground black
   pepper

Preheat oven to 450 degrees. Wash and drain shrimp. Place in a shallow baking pan. Melt butter in a saucepan. Add garlic and sauté 3 to 4 minutes. Pour over shrimp and toss to coat. Pepper shrimp until shrimp are covered well. Bake until pink (about 5 minutes), turn, bake a few minutes longer, and pepper again. This will not be good unless you use a heavy hand with the pepper. Serve with a fresh garden salad and hot French bread. Dip bread in the pan juices for an extra treat.

❦ ❦ ❦   **The Lady & Sons**

Savory Salmon

SERVES 4

One 2-pound salmon fillet
House Seasoning (see page 325)
Juice of 2 lemons
1 medium orange, sectioned and
   seeded
1 medium onion, sliced thin
1 small red bell pepper, julienned
1 small green bell pepper, julienned

1 pint strawberries, cleaned and
   sliced
½ cup water
½ cup honey
½ cup chopped fresh chervil or
   baby dill
4 cloves garlic, minced
1 bunch chives, chopped

Preheat oven to 350 degrees. Place salmon fillet on a foil-lined pan. Season with House Seasoning and lemon juice, then cover and surround fish with orange, onion, and red and green bell pepper. Mix strawberries, water, honey, chervil or dill, garlic, and chives together. Pour evenly over salmon. Cover with foil and pierce foil, allowing salmon to steam. Bake for 25 to 30 minutes. Serve with rice.

Savannah Crab Cakes

SERVES 4 TO 6

1 pound crabmeat, picked free of
   shell
½ cup crushed Ritz crackers
3 green onions, finely chopped,
   with tops
½ cup finely chopped bell pepper

¼ cup mayonnaise
1 egg
1 teaspoon Worcestershire sauce
1 teaspoon dry mustard
Juice of ½ lemon
¼ teaspoon garlic powder

| 1 teaspoon salt | Flour for dusting |
| Dash of cayenne pepper | ½ cup peanut oil |

Mix all ingredients together except flour and peanut oil. Shape into patties and dust with flour. Panfry in hot peanut oil over medium heat until browned, for 4 to 5 minutes. Flip and panfry other side until golden brown.

TARTAR SAUCE

½ cup chopped green onion	½ teaspoon House Seasoning (see
½ cup chopped dill pickle	page 325)
1 cup mayonnaise	

In a bowl, combine chopped onion, pickle, mayonnaise, and House Seasoning and mix well. Serve alongside crab cakes with lemon wedges.

❦ ❦ ❦ **The Lady & Sons**

VARIATION: Substitute ⅓ cup capers for ½ cup pickles and add a dash of cayenne pepper.

Spicy Shrimp and Pasta Casserole

SERVES 8

2 eggs	1 teaspoon dried oregano, crushed
1½ cups half-and-half	9 ounces angel hair pasta, cooked
1 cup plain yogurt	16 ounces mild salsa, thick and
½ cup grated Swiss cheese	chunky
⅓ cup crumbled feta cheese	2 pounds shrimp, cleaned, peeled,
⅓ cup chopped fresh parsley	and deveined
1 teaspoon dried basil, crushed	½ cup grated Monterey Jack cheese

Preheat oven to 350 degrees. Grease a 12 × 8-inch pan or glass dish with butter. Combine eggs, half-and-half, yogurt, Swiss and feta cheeses, parsley, basil, and oregano in medium bowl; mix well. Spread half the pasta on bottom of prepared pan. Cover with salsa. Add half of the shrimp. Cover with Monterey Jack cheese. Cover with remaining pasta and shrimp. Spread egg mixture over top. Bake for 30 minutes or until bubbly. Let stand for 10 minutes.

Scallops Charleston

SERVES 4

1½ pounds fresh sea scallops
Salt and pepper to taste
½ teaspoon garlic powder
¼ teaspoon paprika
¼ cup finely chopped fresh basil
Flour for dusting
¾ cup sherry or dry white wine

1 shallot, finely chopped
8 ounces fresh mushrooms, quartered
2 tablespoons butter
3 tablespoons all-purpose flour
1 cup grated Gruyère cheese

Season scallops with salt, pepper, garlic powder, paprika, and basil. Dust scallops with flour. Sauté in a pan that has been lightly coated with nonstick cooking spray and a small amount of olive oil. Cook scallops on both sides until browned. Remove scallops from pan. To the drippings in the pan, add sherry, shallots, and mushrooms; cook for approximately 3 to 4 minutes. In a separate saucepan, melt butter over medium heat and add 3 tablespoons flour. Mix well and cook for 2 minutes over low heat, stirring constantly. Pour shallots, mushrooms, and liquid from scallops into flour mixture. Mix well. Stir scallops into sauce. (If too thick, you can thin with clam juice or fish or chicken stock.) Transfer to four individual baking dishes, top with cheese, and broil for 1 minute, until browned. Serve with wild rice.

Deviled Seafood Casserole

SERVES 8

1½ pounds shrimp, cleaned, peeled, and deveined

1 pound fresh sea scallops

12 tablespoons (1½ sticks) butter

One 1-pound haddock fillet

½ cup plus 1 tablespoon all-purpose flour

1 cup evaporated milk

1 cup consommé or beef broth

2 tablespoons cornstarch

⅓ cup milk

1 teaspoon garlic powder

1 tablespoon horseradish

½ teaspoon salt

1 teaspoon soy sauce

2 tablespoons chopped fresh parsley

1 tablespoon Worcestershire sauce

1 teaspoon dry mustard

¼ teaspoon cayenne pepper

1 tablespoon lemon juice

4 teaspoons ketchup

½ cup sherry

Preheat oven to 400 degrees. Sauté shrimp and scallops in 4 tablespoons butter for 3 to 5 minutes, until tender. In a saucepan, steam fish in small amount of water for 3 minutes, until tender, and cut into bite-size pieces. In a saucepan, melt remaining 8 tablespoons butter; add flour and evaporated milk; mix and add consommé. Cook over medium heat until thick. Mix cornstarch in ⅓ cup of milk and add remaining ingredients except sherry. Add to sauce and stir well. Add seafood and stir in sherry. Pour into a casserole and bake for 30 minutes.

Mushroom-Stuffed Baked Red Snapper

SERVES 4

½ pound fresh mushrooms, or one 8-ounce can stems and pieces

4 tablespoons (½ stick) butter

½ cup finely chopped celery

5 tablespoons minced onion

One 8-ounce can water chestnuts, drained and chopped

½ cup soft bread crumbs

1 egg, lightly beaten

1 tablespoon soy sauce

1 tablespoon chopped fresh parsley

Salt and pepper to taste

Two 2½-pound oven-ready whole red snappers, gutted, scaled, and cleaned

½ cup dry white wine

¾ cup water

Preheat oven to 350 degrees. Rinse, pat dry, and finely chop ¼ pound mushrooms. Quarter remaining mushrooms or drain canned mushrooms. Set aside. In a small skillet, melt 2 tablespoons butter; add celery and 3 tablespoons of the onion. Sauté for 5 minutes. Combine sautéed celery mixture with mushrooms, water chestnuts, bread crumbs, egg, soy sauce, parsley, and salt and pepper. Mix well and spoon into fish cavities. Secure openings with skewers or toothpicks. Sprinkle both sides of each fish with salt and pepper. Place in a large baking dish. Dot with remaining 2 tablespoons of butter, 2 tablespoons onion, the wine, and water. Bake uncovered for 45 to 50 minutes. Baste occasionally. Test with a fork. When fish flakes, it's done.

Shrimp and Scallop Fraîche

SERVES 4

½ cup crème fraîche
1 pound shrimp, cleaned, peeled, and deveined
1 pound fresh sea scallops
4 tablespoons (½ stick) butter
Juice of 1 lemon

3 cloves garlic, minced
1 tablespoon cognac or wine
1 tablespoon cornstarch
2 tablespoons fish or chicken stock
4 sprigs fresh basil

CRÈME FRAÎCHE

1 cup heavy cream

2 tablespoons sour cream

Prepare crème fraîche ahead of time by combining heavy cream and sour cream. Cover with plastic wrap and let stand at room temperature for 12 to 24 hours. Clean and devein shrimp, leaving tails on. Pat scallops dry with paper towels. Melt butter in a large skillet. Add lemon juice and garlic. Place shrimp and scallops in butter and sauté until scallops are opaque, 3 to 4 minutes per side. Remove to a warm platter. Add cognac or wine to pan juice. Dissolve cornstarch in stock and add along with crème fraîche to pan. Simmer until thickened. Pour sauce over shellfish and garnish with basil sprigs.

Fillet of Sole Paprika

SERVES 3 TO 4

1½ pounds fillet of sole
1 onion, sliced thin
1 cup sour cream
⅓ cup white table wine

1 tablespoon all-purpose flour
Juice of ½ lemon
½ teaspoon paprika
Salt and pepper to taste

Preheat oven to 375 degrees. Arrange fillets in a greased shallow baking dish. Cover with onion slices. Blend sour cream, wine, flour, lemon juice, and seasonings and pour over entire baking dish. Bake for about 25 minutes, or until fish is tender.

Shrimp with Rice

SERVES 8

Two 6-ounce boxes Uncle Ben's
long-grain and wild rice
2 pounds shrimp, cleaned, peeled,
and deveined
1 onion, diced and sautéed in 2
tablespoons butter
1 bell pepper, chopped

Two 10¾-ounce cans condensed
cream of mushroom soup
16 ounces grated Cheddar cheese;
reserve ½ cup for top
1 tablespoon Worcestershire sauce
½ teaspoon dry mustard

Remove seasoning mix from rice; do not use. Cook rice as directed on box. Preheat oven to 375 degrees. Mix rice with remaining ingredients in a baking dish and sprinkle reserved cheese on top. Bake for 45 minutes.

Shrimp Gumbo Casserole

SERVES 6

This Southern dish usually is prepared and served in an iron skillet, but may be cooked in a frying pan with an ovenproof handle.

1 cup finely chopped onion
1 cup finely chopped celery
2 tablespoons olive oil
One 14½-ounce can diced tomatoes
2 bay leaves
½ teaspoon dried thyme
One 10-ounce package frozen
   cut okra

1 teaspoon lemon-pepper seasoning
1½ teaspoons House Seasoning
   (see page 325)
1 cup chicken or fish stock
2 cups shrimp, cleaned, peeled,
   and deveined

In an iron skillet sauté onion and celery in oil. Add tomatoes, bay leaves, thyme, okra, lemon-pepper seasoning, and House Seasoning. Pour in stock. Cover pot and gently simmer for 30 minutes. Remove from heat and stir in shrimp. Prepare topping.

TOPPING

1 egg, beaten
⅓ cup milk

One 12-ounce package corn
   muffin mix

Preheat oven to 400 degrees. Mix together egg and milk. In separate bowl, place muffin mix and add egg-milk mixture. Mix until just well blended. Drop by tablespoonfuls on top of hot shrimp mixture, leaving the center uncovered. Bake 15 to 20 minutes.

Lemon Mackerel

SERVES 4

2 pounds Spanish mackerel fillets,
   skin on

¼ cup olive oil
½ cup lemon juice

2 tablespoons butter
1 teaspoon salt

1 teaspoon lemon-pepper seasoning
Lemon slices

Preheat oven to 350 degrees. Rinse fish fillets and lay on paper towels to dry. Rub a glass casserole dish with olive oil. Also rub fish fillets with olive oil. Lay fillets skin side down in dish. Pour lemon juice on fish (¼ inch in dish) and spread fish with butter. Sprinkle with salt and lemon-pepper seasoning. Put about three slices of lemon on each fillet. Bake for 20 to 30 minutes, until fish flakes easily with fork. If you would like your fillet to brown more, put it under the broiler for 2 to 3 extra minutes.

Shrimp and Mushroom Casserole

SERVES 4

This recipe can be served as a main dish with a green salad and French bread or as a side dish with steak or seafood.

8 tablespoons (1 stick) butter
¾ cup all-purpose flour
1½ cups half-and-half
One 10¾-ounce can condensed
    cream of mushroom soup
One 13¼-ounce can sliced
    mushrooms, drained

½ cup grated Parmesan cheese
1 pound cooked shrimp, peeled,
    deveined, and coarsely diced
Garlic powder
Buttered bread crumbs for topping

Preheat oven to 350 degrees. In saucepan over medium heat, melt butter and stir in flour, then slowly blend in half-and-half, stirring constantly. Sauce will be thick. Do not brown. Add mushroom soup, sliced mushrooms, and Parmesan cheese. Fold in shrimp. Add garlic powder to taste. Pour mixture into buttered casserole dish and top with buttered bread crumbs. Bake for 25 to 30 minutes.

Red Snapper Stuffed with Crabmeat

SERVES 8

*1 whole dressed red snapper, at
   least 7 pounds*
Salt and pepper to taste
Garlic powder to taste
Onion salt to taste
*2 pounds crabmeat, picked free of
   shell*

2 eggs, beaten
1 medium onion, chopped
1 sleeve saltine crackers, crushed
6 slices bacon
2 slices lemon
*¼ teaspoon dried dill or
   1 tablespoon chopped fresh dill*

Preheat oven to 350 degrees. Line a baking pan with aluminum foil. Grease the foil so the fish won't stick. Lay the fish in the pan. Season inside and out with salt, pepper, garlic powder, and onion salt. Make two slits on the side of the fish facing up. To stuff the fish, mix the crabmeat, beaten eggs, chopped onion, saltines, salt, and pepper to taste. Stuff this mixture in the cavity of the fish. If it is more than the fish will hold, put it all around the cavity. Lay bacon and lemon slices on fish and lightly sprinkle with dill. Bake, covered, for 1 hour. Remove cover for the last few minutes to brown.

Shrimp and Artichoke Bake

SERVES 4

2 tablespoons butter
2 tablespoons all-purpose flour
1½ cups half-and-half
¼ cup grated Parmesan cheese
¼ cup sherry
1 tablespoon Worcestershire sauce
*1 teaspoon House Seasoning (see
   page 325)*
2 egg yolks, lightly beaten

*One 13¾-ounce can artichoke
   hearts, drained and chopped*
*1 pound shrimp, cleaned, peeled,
   and deveined*
¼ pound fresh mushrooms
*¾ cup grated Cheddar and
   Monterey Jack cheese
   (combined)*
Paprika to taste

Preheat oven to 350 degrees. Melt butter in saucepan over medium heat. Blend in flour to make a paste. Add half-and-half all at once, stirring constantly until thickened and smooth. Add Parmesan cheese, sherry, Worcestershire sauce, and garlic powder, salt, and pepper. Temper egg yolks with 2 tablespoons of hot mixture and add back to remaining cheese sauce. Set aside. Mix artichoke hearts, shrimp, and mushrooms together. Put in baking dish and pour sauce over top. Sprinkle top with grated cheese and paprika. Bake for 30 to 35 minutes. Serve over rice.

Bourbon Beef Tenderloin

SERVES 8 TO 10

This recipe is for the grill. Beef can also be cooked in the oven at 350 degrees for 45 minutes to 1 hour. Use a meat thermometer: rare—115 to 120 degrees; medium rare—130 to 135 degrees; medium—140 to 145 degrees. Buy a whole tenderloin, about 4½ to 5 pounds, and have the butcher remove the "silver" connective tissue.

1 cup bourbon
1 cup brown sugar
⅔ cup soy sauce
1 bunch cilantro, chopped
½ cup lemon juice
1 tablespoon Worcestershire sauce

2 cups water
3 to 4 sprigs fresh thyme, chopped
*1 beef tenderloin, silver connective
    tissue removed*
Oil for grill

Prepare marinade by combining bourbon, brown sugar, soy sauce, cilantro, lemon juice, Worcestershire sauce, water, and thyme. Be sure tenderloin is completely trimmed of any fat and connective tissue. Fold the tail end of the beef back underneath itself so that it is of uniform thickness. Secure with butcher's string. Pour marinade over meat, cover, and refrigerate 8 to 12 hours. Turn meat over several times during that time. Prepare grill for cooking (or preheat oven to 350 degrees). When fire is ready, place meat on oiled grill, reserving marinade. Cook over high heat with lid closed, turning often; occasionally baste. Cooks rare in about 30 or 45 minutes in the oven. Serve with Horseradish Cream on the side.

HORSERADISH CREAM

1 cup heavy cream   ¼ cup horseradish, drained

Whip cream until stiff. Stir in horseradish, mixing well.

Old-Time Beef Stew

SERVES 6

2 pounds stew beef   ½ teaspoon pepper
2 tablespoons vegetable oil   ½ teaspoon paprika
2 cups water   Dash of ground allspice or ground
1 teaspoon Worcestershire sauce   cloves
1 clove garlic, peeled   3 large carrots, sliced
1 or 2 bay leaves   4 red potatoes, quartered
1 medium onion, sliced   3 ribs celery, chopped
1 teaspoon salt   2 tablespoons cornstarch
1 teaspoon sugar

Brown meat in hot oil. Add water, Worcestershire sauce, garlic, bay leaves, onion, salt, sugar, pepper, paprika, and allspice. Cover and simmer 1½ hours. Remove bay leaves and garlic clove. Add carrots, potatoes, and celery. Cover and cook 30 to 40 minutes longer. To thicken gravy, remove 2 cups hot liquid. Using a separate bowl, combine ¼ cup water and cornstarch until smooth. Mix with hot liquid and return mixture to pot. Stir and cook until bubbly.   ❦ ❦ ❦   **The Lady & Sons**

Basic Meat Loaf

SERVES 4

1 pound ground beef   1 egg, lightly beaten
1¼ teaspoons salt   8 ounces canned diced tomatoes,
¼ teaspoon ground black pepper   with juice
½ cup chopped onion   ½ cup quick-cooking oats
½ cup chopped bell pepper

Preheat oven to 375 degrees. Mix all meat loaf ingredients well and place in a baking dish. Shape into a loaf.

TOPPING

⅓ cup ketchup

2 tablespoons brown sugar

1 tablespoon prepared mustard

Mix ingredients for topping and spread on loaf. Bake for 1 hour.

❦ ❦ ❦ *The Lady & Sons*

Barbecue-Style Pork Chops

SERVES 6

6 center-cut pork chops, trimmed
   of fat

1 tablespoon vegetable oil

One 14½-ounce can whole
   tomatoes, crushed

½ cup ketchup

¼ cup dark brown sugar

2 tablespoons Worcestershire sauce

2 tablespoons prepared mustard

½ teaspoon salt

Preheat oven to 350 degrees. Brown pork chops in oil. Drain, then place in a 13 × 9-inch baking dish. Combine remaining ingredients and spoon over chops. Bake for 45 minutes. Great served with macaroni and cheese!

Pot Roast

SERVES 6

Put this on to cook in a Crock-Pot before leaving for work and come home in the evening to a mouthwatering dinner.

One 3-pound boneless chuck roast

1½ teaspoons House Seasoning (see
   page 325)

¼ cup vegetable oil

1 onion, thinly sliced

3 bay leaves

3 or 4 beef bouillon cubes, crushed

2 cloves garlic, crushed

One 10¾-ounce can condensed
   cream of mushroom soup

¼ to ½ cup Chardonnay wine

Sprinkle roast on all sides with House Seasoning; season well. In moderately hot skillet, brown roast on all sides in oil. Place roast in Crock-Pot. On top of the roast, layer onion, bay leaves, crushed beef bouillon cubes, crushed garlic, and cream of mushroom soup. Add Chardonnay. Cover with just enough water to cover all the ingredients sufficiently. Cook on low setting approximately 8 hours.

Pepper Steak

SERVES 4

One 1½-pound round steak	*1 large onion*
Sprinkle of paprika	*1 large bell pepper*
2 tablespoons butter	*2 tablespoons cornstarch*
Garlic salt to taste	*¼ cup water*
One 10½-ounce can beef broth	*¼ cup soy sauce*

Pound round steak and cut into ¼-inch strips; sprinkle with paprika. Brown meat in butter; add garlic salt and beef broth. Cover; simmer for 30 minutes. Cut onion and pepper into strips. Add to meat and simmer for 5 minutes. Mix cornstarch, water, and soy sauce and add to meat mixture. Simmer until sauce thickens slightly. Serve over rice.

❦ ❦ ❦ **The Lady & Sons**

Burgundy Beef Roast

YIELD DEPENDS ON SIZE OF ROAST (6 TO 8 OUNCES PER SERVING)

1 eye of round roast (be sure you know exact weight)	*⅓ cup soy sauce*
½ cup red Burgundy wine	*2 tablespoons cracked black pepper*

Place roast in glass container large enough to hold it comfortably. Make marinade of Burgundy wine, soy sauce, and pepper. Pour over meat and marinate overnight. Next day, place roast in shallow pan with just a little of the marinade. Preheat oven to 500 degrees. Cook uncovered for 5 minutes per pound of meat. Turn off oven and cover roast with foil. Leave in oven for 40 minutes for medium-rare roast. Let cool and slice very thin.

Sausage-Rice Casserole

SERVES 4

One 6-ounce box Uncle Ben's
   long-grain and wild rice
1 pound ground sausage
2 small onions, chopped

One 4-ounce can mushroom pieces
One 10¾-ounce can condensed
   cream of mushroom soup
4 tablepoons (½ stick) butter

Preheat oven to 350 degrees. Cook rice according to directions on box. In a heavy skillet over medium heat, cook sausage until thoroughly done, about 4 to 5 minutes; drain. Combine all ingredients except butter and pour into casserole dish. Dot top with butter. Bake until bubbly, about 25 minutes.   🍀 🍀 🍀   **The Lady & Sons**

Beef Stroganoff

SERVES 4 TO 6

6 tablespoons all-purpose flour
⅔ cup water
4 tablespoons (½ stick) butter
2 pounds round steak
1 teaspoon House Seasoning
   (see page 325)

One 10¾-ounce can condensed
   cream of mushroom soup
One 10¾-ounce can condensed
   French onion soup
1 cup sour cream

Mix flour and water and set aside. Heat butter in a large, heavy skillet. Season steak with House Seasoning and cook until brown on both sides. Remove from pan and cut into thin strips. Add to pan drippings cream of mushroom soup, French onion soup, 1 soup can water, and flour mixture. Simmer and stir constantly until thickened (if too thick, add a small amount of water). Add steak and simmer for 45 minutes. Add sour cream and heat until bubbling. Serve over cooked noodles.

🍀 🍀 🍀 **The Lady & Sons**

Cheeseburger Meat Loaf and Sauce

SERVES 6 TO 8

2 pounds ground beef
2 teaspoons House Seasoning
   (see page 325)
1 medium onion, chopped
1 medium bell pepper, chopped
1 cup grated Cheddar cheese

¼ cup Worcestershire sauce
1 cup sour cream
1 cup crushed Ritz crackers
1 teaspoon Lawry's Seasoned Salt
8 to 10 slices white bread

Preheat oven to 325 degrees. Mix all ingredients except bread slices well. Shape into loaf. Place loaf on 1-inch-deep jelly roll pan lined with white bread slices. Bake loaf for 45 to 60 minutes. The bread absorbs the grease and should be discarded after loaf is removed from oven.

SAUCE

One 10¾-ounce can condensed
   cream of mushroom soup

1 soup-can measure of milk
1½ cups grated Cheddar cheese

Heat soup and milk over medium heat; add cheese. Pour over meat loaf or pass at the table.

🍀 🍀 🍀 **The Lady & Sons**

Veal and Creamed Spinach

SERVES 4 TO 6

4 to 6 veal scallopini
1 egg, beaten
1 teaspoon House Seasoning
   (see page 325)

1 sleeve from one 16-ounce box
   Ritz crackers, crushed
3 tablespoons olive oil
½ cup white wine

1 large onion, chopped
1 bunch fresh spinach, trimmed at
  stems, soaked, and cleaned
  thoroughly

¼ cup heavy cream (optional)
Salt and pepper to taste

Between sheets of wax paper, pound veal into ¼-inch-thick slices. Beat egg with House Seasoning. Dip veal in egg, then dip into Ritz cracker crumbs. Sauté in heated oil for about 2 minutes on each side over medium heat. Pour wine into pan and cook for another minute or two. Remove veal. Add chopped onion and fresh spinach to pan and sauté until spinach is done, 2 to 3 minutes (don't overcook). Add cream and continue to sauté for 1 more minute or until hot. Season with salt and pepper. Pour onto platter. Place veal on top of spinach. Garnish as you wish and serve from the platter at the table. If you're looking to cut back on calories, don't add the cream.

Foolproof Standing Rib Roast

SERVES 6 TO 8

One 5-pound standing rib roast

1 tablespoon House Seasoning (see page 325)

Follow this method for a rib roast that is lusciously browned on the outside and rare on the inside—regardless of size. Allow roast to stand at room temperature for at least 1 hour. If roast is frozen, thaw completely; bring to room temperature. Preheat oven to 375 degrees. Rub roast with House Seasoning; place roast on rack in pan—rib side down, fatty side up. Roast for 1 hour. Turn off oven. Leave roast in oven but *do not open oven door.* Thirty to 40 minutes before serving time, turn oven to 375 degrees and reheat roast. Important: Do not remove roast or open oven door from time roast is put in until ready to serve.

❧ ❧ ❧ **The Lady & Sons**

Swiss Steak

SERVES 4

1 round steak (approximately
   1½ pounds) (see Note)
1 teaspoon garlic powder
Salt and pepper to taste
Flour for dusting
⅓ cup vegetable oil

2 cloves garlic, crushed
One 14½-ounce can diced
   tomatoes
1 medium onion, cut into strips
1 medium bell pepper, cut into
   strips

Cut steak into serving-size pieces. Season to taste with garlic powder
and salt and pepper. Dust meat with flour. In heavy skillet, brown both
sides of meat in vegetable oil. Transfer to Dutch oven. Combine garlic, tomatoes, onion, bell pepper, and 1 tomato-can measure of water.
Pour over steak and simmer until meat is tender. Season to taste with
additional salt and pepper. Hint: This is good to cook in Crock-Pot on
low for a most fabulous dinner.

NOTE: To ensure tenderness, it is necessary to have the butcher run
the round steak through a cuber.

Farmer's Pork Chops

SERVES 8

8 medium potatoes
½ medium onion
Salt and pepper to taste
White sauce (see recipe below; you
   may also use your own)
1 cup all-purpose flour

2 tablespoons Lawry's Seasoned
   Salt
8 center-cut pork chops, about
   ½ inch thick
⅓ cup vegetable oil

Preheat oven to 350 degrees. Peel potatoes; slice ¼ inch thick and
cover with cold water. Slice onion into very thin slices. Cut slices in
half. Drain potatoes; layer half the potatoes in a well-greased 15 × 10-
inch casserole dish. Sprinkle with salt and pepper to taste. Scatter half

of onion slices on top of potatoes. Repeat with remaining potatoes and onions. Cover potatoes with white sauce. Cover casserole dish with plastic wrap and microwave for 5 minutes on high or bake uncovered for 15 minutes. Mix together flour and seasoned salt and dredge pork chops in flour mixture. Lightly brown chops in vegetable oil. *Do not cook them completely.* As chops are removed from frying pan, lay them on top of potatoes. Bake at 350 degrees for 45 to 60 minutes. The juices from the pork chops will drip down into the potatoes. Delicious!

WHITE SAUCE

8 tablespoons (1 stick) butter
½ cup all-purpose flour
1 to 2 teaspoons salt
½ to ¾ teaspoon pepper

4 cups milk
¼ cup chopped fresh parsley or
    chives (optional)

Melt butter; remove from heat. Stir in flour; add salt and pepper. Return to heat and cook, stirring constantly, until mixture is bubbly. Add milk, 1 cup at a time. Bring to a boil over medium heat, stirring frequently. Reduce heat and simmer 1 to 2 minutes, then let stand at least 1 to 2 minutes. Stir in parsley or chives, if desired.

Steak and Greens

SERVES 6

For the best flavor, you must use at least three types of greens—turnip, collard, mustard, and spinach are all good. When you brown the flour, you should stir it about five minutes. (I always keep a batch in the fridge.)

1½ pounds beef flank or round
    steak, sliced thin
2 tablespoons vegetable oil
2 cups chopped onion
12 to 15 cups greens, washed and
    chopped

6 cups beef stock
5 tablespoons all-purpose flour,
    browned in hot, dry skillet

SEASONING MIX

1 tablespoon paprika
2 teaspoons salt
2 teaspoons dry mustard
1½ teaspoons onion powder
1 teaspoon garlic powder
1 teaspoon dried thyme

¾ teaspoon white pepper
½ teaspoon ground black pepper
¼ teaspoon cayenne pepper
½ teaspoon ground cumin
1 teaspoon ground ginger

Mix together seasoning mix. Sprinkle 2 tablespoons on sliced steak, tossing to insure the meat is covered. (Set aside remaining seasoning for later use.) Heat heavy 5-quart pot; add oil. Brown seasoned meat 2 or 3 minutes, turning once. Add onion, rest of seasoning mix, and ½ cup of each type of greens. Cook, scraping bottom of pot to clear all brown bits, for 5 to 10 minutes. Add 1 cup stock, cover, and cook for 15 minutes. Add browned flour and mix until completely absorbed and no longer visible. Add remaining stock and greens; bring to a boil, reduce heat, and cook until greens and meat are tender, about 20 minutes. Serve over creamy grits, rice, or with boiled new potatoes. Additional broth would make it a great soup. However served, it needs a good, crusty bread. This is a sopping dish.

The Lady's Oven-Roasted Ribs

SERVES 6

One 5-pound slab pork ribs
4 teaspoons liquid smoke
    (available in a bottle at
    grocery store)

2 teaspoons House Seasoning (see
    page 325)
2 teaspoons seasoned salt

Preheat oven to 325 degrees. Wash ribs and drain. Rub each side with liquid smoke, garlic powder, salt, pepper, and seasoned salt. Refrigerate for 4 to 24 hours. Roast uncovered for 1½ hours.

❦ ❦ ❦ **The Lady & Sons**

Sausage and Grits

SERVES 10

1 cup uncooked grits
1 pound ground sausage
1 onion, chopped
Two 4½-ounce cans green chilies,
    chopped
8 tablespoons (1 stick) butter

2 eggs, beaten
2 cups grated Cheddar cheese
10 dashes Tabasco
1 teaspoon paprika
¼ cup chopped fresh parsley

Preheat oven to 325 degrees. Cook grits in 4 cups salted water until thick. Sauté sausage, breaking it into small pieces. Sauté onion in sausage fat; drain. Add onion and chilies to sausage. Add butter, eggs, cheese, and Tabasco to grits. Combine grits mixture with sausage mixture. Pour into a 13 × 9-inch casserole dish and garnish with additional small amounts of cheese, chilies, paprika, and parsley. Bake for 1 hour. Can be refrigerated up to 2 days before baking. Freezes well.

Piggy Pudding

SERVES 4 TO 5

This is a great no-fuss recipe—wonderful for a brunch or Sunday-night supper.

16 link pork sausages
4 to 5 tart apples, peeled, cored,
    and sliced

One 7½-ounce package corn bread
    mix (prepare batter according
    to directions on package)

Preheat oven to 450 degrees. Cook sausages until done, piercing with fork to let out fat. Drain, then arrange in a 9-inch square baking dish. Layer sliced apples on top. Pour corn bread batter over all and bake for approximately 30 minutes or until corn bread is done. Serve with warm maple syrup.

Southern Fried Chicken

SERVES 4

My Grandmother Paul always said to season chicken and return it to the refrigerator and let it sit as long as time permits, at least 2 to 3 hours. At the restaurant, we season ours with House Seasoning and Lawry's Seasoned Salt. Always use small chickens. I find that a Dutch oven works best for frying chicken.

3 eggs
⅓ cup water
2 cups self-rising flour
1 teaspoon pepper

One 1- to 2½-pound chicken, cut
 into pieces
Crisco shortening for frying

Beat eggs with water. To just enough self-rising flour to coat all the chicken, add black pepper. Dip seasoned chicken in egg; coat well in flour mixture. Fry in moderately hot shortening (350°) until brown and crisp. Remember that dark meat requires longer cooking time (about 13 to 14 minutes, compared to 8 to 10 minutes for white meat).

❧ ❧ ❧ *The Lady & Sons*

Chicken Pot Pie

SERVES 6 TO 8

One 10¾-ounce can condensed
 Cheddar cheese soup
One 10¾-ounce can condensed
 cream of celery soup
½ cup milk
1 chicken, skinned, cooked, boned,
 and cubed
1 medium onion, diced
One 10-ounce package frozen
 green peas (or one 8-ounce can,
 drained)

3 carrots, sliced, cooked, and
 drained
Salt and pepper to taste
1 pastry for top and bottom (see
 next page)
Butter to dot pastry

In a large saucepan, heat soups and milk. Stir in chicken, onion, peas, carrots, and salt and pepper. Cook until mixture boils. Remove from heat. Preheat oven to 350 degrees. Pour into a pastry-lined 13 × 9 × 2-inch pan. Cut pastry for top into strips. Lay over pie filling in a lattice style. Dot with butter. Bake for 45 minutes until golden brown.

PASTRY

3 cups all-purpose flour
1 teaspoon salt
¼ teaspoon baking powder

¾ cup Crisco shortening
Ice water

Sift together flour, salt, and baking powder. Cut in shortening with pastry blender until pieces are the size of small peas. Sprinkle 1 to 2 tablespoons of ice water over part of mixture. Gently toss with fork; push to side of bowl. Repeat until all is moistened. Form into 2 balls. Flatten each on a lightly floured surface by pressing with edge of hand three times across in both directions. With a floured rolling pin, roll out on floured surface. Roll from center to edge until ⅛ inch thick.

❧ ❧ ❧ *The Lady & Sons*

Chicken Brunswick Stew

SERVES 6 TO 8

One 2½-pound fryer
One 28-ounce can crushed toma-
toes, sweetened with ⅓ cup sugar
One 16-ounce can creamed corn
1 cup ketchup
½ cup prepared barbecue sauce
1 tablespoon liquid smoke
(available in a bottle at grocery
store)

1 onion, chopped
1 tablespoon vinegar
1 tablespoon Worcestershire sauce
Salt and pepper to taste
Celery salt to taste

In a large pot, boil chicken until meat falls off bone, approximately 45 minutes; drain (reserve 1 to 2 cups of stock). Remove skin and bones;

chop meat. In a separate pot, mix chicken and remaining ingredients. Simmer slowly for about 30 minutes, stirring often to prevent sticking. (Add a little bit of stock if stew gets too thick.) Serve over steamed rice.

❦ ❦ ❦ *The Lady & Sons*

Baked Hen and Dressing

SERVES 8 TO 10

One 6-pound hen
4 to 6 ribs celery, cut into large
  pieces
2 tablespoons salt
1 tablespoon whole peppercorns

4 bay leaves
1 large onion, peeled and left
  whole
3 chicken bouillon cubes

Remove giblets from bird. Wash giblets and bird well, inside and out. Place all ingredients including giblets in large pot, cover with water, and bring to a boil. Reduce heat and simmer until tender, approximately 2 to 2½ hours. Skim fat from pot at end of cooking time. (You will need to reserve stock for stuffing and gravy.) In the meantime, prepare and cook corn bread.

CORN BREAD

1 cup self-rising cornmeal
½ cup self-rising flour
¾ cup buttermilk

2 eggs
2 tablespoons vegetable oil

Preheat oven to 350 degrees. Combine all ingredients and pour into a greased shallow baking dish. Bake for approximately 20 to 25 minutes. Remove from oven and let cool.

SOUTHERN CORN BREAD STUFFING

7 slices white bread (dried in
  warm oven)
Corn bread

1 sleeve saltine crackers
2 cups chopped celery
1 large onion, chopped

8 tablespoons (1 stick) butter
7 cups stock reserved from cooking
   hen
1 teaspoon salt
½ teaspoon pepper

1 teaspoon sage (optional)
1 tablespoon poultry seasoning
   (optional)
5 eggs, beaten

Preheat oven to 350 degrees. Crumble dried white bread slices, corn-bread, and saltines; mix together and set aside. Sauté chopped celery and onion in butter until transparent, approximately 5 to 10 minutes. Pour over corn bread mixture. Add stock; mix well and taste; add salt, pepper, sage, and poultry seasoning. Add beaten eggs and mix well. Reserve 2 heaping tablespoons of this mixture for the giblet gravy. Pour into a greased pan. Place bird on top of dressing and bake until dressing is done, about 45 minutes. If hen browns too quickly, make a tent of foil and place over bird.

GIBLET GRAVY

4 cups stock reserved from cooking
   hen
Giblets from hen (liver, gizzard,
   and neck), chopped
2 chicken bouillon cubes
2 heaping tablespoons reserved
   uncooked corn bread stuffing
   mix

3 tablespoons cornstarch
⅓ cup cold water
1 hard-boiled egg, sliced
Salt and pepper to taste

Bring stock to a boil along with giblets and the meat that has been re-moved from the neck. Add bouillon cubes and raw stuffing mixture. Mix cornstarch with water and add to boiling stock, stirring constantly. Reduce heat and continue to cook for 2 to 3 minutes. Add salt and pepper to taste, and add sliced boiled egg. Serve with hen.

❧ ❧ ❧ *The Lady & Sons*

Chicken in Wine Sauce

SERVES 4

*4 large skinless boneless chicken
 breasts*
6 ounces Swiss cheese slices
*One 10¾-ounce can condensed
 cream of chicken soup*
¼ cup white wine (more if desired)

Salt and pepper to taste
*1 cup herb-flavored Pepperidge
 Farm stuffing mix, crushed*
*4 tablespoons (½ stick) butter,
 melted*

Preheat oven to 350 degrees. Place chicken in shallow buttered casserole. Layer cheese on top. Mix soup, wine, salt, and pepper; pour over cheese. Sprinkle stuffing mix on top and drizzle with melted butter. Bake for 45–60 minutes.

Chicken Paprika

SERVES 6 TO 8

1 large onion, chopped
1 clove garlic, minced
4 tablespoons olive oil
One 4- to 5-pound chicken, cut up
2 tablespoons paprika
1 teaspoon pepper

2 teaspoons salt
1½ cups water
1 cup sour cream
1 tablespoon all-purpose flour
Dumplings (optional)

In a deep skillet over medium heat, brown onion and garlic in oil. Add chicken and brown on all sides, about 10 minutes. Sprinkle paprika, pepper, and salt on chicken. Turn meat once. Add water, cover, and simmer on low heat for approximately 30 minutes or until meat is tender. Remove from liquid. In a small bowl, mix sour cream, flour, and 1 cup of hot liquid from chicken until smooth. Pour mixture into skillet and blend with remaining liquid. Add dumplings if desired and heat through. This dish may be served over noodles or rice instead of dumplings.

DUMPLINGS

3 eggs, beaten
3 cups all-purpose flour

1 teaspoon salt
½ cup water

Blend all ingredients and mix well. Drop batter by teaspoonfuls into boiling water. Cook about 10 minutes and drain. Rinse with cold water and drain again.

Chicken Georgia

SERVES 4 TO 6

4 tablespoons (½ stick) butter
4 skinless boneless chicken breast
 halves
1 cup sliced fresh mushrooms

2 tablespoons minced shallots
¼ teaspoon salt
¼ teaspoon pepper
4 ounces grated mozzarella cheese

Melt butter over medium heat. Add mushrooms and shallots and sprinkle with salt and pepper. Cook 10 minutes. Add chicken and cook 10 minutes on each side, or until tender. Transfer chicken to platter and sprinkle with grated cheese. Top with mushroom mixture. Cover and let stand 5 minutes or until cheese melts.

Herbed Stuffed Chicken Breasts

SERVES 4

4 whole skinless boneless chicken
 breasts (approximately 5 to 7
 ounces each)
One 3-ounce package cream
 cheese, softened
3 ounces feta cheese, crumbled
½ teaspoon dried sweet basil

½ teaspoon dried oregano
½ teaspoon House Seasoning
 (see page 325)
4 slices bacon
1 leek (optional)
4 tablespoons (½ stick) butter,
 melted

Preheat oven to 275 degrees. Wash and pound each chicken breast flat. Lay chicken breast on cookie sheet or large platter and spread it with cream cheese, followed by a quarter of the feta cheese. Mix together basil, oregano, and House Seasoning and sprinkle over chicken. Roll up each breast and wrap with a slice of bacon. At this time, if desired, you can tie up each rolled chicken breast with the green top of a leek. Cut the green top off the vegetable, leaving it long enough to tie around the breast and allowing a couple of extra inches for a knot. Place chicken breasts in a casserole dish and pour melted butter over all. Cover casserole dish with foil and bake for 1½ hours. Uncover dish and increase temperature to 350 degrees. Continue to bake, allowing the bacon to brown, for 15 to 20 minutes. Or you could place dish under broiler for a few minutes to brown. Serve over rice, with pan juices poured on top.

Honey Game Hens

SERVES 6

6 Cornish game hens (about ¾ to 1 pound each)	*½ cup soy sauce*
4 cloves garlic, chopped	*½ cup honey*
One 1-inch piece of ginger, peeled and chopped	*2 tablespoons peanut oil*
	2 tablespoons orange juice
	1 tablespoon orange zest, minced

Rinse hens, trim off excess fat, and pat dry; place in bowl. Put garlic and ginger in food processor and process until nearly smooth. In another bowl, combine soy sauce, honey, oil, orange juice, and zest. Add the garlic and ginger. Pour mixture over game hens, coating well. Refrigerate overnight, turning in marinade several times. Preheat oven to 350 degrees. Place game hens in shallow roasting pan; pour marinade on top. Bake for 1 hour, basting every 15 minutes. Remove hens to serving platter. Pour cooking juices into small, heavy saucepan and boil for 5 minutes, or until sauce thickens. Pour over hens just before serving. Serve with sesame noodles or rice pilaf. These hens can also be grilled—just remember to baste often.

Pecan Chicken

SERVES 8

8 tablespoons (1 stick) butter
1 cup buttermilk
1 egg, lightly beaten
1 cup all-purpose flour
1 cup ground pecans
1 tablespoon salt

1 tablespoon paprika
⅛ teaspoon pepper
¼ cup sesame seeds
Two 2½-pound chickens, cut into
    quarters or pieces
¼ cup pecan halves

Preheat oven to 350 degrees. Melt butter in a 10 × 15-inch baking pan. In a shallow dish, combine buttermilk and egg. In another dish combine flour, pecans, salt, paprika, pepper, and sesame seeds. Dip chicken in buttermilk, then in flour. Place skin side down in melted butter. Turn to coat and leave skin side up. Sprinkle with pecan halves. Bake for 1¼ hours.

Chicken and Rice Casserole

SERVES 6 TO 8

3 cups diced cooked chicken
1 medium onion, diced and
    sautéed
One 8-ounce can water chestnuts,
    drained and chopped
Two 14½-ounce cans French green
    beans, rinsed and drained
One 4-ounce can pimentos, rinsed
    and drained

One 10¾-ounce can condensed
    cream of celery soup
1 cup mayonnaise
One 6-ounce box Uncle Ben's long-
    grain and wild rice, cooked
    according to package directions
1 cup grated sharp Cheddar cheese

Preheat oven to 300 degrees. Mix all ingredients together and pour into a 3-quart casserole. Bake for 25 minutes.

❧ ❧ ❧ **The Lady & Sons**

Chicken and Dumplings

SERVES 4 TO 6

One 2½-pound chicken
3 ribs celery, chopped
1 large onion, chopped
2 bay leaves
2 chicken bouillon cubes
1 teaspoon House Seasoning
  (see page 325)

4 quarts water
One 10¾-ounce can condensed
  cream of celery or cream of
  chicken soup

Cut up chicken, but do not remove skin. The skin and bones can be removed later. Place chicken, celery, onion, bay leaves, bouillon, and House Seasoning in water and boil at a rolling boil for 30 to 45 minutes, until meat begins to fall off the bones. Remove skin and bones at this point, along with bay leaves. Return chicken to pan. Prepare dumplings and set them aside for a few minutes. Add cream soup to chicken and continue to boil. If desired, you can thicken the stock a little by mixing 2 tablespoons cornstarch with ¼ cup of water and adding it to the stock. Drop dumplings into boiling stock. Never stir dumplings. Shake the pot gently in a circular motion to submerge dumplings in stock. Cook for a few minutes more, until dumplings are done. Do not overcook.

DUMPLINGS

2 cups all-purpose flour mixed
  with 1 teaspoon salt

¾ cup ice water

Put flour in a mixing bowl. Beginning in center of flour, dribble small amount of ice water. Work mixture with fingers from center of bowl to sides of bowl, incorporating small amounts of water at a time. Continue until all flour is used up. Batter will feel as if it is going to be tough. Knead dough and form into ball. Dust a good amount of flour onto dough board and rolling pin. Roll out dough, working from center. Dough will be firm. Roll to ⅛ inch thinness. Let it air-dry for a minute or two while you return your attention to the boiling pot at the point at which you add the canned soup to the chicken mixture. Cut dumplings into 1-inch strips. Working with one strip at a time, hold strip over pot, pull it in half, and drop into the boiling stock. Remember, do not stir mixture after dumplings have been added to pot.

❦ ❦ ❦ *The Lady & Sons*

NOTE: Frozen dumplings are available in most supermarkets if you don't have the time to make them.

Marinated Cornish Hens

SERVES 2 TO 4

2 split Cornish hens
1 onion, diced
1 clove garlic, minced
8 tablespoons (1 stick) butter
One 10¾-ounce can beef broth

1 bay leaf
¼ teaspoon dried thyme
2 tablespoons sherry
Salt and pepper to taste
16 ounces fresh mushrooms, sliced

Wash, pat dry, and salt and pepper hens. Place in long, flat baking dish. Sauté onion and garlic in butter. Add remaining ingredients except the mushrooms. Stir and pour over hens; cover and refrigerate overnight. Preheat oven to 350 degrees. Add mushrooms and bake for 1 hour, basting frequently. Serve with wild rice.

VARIATION: Chicken can be substituted for Cornish hens.

Herb-Baked Chicken

SERVES 4

One 1- to 2-pound chicken, cut in
   quarters, skin removed
3 to 4 tablespoons olive oil
¼ cup teriyaki sauce
¼ teaspoon dried oregano

¼ teaspoon dried rosemary
1 teaspoon chopped fresh ginger
½ teaspoon salt
⅛ teaspoon pepper
1 lemon, sliced thin

Preheat oven to 350 degrees. Coat chicken with oil and place in baking dish. Sprinkle with teriyaki sauce. Combine oregano, rosemary, ginger, salt, and pepper; sprinkle over chicken. Top with lemon slices. Bake for about 1 hour.

Chicken Breasts in Sour Cream Sauce

*Very easy/good
& quite good*

SERVES 6 TO 8

8 slices dried beef (in a jar)

8 skinless boneless chicken breast halves (7 ounces each)

4 slices bacon, cut in half

1 cup sour cream

One 10¾-ounce can condensed cream of mushroom soup

2 cups sliced fresh mushrooms

Preheat oven to 300 degrees. Lay one piece of dried beef on each chicken breast and wrap with a half slice of bacon. Place in a 13 × 9-inch casserole dish, seam side down. Mix sour cream, soup, and mushrooms together. Pour over chicken breasts. Cover and bake for 1½ hours. Serve with rice.

Duck Burgundy

SERVES 4 TO 6

The flavor in this recipe really comes out if you can let the duck marinate in the seasoning for a few hours or overnight.

4 whole ducks

Salt and pepper to taste

Garlic powder to taste

Poultry seasoning to taste

1 large onion, quartered

1 apple, quartered

1 orange, quartered

4 ribs celery, cut into 1-inch pieces

⅓ cup soy sauce

⅓ cup vegetable oil

½ cup red Burgundy wine

Preheat oven to 450 degrees. Clean ducks well and rub body cavities lightly with salt, pepper, garlic powder, and poultry seasoning. Stuff cavities with pieces of onion, apple, orange, and celery. Rub ducks with soy sauce and oil. Place in baking pan. Roast uncovered, basting often with Burgundy wine. Allow 10 to 15 minutes baking time per pound of duck. Remove stuffing before serving.

Chicken Casserole

SERVES 6 TO 8

1 fryer, cooked, boned, and cut
   into small pieces (reserve broth)
½ cup mayonnaise
½ cup chopped onion
4 eggs
8 tablespoons (1 stick) butter,
   melted

2½ cups chicken broth
1 package Pepperidge Farm corn
   bread stuffing mix
1 cup milk
One 10¾-ounce can condensed
   cream of chicken soup

Combine chicken, mayonnaise, and chopped onion and set aside. Combine 2 eggs, the butter, chicken broth, and corn bread stuffing mix and set aside. In small bowl, lightly beat 2 eggs and milk. Spray large casserole dish with nonstick cooking spray. In bottom of dish, spread half the stuffing mixture; then layer with chicken mixture. Add second layer of stuffing mixture. Pour egg and milk mixture over top layer of stuffing mixture. Refrigerate overnight. Preheat oven to 350 degrees. Spread cream of chicken soup on top of casserole and bake for 45 minutes.

Vegetables and Side Dishes

Cheesy Broccoli Bake

Baked Grits

Squash Casserole

Sherry-Glazed Sweet Potatoes

Turnip Greens with Cornmeal Dumplings

Steakside Mushrooms

The Lady's Cheesy Mac

Twice-Baked Potatoes

Savannah Red Rice

Collard Greens

Eggplant Casserole

Vidalia Onion Pie

Sweet Potato Chips

Broccoli Soufflé

Boursin Cheese Potatoes

Fried Green Tomatoes

Southern Baked Beans

Zucchini and Corn Casserole

Savory Rice

Mashed Potatoes

Fresh Corn Scallop

Sweet Potato Bake

Tomato Pie

Broccoli Casserole

Susan's Baked Rice

Potato Casserole

Creamed Corn

Pattypan Summer Squash Casserole

Hoppin' John

Mashed Potatoes with Sautéed Mushrooms

Pineapple Casserole

Zucchini Custard Bake

Rutabagas

Cheesy Broccoli Bake

SERVES 8 TO 10

2 pounds fresh broccoli, trimmed
   and cut up
¼ cup chopped celery
¼ pound fresh mushrooms, sliced
¼ cup chopped onion
2 tablespoons butter
One 8-ounce can sliced water
   chestnuts

One 10¾-ounce can condensed
   cream of mushroom soup
½ pound Velveeta
½ teaspoon garlic salt
¼ teaspoon pepper
1 cup grated Cheddar cheese

Preheat oven to 350 degrees. Steam broccoli for 10 minutes. Sauté celery, mushrooms, and onion in butter for 10 minutes; drain. Combine broccoli, sauté mixture, and water chestnuts. Heat soup and Velveeta in saucepan over low heat until cheese melts. Pour over broccoli mixture. Stir in garlic salt and pepper. Place in greased casserole dish. Bake for 25 minutes. Sprinkle top with grated Cheddar.

Baked Grits

SERVES 6

4 cups water
1½ teaspoons salt
1 cup uncooked grits
2 eggs, beaten
8 tablespoons (1 stick) butter

1½ cups grated Monterey Jack and
   Cheddar cheese (combined)
2 cloves garlic, crushed
Dash of cayenne pepper

Preheat oven to 350 degrees. Bring water and salt to a boil. Add grits to boiling water, stirring constantly for a minute. Cover and cook, stirring occasionally, until grits are thick and creamy. Temper eggs with a small amount of hot cooked grits, then add back to remaining grits. Combine remaining ingredients with grits and pour into a 2-quart casserole dish. Bake for 45 minutes. Top with additional cheese, if desired.   ❧ ❧ ❧ **The Lady & Sons**

Squash Casserole

SERVES 6

1 large onion, chopped
4 tablespoons (½ stick) butter
3 cups cooked squash, drained,
   with all water squeezed out
1 cup crushed Ritz crackers, plus
   additional for topping

½ cup sour cream
1 teaspoon House Seasoning
   (see page 325)
1 cup grated Cheddar cheese

Preheat oven to 350 degrees. Sauté onion in butter for 5 minutes. Remove from pan and mix all ingredients together. Pour into buttered casserole dish and top with cracker crumbs. Bake for 25 to 30 minutes.

❦ ❦ ❦   *The Lady & Sons*

VARIATION: For a different taste in this casserole, layer slices of cooked red potatoes in the bottom of the casserole dish, followed by squash mixture; repeat layers. Top with about 1 cup Ritz crumbs tossed with melted butter.

Sherry-Glazed Sweet Potatoes

SERVES 6

3 large sweet potatoes or yams
6 slices canned pineapple
4 tablespoons (½ stick) butter

½ cup brown sugar
½ cup sherry

Preheat oven to 375 degrees. Boil potatoes, with skins on, for 20 to 30 minutes, or until tender. Drain and allow to cool. Peel and cut lengthwise into halves. Arrange slices of pineapple in a single layer in a greased shallow baking dish; place a potato half (cut side down) on top of each pineapple slice. Heat butter, brown sugar, and sherry together until sugar is dissolved; pour over potatoes and pineapple. Bake for 30 minutes, basting often with syrup in dish.

Turnip Greens with Cornmeal Dumplings

SERVES 4 TO 6

¾ pound smoked meat (smoked
　turkey wings are excellent)
4 quarts water
1 teaspoon House Seasoning
　(see page 325)
2 chicken bouillon cubes

¼ teaspoon ground ginger
1 bunch turnip greens with roots
4 tablespoons (½ stick) butter
1 teaspoon sugar (optional; may be
　used if greens are bitter)

Place smoked meat in water along with House Seasoning, bouillon, and ginger. Cook over low heat for 1½ hours. Strip turnip leaves free of the big stem that runs down the center of each leaf. Wash in a sink full of clean water. Drain and wash twice more, since greens can often be sandy. Peel and slice or quarter roots. Add greens to meat; cook for another 30 minutes, stirring often. Add roots and continue to cook for approximately 15 minutes or until roots are tender. (Reserve ⅔ cup liquid after cooking if making dumplings.) Add butter and dumplings (if desired) and serve.

CORNMEAL DUMPLINGS

1 cup all-purpose cornmeal
½ teaspoon salt
1 small onion, chopped

1 egg
⅔ cup liquid from cooked turnips

Mix all ingredients together. Dipping by teaspoonfuls, gently roll batter in the palms of your hands into approximately 1-inch balls; drop into boiling turnip liquid. Make sure each dumpling is completely covered in liquid by shaking the pot gently; do not stir. Boil for about 10 minutes.

Steakside Mushrooms

SERVES 8

1½ pounds fresh mushrooms, sliced
    lengthwise
8 tablespoons (1 stick) butter

Jane's Krazy Mixed-Up Salt
¼ cup Worcestershire sauce
¼ cup water

In large skillet, sauté sliced mushrooms in butter until brown. Sprinkle liberally with Krazy salt. Add Worcestershire sauce and simmer until almost all sauce is absorbed by mushrooms. Add water and continue to simmer until mushrooms are tender. Great with steak or roast beef.

The Lady's Cheesy Mac

SERVES 6 TO 8

4 cups cooked elbow macaroni,
    drained (approximately 2 cups
    uncooked)
2 cups grated Cheddar cheese
3 eggs, beaten
½ cup sour cream

4 tablespoons (½ stick) butter, cut
    into pieces
½ teaspoon salt
1 cup milk, or equivalent in
    evaporated milk

Preheat oven to 350 degrees. After macaroni has been boiled and drained, add Cheddar cheese while macaroni is still hot. Combine remaining ingredients and add to macaroni mixture. Pour into casserole dish and bake for 30 to 45 minutes. Top with additional cheese, if desired.

Twice-Baked Potatoes

SERVES 6

This recipe can be frozen and whipped out whenever company comes over. Also try stuffing the potatoes with different kinds of cheese, sautéed shrimp, etc. Makes a great meal with a green salad.

6 large Idaho potatoes (as large and oval as possible)
Vegetable oil to coat
8 tablespoons (1 stick) butter

2 cups sour cream
Salt and pepper to taste
1 teaspoon dried parsley
Paprika

Preheat oven to 350 degrees. Wash potatoes, pat dry, prick sides gently with fork, and coat each potato entirely with oil. Place on foil-covered pan. Bake for at least 1 hour. In large bowl, place 1 stick of butter. Remove potatoes from oven and slice off top third of each one. Gently scoop out potato with spoon (potato skins should be crisp) and place into bowl. With mixer on high, mix potatoes, butter, sour cream, salt, and pepper. Add parsley and continue mixing until smooth. Gently stuff mixture back into potato shells, being careful not to break them. Pile potato mixture as high as you can above top of potato shell. Sprinkle with paprika for color. (Can be frozen at this point for serving later.) Bake again for about 20 to 30 minutes. Should be lightly browned on top.

Savannah Red Rice

SERVES 4 TO 6

1 cup chopped onion

1 cup chopped bell pepper

2 tablespoons butter

1 cup diced Hillshire Farms sausage

One 14½-ounce can crushed tomatoes with juice

1 tablespoon Texas Pete or red hot sauce

1 cup tomato sauce

1 cup water

3 chicken bouillon cubes

Pepper to taste; add salt to taste if desired

1 cup uncooked white rice

Preheat oven to 350 degrees. In a saucepan over medium heat, sauté onion and bell pepper in butter. Add sausage; heat until mixture is slightly browned. Add tomatoes, hot sauce, tomato sauce, water, and bouillon cubes. Season with pepper and salt as needed. Stir in rice. Pour mixture into a greased casserole and bake for 45 minutes.

❦ ❦ ❦ **The Lady & Sons**

Collard Greens

SERVES 4 TO 6

½ pound smoked meat (ham hocks, smoked turkey wings, or smoked neck bones)

1 tablespoon House Seasoning (see page 325)

1 tablespoon seasoned salt

1 tablespoon Texas Pete hot sauce

1 large bunch of collards

8 tablespoons (1 stick) butter

In a large pot, bring 3 quarts of water to a boil and add smoked meat, House Seasoning, seasoned salt, and hot sauce. Reduce heat to medium and cook for 1 hour. In the meantime, wash collard greens thoroughly. Remove the thick stem that runs down the center of the greens by holding the leaf in your left hand and stripping the leaf down with your right hand (the tender young leaves in the heart of the collards don't need to be stripped). Stack 6 to 8 stripped leaves on top of each other, roll up, and slice into ½- to 1-inch-thick slices. Place greens in pot with cooked smoked meat. Add butter after greens. Cook for 45 to 60 minutes, stirring occasionally. When done, taste and adjust seasoning.

Eggplant Casserole

SERVES 4

1 large eggplant
1¾ cups crushed Ritz crackers
1½ cups grated American cheese
8 tablespoons (1 stick) butter,
    melted

2 eggs
⅔ cup milk
1 teaspoon House Seasoning (see
    page 325)

Preheat oven to 350 degrees. Peel, slice, and boil eggplant for 10 to 15 minutes, until tender; drain. Divide cracker crumbs, cheese, and butter in half. To eggplant, add eggs, milk, House Seasoning, and half the crumbs, cheese, and butter. Mix well; pour into baking dish. Top with remaining half of the crumbs, cheese, and butter. Bake for 20 to 30 minutes. 🌸 🌸 🌸 *The Lady & Sons*

Vidalia Onion Pie

SERVES 8

Vidalia onions are Georgia's most famous taste. This sweet onion is grown in southeast Georgia, just a few miles west of Savannah. They can be stored in a cool dry place to use throughout the year.

3 cups thinly sliced Vidalia onion
3 tablespoons butter, melted
One 9-inch prebaked deep-dish pie
    shell
½ cup milk
1½ cups sour cream

1 teaspoon salt
2 eggs, beaten
3 tablespoons all-purpose flour
4 slices bacon, crisply cooked and
    crumbled

Preheat oven to 325 degrees. Sauté onion in butter until lightly browned. Spoon into pie shell. Combine milk, sour cream, salt, eggs, and flour. Mix well and pour over onion mixture. Garnish with bacon. Bake for 30 minutes or until firm in center. Pie has taste and texture of a quiche.   ❦ ❦ ❦   **The Lady & Sons**

Sweet Potato Chips

SERVES 4

2 large sweet potatoes
8 tablespoons (1 stick) butter,
*   melted*

1 cup honey-roasted peanuts,
*   chopped*
Salt to taste

Preheat oven to 450 degrees. Line two large baking sheets with foil; lightly grease. Slice potatoes to ¼ inch thick. Dip potatoes in melted butter and arrange on baking sheet so that chips do not overlap. Sprinkle with peanuts. Bake for 15 to 20 minutes. Sprinkle with salt.

Broccoli Soufflé

SERVES 10

Three 10-ounce packages frozen
*   chopped broccoli*
¾ cup chicken stock
¾ cup whipping cream
8 tablespoons (1 stick) butter
½ cup all-purpose flour

4 eggs, separated
2 teaspoons chopped fresh parsley
3 tablespoons minced onion
Salt and pepper to taste
½ cup grated Monterey Jack or
*   Cheddar cheese*

Preheat oven to 425 degrees. Cook and drain broccoli. Add stock to cream and scald. Melt butter and blend in flour. Gradually add to cream mixture. Stir over medium heat until thick. Remove from heat and beat in egg yolks, parsley, onion, salt, and pepper. Stir in broccoli and cheese. When ready to serve, add stiffly beaten egg whites and pour into a buttered casserole dish. Bake for 25 to 30 minutes.

Boursin Cheese Potatoes

SERVES 8

3 pounds red potatoes, unpeeled
Salt and pepper to taste
1 pint heavy cream

One 5-ounce package Boursin
cheese
Fresh chives or parsley, chopped

Preheat oven to 350 degrees. Wash and slice potatoes into ¼-inch-thick rounds. Toss potatoes with salt and pepper. Heat cream and cheese together, on top of stove or in microwave, until cheese has melted. Stir mixture until thoroughly blended. Layer half of the potatoes into a 2-quart baking dish (this is best if done in a deep dish instead of a long, flat dish). Cover potatoes with half of the cream mixture. Repeat with remaining potatoes and cream mixture. Cover and bake for 1 hour. Sprinkle top with chopped chives or parsley.

Fried Green Tomatoes

SERVES 6

Quite frequently I walk the dining room with a plate piled high with this wonderful fried fruit. The guests seem to enjoy this extra treat. My grandmother always used cornmeal, but I prefer flour.

3 or 4 large, firm green tomatoes
Salt
2 cups self-rising flour or cornmeal

1 to 2 teaspoons pepper
Vegetable oil for frying

Slice tomatoes to desired thickness (I prefer mine thin). Lay out on a pan and sprinkle with salt. Place in a colander and allow time for salt to pull the water out of tomatoes. Mix flour with pepper. Coat tomatoes with flour mixture and deep-fry until golden brown.

❦ ❦ ❦ **The Lady & Sons**

Southern Baked Beans

SERVES 3 TO 4

½ pound bacon
1 large onion, diced
One 16-ounce can pork and beans
3 tablespoons yellow mustard

5 tablespoons maple or pancake
syrup
4 tablespoons ketchup

Preheat oven to 325 degrees. Fry bacon until crisp; crumble. In bacon drippings, sauté onion until brown. Mix bacon, onion, and drippings with remaining ingredients. Pour into casserole dish and bake covered for 45 to 60 minutes.   ✿ ✿ ✿   **The Lady & Sons**

Zucchini and Corn Casserole

SERVES 4 TO 5

1½ pounds small zucchini
One 8-ounce can cream-style corn
2 eggs, lightly beaten
1 small onion, chopped
1 small bell pepper, chopped

1 tablespoon butter
½ teaspoon salt
¼ teaspoon ground black pepper
½ cup grated sharp Cheddar cheese
Paprika to taste

Preheat oven to 350 degrees. Cook zucchini in boiling salted water to cover until just tender, about 6 minutes. Drain, cut into chunks, and combine with corn and eggs. Meanwhile, sauté onion and bell pepper in butter until golden brown, about 5 minutes. Add to zucchini and corn mixture; add salt and pepper. Pour mixture into a greased casserole. Sprinkle cheese on top, then sprinkle with paprika. Bake uncovered for about 30 minutes, or until lightly browned and bubbly.

Savory Rice

SERVES 4

1 cup chopped onion
8 tablespoons (1 stick) butter
One 10¾-ounce can beef broth
One 10¾-ounce can condensed
   French onion soup

One 4½-ounce can mushroom
   pieces, drained
1 cup uncooked white rice

Preheat oven to 350 degrees. In saucepan over medium heat, sauté onion in butter until almost tender. Remove from heat. Stir in broth, onion soup, mushrooms, and uncooked rice. Pour into casserole dish. Bake for about 1 hour, or until done.

Mashed Potatoes

SERVES 8

8 to 10 medium red new potatoes,
   skin on
½ cup hot milk

8 tablespoons (1 stick) butter
½ cup sour cream
Salt and pepper to taste

Slice potatoes ¼ inch thick. Cook in boiling water for 15 minutes or until fork-tender. Whip unpeeled cooked potatoes with electric mixer; mix until moderately smooth. Don't overbeat them; a few lumps are nice. Add hot milk, butter, and sour cream. Salt and pepper to taste. Whip until mixed. Adjust thickness by adding more milk, if desired.

❧ ❧ ❧ **The Lady & Sons**

Fresh Corn Scallop

SERVES 6

6 ears fresh corn
2 tablespoons all-purpose flour
1 teaspoon sugar
1¼ teaspoons salt

⅛ teaspoon pepper
½ cup milk
¾ cup buttered dry bread crumbs

Preheat oven to 375 degrees. Cut corn off cob, being careful not to cut too deep. This should make 2½ to 3 cups of corn. Combine corn, flour, sugar, salt, pepper, and milk. Sprinkle half the crumbs over bottom of 1-quart casserole dish. Add corn mixture. Bake covered for 30 minutes. Remove cover and sprinkle with remaining crumbs. Bake uncovered 20 minutes more.

Sweet Potato Bake

SERVES 8

3 cups peeled, cooked, and mashed
    sweet potatoes or yams
1 cup sugar
⅓ cup butter, melted
2 eggs

1 teaspoon vanilla
1 teaspoon ground cinnamon
¼ teaspoon ground nutmeg
¼ cup heavy cream, half-and-half,
    or whole milk

Preheat oven to 325 degrees. Mix all ingredients together except for cream. Beat with electric mixer until smooth. Add cream; mix well. Pour into greased casserole dish. Add topping. Bake for 25 to 30 minutes.

TOPPING

1 cup brown sugar
1 cup walnuts, chopped

⅓ cup all-purpose flour
3 tablespoons butter, melted

Mix together with fork; sprinkle over top of casserole.

Tomato Pie

SERVES 6

4 tomatoes, peeled and sliced
8 to 10 fresh basil leaves, chopped
⅓ cup chopped green onion
One 9-inch prebaked deep-dish pie
    shell

Salt and pepper to taste
2 cups grated mozzarella and
    Cheddar cheese (combined)
1 cup mayonnaise

Preheat oven to 350 degrees. Layer tomato slices, basil, and onion in pie shell. Add salt and pepper to taste. Mix together grated cheese and mayonnaise. Spread on top of tomatoes. Bake for 30 minutes or until lightly browned.

Broccoli Casserole

SERVES 2 TO 3

One 10-ounce package frozen
    chopped broccoli
1 small onion, chopped
4 tablespoons (½ stick) butter
½ cup grated Cheddar cheese
½ cup crushed Ritz crackers

½ cup condensed cream of mush-
    room soup
¼ cup mayonnaise
House Seasoning (see page 325) to
    taste

Preheat oven to 350 degrees. Steam broccoli until limp, about 10 minutes. Remove from heat; drain. Sauté onion in butter and add to broccoli. Add all remaining ingredients; mix well. Pour mixture into a casserole dish. Add topping.

TOPPING

½ cup crushed Ritz crackers   1 tablespoon butter, melted

Combine crackers and melted butter for topping; sprinkle on top of casserole. Bake for 20 to 25 minutes. 🍀 🍀 🍀 ***The Lady & Sons***

Susan's Baked Rice

SERVES 4

1 large onion, chopped
1 large bell pepper, chopped
8 tablespoons (1 stick) butter
4 or 5 chicken bouillon cubes

1 cup uncooked white rice
2 cups water
Ground black pepper to taste

Preheat oven to 350 degrees. Sauté onion and bell pepper in butter; add bouillon cubes. Stir until dissolved. Combine rice and water and add to mixture. Pour into a 13 × 9-inch baking dish. Sprinkle with pepper. Bake for 45 minutes. Goes great with baked or fried chicken.

❧ ❧ ❧ **The Lady & Sons**

Potato Casserole

SERVES 6

Leftover mashed potatoes work wonderfully in this recipe.

2 cups mashed potatoes
½ cup sour cream
House Seasoning (see page 325)
   to taste
1 small onion, sliced thin

1 small bell pepper, sliced thin
8 tablespoons (1 stick) butter
1½ cups grated Cheddar cheese
4 medium potatoes, cooked
6 slices bacon, cooked crisp

Preheat oven to 350 degrees. Spread mashed potatoes evenly on bottom of casserole dish. Layer sour cream evenly over top. (Each time you add a layer, sprinkle on a little House Seasoning.) Sauté onion and bell pepper in butter; evenly layer over top of sour cream. Next, layer with ½ cup Cheddar cheese. Slice potatoes and layer over cheese until top is completely covered with potatoes. Finally, top with remaining 1 cup cheese. Bake for 25 to 30 minutes. Remove from oven and crumble bacon over top.

❧ ❧ ❧ **The Lady & Sons**

Creamed Corn

SERVES 3 TO 4

1 dozen ears fresh corn	*Salt and pepper to taste*
8 tablespoons (1 stick) butter	

Remove corn from cob using a corn grater. (If you have to cut corn with a knife, avoid whole kernels; try mashing a little.) Put corn in glass dish and put stick of butter on top. Cook in microwave on high about 7 to 10 minutes, stopping to turn and stir a couple of times. Be careful not to overcook corn. If it seems too dry, add a little milk or water. Season with salt and pepper to taste.   ❀ ❀ ❀   **The Lady & Sons**

Pattypan Summer Squash Casserole

SERVES 6

4 medium white pattypan sum-	*1 medium bowl ice water*
mer squash	*1 egg*
2 small onions, chopped	*Salt and pepper to taste*
1 clove garlic, minced	*2 tablespoons chopped fresh parsley*
4 tablespoons (½ stick) butter	*1 cup cracker crumbs (or enough*
2 slices white bread	*to cover casserole)*

Preheat oven to 350 degrees. Peel and cut squash into cubes. Boil until tender, about 5 to 7 minutes, and drain. Brown onion and garlic in 2 tablespoons butter. Soak bread in ice water and wring out; chop fine. Add to onion and garlic; cook, stirring, for 2 to 3 minutes. Add drained squash and cook 2 to 3 minutes more, stirring. Beat egg and add, allowing it to absorb into the mixture. Cook 3 to 4 minutes. Season with salt and pepper and add parsley. Stir and remove from heat. Place in casserole dish or baking pan. Cover top with cracker crumbs and dot with remaining butter. Bake for 20 to 25 minutes, until the crumbs brown.

Hoppin' John

SERVES 6 TO 8

2 cups black-eyed peas, cooked
2 cups cooked rice
1 small onion, chopped

1 small bell pepper, chopped
Garlic powder to taste

Heat the black-eyed peas and add the rice. Add remaining ingredients and cook an additional 10 to 15 minutes. Do not overcook. This dish is best if the bell pepper and onion still have a crunch to them.

❧ ❧ ❧   *The Lady & Sons*

Mashed Potatoes with Sautéed Mushrooms

SERVES 6 TO 8

8 tablespoons (1 stick) butter
1 cup sliced fresh mushrooms
½ cup diced onion
2 tablespoons chopped fresh chives
1 clove garlic, chopped

1 cup white wine
6 cups (about 2 pounds) diced new
   potatoes
½ cup sour cream
Small amount whole milk

In a saucepan, melt butter and sauté mushrooms, onion, chives, and garlic. Add wine and simmer for about 15 minutes. In a pot, boil potatoes until done; drain. Combine all ingredients and mix. Whip until thick and creamy. Add milk for desired consistency.

Pineapple Casserole

SERVES 8

1 cup sugar
6 tablespoons all-purpose flour

2 cups grated sharp Cheddar
   cheese

Two 20-ounce cans pineapple
  chunks, drained (reserve
  6 tablespoons juice)

1 cup Ritz cracker crumbs
8 tablespoons (1 stick) butter,
  melted

Preheat oven to 350 degrees. In a mixing bowl, combine sugar and flour. Gradually stir in cheese. Add pineapple and stir well. Pour mixture into a greased casserole dish. Combine cracker crumbs, butter, and pineapple juice and spread on top of pineapple mixture. Bake for 25 to 30 minutes or until golden brown.   ❦ ❦ ❦ **The Lady & Sons**

Zucchini Custard Bake

SERVES 4 TO 6

4 tablespoons (½ stick) butter,
  melted
2 pounds zucchini, cut into small
  pieces
3 eggs
½ cup undiluted evaporated milk
  or light cream
2 tablespoons fine dry bread
  crumbs

1 teaspoon instant minced onion
1 teaspoon Worcestershire sauce
Dash of liquid hot pepper sauce
¾ teaspoon salt
⅛ teaspoon pepper
⅓ cup grated Parmesan cheese

Preheat oven to 350 degrees. In a large saucepan with a tight-fitting lid, combine melted butter and zucchini. Cover and cook over low heat, stirring occasionally, until tender (5 to 7 minutes). Remove from heat and set aside. Beat eggs with milk; add bread crumbs, onion, Worcestershire sauce, hot pepper sauce, salt, pepper, and 2 tablespoons of the Parmesan. Mix well. Combine mixture with zucchini, stirring until blended. Turn into a buttered 1½-quart casserole. Sprinkle top with remaining Parmesan cheese. Bake uncovered for 35 to 40 minutes. If the dish has been refrigerated, allow about 10 minutes longer baking time.

Rutabagas

SERVES 4 TO 6

Clint Eastwood was in for dinner one night while he was here in Savannah filming Midnight in the Garden of Good and Evil. *That particular night, we had rutabagas on the buffet. He made a point to tell me that he was a ten-year-old boy the last time he had tasted this wonderful vegetable. He said that he really enjoyed them again after all those years. Rutabagas are a winter vegetable, and not always available, so enjoy them while you can.*

1 chunk of streak-o'-lean (approximately ½ pound) (see Note) Pinch of sugar	Salt and pepper to taste 1 rutabaga 2 tablespoons butter

Wash and cut streak-o'-lean to your liking. (You could use ham hock or smoked wings or even cut-up bacon, but I just prefer streak-o'-lean.) Place in a pot with enough water to cook meat. Add sugar, salt, and pepper. The water will cook out, so it might be necessary to add more during cooking. Cook meat while you prepare the rutabaga. Peel rutabaga and cut into cubes (as you would cut up potatoes for potato salad—about the same size). Add rutabaga to the meat; add more water if needed. Cover pot and cook until tender; this may take about 45 minutes. When done, remove from pot, add butter, and serve.

❧ ❧ ❧ *The Lady & Sons*

NOTE: Streak-o'-lean is very similar to bacon. You can get it from the butcher.

Breads

Zucchini Bread

Banana Nut Bread

Easy Rolls

Pumpkin Bread

Basic Biscuits

Hoecakes

Corny Corn Bread

Pear Fritters

Mother's Rolls

Cheese Biscuits

Cracklin' Corn Bread

Dutch Bread

Bubba's Beer Biscuits

Applesauce Bread

Herb Corn Bread

Peanut Butter Bread

Pineapple Cheese Bread

Zucchini Bread

YIELDS 2 LOAVES

The flavor improves with age and the bread keeps well frozen. You can also substitute pumpkin for zucchini.

3¼ cups all-purpose flour
1½ teaspoons salt
1 teaspoon ground nutmeg
2 teaspoons baking soda
1 teaspoon ground cinnamon
3 cups sugar

1 cup vegetable oil
4 eggs, beaten
⅔ cup water
2 cups grated zucchini
1 teaspoon lemon juice
1 cup chopped walnuts or pecans

Preheat oven to 350 degrees. Mix dry ingredients except for nuts in a large bowl. In a separate bowl, mix wet ingredients; fold into dry, and add nuts. Bake in two loaf pans for 1 hour, or until done.

Banana Nut Bread

YIELDS 1 LOAF

½ cup Crisco shortening
1 cup sugar
2 cups all-purpose flour
1 teaspoon salt
2 teaspoons baking powder

½ teaspoon baking soda
2 eggs, beaten
3 bananas, mashed
⅓ cup buttermilk
½ cup chopped walnuts or pecans

Preheat oven to 350 degrees. Cream shortening and sugar. Sift together flour, salt, baking powder, and baking soda and add to creamed mixture. Add remaining ingredients; mix well. Pour into a well-greased loaf pan. Bake for 40 to 45 minutes.

Easy Rolls

YIELDS 6 ROLLS

1 cup self-rising flour
½ cup milk

1 teaspoon sugar
2 tablespoons mayonnaise

Preheat oven to 350 degrees. Mix together flour and milk. Add sugar and mayonnaise. Pour into slightly greased muffin tins and bake for 12 to 15 minutes.

Pumpkin Bread

YIELDS 2 LOAVES

3 cups sugar
1 cup vegetable oil
4 eggs
2 cups canned pumpkin
⅔ cup water
3⅓ cups all-purpose flour

2 teaspoons baking soda
1½ teaspoons salt
1 teaspoon ground cinnamon
1 teaspoon ground nutmeg
½ to ¾ cup chopped pecans or
    walnuts

Preheat oven to 350 degrees. Grease and flour two loaf pans. Mix sugar and oil with mixer. Add eggs and blend. Add pumpkin and blend. Add water and blend. Combine remaining ingredients and add slowly. Fill pans equally and bake for 1 hour or until golden brown.

VARIATIONS: For the oil, substitute ½ cup oil and add ½ cup applesauce. For banana bread, substitute 2 cups mashed, ripe bananas for pumpkin and omit nutmeg.

Basic Biscuits

YIELDS APPROXIMATELY 3 DOZEN BISCUITS

1 package yeast
½ cup lukewarm water
5 cups all-purpose flour
1 teaspoon baking soda
1 teaspoon salt

1 tablespoon baking powder
2 tablespoons sugar
¾ cup Crisco shortening
2 cups buttermilk

Preheat oven to 400 degrees. Dissolve yeast in warm water; set aside. Mix dry ingredients together. Cut in shortening. Add yeast and buttermilk and mix well. Turn dough onto lightly floured surface and roll out to desired thickness. Cut with small biscuit cutter and place on greased baking sheet. Bake for 12 minutes or until golden brown.

Hoecakes

YIELDS APPROXIMATELY 17 CAKES

These hoecakes have become a favorite with our guests. Use them to soak up that good pot liquor from turnip or collard greens. After the plate is completely sopped clean, save one to eat as a dessert along with maple syrup.

1 cup self-rising flour
1 cup self-rising cornmeal
2 eggs
1 tablespoon sugar

¾ cup buttermilk
⅓ cup plus 1 tablespoon water
¼ cup vegetable oil or bacon grease
Oil or butter for frying

Mix all ingredients well except for frying oil. Heat oil in a skillet over medium heat. Drop mixture by tablespoonfuls into hot skillet. Use approximately 2 tablespoons batter per hoecake. Brown until crisp; turn and brown on other side. Drain on paper towels. Leftover batter will keep in refrigerator for up to 2 days. ❧ ❧ ❧ **The Lady & Sons**

Corny Corn Bread

SERVES 8

1 cup self-rising cornmeal
¾ cup self-rising flour
½ cup vegetable oil plus ¼ cup for
   skillet
One 8-ounce can cream-style corn

2 eggs
1 cup sour cream
1 cup grated sharp Cheddar cheese
½ teaspoon cayenne pepper
   (optional)

Preheat oven to 375 degrees. Mix all ingredients together. Pour into a heated cast-iron skillet that has been well greased with oil. Bake until golden brown, approximately 30 minutes.

Pear Fritters

YIELDS APPROXIMATELY 21 PIECES

This fritter batter may be used for sliced fresh apples or bananas, or canned pineapple.

1 egg, beaten
½ cup milk
2 teaspoons sugar
1 teaspoon ground cinnamon
1 cup self-rising flour

1 cup sour cream
¼ cup vegetable oil
3 pears, peeled, cored, and sliced
   horizontally

Combine beaten egg, milk, sugar, cinnamon, and flour. Mix well and add sour cream. Heat 2 tablespoons oil to 375 degrees. Dip pears in batter, carefully place in oil, and cook 1 to 2 minutes. Turn and cook 1 to 2 minutes more. Add oil as needed. Remove fritters and drain. May be sprinkled with powdered sugar or cinnamon sugar. Serve warm.

Mother's Rolls

YIELDS APPROXIMATELY 2 DOZEN ROLLS

½ cup Crisco shortening

¼ cup sugar

1 heaping teaspoon salt

½ cup boiling water

1 package yeast

½ cup lukewarm water

1 egg

3 cups sifted all-purpose flour

Cream together shortening, sugar, and salt. Add boiling water. Dissolve yeast in ½ cup lukewarm water; beat egg and add. Combine with shortening and mix all together with flour. Beat well. Set aside at room temperature for 30 minutes, then refrigerate until needed. Preheat oven to 350 degrees. Roll out dough and cut into rolls. Place on greased cookie sheet. Bake for 15 minutes or until brown.

Cheese Biscuits

YIELDS 8 LARGE BISCUITS

These biscuits have become one of our signature items at The Lady & Sons Restaurant. Everyone really looks forward to us bringing them out, whether it be after they are seated or while they are waiting in line.

2 cups self-rising flour

1 teaspoon baking powder

1 teaspoon sugar

⅓ cup Crisco shortening

¾ cup grated Cheddar cheese

1 cup buttermilk

Preheat oven to 350 degrees. Mix flour, baking powder, and sugar together using a fork; cut in shortening until it resembles cornmeal. Add cheese. Stir in buttermilk all at one time just until blended. Do not overstir. Drop by tablespoonfuls (I use an ice cream scoop to give biscuits a nicer shape) onto a well-greased baking sheet. Bake for 12 to 15 minutes.

GARLIC BUTTER

8 tablespoons (1 stick) butter,
   melted

2 cloves garlic, crushed

Combine butter and garlic over medium heat until butter absorbs garlic; brush over tops of warm biscuits. Store leftover butter for next baking.

❦ ❦ ❦   *The Lady & Sons*

VARIATION: For breakfast, brush with plain butter or honey butter.

Cracklin' Corn Bread

YIELDS 4 PONES

1 cup cracklings
½ cup hot water
2 cups sifted yellow cornmeal

1 teaspoon salt
Small amount of cold water
Vegetable oil for skillet

Preheat oven to 425 degrees. Mash or break cracklings. Mix with hot water and pour into cornmeal; add salt. Use sufficient amount of cold water to make dough. Let stand 5 minutes. Shape into pones and place in a cast-iron skillet that has been heated with a few tablespoons of oil. Bake until brown, for about 15 minutes, then reduce heat to 350 degrees and bake for 30 to 45 minutes. The skillet should be placed near the top of the oven.

Dutch Bread

YIELDS 2 LOAVES

1 package yeast
½ cup warm water
2 tablespoons sugar
1½ teaspoons salt

6 cups all-purpose flour
2 cups scalded milk
2 tablespoons Crisco shortening

Preheat oven to 375 degrees. Mix yeast in water and set aside to dissolve. Combine dry ingredients. Add milk, shortening, and yeast. Pour into two greased 8 × 4 × 3-inch pans. Bake for approximately 45 to 50 minutes.

Bubba's Beer Biscuits

YIELDS 12 TO 16 BISCUITS

My brother Bubba confines most of his cooking to his charcoal grill, but he does come into the kitchen quite often to bake up these great biscuits.

4 cups Bisquick
¼ to ½ cup sugar

One 12-ounce can of beer
2 tablespoons butter, melted

Preheat oven to 400 degrees. Mix all ingredients well, adjusting the sugar according to how sweet a biscuit you prefer. Pour into well-greased muffin tins. Bake for 15 to 20 minutes. Serve with honey butter.   ❦ ❦ ❦   *The Lady & Sons*

Applesauce Bread

YIELDS 1 LOAF

2 cups all-purpose flour
¼ cup dark brown sugar
1 teaspoon baking powder
1 teaspoon baking soda
¾ teaspoon salt
1 teaspoon ground cinnamon
½ teaspoon ground nutmeg

1 teaspoon vanilla
8 tablespoons (1 stick) butter,
* softened*
1 cup applesauce
2 eggs
1 cup raisins
½ cup chopped walnuts

Preheat oven to 350 degrees. Combine all ingredients except raisins and nuts. Mix well until blended. Stir in raisins and nuts. Pour into greased and floured 8 × 4 × 3-inch loaf pan. Bake for 60 to 65 minutes.

Herb Corn Bread

SERVES 9

1¼ cups self-rising cornmeal
¾ cup self-rising flour
1 teaspoon sugar
½ teaspoon dried marjoram
½ teaspoon dried thyme

¼ teaspoon celery seed
2 eggs, beaten
1¼ cups milk
6 tablespoons butter, melted

Preheat oven to 425 degrees. Combine dry ingredients in a large bowl. Combine eggs, milk, and butter. Add to dry ingredients, stirring until just moistened. Pour batter into a lightly greased 9-inch square pan. Bake for 25 minutes or until golden brown.

Peanut Butter Bread

YIELDS 1 LOAF

2 cups all-purpose flour
⅓ cup sugar
1 teaspoon salt

4 teaspoons baking powder
1½ cups milk
½ cup peanut butter

Preheat oven to 375 degrees. Combine dry ingredients. Add milk and peanut butter. Pour into a greased 8 × 4 × 3-inch loaf pan. Bake for approximately 50 minutes. Great with homemade jam.

Pineapple Cheese Bread

YIELDS 1 LOAF

2 cups self-rising flour
¾ cup sugar
1 cup canned crushed pineapple,
    with juice
2 eggs

2 tablespoons vegetable oil
¾ cup grated sharp Cheddar cheese
½ cup chopped walnuts
½ teaspoon pineapple extract

Preheat oven to 350 degrees. Sift flour into a large mixing bowl and add sugar. Mix together. In a separate bowl, mix pineapple, eggs, and oil and add to flour mixture, mixing well. Fold in cheese, nuts, and pineapple extract. Pour into a greased 9 × 3-inch loaf pan. Bake for 1 hour. Cool and turn out from pan, allowing to cool completely before slicing.

Sauces, Dressings, and Preserves

Daddy's Tangy Grilling Sauce
Oriental Marinade
Chicken or Shrimp Marinade
Spicy Barbecue Sauce
The Lady's Barbecue Sauce
Egg and Lemon Sauce
Lemon Shrimp Cocktail Sauce
Savory Grilled Chicken Sauce
Lemon Butter for Fish
Lemon Butter for Steak
Sweet-and-Sour Dressing
Poppy Seed Dressing
Aunt Peggy's Italian Dressing
Honey Mustard Dressing
Buttermilk Dressing
Pear Honey
Mint Julep Jelly
Port Wine Jelly
Strawberry Fig Preserves
Pepper Jelly
Honey Butter

Daddy's Tangy Grilling Sauce

YIELDS 1½ CUPS

For good charcoal grilling, brush sauce over the meat during the last 10 or 15 minutes of grilling time. Turn often to prevent burning.

1 cup Worcestershire sauce
4 tablespoons (½ stick) butter

Juice of 2 lemons

Mix ingredients together and simmer for 10 minutes.

Oriental Marinade

YIELDS 1 CUP

½ cup soy sauce
¼ cup water
2 tablespoons vinegar
1 tablespoon vegetable oil

1 teaspoon sugar
¼ teaspoon ground ginger
Garlic powder to taste

Combine all ingredients. Use to marinate beef, chicken, or fish.

Chicken or Shrimp Marinade

YIELDS 1½ CUPS

3 cloves garlic, crushed
1½ teaspoons salt
½ cup packed brown sugar
3 tablespoons Dijon mustard
¼ cup apple cider vinegar

6 tablespoons olive oil
Juice of 1 lime
Juice of ½ lemon
Dash of cayenne or ground black
    pepper

Mix all ingredients with a whisk. Pour over chicken or shrimp. Refrigerate overnight. Grill over hot coals or broil in oven.

Spicy Barbecue Sauce

YIELDS 2 CUPS

1½ cups apple cider vinegar
1 to 2 tablespoons Worcestershire
   sauce
1 to 2 tablespoons peanut butter
1 teaspoon salt

Juice of 2 lemons
1 teaspoon pepper
2 tablespoons celery seed
2 tablespoons chili powder
4 tablespoons (½ stick) butter

Bring all ingredients to a boil until peanut butter dissolves. Stir to avoid sticking. Lower heat and simmer for 20 minutes.

The Lady's Barbecue Sauce

YIELDS 2 CUPS

½ cup oil
¼ cup lemon juice
1 teaspoon pepper
¾ cup ketchup
3 tablespoons brown sugar
Pinch of garlic salt or garlic
   powder

2 teaspoons salt
½ cup apple cider vinegar
3 tablespoons Worcestershire sauce
2 teaspoons paprika
¾ cup water
3 tablespoons prepared mustard
½ onion, finely chopped

Mix all ingredients together and simmer over medium heat for 15 minutes.   ❦ ❦ ❦   **The Lady & Sons**

Egg and Lemon Sauce

YIELDS 1 CUP

This is a tasty sauce that goes great with broccoli, cauliflower, asparagus, and fish.

3 eggs, separated	1 tablespoon cornstarch
Juice of 2 lemons	1 cup chicken stock

Beat egg whites until stiff; add egg yolks and continue beating. Add lemon juice slowly. Beat constantly to prevent curdling. Dissolve cornstarch in ¼ cup water; add to broth and cook over medium heat until it thickens. Slowly add hot stock to egg mixture, beating constantly. Sauce should be smooth and creamy.

Lemon Shrimp Cocktail Sauce

YIELDS ½ CUP

6 tablespoons mayonnaise	1 teaspoon prepared mustard
1 tablespoon horseradish	2 tablespoons lemon juice
½ teaspoon grated onion	

Combine all ingredients and chill before serving. Serve with cold shrimp, crab claws, or raw oysters.

Savory Grilled Chicken Sauce

YIELDS 1½ CUPS

½ cup distilled vinegar	¼ teaspoon ground black pepper
½ cup lemon juice	1½ tablespoons dry mustard
½ cup corn oil	Sprinkle of cayenne pepper
1 tablespoon salt	

Mix ingredients together. Bring to boil over medium heat. Stir frequently. Remove from heat; brush chicken with sauce while on the grill. Makes enough sauce for 2 chickens.

Lemon Butter for Fish

YIELDS ½ CUP

4 tablespoons (½ stick) butter
1 clove garlic, minced
2 tablespoons lemon juice

Dash of Worcestershire sauce
Salt and pepper to taste

Melt butter in a saucepan. Sauté garlic for 2 to 3 minutes. Add remaining ingredients and mix well. Serve warm over broiled fish.

Lemon Butter for Steak

YIELDS ½ CUP

2 tablespoons lemon juice
3 tablespoons butter
¼ teaspoon salt

¼ teaspoon paprika
1 tablespoon finely chopped fresh
   parsley

Combine all ingredients. Pour over cooked steaks and garnish with lemon wedges.

Sweet-and-Sour Dressing

YIELDS 3 CUPS

1½ cups vegetable oil
¾ cup vinegar
¾ cup sugar
1½ teaspoons salt

1½ teaspoons celery seed
1½ teaspoons dry mustard
1½ teaspoons paprika
1½ teaspoons grated onion

Combine all ingredients in a jar. Chill. Shake and serve over salad.

Poppy Seed Dressing

YIELDS 1¼ CUPS

⅓ cup honey
¼ cup red wine vinegar
1 tablespoon Dijon mustard
1 tablespoon minced onion

1 teaspoon House Seasoning
  (see page 325)
1 tablespoon poppy seeds
¾ cup olive oil

Combine ingredients except oil in a blender. Process on low, gradually adding oil. Chill; shake or stir before serving.

❧ ❧ ❧ **The Lady & Sons**

Aunt Peggy's Italian Dressing

YIELDS 2½ CUPS

4 cloves garlic, minced
½ teaspoon salt, or to taste
⅛ teaspoon pepper
¼ teaspoon dried basil
¼ teaspoon dried oregano
½ teaspoon paprika
⅛ teaspoon dried dill

Pinch of dill seed
½ teaspoon sugar
½ teaspoon grated Parmesan cheese
1 teaspoon lemon juice
1¾ cups vinegar
¾ cup olive oil

Combine all ingredients and mix well.

Honey Mustard Dressing

YIELDS 1¼ CUPS

¾ cup mayonnaise
3 tablespoons honey
2 tablespoons yellow mustard
1 tablespoon lemon juice or juice
  from ½ lemon

Horseradish to taste
2 tablespoons orange juice (more
  or less as needed)

Combine all ingredients except orange juice; stir well. Thin to pouring consistency with orange juice. Cover and chill for 2 to 3 hours.

❧ ❧ ❧ **The Lady & Sons**

Buttermilk Dressing

YIELDS 2 CUPS

½ cup sour cream
1 cup mayonnaise
½ cup buttermilk
1 teaspoon House Seasoning
  (see page 325)

2 tablespoons minced fresh parsley
1 tablespoon minced onion

Mix ingredients together and chill overnight.

❧ ❧ ❧ **The Lady & Sons**

Pear Honey

YIELDS 12 TO 16 HALF-PINT JARS

One 20-ounce can crushed
  pineapple with syrup
8 cups (about 3 pounds) peeled,
  cored, and chopped pears

10 cups sugar
1 tablespoon lemon juice

Mix all ingredients and cook until pears are tender and mixture thickens, approximately 30 minutes. Place in sterilized jars and seal while still hot.

Mint Julep Jelly

YIELDS 4 TO 5 HALF-PINT JARS

1½ cups bourbon
½ cup water
3 cups sugar

6 tablespoons Certo
4 to 5 fresh mint sprigs

Combine bourbon, water, and sugar in double boiler over medium heat. Stir until sugar is dissolved. Remove from heat; add Certo. Pour into sterilized jars. Add mint sprig to each jar and seal.

Port Wine Jelly

YIELDS 5 HALF-PINT JARS

1 cup port wine
1 cup cranberry juice

3½ cups sugar
½ bottle Certo

Stir wine, juice, and sugar together in double boiler over medium heat until sugar is dissolved. Remove from heat and add Certo. Pour into sterilized jars and seal immediately.

Strawberry Fig Preserves

YIELDS 8 HALF-PINT JARS

3 cups mashed ripe figs
3 cups sugar

Two 3-ounce packages strawberry Jell-O

Mix all ingredients together in saucepan and cook 4 minutes at rolling boil. Stir frequently. Skim. Pour into sterilized jars; seal.

Pepper Jelly

YIELDS 6 HALF-PINT JARS

¾ cup chopped green bell pepper
¼ cup chopped fresh hot green pepper
1½ cups apple vinegar

6 cups sugar
4 ounces Certo
4 drops green food coloring

Process bell and hot pepper in food processor, then mix all ingredients except Certo and food coloring. Bring to rolling boil. Remove from heat and add Certo and coloring. Pour into sterilized jars and seal.

Honey Butter

YIELDS 1 CUP

½ *pound (2 sticks) butter*   2 *tablespoons honey*

Allow butter to soften slightly at room temperature. Using an electric mixer, whip butter and honey together in a bowl until well mixed.

To give the butter an extra flair, you can:

- put the mixture in a butter mold and allow to chill;
- roll butter up in wax paper, allow it to chill, and slice when ready to use;
- spread softened butter in a shallow pan, chill, and, when it is firm, use a miniature cookie cutter to make different shapes;
- run semichilled butter through a pastry bag, using a star tip.

You can also adapt the above to suit your needs. For example, you could add fresh strawberries, blueberries, peaches, or other fruit. Fresh herbs like basil, thyme, and oregano—as well as fresh garlic—help make wonderful herbed butter (for this you should omit the honey).

❧ ❧ ❧ *The Lady & Sons*

Desserts

CAKES AND PIES

Caramel Apple Cake with Caramel Topping

Rum Cake

Coconut Cake

Chocolate Strawberry Shortcake

Low-Fat Peach Cake

Savannah Chocolate Cake with Hot Fudge Sauce

Mama's Pound Cake

Chocolate Chip Nut Cake

Luscious Lime Cheesecake

Grandmother Paul's Sour Cream Pound Cake

Gooey Butter Cakes

Grandmother Paul's Red Velvet Cake

Cheesecake

Pineapple Cake

Chocolate Sheet Cake

Banana Split Cake

Grandmama Hiers's Carrot Cake

Tunnel of Fudge Cake

Old-Time Lemon "Cheesecake"

Better Than Sex? Yes!

Punch Bowl Cake

Chocolate Pound Cake

Easy Coffee Cake

Applesauce Cupcakes

Chocolate Damnation

Peanut Butter Cake

French Coconut Pie

Butterscotch Pie

Corrie's Kentucky Pie

Mini Pecan Pies

Praline Pumpkin Pie

Chocolate Chip Pie

Chocolate Almond Pie

Strawberry and Cream Pie

Thanksgiving Pie

Mama's Chess Pie

Lemon Meringue Pie

Banana Cream Pie

Million-Dollar Pie

Pastry for Two-Crust Pie

COOKIES AND BROWNIES

Chewy Pecan Cookies

Snickerdoodles

Lady Lock Cookies

Southern Tea Cakes

Sliced Nut Cookies

Butter Fingers

Goodies

Low Country Cookies

Thumb Print Cookies

Butter Cookies

Grandma's Iced Georgia Squares

Fudgie Scotch Ring

Lady Brownies

Cream Cheese Brownies

Peanut Butter Bars

Aunt Glennis's Blonde Brownies

OTHER CONFECTIONS

Peanut Butter Buckeyes

Pecan Clusters

Peanut Butter Balls

Old-Time Chocolate Fudge

Five-Minute Fudge

Baked Apples

Strawberry Mold

Walnut Praline Brie with Fruit

Crème Caramel

Rice Pudding

Banana Pudding

Savannah "Tiramisu"

Peach Cobbler

Caramel Apple Cake with Caramel Topping

SERVES 15 TO 20

2½ cups sugar
3 eggs
1½ cups vegetable oil
3 cups all-purpose flour

2 teaspoons vanilla
1 cup chopped walnuts
2½ cups diced apples, canned or
   fresh

Preheat oven to 350 degrees. Cream together sugar, eggs, and oil. Add flour; mix together until well blended. Add vanilla, nuts, and diced apples. Spread into a lightly greased and floured 13 × 9-inch baking dish; bake for 45 to 60 minutes. Cake is done when toothpick inserted in center comes out clean. When cake is done, punch holes in it with a knife and pour topping over.

CARAMEL TOPPING

¾ pound (3 sticks) butter
2 cups brown sugar

¼ cup milk

Heat all ingredients together over medium heat. Bring to boil, stirring constantly. Let boil for about 2 minutes. Pour over warm cake.

❦ ❦ ❦   *The Lady & Sons*

Rum Cake

SERVES 12 TO 16

1 cup chopped walnuts
One 18¼-ounce package yellow
   cake mix
One 3½-ounce package instant
   vanilla pudding mix

4 eggs
½ cup buttermilk
½ cup vegetable oil
½ cup dark rum

Preheat oven to 325 degrees. Grease and flour a 10-inch tube pan. Sprinkle nuts over bottom of pan. Mix remaining ingredients together. Pour batter over nuts. Bake for 1 hour. Cool. Invert on service plate. Prick top with fork or toothpick. Drizzle and smooth glaze evenly over top and sides. Allow cake to absorb glaze. Use all the glaze.

GLAZE

4 tablespoons (½ stick) butter
¼ cup water

1 cup sugar
½ cup dark rum

Melt butter in saucepan. Stir in water and sugar. Boil 5 minutes, stirring constantly. Remove from heat; stir in rum.

Coconut Cake

SERVES 12 TO 16

One 18¼-ounce package yellow
  pudding cake mix
1 cup sour cream

1½ cups sugar
12 ounces canned or frozen
  shredded coconut

Preheat oven to 350 degrees. Make cake by following directions on package, substituting milk for water. Divide and bake in three 9-inch round cake pans for 20 minutes. Remove from oven and allow to cool for 5 minutes. Remove from pans. Stir together sour cream, sugar, and coconut. Spread between slightly warm cake layers, piercing each layer as you stack them. Store cake in container in refrigerator for 2 to 3 days. This allows cake to soak up moisture from the coconut. On the third day, prepare icing for cake.

ICING

2 unbeaten egg whites
1½ cups sugar
2 teaspoons light corn syrup, or ¼
  teaspoon cream of tartar
⅓ cup cold water

Dash of salt
1 teaspoon vanilla
Additional coconut to top icing
  (about ½ cup)

Place all ingredients except vanilla and additional coconut in top of double boiler, but do not place over heat; beat 1 minute with electric hand mixer. Place over boiling water and cook, beating constantly, until frosting forms stiff peaks (about 7 minutes). Remove from boiling water; add vanilla and beat until it reaches spreading consistency (about 2 minutes). Frost top and sides of cake; sprinkle with additional coconut. Cover and store at room temperature.

Chocolate Strawberry Shortcake

SERVES 15 TO 20

2 cups cake flour
1½ cups sugar
⅔ cup cocoa
½ cup Crisco shortening
1½ cups buttermilk
1½ teaspoons baking soda
1 teaspoon salt

1 teaspoon vanilla
2 whole eggs or 3 egg whites
1 quart fresh strawberries, rinsed
  and sliced
1 cup whipped cream or
  Cool Whip

Preheat oven to 350 degrees. In a mixing bowl, combine all ingredients in order listed, except strawberries and whipping cream. Beat with mixer on low speed, scraping bowl constantly, for 30 seconds. Beat on high speed, scraping bowl occasionally, for 3 minutes. Pour into greased and floured 13 × 9-inch pan. Bake for 30 to 35 minutes. Cool cake completely. Cut into squares. Place 2 or 3 squares in dessert cups and layer with small amount of strawberries and whipped cream. Garnish with strawberries. *A heavenly treat!*

Low-Fat Peach Cake

SERVES 12 TO 16

¼ teaspoon sugar

1 teaspoon ground cinnamon

CAKE

2 cups all-purpose flour
1½ cups sugar
½ cup Crisco shortening
½ cup milk
One 15-ounce can cling peaches,
    drained (reserve ½ cup juice)

3 egg whites
3½ teaspoons baking powder
½ teaspoon ground cinnamon
1 teaspoon vanilla
1 teaspoon salt

Preheat oven to 350 degrees. Use no-stick cooking spray in Bundt pan. Mix together sugar and cinnamon. Sprinkle mixture over bottom and sides of pan. Combine all cake ingredients together, including reserved juice. Beat with mixer on low speed for 30 seconds, scraping bowl constantly. Beat on high speed for 2 minutes. Pour into Bundt pan. Bake for 40 to 45 minutes. Remove from oven; cool completely. Frost with icing immediately before serving.

ICING

One 6-ounce container nonfat
    peach yogurt

One 8-ounce container Lite
    Cool Whip

Mix together. Frost cake.

Savannah Chocolate Cake
with Hot Fudge Sauce

SERVES APPROXIMATELY 20

2 cups brown sugar
½ cup Crisco shortening
1 cup buttermilk
1 teaspoon vanilla
2 ounces unsweetened chocolate,
    melted

3 eggs
2 cups sifted all-purpose flour
1 teaspoon baking soda
½ teaspoon salt

Preheat oven to 350 degrees. Cream together brown sugar and shortening; add buttermilk and vanilla. Add melted chocolate, then add eggs one at a time; beat for 2 minutes. Sift together flour, baking soda, and salt and add to creamed mixture. Beat an additional 2 minutes. Pour into a 13 × 9 × 2-inch greased, floured pan. Bake for 40 to 45 minutes.

HOT FUDGE SAUCE

One 4-ounce bar German chocolate
½ ounce unsweetened chocolate
8 tablespoons (1 stick) butter

3 cups powdered sugar
1⅔ cups evaporated milk
1¼ teaspoons vanilla

Melt chocolate and butter in saucepan over very low heat. Stir in powdered sugar, alternating with evaporated milk, blending well. Bring to a boil over medium heat, stirring constantly. Cook and stir until mixture becomes thick and creamy, about 8 minutes. Stir in vanilla; serve warm over Savannah Chocolate Cake (or your favorite sheet cake).

Mama's Pound Cake

SERVES 16 TO 20

½ pound (2 sticks) butter
½ cup Crisco shortening
3 cups sugar
5 eggs
3 cups all-purpose flour

½ teaspoon salt
½ teaspoon baking powder
1 cup milk
1 teaspoon vanilla

Preheat oven to 325 degrees. Cream butter and shortening together. Add sugar, a little at a time. Add eggs, one at a time, beating after each. Sift together dry ingredients and add to mixture alternately with milk, starting with flour and ending with flour. Add vanilla. Pour into greased and floured tube pan and bake for 1½ hours.

Chocolate Chip Nut Cake

SERVES 16 TO 20

½ cup Crisco shortening
½ pound (2 sticks) butter
2¾ cups sugar
6 large eggs
3 cups all-purpose flour
1 teaspoon baking powder

1 cup milk
1 teaspoon vanilla
One 12-ounce package semisweet
  chocolate chips
1½ cups chopped pecans or walnuts

Cream shortening, butter, and sugar. Add eggs, one at a time, beating thoroughly after each. Sift flour with baking powder. Add to creamed mixture, alternating with milk. Roll nuts and chocolate chips in a little flour and add to mixture, then add vanilla. Pour into a greased and floured tube pan. Place in cold oven and bake at 325 degrees for about 1½ hours, or until done.

Luscious Lime Cheesecake

SERVES 15 TO 20

One 18¼-ounce package yellow
  cake mix
4 eggs
¼ cup vegetable oil
Two 8-ounce packages cream
  cheese, at room temperature
One 14-ounce can sweetened condensed milk

2 teaspoons grated lime zest
⅓ cup fresh lime juice
1 teaspoon vanilla
One 8-ounce container Cool Whip,
  or 2 cups heavy cream, whipped
  with ½ cup sugar until stiff
Lime slices, for garnish

Preheat oven to 300 degrees. Reserve ½ cup dry cake mix. In large bowl, combine remaining cake mix, 1 egg, and oil. Mix well (mixture will be crumbly). Press evenly in bottom and 1½ inches up sides of greased 13 × 9-inch pan. In same bowl, beat cheese until fluffy. Beat in condensed milk until smooth. Add remaining eggs and reserved cake mix and beat 1 minute at medium speed. Stir in lime zest, lime juice, and vanilla. Pour into prepared crust. Bake for 50 to 55 minutes or until center is firm. Cool to room temperature. Chill thoroughly. Spread Cool Whip over top. Cut into squares to serve. Garnish with lime slices.

Grandmother Paul's Sour Cream Pound Cake

SERVES 16 TO 20

½ pound (2 sticks) butter
3 cups sugar
1 cup sour cream
3 cups all-purpose flour

½ teaspoon baking soda
6 eggs
1 teaspoon vanilla

Preheat oven to 325 degrees. Cream butter and sugar together; add sour cream. Sift flour and baking soda together. Add to creamed mixture, alternately with eggs, one at a time, beating after each. Add vanilla. Pour into a greased and floured tube pan and bake for 1 hour 20 minutes. 🌼 🌼 🌼 **The Lady & Sons**

Gooey Butter Cakes

SERVES 15 TO 20

I could write a full chapter on this dessert. It is the number-one choice in our restaurant.

One 18¼-ounce package yellow cake mix
1 egg

8 tablespoons (1 stick) butter, melted

Preheat oven to 350 degrees. Combine ingredients and mix well. Pat into a lightly greased 13 × 9-inch baking pan. Prepare filling.

FILLING

*One 8-ounce package cream
    cheese, softened*
2 eggs
1 teaspoon vanilla

*8 tablespoons (1 stick) butter,
    melted*
One 16-ounce box powdered sugar

Beat cream cheese until smooth. Add eggs and vanilla. Add butter; beat. Add powdered sugar and mix well. Spread over cake mixture. Bake for 40 to 50 minutes. You want the center to be a little gooey, so do not overbake.

VARIATIONS:

1. For the holidays, add a 15-ounce can of pumpkin to the filling; add cinnamon and nutmeg.
2. Add a 20-ounce can of drained crushed pineapple to the filling.
3. Use a lemon cake mix. Add lemon juice and zest to the filling.
4. Use a chocolate cake mix with cream cheese filling. Add chocolate chips and nuts on top.
5. Use a spiced carrot cake mix. Add chopped nuts and shredded carrots to the filling.
6. Use mandarin oranges, bananas, blueberries, or strawberries—just coordinate your extract flavorings.
7. Use a chocolate cake mix. Add ¾ to 1 cup peanut butter and nuts to the filling.

❧ ❧ ❧ *The Lady & Sons*

Grandmother Paul's Red Velvet Cake

SERVES 16 TO 20

2 eggs
2 cups sugar
1 teaspoon cocoa
2 ounces red food coloring
½ pound (2 sticks) butter
2½ cups cake flour

1 teaspoon salt
1 cup buttermilk
1 teaspoon vanilla
½ teaspoon baking soda
1 tablespoon vinegar

Preheat oven to 350 degrees. Beat eggs; add sugar. Mix cocoa and food coloring. Add butter and egg mixture; mix well. Sift together flour and salt. Add to creamed mixture alternately with buttermilk. Blend in vanilla. In a small bowl, combine soda and vinegar and add to mixture. Pour into three 9-inch round greased and floured pans. Bake for 20 to 25 minutes, or until tests done.

ICING

2 egg whites
1½ cups sugar
5 tablespoons cold water
2 tablespoons light corn syrup

1 cup miniature marshmallows
1 cup or 3½-ounce can shredded
coconut
1 cup chopped pecans

Cook egg whites, sugar, water, and corn syrup in double boiler for 5 minutes and beat. Add marshmallows; stir until melted. Fold in coconut and nuts. Spread between layers and on top and sides of cooled cake.   ❦ ❦ ❦ *The Lady & Sons*

Cheesecake

SERVES 10 TO 12

1 cup graham cracker crumbs
¼ cup sugar

4 tablespoons (½ stick) butter,
melted

Preheat oven to 350 degrees. Mix ingredients together and pat onto bottom and sides of an 8-inch springform cake pan. Prepare filling.

FILLING

2 eggs
12 ounces cream cheese, softened

1 cup sugar
½ teaspoon vanilla

Beat eggs and softened cream cheese together. Add sugar and vanilla. Beat until well blended. Pour into prepared crust. Bake for 25 to 30 minutes. Let cool for 10 minutes. Add topping (recipe follows).

TOPPING

½ cup sugar   ½ teaspoon vanilla
1 cup sour cream

Combine ingredients and put on top of cake; return to oven for 10 minutes.

OPTIONAL FRESH FRUIT TOPPING

2 cups fresh raspberries, blueberries,   ¾ cup water
  strawberries, cherries, etc.   1 tablespoon butter
½ cup sugar   2 tablespoons cornstarch

In small saucepan, bring fruit, sugar, ½ cup water, and butter to a boil. Mix cornstarch and ¼ cup water together. Add to boiling pot, cooking and stirring constantly for 1 minute or until thick. Cool to room temperature. Serve dollop on each slice of cheesecake, with a sprig of fresh mint for garnish.   ❦ ❦ ❦ **The Lady & Sons**

NOTE: You can use a canned pie filling (blueberry, strawberry, or cherry) instead of fresh fruit.

Pineapple Cake

SERVES 16 TO 20

One 16-ounce can crushed   ¾ cup sour cream
  pineapple in heavy syrup   8 tablespoons (1 stick) butter
2 cups Bisquick   2 teaspoons vanilla
1 cup sifted all-purpose flour   2 large eggs
1 teaspoon baking soda   2 tablespoons rum
1 cup sugar

Preheat oven to 350 degrees. Drain pineapple well, reserving syrup for glaze. Stir Bisquick, flour, and baking soda together and set aside. Beat sugar, sour cream, butter, and vanilla together for 2 minutes. Add eggs and beat 1 additional minute. Add flour mixture and beat 1 minute longer. Mix in drained pineapple and rum. Pour into well-greased 9-inch Bundt pan. Bake for about 45 minutes or until cake tests done. Remove from oven and spoon about half the glaze over cake. Let stand 10 minutes and then turn onto serving plate. Spoon on remaining glaze. Cool before cutting.

GLAZE

¾ *cup sugar*	¼ *cup reserved pineapple syrup*
4 *tablespoons butter*	2 *tablespoons rum (optional)*

Combine sugar, butter, and syrup. Stir over low heat until sugar is dissolved and butter is melted. Remove from heat and add rum, if desired.   🌸 🌸 🌸 *The Lady & Sons*

Chocolate Sheet Cake

SERVES 15 TO 20

2 *cups sugar*	¼ *cup cocoa*
½ *teaspoon salt*	2 *eggs*
2 *cups all-purpose flour*	1 *teaspoon baking soda*
8 *tablespoons (1 stick) butter*	½ *cup buttermilk*
½ *cup vegetable oil*	1 *teaspoon vanilla*
1 *cup water*	

Preheat oven to 350 degrees. Combine sugar, salt, and flour in a large mixing bowl. In a saucepan, bring to a boil butter, oil, water, and cocoa. Add to flour mixture. Beat eggs, baking soda, buttermilk, and vanilla. Add to dry ingredients. Pour into greased and floured 13 × 9 × 2-inch pan. Bake for 25 minutes.

ICING

8 *tablespoons (1 stick) butter*	1 *teaspoon vanilla*
3 *tablespoons cocoa*	*One 16-ounce box powdered sugar*
6 *tablespoons milk*	1 *cup chopped pecans or walnuts*

Melt together butter and cocoa. Add milk and vanilla. Stir in powdered sugar and nuts. Spread on warm cake.   🌸 🌸 🌸   **The Lady & Sons**

Banana Split Cake

SERVES 15 TO 20

2 cups crushed graham crackers
¾ pound (3 sticks) butter
2 eggs
One 16-ounce box powdered sugar

One 20-ounce can crushed
    pineapple, drained
2 to 3 bananas, sliced
One 12-ounce container Cool Whip

For crust, mix crushed graham crackers and 1 stick of butter. Line bottom and sides of a 13 × 9-inch pan with mixture. Beat until fluffy eggs, 2 sticks butter, and the powdered sugar. Spread mixture on crust. Add layer of crushed pineapple (drained) and layer of sliced bananas. Cover with Cool Whip. Sprinkle with nuts or graham crackers. Refrigerate for 1 hour.   🌸 🌸 🌸   **The Lady & Sons**

Grandmama Hiers's Carrot Cake

SERVES 16 TO 20

2 cups all-purpose flour
2 cups sugar
2 teaspoons baking soda
2 teaspoons cinnamon
1 teaspoon salt

4 eggs
1½ cups vegetable oil
3 cups grated carrots
1½ cups chopped pecans (optional)

Preheat oven to 350 degrees. In a large bowl, combine flour, sugar, baking soda, cinnamon, and salt. Add eggs and vegetable oil and mix well; add carrots and pecans. Pour into three 9-inch round greased, floured pans. Bake for approximately 40 minutes. Remove from oven and cool for 5 minutes. Remove from pans, place on waxpaper, and allow to cool completely before frosting.

FROSTING

One 8-ounce package cream cheese
8 tablespoons (1 stick) butter
One 16-ounce box powdered sugar

1 teaspoon vanilla
½ cup chopped pecans

Combine all ingredients except for nuts and beat until fluffy. Stir in nuts. Frost cake.   🌸 🌸 🌸 **The Lady & Sons**

Tunnel of Fudge Cake

SERVES 16 TO 20

¾ pound (3 sticks) butter
6 eggs
1½ cups sugar
One 12½-ounce can creamy
    double Dutch frosting

2 cups all-purpose flour
2 cups chopped walnuts or pecans

Preheat oven to 350 degrees. Cream butter in large bowl on high speed. Add eggs one at a time, beating well. Add sugar gradually, creaming at high speed, until light and fluffy. Gradually add flour. By hand, stir in frosting mix and nuts until well blended. Pour batter in well-greased and floured Bundt pan. Bake for 60 to 65 minutes. Cool 2 hours before removing from pan. Cake will have a dry, brownie-type crust and a moist center with a tunnel of fudge running through it.

Old-Time Lemon "Cheesecake"

SERVES 16 TO 20

While the recipe contains no actual cheese, Southerners have referred to this dessert as lemon cheesecake for generations. Go figure!

1½ sticks butter
2 cups sugar
3½ cups all-purpose flour
3½ teaspoons baking powder

1 cup milk
1 teaspoon vanilla
6 egg whites, beaten to stiff peaks

Preheat oven to 375 degrees. Cream butter; add sugar. Sift flour and baking powder together three times and add to butter alternately with milk and vanilla. Fold in egg whites. Bake in three greased 8-inch round pans for 35 minutes.

ICING

9 egg yolks
1½ cups sugar

¾ pound (3 sticks) butter
Juice and zest of 4 lemons

Mix all ingredients together and cook in double boiler until thick, approximately 20 minutes. Allow cake to cool. Spread icing in between layers and on entire outside of cake.

Better Than Sex? Yes!

SERVES 15 TO 20

One 18½-ounce package chocolate cake mix
One 14-ounce can sweetened condensed milk
One 6-ounce jar caramel or hot fudge topping

8 ounces Cool Whip
4 Skor candy bars, crushed

Prepare cake according to directions and bake in 9 × 13-inch pan. Pierce warm cake all over with toothpick. Pour milk over cake. Pour caramel over cake. Chill. Before serving, top with whipped topping and sprinkle with crushed candy. 🌼 🌼 🌼 *The Lady & Sons*

Punch Bowl Cake

SERVES 16 TO 20

One 18¼-ounce package yellow cake mix

Two 3½-ounce packages instant vanilla pudding mix (prepared according to instructions on box)

One 20-ounce can crushed pineapple, drained

6 medium bananas, sliced

2 pints strawberries (crush one pint, slice one pint, and mix both together)

One 24-ounce container Cool Whip (thawed), or fresh whipped cream (1 quart heavy cream whipped with 1 cup sugar till stiff)

Prepare cake in two 9-inch round pans according to directions. Put one layer of cake in the bottom of a punch bowl. Add half of the pudding, half of the pineapple, 3 sliced bananas, half of the strawberries, and half of the Cool Whip. Put another layer of cake in punch bowl along with remaining pudding, pineapple, bananas, and strawberries. Top off with Cool Whip and sprinkle strawberry juice on top.

Chocolate Pound Cake

SERVES 16 TO 20

3 cups sugar

½ pound (2 sticks) butter

¼ pound (1 stick) margarine

5 eggs

3 cups cake flour

4 tablespoons cocoa

½ teaspoon salt

½ teaspoon baking powder

1 cup milk

1 tablespoon vanilla

Preheat oven to 350 degrees. Mix sugar with butter and margarine; add eggs one at a time, beating after each. Mix together dry ingredients. Add dry ingredients alternately with milk to butter mixture, beginning with flour and ending with flour. Add vanilla. Bake in a greased and floured tube pan for about 1 hour.

Easy Coffee Cake

SERVES 12 TO 15

Two 8-ounce cans refrigerated
   crescent rolls
1 cup sugar
Two 8-ounce packages cream
   cheese, softened

1 teaspoon vanilla
1 egg, separated
½ cup chopped pecans

Preheat oven to 350 degrees. Spread one can of crescent rolls in bottom of 13 × 9-inch pan. Cream together ¾ cup sugar, cream cheese, vanilla, and egg yolk. Spread mixture over rolls. Top with second package of crescent roll dough. Beat egg white until frothy and spread on top. Sprinkle top with remaining sugar and nuts. Bake for 30 to 35 minutes.

Applesauce Cupcakes

YIELDS APPROXIMATELY 2 DOZEN

1 egg
2 cups all-purpose flour
½ teaspoon ground cloves
¼ teaspoon salt
1½ teaspoons ground nutmeg
1 teaspoon ground cinnamon
1½ sticks butter, melted

1 teaspoon vanilla
1 cup chopped pecans
1½ cups sugar
1 cup raisins
1½ cups hot applesauce with
   2 teaspoons baking soda added

Preheat oven to 350 degrees. Mix above ingredients in bowl by hand except for applesauce. Last, add hot applesauce and baking soda. Pour batter into paper-lined cupcake pans. Bake for 25 minutes or until done.

Chocolate Damnation

SERVES 15 TO 20

One 19.8-ounce package brownie
   mix
12 ounces semisweet chocolate
¼ cup strong black brewed coffee

2 eggs, separated
¼ cup coffee liqueur
3 tablespoons sugar
¼ cup heavy cream

Prepare brownie batter according to directions on box. Pour into a greased 13 × 9 × 2-inch pan. Bake according to instructions on box. When cool, cut into squares and remove from pan. Clean pan thoroughly and grease once more. Place brownies back in greased pan. Combine chocolate and coffee in top of double boiler, and melt over boiling water. Remove from heat. Beat egg yolks and stir in small amount of chocolate mixture; pour mixture into balance of chocolate mixture; stir until smooth. Stir in liqueur and set aside to cool. Beat egg whites until foamy; gradually add sugar and beat until stiff. Whip cream until stiff. Fold cream into chocolate mixture; fold in egg whites. Pour filling over brownies. Cover with plastic wrap and chill 3 to 4 hours, until firm. Invert onto serving platter and drizzle on glaze. Let set and decorate with chocolate curls, if desired.

CHOCOLATE GLAZE

4 ounces semisweet chocolate

3 tablespoons strong black brewed
   coffee

Combine chocolate and coffee in double boiler. Heat until melted. Stir well.

Peanut Butter Cake

SERVES 12 TO 16

1 cup all-purpose flour
1 cup plus 2 tablespoons sugar
3½ teaspoons baking powder
¾ teaspoon salt
2 cups graham cracker crumbs
Peanut butter to taste (at least ½
   cup; if using more, decrease
   shortening by an equal amount)

¾ cup Crisco shortening
1 cup plus 2 tablespoons milk
1½ teaspoons vanilla
3 eggs

Preheat oven to 375 degrees. Sift flour, sugar, baking powder, and salt together. Add graham cracker crumbs, peanut butter, shortening, milk, and vanilla. Beat mixture with electric mixer on low until moistened, then beat on medium for 2 minutes. Add eggs and beat for 1 minute. Bake in a greased 9 × 13-inch pan for 30 to 35 minutes. Do not remove from pan.

FROSTING

2 cups sugar
½ cup cocoa

8 tablespoons (1 stick) butter
½ cup milk

Mix all ingredients together. Heat in a saucepan and bring to a boil. Boil for 1 minute. Cool slightly. With a wooden spoon handle, poke a few holes in the cake, then pour warm frosting over it.

❧ ❧ ❧ *The Lady & Sons*

French Coconut Pie

SERVES 6 TO 8

4 tablespoons (½ stick) butter
2 eggs, beaten

1 tablespoon all-purpose flour
¾ cup sugar

1 cup or 3½-ounce can shredded
    coconut

1 cup milk
One 9-inch unbaked pie shell

Preheat oven to 400 degrees. Melt butter; add remaining ingredients. Pour into pie shell. Bake until firm, about 45 to 60 minutes.

Butterscotch Pie

SERVES 6 TO 8

¾ cup brown sugar
5 tablespoons all-purpose flour
½ teaspoon salt
2 cups milk

2 egg yolks, lightly beaten
2 tablespoons butter
1 teaspoon vanilla
One 9-inch prebaked pie shell

Combine sugar, flour, and salt and stir in milk slowly. Cook in double boiler over boiling water until thickened, stirring constantly. Cover and cook 10 minutes longer, stirring occasionally. Add small amount of hot mixture to egg yolks, stirring rigorously. Add back to pot and cook 1 minute longer. Add butter and vanilla and cool. Place filling in pastry shell and cover with whipped cream or meringue.

Corrie's Kentucky Pie

SERVES 16 TO 22

4 eggs, lightly beaten
2 cups sugar
One 12-ounce package semisweet
    chocolate chips, melted
1 cup sifted self-rising flour
½ pound (2 sticks) butter, melted

2 teaspoons vanilla
2 cups chopped pecans
Two 9-inch unbaked deep-dish
    pie shells or 3 regular 9-inch
    unbaked pie shells

Preheat oven to 350 degrees. Combine eggs, sugar, and melted chocolate in large bowl. Add flour and mix well; stir in remaining ingredients except for pie shells. Spread mixture into pie shells. Bake for 30 minutes. Serve warm with ice cream. Freezes well!

Mini Pecan Pies

YIELDS 24

8 tablespoons (1 stick) butter   One 3-ounce package cream cheese
1 cup all-purpose flour

Preheat oven to 325 degrees. Soften cheese and butter and blend well. Stir in flour. Chill 1 hour. Shape into twenty-four 1-inch balls. Place in ungreased small muffin tins. Press down to form crust.

FILLING

1 egg   1 teaspoon vanilla
¾ cup brown sugar   Dash of salt
1 tablespoon butter   ⅔ cup chopped pecans

Beat egg, sugar, butter, vanilla, and salt until smooth. Divide half the nuts among pastry cups. Add egg mixture. Top with remaining nuts. Bake for 25 minutes or until filling hardens.

Praline Pumpkin Pie

SERVES 6 TO 8

⅓ cup finely chopped pecans   ¼ cup dark rum
⅓ cup plus ½ cup brown sugar   ½ teaspoon salt
2 tablespoons butter, softened   1 teaspoon ground cinnamon
One 9-inch unbaked pie shell   ¼ teaspoon ground cloves
3 whole eggs   ¼ teaspoon ground ginger
2 eggs, separated   ¼ teaspoon ground mace
1 cup canned pumpkin   (optional)
1½ cups heavy cream   2 tablespoons granulated sugar

Preheat oven to 400 degrees. Blend pecans with ⅓ cup brown sugar and softened butter. Press gently with the back of a spoon into bottom of pie shell. Blend all remaining ingredients except egg whites and granulated sugar. Pour into pie shell. Bake for about 50 minutes. Make a meringue by beating egg whites until stiff, adding the granulated sugar while beating. After pie has baked, remove from oven and cover with meringue. Return to 425-degree oven just to brown meringue.

Chocolate Chip Pie

SERVES 6 TO 8

2 eggs
½ cup all-purpose flour
½ cup packed brown sugar
½ cup granulated sugar
8 tablespoons (1 stick) butter,
* melted*

One 6-ounce package semisweet
* chocolate chips*
1 cup chopped pecans or walnuts
One 9-inch unbaked pie shell
Whipped topping (optional)

Preheat oven to 325 degrees. In large bowl, beat eggs until foamy. Add flour and brown sugar; beat until well blended. Blend in granulated sugar and butter. Stir in chocolate chips and nuts. Pour into pie shell. Bake for 1 hour. Cover with whipped topping, if desired.

Chocolate Almond Pie

SERVES 6 TO 8

16 to 20 large marshmallows
Four 1½-ounce Hershey chocolate
* bars with almonds*
½ cup milk

1 cup heavy cream
1 teaspoon vanilla
One 8-inch graham cracker crust

Melt marshmallows and candy bars in milk in double boiler. Remove from heat and cool. Whip cream until stiff and fold into cooled mixture. Add vanilla. Pour into prepared crust and chill. Good as is or top with whipped cream.

Strawberry and Cream Pie

SERVES 6 TO 8

8 tablespoons (1 stick) butter
1½ cups powdered sugar

2 eggs, beaten
One 8-inch graham cracker crust

Cream together butter and powdered sugar; add eggs. Beat ingredients until fluffy. Spread over crust. Chill. Add topping.

TOPPING

1½ cups sliced and sweetened
  strawberries, drained

1 cup whipped cream

Fold strawberries into whipped cream. Spread over chilled pie. Chill for at least 8 hours. Garnish with whole berries and mint leaves.

Thanksgiving Pie

SERVES 6 TO 8

3 eggs
1 cup dark corn syrup
½ cup sugar
4 tablespoons (½ stick) butter,
  melted

1 cup canned pumpkin
1 teaspoon vanilla
1 cup chopped pecans
One 9-inch unbaked pie shell
Whipped cream

Preheat oven to 350 degrees. With hand beater, beat eggs well. Beat in corn syrup, sugar, butter, pumpkin, and vanilla until well blended. Arrange pecans in bottom of pie shell. Slowly pour egg mixture over them. Bake for 1 hour or until knife inserted 1 inch from edge comes out clean. Serve with whipped cream.

Mama's Chess Pie

SERVES 6 TO 8

8 tablespoons (1 stick) butter
2 cups sifted cake flour

¼ teaspoon salt
3 to 6 tablespoons ice water

Cut butter into dry ingredients. Slowly add ice water. Knead dough and roll out on dough board, or press into bottom and sides of a 9-inch pie plate.

FILLING

½ pound (2 sticks) butter
2 cups sugar
7 egg yolks, beaten

1½ teaspoons vanilla
½ cup heavy cream
2 tablespoons cornmeal

Preheat oven to 350 degrees. Cream butter and sugar; add egg yolks, vanilla, and cream. Gently blend in cornmeal. Pour into chess pie pastry. Bake until light brown on top, about 35 to 45 minutes.

Lemon Meringue Pie

SERVES 6 TO 8

One 14-ounce can sweetened
* condensed milk*
½ cup lemon juice
1 teaspoon grated lemon zest

3 egg yolks
One 8-inch prebaked pie shell or
* crumb crust*

In medium bowl, combine milk, lemon juice, and zest; blend in egg yolks. Pour into cooled crust.

MERINGUE

3 egg whites
¼ teaspoon cream of tartar

¼ cup sugar

Preheat oven to 325 degrees. Beat egg whites with cream of tartar until soft peaks form. Gradually beat in sugar until stiff. Spread over filling; seal to edge of crust. Bake for 12 to 15 minutes or until meringue is golden brown.

Banana Cream Pie

SERVES 6 TO 8

⅓ cup plus ¼ cup sugar
3 tablespoons cornstarch
¼ teaspoon salt
1½ cups milk
2 egg yolks, lightly beaten

2 tablespoons butter
2 teaspoons vanilla
2 egg whites
2 bananas, sliced
One 9-inch prebaked pie shell

In a saucepan over medium heat, combine ⅓ cup sugar with the cornstarch and salt. Blend in milk, then egg yolks. Cook and stir until mixture thickens. Remove from heat; stir in butter and vanilla. Cool to room temperature. Beat egg whites until soft peaks form; gradually add ¼ cup sugar and beat until stiff peaks form. Fold into egg yolk mixture. In pie shell, alternate layers of banana slices and cream filling. Cover and chill. Top with whipped cream and additional sliced bananas, if desired.

Million-Dollar Pie

SERVES APPROXIMATELY 20

8 tablespoons (1 stick) butter
1 cup all-purpose flour
½ cup chopped pecans
One 8-ounce package cream cheese
1 cup powdered sugar

1 quart heavy cream, whipped
  with 1 cup sugar until stiff
Two 3.4-ounce packages instant
  chocolate pudding mix
3 cups milk

Preheat oven to 350 degrees. In a 13 × 9 × 2-inch glass dish, melt butter and stir in flour and ¼ cup of the nuts. Bake about 20 minutes, until firm. Let cool.

First layer: Combine cream cheese, powdered sugar, and 1 cup of whipped cream. Layer over cooked nut crust.

Second layer: Combine instant pudding mix and milk. Layer over first layer.

Third layer: Combine remaining whipped cream and remaining chopped nuts. Layer over top. Keep refrigerated.   ❧ ❧ ❧   **The Lady & Sons**

Pastry for Two-Crust Pie

For extra-tender pastry, cut in half of the shortening until the mixture is like cornmeal; then cut in the remaining shortening until it is like small peas.

2 cups sifted all-purpose flour	*⅔ cup Crisco shortening*
1 teaspoon salt	*5 to 7 tablespoons cold water*

Sift together flour and salt; cut in shortening with pastry blender until pieces are the size of small peas. Sprinkle 1 tablespoon water over part of mixture. Gently toss with fork; push to side of bowl. Repeat until all is moistened. Form into 2 balls. Flatten each on lightly floured surface by pressing with edge of hand three times across in both directions. Roll from center to edge until ⅛ inch thick.

Chewy Pecan Cookies

YIELDS APPROXIMATELY 5 DOZEN

8 tablespoons (1 stick) butter	*2 cups all-purpose flour*
One 16-ounce box brown sugar	*1½ teaspoons baking powder*
4 eggs, lightly beaten	*Pinch of salt*
½ teaspoon vanilla	*2 cups chopped pecans*

Preheat oven to 300 degrees. Melt butter and sugar together in the top of a double boiler; remove from heat. Add eggs and vanilla. In a bowl, combine flour, baking powder, and salt. Add to egg mixture; mix well. Stir in nuts. Drop spoonfuls onto greased cookie sheet and bake for 15 to 20 minutes.   ❧ ❧ ❧   **The Lady & Sons**

Snickerdoodles

YIELDS APPROXIMATELY 4 DOZEN

1 cup Crisco shortening
1½ cups plus 2 tablespoons sugar
2 eggs
2¾ cups sifted all-purpose flour

2 teaspoons cream of tartar
1 teaspoon baking soda
½ teaspoon salt
2 teaspoons ground cinnamon

Preheat oven to 350 degrees. Cream shortening, 1½ cups sugar, and eggs. Sift together flour, cream of tartar, baking soda, and salt. Combine with egg mixture. Chill dough thoroughly and then roll into balls the size of a small walnut. Roll in mixture of 2 tablespoons sugar and the cinnamon. Bake for 8 to 10 minutes on an ungreased baking sheet until lightly browned but still soft.

Lady Lock Cookies

APPROXIMATELY 4 DOZEN

1 pound (4 sticks) butter
4 cups all-purpose flour
1 teaspoon salt

1 cup sour cream
1 cup buttermilk

Cut butter into dry ingredients. Add sour cream and buttermilk. Mix well. Divide into four parts, flour well, and fold like a rectangular envelope. Refrigerate overnight. Preheat oven to 375 degrees. Remove one part at a time, and roll thin. Make strips 1 inch wide and 7 inches long. Wrap around foil-covered clothespins. Bake for 15 minutes, or longer if needed. Set aside to cool.

FILLING

1½ cups Crisco shortening
8 tablespoons (1 stick) butter
1 cup sugar

1 egg white
2 teaspoons vanilla
½ cup hot milk

Cream together shortening and butter. Add sugar and beat well. Add egg white and vanilla; beat thoroughly. Add hot milk, 1 tablespoon at a time, and beat until creamy. Put into cookie press or pastry tube and fill cookies.

Southern Tea Cakes

YIELDS 6 TO 8 DOZEN

This is a very old Southern recipe that has been handed down from one generation to another.

4 cups all-purpose flour	*2 eggs*
1 teaspoon baking soda	*½ cup buttermilk*
2 teaspoons baking powder	*½ pound (2 sticks) butter, softened*
2 cups sugar	*1 teaspoon vanilla*

Preheat oven to 350 degrees. In a large bowl sift flour, baking soda, and baking powder together. Add remaining ingredients and blend well. Dough should be soft. Roll dough out onto a floured surface until approximately ¼ inch thick. Cut dough into desired shapes and bake on a slightly greased sheet for 10 to 12 minutes.

Sliced Nut Cookies

YIELDS APPROXIMATELY 8 DOZEN

1 cup granulated sugar	*1 teaspoon baking powder*
1 cup brown sugar	*1 teaspoon salt*
1½ cups Crisco shortening	*1 teaspoon ground cinnamon*
3 eggs, beaten	*1 teaspoon ground nutmeg*
4½ cups all-purpose flour	*½ teaspoon ground cloves*
1 teaspoon baking soda	*1 cup ground pecans*

Cream sugars and shortening; add eggs. Sift together flour, baking soda, baking powder, and salt; add to sugar mixture. Add cinnamon, nutmeg, cloves, and nuts. Roll into several small, oblong rolls. Chill until cold. Preheat oven to 375 degrees. Slice dough into thin cookies. Bake for 12 minutes.

Butter Fingers

YIELDS APPROXIMATELY 100

1 cup chopped pecans
2½ cups all-purpose flour
¾ cup granulated sugar

½ pound (2 sticks) butter
1 teaspoon vanilla
One 16-ounce box powdered sugar

Preheat oven to 325 degrees. Combine all ingredients except for powdered sugar. Roll into small "fingers" or balls. Bake for 20 to 30 minutes. Roll immediately in powdered sugar.

Goodies

YIELDS APPROXIMATELY 20

½ pound (2 sticks) butter
2 cups packed brown sugar
1 cup light corn syrup
½ teaspoon salt
1 teaspoon vinegar

1 teaspoon vanilla
⅓ cup peanut butter
1½ cups uncooked rolled oats
½ cup chopped pecans

Melt butter in large saucepan. Stir in brown sugar, syrup, salt, and vinegar. Cook over high heat to firm ball stage. Remove from heat. Stir in remaining ingredients; pour into greased 8-inch square pan and chill. Cut into squares. Wrap each piece in wax paper.

Low Country Cookies

YIELDS 15 TO 20

One 16-ounce box graham crackers
12 tablespoons (1½ sticks) butter
1 cup sugar
1 egg

½ cup milk
1 cup chopped pecans
1 cup or 3½-ounce can shredded
coconut

Line a 13 × 9-inch pan with whole graham crackers. Melt butter in saucepan and add sugar. Beat egg and milk together; add to butter mixture. Bring to a boil, stirring constantly. Remove from heat. Add nuts, coconut, and 1 cup graham cracker crumbs. Pour over crackers in pan. Cover with another layer of whole graham crackers. Prepare topping.

TOPPING

2 cups powdered sugar
1 teaspoon vanilla

4 tablespoons (½ stick) butter
3 tablespoons milk

Beat all ingredients together and spread over top layer of crackers. Chill. Cut into squares.

Thumb Print Cookies

YIELDS 5 DOZEN

¾ pound (3 sticks) butter, softened
1 cup sugar
2 egg yolks
3¾ cups all-purpose flour

¼ teaspoon salt
1 teaspoon vanilla
Any tart preserves (plum, for
example)

Cream butter and sugar. Add egg yolks. Sift flour and salt; blend into butter mixture. Add vanilla. Chill dough thoroughly. Preheat oven to 350 degrees. Shape dough into 1-inch balls and place on an ungreased cookie sheet. Make indentation in center of each with thumb; fill with preserves (jelly or pecan halves will also work). Bake for 15 minutes or until lightly browned. Cool slightly; remove to rack to finish cooling. These keep well in a tightly closed container.

Butter Cookies

YIELDS 6 TO 7 DOZEN

3 cups sugar
¾ pound (3 sticks) butter
2 egg yolks

1 tablespoon vanilla
3 cups bread flour

Gradually cream 1 cup sugar into butter. Add egg yolks and vanilla. Mix well. Add flour, gradually. Decide whether you want to use the dough in a cookie press, roll it out and use cookie cutters, or slice cookies. Shape the dough accordingly. Refrigerate for 2 hours or until ready to bake. Preheat oven to 375 degrees. Form dough into cookies, using whatever method you chose, and place on an ungreased cookie sheet. Bake for 10 to 15 minutes. Do not let them get brown. Use spatula to remove and place on rack to cool. When cool, dip in remaining sugar.

Grandma's Iced Georgia Squares

YIELDS APPROXIMATELY 20

¼ cup sugar
8 tablespoons (1 stick) butter
1 egg
1 cup all-purpose flour

½ teaspoon baking soda
1 teaspoon cream of tartar
Pinch of salt

Preheat oven to 350 degrees. Cream together sugar, butter, and egg. Sift dry ingredients together; add to egg mixture. Pour into greased 13 × 9 × 2-inch baking pan. Bake for 10 to 12 minutes. Cool. Prepare icing.

ICING

1 cup powdered sugar
4 tablespoons (½ stick) butter

½ teaspoon vanilla
Small amount of milk

Combine sugar and butter; add vanilla. Add just enough milk for desired consistency. Pour onto cooled baked batter. Cut into squares.

Fudgie Scotch Ring

YIELDS 36 SLICES

One 6-ounce package semisweet
    chocolate chips
One 6-ounce package butterscotch
    morsels
One 14-ounce can sweetened
    condensed milk

1 cup coarsely chopped walnuts,
    plus 1 cup walnut halves
½ teaspoon vanilla

In top of double boiler, melt chocolate and butterscotch together with milk. Stir occasionally until mixture begins to thicken. Remove from heat; add chopped walnuts and vanilla. Blend well. Chill for 1 hour until mixture thickens. Line bottom of a 9-inch pan with a 12-inch square of foil. Place ¾ cup walnut halves in bottom of pan, forming a 2-inch-wide flat ring. Spoon chocolate mixture in small mounds on top of walnuts to form a ring. Garnish with remaining walnut halves. Chill until firm enough to slice.

Lady Brownies

YIELDS 15 TO 20

2 cups sugar
1 cup vegetable oil
4 eggs
6 tablespoons cocoa

1 teaspoon vanilla
1½ cups self-rising flour
1 cup chopped walnuts or pecans

Preheat oven to 325 degrees. Blend together sugar, oil, eggs, cocoa, and vanilla. Add flour; mix. Add nuts; spread into greased 13 × 9-inch baking dish. Bake for 25 to 30 minutes.   ❧ ❧ ❧   *The Lady & Sons*

Cream Cheese Brownies

YIELDS 15 TO 20

Use Lady Brownies recipe above. Pour half the batter into a greased pan. Layer with this cream cheese mixture, then top with remaining batter, swirling it with a knife.

8 tablespoons (1 stick) butter, softened

One 8-ounce package cream cheese, softened

½ cup sugar

2 eggs

1 tablespoon all-purpose flour

1 cup chopped walnuts or pecans

Cream together butter and cream cheese. Add remaining ingredients; blend well. Swirl into brownie batter with knife edge.

❧ ❧ ❧   *The Lady & Sons*

Peanut Butter Bars

YIELDS 15 TO 20

8 tablespoons (1 stick) butter

½ cup peanut butter

1½ cups sugar

2 eggs

1 teaspoon vanilla

1 cup self-rising flour

Preheat oven to 350 degrees. Grease and flour a 13 × 9 × 2-inch pan. Melt butter and peanut butter in bowl over hot water. Add remaining ingredients. Stir until blended. Pour into prepared pan and bake for 25 to 30 minutes. Cool and cut into squares.

Aunt Glennis's Blonde Brownies

YIELDS 15 TO 20

3 eggs
8 tablespoons (1 stick) butter
One 16-ounce box brown sugar
2 cups self-rising flour
1 tablespoon vanilla

2 cups chopped walnuts or pecans
1 cup or 3½-ounce can shredded
   coconut (optional)
One 6-ounce package semisweet
   chocolate chips

Preheat oven to 375 degrees. Beat eggs and butter together; add sugar. Gradually add flour; mix well. Stir in vanilla. Fold in nuts, coconut, and chocolate chips. Bake in greased and floured 13 × 9-inch sheet pan for 25 to 30 minutes. Cool and cut into squares.

❦ ❦ ❦ **The Lady & Sons**

Peanut Butter Buckeyes

YIELDS 6 TO 7 DOZEN

One 12-ounce jar crunchy peanut
   butter (1½ cups)
One 16-ounce box powdered sugar
½ pound (2 sticks) butter

One 12-ounce package semisweet
   chocolate chips
1 bar paraffin

Mix together peanut butter, sugar, and butter and form into small balls; chill. Over medium heat in the top of a double boiler, melt together the chocolate and paraffin. Using a toothpick, dip each ball into chocolate and cover about three-quarters of the ball, leaving a brown round eye. Place on wax paper to cool.

Pecan Clusters

YIELDS 12 DOZEN

One 7-ounce jar marshmallow
   fluff
1½ pounds chocolate kisses
5 cups sugar

One 12-ounce can evaporated
   milk
8 tablespoons (1 stick) butter
6 cups pecan halves

Place marshmallow fluff and kisses into a large bowl. Set aside. Combine sugar, milk, and butter in a saucepan. Bring to a boil and cook for 8 minutes. Pour over marshmallow and chocolate, stirring until well blended. Stir in pecans. Drop by teaspoonfuls onto wax paper.

Peanut Butter Balls

YIELDS 18 TO 24

1 cup peanut butter
1 cup honey
2 cups powdered milk

1½ cups crushed cornflakes,
   1½ cups finely chopped walnuts
   or pecans, or 1 cup powdered
   sugar

Mix peanut butter, honey, and milk together to form very thick mixture. Roll out in small balls about the size of a walnut. Then roll in crushed cornflakes, finely chopped nuts, or powdered sugar. Place on wax paper and refrigerate.

Old-Time Chocolate Fudge

YIELDS 36 PIECES

3 cups sugar
4 heaping tablespoons cocoa
3 tablespoons light corn syrup
1 cup evaporated milk

6 tablespoons butter
1 cup chopped pecans
1½ teaspoons vanilla

Mix sugar and cocoa; add syrup and milk. Cook in saucepan over medium heat until a small drop forms a soft ball in cold water (234 to 240 degrees on a candy thermometer). Remove from heat. Add butter, pecans, and vanilla. Beat with mixer or by hand. Pour into a slightly buttered oblong glass dish and cut into squares. Work fast, as mixture thickens quickly.

Five-Minute Fudge

YIELDS APPROXIMATELY 16 TO 24 PIECES,
OR ABOUT 2½ POUNDS OF CANDY

1⅔ cups sugar
⅔ cup evaporated milk
1 tablespoon butter
½ teaspoon salt
One 6-ounce bag semisweet
   chocolate chips

16 large marshmallows
1 teaspoon vanilla
1 cup chopped pecans

Combine sugar, milk, butter, and salt in a saucepan. Bring to a boil and cook for 5 minutes, stirring constantly. Add chocolate chips and continue to heat until chocolate is melted. Remove from heat and stir in marshmallows, vanilla, and nuts; mix well. Pour into shallow 8-inch square pan to cool; cut into squares.

Baked Apples

YIELDS 6 APPLES

Baked apples are so very good and can be served along with baked ham or roasted turkey as part of the meal. They may also be served as a dessert with caramel sauce.

6 same-size Granny Smith apples
1 teaspoon ground cinnamon
¼ teaspoon ground nutmeg
½ cup sugar

2 tablespoons butter
1 cup apple juice
6 sprigs fresh mint

Preheat oven to 325 degrees. Core apples, being sure not to puncture bottom of apples, so the juices will remain. Skin ½ inch around top of apples at the opening. Fill each cavity with a mixture of cinnamon, nutmeg, and sugar. Top each apple with a teaspoon of butter. Place apples in casserole dish and pour apple juice around them. Bake for approximately 1½ hours.

CARAMEL SAUCE

8 tablespoons (1 stick) butter
1 cup light brown sugar

¼ cup evaporated milk
½ teaspoon vanilla

Melt butter; add brown sugar and evaporated milk in saucepan over medium heat. Cook until bubbly, stirring constantly. Continue to cook for 2 to 3 minutes. Remove from heat. Add vanilla. Place apples in individual compote dishes and top each with an ample amount of caramel sauce and a sprig of mint. Serve immediately.

❦ ❦ ❦ *The Lady & Sons*

Strawberry Mold

SERVES 12

I serve this as a congealed salad at holiday meals.

Two 3-ounce packages strawberry
* Jell-O*
1 cup boiling water
Two 10-ounce cartons frozen
* strawberries*

1 cup chopped pecans
3 medium bananas, sliced
1 cup crushed pineapple, drained
1 cup sour cream

Dissolve Jell-O in boiling water. Add remaining ingredients except sour cream. Pour half of mixture in salad mold; let chill. Cover with layer of sour cream, then top with remaining half of mixture. Refrigerate; chill until firm.

Walnut Praline Brie with Fruit

SERVES 4 TO 6

1 pound red or green grapes
¼ cup dark brown sugar
4 teaspoons butter

2 teaspoons light corn syrup
2 ounces chopped walnuts
1 small wheel of Brie (8 ounces)

Wash and divide grapes into clusters. Make praline: Place sugar, butter, corn syrup, and 1 teaspoon water in a small saucepan. Simmer for 3 minutes. Stir in walnuts. Cut Brie into wedges; arrange on round serving tray. Spoon 1 teaspoon praline mixture over each wedge. Garnish with grapes.

Crème Caramel

SERVES 8

1 cup sugar
5 eggs
¼ teaspoon salt

3 cups milk
1½ teaspoons vanilla

Preheat oven to 350 degrees. Butter eight 6-ounce custard cups. In a small skillet over medium heat, melt ½ cup sugar, stirring constantly until it is a light brown syrup. Pour syrup into buttered cups. Place cups in baking pan for easy handling. In large bowl with mixer at low speed, beat eggs, salt, and remaining ½ cup sugar until lemon-colored. Gradually beat in milk and vanilla. Once mixture has settled, with all air bubbles out, pour mixture into cups. Put hot water into baking pan to within 1 inch of top of cups. Bake 1 hour or until knife inserted in center comes out clean. Cool, loosen custard with knife; invert.

VARIATION: Sprinkle ground nutmeg on top of each custard before baking.

Rice Pudding

SERVES 8

½ cup uncooked rice
3 cups boiling water
½ teaspoon salt
One 14-ounce can sweetened
  condensed milk

4 tablespoons (½ stick) butter
½ cup raisins
1 tablespoon vanilla

Measure rice, boiling water, and salt into top of double boiler. Cook over rapidly boiling water until rice is tender, about 40 minutes. Stir in condensed milk, butter, and raisins. Cook, stirring frequently, over boiling water until slightly thickened, about 20 minutes. Remove from heat and stir in vanilla. Serve warm or cold.

❦ ❦ ❦   **The Lady & Sons**

Banana Pudding

SERVES 8 TO 10

At the restaurant, I no longer prefer the meringue topping but instead like fresh whipped. Of course, the pudding must be very cold before you add the whipped cream. Otherwise, the warmth from the pudding will break down the ingredients of the whipped cream.

¾ cup sugar
3 tablespoons all-purpose flour
2 cups milk
3 egg yolks

1 teaspoon vanilla
4 tablespoons (½ stick) butter
3 medium bananas, sliced
Vanilla wafers

Mix together sugar and flour and slowly add milk. This should be cooked in the top of a double boiler, but you can cook it over low to medium heat, stirring constantly until it thickens—do not leave it unattended. Slightly beat egg yolks and temper with a small amount of the hot custard; stir well. Add egg mixture to custard pot and cook 2 more minutes. Remove from heat and add vanilla and butter. Let cool. In a 13 × 9-inch casserole dish, alternate pudding, bananas, and wafers, beginning with pudding and ending with pudding. Add topping, if desired.

MERINGUE TOPPING

3 egg whites
¼ teaspoon cream of tartar

6 tablespoons sugar
1 teaspoon vanilla

Preheat oven to 350 degrees. Beat egg whites with cream of tartar and sugar until stiff. Add vanilla. Spread over pudding mix; completely seal around edge. Bake until desired brownness on top.

❦ ❦ ❦ ***The Lady & Sons***

Savannah "Tiramisu"

SERVES 12 TO 16

2 dozen macaroons, crumbled
½ cup bourbon or rum
½ pound (2 sticks) butter
1 cup sugar
6 eggs, separated
2 ounces unsweetened chocolate,
  melted

½ teaspoon vanilla
½ cup chopped pecans
1 dozen double ladyfingers
¾ cup heavy cream, whipped with
  3 tablespoons sugar until stiff

Soak crumbled macaroons with bourbon or rum. Cream butter with sugar. Beat in lightly beaten egg yolks; add melted chocolate, vanilla, nuts, and macaroons. Beat egg whites until stiff; fold into chocolate mixture. Grease a springform pan; line with separated ladyfingers. Alternate layers of chocolate mixture with remaining ladyfingers. Chill overnight. Remove from pan and decorate with whipped cream.

Peach Cobbler

SERVES 8 TO 10

8 tablespoons (1 stick) butter
1 cup sugar
¾ cup self-rising flour
¾ cup milk

One 28-ounce can sliced peaches
in syrup, undrained (see
Variation)

Preheat oven to 350 degrees. Put butter in deep baking dish and place in oven to melt. Mix sugar and flour; add milk slowly to prevent lumping. Pour over melted butter. Do not stir. Spoon fruit on top, gently pouring in syrup. Still do not stir; batter will rise to top during baking. Bake for 30 to 45 minutes. Good with fresh whipped cream or vanilla ice cream.   🍀 🍀 🍀 *The Lady & Sons*

VARIATION: When available, fresh fruit is wonderful. You may use fresh blueberries, strawberries, blackberries, cherries, apples, peaches, or pears. Simply clean, peel, and core 2 cups of fruit and mix with 1 cup of sugar and 1 cup of water. In a saucepan, bring mixture to a boil and then simmer for about 10 minutes. Stir often, making sure sugar is completely dissolved. Substitute this for the canned peaches.

Cooking Tips from The Lady

1. Unless specifically instructed to put your dish in a cold oven to begin baking, you should *always preheat* the oven to the temperature required.

2. Always beat eggs before adding sugar.

3. Combine dry ingredients together when baking.

4. Add flour and milk to egg mixture alternately, beginning with flour mixture and ending with flour mixture for a lighter cake, muffin, or biscuit.

5. To eliminate odor from collards being cooked, add one washed, unshelled pecan to the collards pot before turning the stove on.

6. To determine whether an egg is fresh or not, place the uncracked egg in a glass of water. If it sinks to the bottom, it's fresh. If it floats, throw it out!

7. To make fluffier scrambled eggs, beat in a small amount of water instead of milk.

8. If baking a double-crust pie, brush top layer lightly with milk for a shiny crust; for a sweet crust, sprinkle with granulated sugar or a mixture of sugar and cinnamon; for a glazed crust, brush lightly with beaten egg. If you place the pie on a hot cookie sheet in the oven during preheating, it will ensure that the bottom crust will bake through.

9. You can always substitute 1⅔ cups all-purpose flour for 2 cups cake flour.

10. No buttermilk? Add 1 teaspoon distilled white vinegar to 1 cup fresh milk; let sour for 5 minutes.

11. Remember, 1½ cups corn syrup equals 1 cup sugar dissolved in ½ cup water.

12. To remove excess grease from soups, drop a lettuce leaf in and watch it absorb the grease. Repeat until the desired amount is removed. Discard lettuce.

13. To keep unused egg yolks fresh for future use, place in bowl and cover with 2 tablespoons of oil. They will remain fresh for 4 to 5 days.

14. If you're out of tomato juice, simply mix ½ cup tomato sauce and ½ cup water to create 1 cup of tomato juice.

15. If you want to achieve a lighter texture in your baking, add a teaspoon of baking powder to any recipe calling for self-rising flour or self-rising cornmeal.

16. Out of sweetened condensed milk? Make your own: Mix 6 cups whole milk with 4½ cups sugar, 1 stick of butter, and 1 vanilla bean (or 1 tablespoon vanilla). Cook over medium heat, reducing liquid, for 1 hour. Stir occasionally. Cool. Yields 4½ cups. This can be stored covered in the refrigerator for several weeks. Cut recipe in half for immediate use.

17. Red potatoes or "new" potatoes are far superior for use in any potato recipe. For great convenience in preparing a variety of potato recipes, keep cooked red potatoes in refrigerator at all times. They can be used on the spur of the moment for potato salad, hash browns, or French fries. They will keep at least a week in the refrigerator if they are well drained.

18. In many of the recipes by The Lady, you will find we make reference to our House Seasoning. The recipe is: 1 cup salt, ¼ cup black pepper, and ¼ cup garlic powder. Mix well. Store in shaker near stove for convenience.

19. If you're watching your fat intake, you can try substituting low-fat cheese, mayonnaise, sour cream, etc.

20. Never throw away chicken stock; fresh vegetables, such as peas, butter beans, turnip greens, collards, and rutabagas, are wonderful cooked in it. Stock may also be frozen for later use in soups and sauces.

Acknowledgments

To all my family, friends, staff, and guests who have given their invaluable help in making this book and restaurant a reality. My most heartfelt thanks goes out to each and every one of you: Mildred C. Ambos, Pat Andres, Ernest Bartley, Trina Bearden, Amy Beaver, John Berendt, Diane Berryhill, Nancy Blood, Holly Brantley, Mike Carnahan, Jamie Chabot, Dora Charles, Joshua Charpentier, Christina Cheves, Bob Christian, Todd Churco, Leroy Clayton, Becky Cohen, Theresa Lynn Creo, Roger Crews, Kevin Crumbley, Carolynn C. Cundiff, Janet Di-Claudio, Jessie Ruth Dixon, Amy Dupuy, Susan Dupuy, Judge Tom Edenfield, Frances Finney, Felicia Gaines, Regina Gaines-Baker, David Gaynor, Lorianne Greenlee, Jean Gregory, Maria Griffin, Ann Schuburger Hanson, Captain Judy Helmey, Corrie Waye Hiers, Don Hiers, Earl "Bubba" W. Hiers Jr., Elizabeth Hiers, Glennis Hiers, Jill R. Hiers, C. McCall Holmes, Cathy Holmes, David Howard, Dion Hurd, Rance Jackson, Ineata "Jellyroll" Jones, Jacklyn Miller, Sheila M. Mims, Jody Moyer, Karen Nangle, George A. Ort III, Kelley P. Ort, Peggy P. Ort, Jacqueline R. Patton, Michael Peay, Shelly Peay, Erick Pineda, Paul Powell, Jeanne Powers, Peggy Richardson, Virginia K. Robertson, Helen Rooks, Bill Schumann, Esther Shaver, Kristen Short, Clark Smith, Dorothy S. Smith, Steven P. Starling, Brendan Sweeney, Charlene Wagner, Suzette Dupuy Wagner, Denise Watson, Claire Watts, Chris White, Melvin Williams, Willie Wilson, and Mary Evelyn Young.

I would especially like to thank the wonderful care and consideration Random House has given me in transforming what started off as a local collection of recipes into a national cookbook—it has been a dream come true. Since discovering The Lady & Sons on a business trip, my editor, Pamela Cannon, has worked tirelessly on the book's behalf, for which I thank her a thousand times over. I would also like to express my gratitude to Beth Pearson, associate copy chief, for her carefully detailed job of overseeing the book's progress; Vicki Wong, senior designer, for her thoughtful design ideas; and art director Andy Carpenter, a fellow Southerner, who made the book jacket come to life.

The Lady & Sons Too!

A WHOLE NEW BATCH
OF RECIPES FROM
SAVANNAH

I'm so fortunate to be blessed with three wonderful men in my life, men who have given to me their unconditional love and support.
These men are my sons, Jamie and Bobby Deen, and my brother, Earl W. Hiers, Jr. (Bubba), to whom this book is most affectionately dedicated.

The Journey Continues . . .

When I look back over my life, I get filled with so much emotion. My early childhood and teen years were so wonderful and safe. My brother, Bubba, and I were protected, guided, and watched over by wonderful parents. You get so secure that you begin to think life is made up of only peaks and almost no valleys. I was nineteen, and Bubba was twelve, when our father, who was our hero, died unexpectedly at the age of forty. This was the beginning of my broken spirit. When our beautiful, sweet, and loving mother died four years later at the age of forty-four, I felt impending doom hanging over me. I thought this valley would last for years.

Being married with two babies under the age of three and a sixteen-year-old brother to finish raising was a big task for a twenty-three-year-old girl. I certainly couldn't classify myself as a woman because I think my mental growth froze at the age of nineteen from the pure shock of the situation. While trying very hard to put up a competent front, I became a scared, nervous shell of my usual self. I lived in dreadful fear of the death of someone I loved, or my own death.

In 1978, due to tremendous financial problems, my husband and I lost our business and also our home. It was at this point, after getting situated into an apartment, that I began to feel safe only within the four walls of my own home. Before long, I had stopped doing anything that required me to leave the apartment. The very thought of having to leave my safety zone sent me into a horrendous panic attack. During these attacks my arms would go numb and my heart would almost pound out of my chest, leaving me weak.

Surely this had to be the death that I had been waiting for. The fear of the fear eventually made me a virtual prisoner. Life continued much the same way for the next nine or ten years. Then, like a miracle, at the age of forty, I got up one day and felt as if a light had been turned on. Yes, one day I would die and I might possibly lose others that I loved, but that was all out of my control. God had given me today, and today I would start the journey of mending. We all know that a certain amount of fear is natural, that healthy fear keeps us safe, but I never again would let myself be a victim of controlling fear.

Sometimes I feel as though I have two birthdays: one January 19, 1947, and the other June 19, 1989. The second date marks the day that I became completely responsible for myself and my actions; it was the day that I, with the help of my sons, Jamie and Bobby, began our business. All those years of being a prisoner in my home were about to pay off, for I had become a pretty good cook. After all, cooking had been my number-one source of entertainment.

The business was started with just two hundred dollars, and today I can still tell you, almost to the penny, how I spent it all. The first year and a half was spent working out of our home, and this proved to be quite a hardship for the family. A divorce after twenty-seven years of marriage was imminent, and we were about to tackle a full-fledged restaurant as well. The next five years would be the hardest, physically, that I had ever experienced. I had taken an available space located in the Best Western Central Motel, and the restaurant required three meals a day, seven days a week.

There was no money to pay employees, so I, along with Jamie, Bobby, and their girlfriends, began the task of providing good, affordable food for our guests. Soon (although it seemed like forever) I was able to employ some very talented women. They were wonderful cooks, and all I needed to do was show them how I wanted things prepared. Almost immediately they were off and running and before long they were teaching me things as well!

Jamie and Bobby were waiters and enjoyed a nice boost to their income through their tips, but the size of the restaurant would not allow me to generate the income I had hoped for. I dreamed of something bigger, a place where my style of food went hand-in-hand with its surroundings. We had met and made friends with many wonderful people on the south side of Savannah, but I knew that we belonged downtown.

It was time to take the next step. I had not a clue just how hard that next step would prove to be. Being naïve, I signed a long-term lease on a wonderful old building in the heart of historic Savannah. It would require total renovation—all at my expense! It's amazing, but when I signed that lease it never dawned on me that I might not be able to get the financing; after all, I had saved and scraped up $20,000, and surely that was good for something. Our nonrenewable lease with the Best Western expired and all we had now was the catering part of the business to keep things going. Bank after bank refused my applications, despite my tears and pleas, until the day I met Doug McCoy, vice president of one of the local banks. Doug listened to my plan and gave me great encouragement. He suggested that with a loan from his bank and the help of SBA and SBAC, we could probably put together a package. The encouragement was short-lived though, because although I had $20,000 in savings, I was still short $25,000. One thing was definite: This was another valley. I had no idea where to turn, but then my mentors and most enthusiastic cheerleaders stepped up and helped clear the way for me and my sons. My aunt Peggy and uncle George Ort did something for which we will be forever grateful. They lent us the remaining money, making it possible for us to open a wonderful restaurant and meet the world—and what a world it was! Our trials were certainly not over, but there was light at the end of the tunnel. On the morning of opening day I received a call from our accountant, Karl Schumacher, who said, "Paula, we're in pretty bad trouble here. Both the construction and restaurant accounts are overdrawn, and we need to take care of this." Well, I hadn't had any money to put in the parking meters that day, much less to cover the overdrafts. In fact, I didn't have a penny to make change with. We were supposed to open our brand-new business in less than an hour—how could I cash a check on an overdrawn account? I made a humbling phone call to my banker and explained the situation and asked him to please allow me to cash just one more check. With a smile in his voice he said, "Yes, Paula, come on down and get your start-up change. We're not going this far with you to stop you now. Good luck!" I'm extremely proud to say that that was the last time we were overdrawn.

That opening lunch was very emotional indeed. It had been almost a year since we had served a guest in-house. The wonderful and loyal friends we had made on the south side magically appeared in an outpouring of support. You all know who you are, and I'll never be able to convey to you my thanks. We enjoyed seeing our old friends, and we soon began adding new friends, some here for only a short visit, some who make their daily living in the downtown area. The number of familiar faces continues to grow.

The next step in my plan was to write and publish a cookbook. Once more I saved $20,000, and soon the cookbook became a reality, not just a dream. My self-published book had been out for only two weeks when another new face appeared. It belonged to a wonderful young woman named Pamela Cannon, an editor at Random House. I can't tell you the surprise and shock I felt the day Pamela called me from New York and said that Random House wanted to publish and distribute my cookbook nationwide. Was I interested? As you probably know by now, the answer was yes.

This was definitely a peak. Pamela has worked tirelessly on my books, and not only do I consider her a talented editor, but a friend who I'm very glad to know. Thank you, Pamela, for being you.

One of the more recent arrivals in our life is a man named Jerry Shriver, who has had a tremendous impact on our business. Jerry is a food and travel writer for *USA Today*. Our meeting was not planned. He was visiting Savannah for the weekend to judge a food extravaganza. When he checked into the Mulberry Inn, Louise Purdy, the concierge, suggested that he might want to drop into The Lady & Sons Restaurant for a sample of "real good" Southern cooking. He did just that. Imagine our amazement on December 17, 1999, when Mr. Shriver's *USA Today* article appeared, declaring that his number-one most memorable meal of the year 1999 had been at The Lady & Sons.

How does one go about expressing one's gratitude for something like that? Along with a heartfelt "thank you" to Jerry, I would also like to say I'm elated that he has been a part of my journey.

In fact, there are many people I would like to thank. Our employees, who give a special piece of themselves every day—you help make it all happen. The guests who come in from far away—you're unbelievable. You all bring such pleasure to us. It's truly been an honor to serve each and every one of y'all. To our local friends—your faces are dear to us, your loyalty and support are so very much appreciated by Jamie, Bobby, me, and the staff. We look forward to serving you all for many years to come.

A very special thanks goes to my dear friend and assistant, Sandra

Cowan. She probably has the hardest job of all, trying to cover my tracks. My lack of organization and order is enough to send anyone over the edge, but Sandra manages it beautifully and always with a smile. Thank you, Sandra, for always being willing to go the extra mile.

I often wonder how one woman could be so blessed. Not only am I no longer a prisoner in my home, but I have been hopping on a plane every six weeks for more than a year now to appear on QVC to promote *The Lady & Sons Savannah Country Cookbook,* and this effort has been hugely successful.

I'm in a business that allows me to stay close to my children and brings wonderful new friends into our lives on a daily basis. Now, at this age and stage of my life, I understand that life does consist of peaks and valleys. The valleys help to mold us into the people we are; without them we would not be able to relish and enjoy the peaks, or be able to know the difference. It is not the destination but the journey.

And so the journey continues . . .

Paula H. Deen

P.S. By the way, my dear brother, Bubba, has made it beautifully through his own peaks and valleys. Our parents would be so proud of him and his precious children.

If you are lucky enough to be in the Savannah area, we would love for you to stop by the restaurant. Please visit us at:

The Lady & Sons
102 West Congress Street
Savannah, GA 31401
(912) 233-2600
www.ladyandsons.com

If you can't get to Savannah to sample the wonderful food at The Lady & Sons, you can still taste the dishes at home. The recipes in this book that we have served at our restaurant or plan on adding to our menu are followed by:

❧ ❧ ❧ *The Lady & Sons*

You can now take the wonderful tastes of The Lady & Sons home with you! We have developed a line of food products that are available from our website (www.ladyandsons.com) or from QVC. Our products include: The Lady's Seasoned Salt, The Lady's House Seasoning, The Lady's Insane Salt, and The Lady's Bake Mix. Many of the recipes in this book use these products, and I certainly recommend them for the most flavor and best results. But if you're in a pinch, you can make do with the following substitutes: For The Lady's House Seasoning, substitute the House Seasoning recipe (see page 325). For The Lady's Seasoned Salt, substitute Lawry's Seasoned Salt. For The Lady's Insane Salt, substitute Jane's Krazy Mixed-Up Salt.

Helpful Hints from The Lady

1. When using muffin tins, if you find you don't have enough batter to fill all the cups, pour a little water into empty ones. This will prevent the pan from scorching.

2. To sanitize cutting boards and countertops, use a mixture of 1 tablespoon bleach to 1 gallon of water.

3. Don't throw away stale bread; cut it up and use it for croutons or breadcrumbs.

4. Find yourself with more eggs than you can use before the date expires? Break the eggs into ice cube trays, separating the white into one cube and the yolk into another cube, mixing with a pinch of salt or sugar per yolk. 3 tablespoons of beaten egg equal 1 whole egg; 2 tablespoons of egg white plus 1 tablespoon of yolk equal 1 large egg. Cover and freeze for future use, up to 1 month.

5. To slice a cheesecake without a lot of mess, use a piece of dental floss a few inches longer than the diameter of the cake. Wrap the floss around your fingers tightly and press down and through the cake. Release one end of the floss and pull through the cake. Repeat until the entire cake is sliced.

6. When baking a pie, if you find your crust is browning too fast, wrap strips of tin foil around the edge of the pie to slow down the browning.

7. When making muffins, avoid overmixing. Use a spoon to mix the batter; never use an electric mixer.

8. If you have overbaked your cake layers, make a simple syrup of 1 cup sugar, 1 cup water, and 1 teaspoon vanilla; boil for 3 to 5 minutes, then brush the cake layers with syrup on both sides until they are "revived."

9. When picking crabmeat free of bits of shell, spread the crabmeat in a thin layer on a baking sheet and place it in a 350-degree oven for about 10 minutes. This will make it easier to see the bits of shell.

10. To deodorize jars, pour in a solution of 1 tablespoon of dry mustard and 1 gallon of warm water. To deodorize plastic containers, wad up newspaper, place it in the containers, cover, and let sit overnight.

11. When making meringue, always have the egg whites at room temperature, and be sure they're free of any trace of yolk. Make sure the bowl and beaters are spotless and totally free of grease.

12. If soup is too salty, add a teaspoon each of cider vinegar and sugar, or a whole peeled raw potato. Leave the potato in the soup and serve from around it.

13. To render more juice from a lemon, warm it in the microwave for 30 seconds on high power.

14. When boiling crab, shrimp, or any shellfish, add 1 tablespoon of vinegar to the water. This helps to loosen the meat from the shell.

15. Don't have any eggs for a baking recipe? Use 2 tablespoons of corn oil plus 1 tablespoon of water as a substitute.

16. Store eggs tapered-side down for longer life.

17. Soak chicken in 1 tablespoon of baking powder with enough water to cover the chicken. Soak for 10 to 15 minutes to discourage bacteria. Rinse chicken and cook thoroughly.

18. Use lemon or lime juice as a marinade to tenderize chicken.

19. Keep a plastic container in the freezer to store small amounts of leftover vegetables. When the container is full, pull it out and make a wonderful pot of vegetable soup.

20. When sautéing, always heat your pan before putting in the fat. This will temper the pan and reduce sticking.

21. For a crisp salad, take special care of your greens. For iceberg lettuce: Hit the bottom of the head of lettuce against your kitchen counter a

few times and then remove the core. Soak the head of lettuce in ice-cold water for 10 to 15 minutes and then drain. For romaine, red, or green leaf lettuce: Trim a thin layer off the bottom of the core; this will allow the lettuce to "drink" when it's soaking. Remove any outer wilted leaves. Soak each head in ice-cold water for 10 to 15 minutes. Store heads of lettuce in plastic bags with a few paper towels to absorb some of the moisture. Remember, when ready to make a salad, never cut your greens with a knife; instead, tear them gently.

22. When deep-fat frying, try adding a tablespoon of vinegar to the fat before heating. This will keep the food from absorbing too much of the fat.

23. Add 1 tablespoon of vinegar to beef stews to tenderize the meat.

24. When cooking green vegetables, add 1 teaspoon of lemon juice to the pot to help retain their color.

25. Don't salt fresh corn during cooking; salt will toughen it. Salt the corn to taste after it's cooked.

26. Add a little oil to the water when cooking pasta to keep the water from boiling over and the pasta from sticking together.

27. For extra-fluffy meringues, add ¼ teaspoon vinegar to 3 egg whites.

28. To make peaches easier to peel, drop them into a pot of boiling water and take them out after 1 minute. This also works for tomatoes: Leave them in for 1 to 2 minutes, or until their skins split.

29. When a recipe calls for chopped celery also include the celery leaves, which lend wonderful flavor and color.

30. To clean a toilet: Pour a can of Coca-Cola into the toilet bowl. Let the "real thing" sit for one hour, then flush clean. The citric acid in Coke removes stains from vitreous china.

31. To remove grease from clothes: Empty a can of Coca-Cola into a load of greasy clothes, add detergent, and run through a regular cycle. The Coca-Cola will help loosen grease stains.

32. And finally, treat your family like company and your company like family.

Appetizers

HOT APPETIZERS

Baked Cheese Spread

Hot Crab Dip

Polynesian Chicken Wings

Spinach and Shrimp Dip

Italian Chicken Sticks

Shore Is Good Seafood Dip

Sugar-and-Nut-Glazed Brie

Tomato Canapés

Mushroom Canapés

Artichoke Frittata

Chicken Nuggets

Black Bean Dip

COLD APPETIZERS

Shrimp Mold

South Georgia "Caviar"

Devilish Cheese Logs

Georgia Spiced Pecans

Tangy Marinated Shrimp

Caviar Spread

Candied Dills

"Boursin Cheese"

Herbed Cheese-and-Cracker Bits

Party Eye-of-Round Steak

Mexican Layered Dip

Salsa Chicken Salad

Smoked Oyster Cheese Balls

Zesty Cheese Straws

Stuffed French Bread

Egg Caviar Mold

Baked Cheese Spread

YIELDS 3 CUPS

1 cup mayonnaise
1 cup grated Colby cheese
1 cup chopped onion

Dash of Tabasco sauce (optional)
Dash of Worcestershire sauce
(optional)

Preheat the oven to 350 degrees. Mix all ingredients in a pie plate. Bake until golden brown on top, about 30 minutes. Serve with crackers or bagel chips.

Hot Crab Dip

YIELDS 4 CUPS

1 pound jumbo lump crabmeat,
picked free of any broken shells
1 cup grated pepper Jack cheese
¾ cup mayonnaise
¼ cup freshly grated Parmesan
¼ cup minced green onions
(optional)
5–6 cloves roasted garlic, or 2
cloves garlic, minced

3 tablespoons Worcestershire sauce
2 tablespoons fresh lemon or lime
juice
1 teaspoon Tabasco sauce
½ teaspoon dry mustard
Salt and pepper

Preheat the oven to 325 degrees. Combine all of the ingredients in a casserole and gently stir until thoroughly mixed. Bake for 40 minutes. Serve hot with crackers or toast points.

Polynesian Chicken Wings

SERVES 12–15

3 pounds chicken wings
1 cup pineapple preserves
½ cup sherry
½ cup frozen orange juice
  concentrate

½ cup soy sauce
½ cup packed brown sugar
¼ cup vegetable oil
1 teaspoon garlic powder
1 teaspoon ground ginger

Chop off the wing tips; discard them, or save them for making soup. Cut each wing into 2 pieces. Place the wings in a glass baking dish. Combine the remaining ingredients and pour this mixture over the wings. Marinate overnight in the refrigerator. Preheat the oven to 350 degrees. Remove the chicken wings from the marinade and place them in a shallow pan (a jelly-roll pan is perfect). Pour 1 cup marinade liquid over. Bake for 1 hour.

Spinach and Shrimp Dip

YIELDS 5 CUPS

1½–2 cups fresh peeled shrimp
1 pound cream cheese, at room
  temperature
1½ cups heavy cream
5 tablespoons butter
4 cloves garlic, minced
1½ cups shredded Monterey Jack
  cheese

1 tablespoon lemon pepper
1 tablespoon fresh lemon juice
1 teaspoon paprika
Salt and pepper
Two 10-ounce packages frozen
  chopped spinach, thawed

Drop the shrimp into a pot of boiling water and cook just until the shrimp turn pink, 2 to 3 minutes. Let cool and chop. Set aside. In a heavy saucepan, over low heat, mix together the cream cheese, heavy cream, 4 tablespoons of the butter, and garlic. Cook, stirring, until the cream cheese is melted. Add the Jack cheese, lemon pepper, lemon juice, paprika, and salt and pepper to taste, and stir until cheese is melted. Melt the remaining tablespoon of butter in another saucepan. Squeeze out any water remaining in the thawed spinach. Add the spinach and cook, 2 to 3 minutes. Drain the spinach and add it to the cream cheese mixture. Stir and simmer for 5 to 8 minutes. Add the shrimp. Serve the dip in a chafing dish along with toast points or French bread for dipping. 🌸 🌸 🌸 *The Lady & Sons*

Italian Chicken Sticks

YIELDS ABOUT 3–3½ DOZEN

1 cup seasoned breadcrumbs
½ cup freshly grated Parmesan
1½ teaspoons dried thyme
1½ teaspoons dried basil
1 teaspoon dried oregano
½ teaspoon salt
¼ teaspoon garlic powder

Pinch of ground red pepper
8 boneless chicken breast halves,
*   cut into ½-inch strips*
½ cup (1 stick) melted butter
Marinara sauce or honey mustard
*   for dipping*

Preheat the oven to 400 degrees. In a pie plate or platter, combine the breadcrumbs, Parmesan, thyme, basil, oregano, salt, garlic powder, and red pepper. Dip the chicken strips in the melted butter, then dredge them in the breadcrumb mixture. Place the chicken strips in a single layer on a lightly greased baking sheet. Bake for 20 minutes, or until the chicken is cooked through. Serve the chicken sticks hot with marinara sauce, or serve hot or cold with honey mustard.

Shore Is Good Seafood Dip

YIELDS 4 CUPS

2 tablespoons butter
1 medium green bell pepper, diced
1 medium onion, diced
2 stalks celery, diced
Half of a 10¾-ounce can cream of
    shrimp soup (discard top half
    and use bottom part of soup)

1 cup mayonnaise
½ pound freshly grated Parmesan
6-ounce can crabmeat, picked free
    of any broken shells, drained
6 ounces shrimp, fresh or canned,
    drained
½ teaspoon white pepper

Preheat oven to 325 degrees. Melt the butter in a skillet over medium heat. Add the bell pepper, onion, and celery, and sauté for 2 minutes. In a bowl, combine the soup, mayonnaise, Parmesan, crabmeat, shrimp, and pepper. Stir the sautéed vegetables into the seafood mixture and spoon this mixture into a lightly greased 8 × 11-inch casserole dish. Bake for 30 minutes. Serve with toast points or crackers.

Sugar-and-Nut-Glazed Brie

SERVES 16–20

¼ cup packed brown sugar
¼ cup chopped macadamia nuts
    or pecans
1 tablespoon brandy
One 14-ounce round of Brie

Apple wedges
Pear wedges
Lemon juice
Crackers

In a small bowl stir together the sugar, nuts, and brandy. Cover and chill for at least 24 hours or up to one week. At serving time, place the Brie on an ovenproof platter or pie plate. Bake at 500 degrees for 4 or 5 minutes or until the Brie is slightly softened. Spread the sugar mixture in an even layer on top of the warm Brie, and bake for 2 to 3 minutes longer, or until the sugar melts. Brush the fruit wedges with lemon juice and arrange them around one side of the Brie. Place crackers around the other side.

Tomato Canapés

YIELDS 15 CANAPÉS

¾ cup finely diced tomatoes
2 teaspoons finely diced onions
1 teaspoon finely chopped fresh
*   basil*
⅛ teaspoon The Lady's House
*   Seasoning*
One 2.1-ounce package Athens

brand mini phyllo shells
½ cup packed shredded mozzarella
¼ cup mayonnaise
2 tablespoons Hormel Real Bacon
*   pieces, or more as needed*

Preheat the oven to 350 degrees. Place the diced tomatoes in a colander. Sprinkle with the onions, basil, and House Seasoning, and toss to coat. Allow to drain, stirring occasionally.

Fill each phyllo shell with 1 teaspoon of the tomato mixture. Stir together the mozzarella and mayonnaise. Frost the top of each shell with 1 teaspoon of the mayonnaise mixture. Sprinkle each shell with ¼ teaspoon of bacon pieces. Bake the filled shells for 10 to 12 minutes. Serve hot. These may be prepared ahead of time and refrigerated until serving time.

Mushroom Canapés

YIELDS 15 CANAPÉS

1 cup mayonnaise
½ cup freshly grated Parmesan
One 4-ounce can mushroom pieces
*   and stems, drained*
One 2.8-ounce can french-fried
*   onion rings*

One 12-ounce loaf of Pepperidge
*   Farm party rye or*
*   pumpernickel*

In a bowl, stir together the mayonnaise, Parmesan, mushrooms, and onion rings. Spread on lightly toasted party rye or pumpernickel. Place the canapés on a baking sheet and broil until the topping is bubbly.

Artichoke Frittata

SERVES 8–10

Two 6-ounce jars marinated
   artichoke hearts
1 small onion, finely chopped
1 clove garlic, minced or mashed
4 eggs, lightly beaten
¼ cup fine breadcrumbs

¼ teaspoon salt
⅛ teaspoon each pepper, oregano,
   and hot sauce
½ pound (2 cups) shredded
   Cheddar cheese
2 tablespoons minced fresh parsley

Preheat the oven to 325 degrees. Drain the artichoke marinade into a large skillet. Chop the drained artichokes and set aside. Heat the marinade over medium heat, add the onion and garlic, and sauté for 5 minutes. Place the beaten eggs in a large bowl. Add the breadcrumbs, salt, pepper, oregano, and hot sauce to the eggs, then stir in the cheese. Add the chopped artichokes and the sautéed onion and garlic, along with the liquid in the skillet. Pour the mixture into a greased 7 × 11-inch pan. Bake for 30 minutes, or until set. To serve, cut into squares. The frittata may be served hot or cold, and may be frozen after baking. Reheat in a 300-degree oven for 10 minutes. Double or triple the recipe, using 2 or 3 pans, for a big party.

Chicken Nuggets

SERVES 12

2 cups crushed sour-cream-and-
   onion-flavored potato chips
1 egg
2 tablespoons milk

6 chicken breast fillets, cut into
   1½-inch cubes
⅓ cup butter

Preheat the oven to 350 degrees. Spread the crushed potato chips in a shallow dish. Beat together the egg and milk in a shallow bowl. Dip the chicken cubes into the egg mixture and then dredge them in the chips. Place the chicken nuggets on a baking sheet and drizzle with melted butter. Bake for 15 to 18 minutes, or until golden brown. The chicken nuggets can be frozen after baking. Serve with your favorite sauce, such as honey mustard or ranch dressing.

Black Bean Dip

SERVES 6–8

2 tablespoons butter
2 tablespoons chopped onion
One 4-ounce can green chilies, chopped
1 tomato, diced
2 teaspoons chopped fresh cilantro (optional)
1 teaspoon The Lady's House Seasoning

One 15-ounce can black beans with jalapeños
1 cup shredded Cheddar cheese
4-ounce block Velveeta Mexican cheese product, diced
1 3-ounce package cream cheese, diced

Melt the butter in a skillet. Add the onions and sauté until tender, about 5 minutes. Add the green chilies, tomato, cilantro, and House Seasoning, and cook for 5 minutes longer. Add the beans and cheeses, and simmer until hot and bubbling. Serve hot with white-corn tortilla chips.

Shrimp Mold

SERVES 12–15

The juice from one 6½-ounce can minced clams, clams reserved for another use
Three ¼-ounce packets unflavored gelatin
1 pound fresh shrimp, cooked
One 8-ounce package cream cheese
1 small onion, grated

1 cup mayonnaise
1 cup chopped celery
1 tablespoon Worcestershire sauce
The Lady's Insane Salt
Fresh chopped parsley and paprika, for garnish

Place the clam juice in a large bowl. Add the gelatin and stir until dissolved. Add the shrimp, cream cheese, onion, mayonnaise, celery, Worcestershire sauce, and Insane Salt to taste. Pour the mixture into a lightly greased 1-quart mold and refrigerate for at least 2 hours or until firm. To serve, turn the mold out onto a platter. Garnish with parsley and paprika. Serve with crackers.

South Georgia "Caviar"

SERVES 15

Two 15-ounce cans black-eyed
  peas, drained
One 15-ounce can whole kernel
  corn, drained
One 10-ounce can Ro-Tel
  tomatoes
2 cups chopped red bell pepper

½ cup chopped fresh jalapeño
  peppers
½ cup chopped onion
One 8-ounce bottle Italian salad
  dressing
One 4-ounce jar chopped pimentos,
  drained

Combine all the ingredients in a large bowl, stir gently to combine, and refrigerate overnight. Serve with corn chips. This recipe will keep in the refrigerator for up to 2 weeks.

Devilish Cheese Logs

SERVES 12

1 cup shredded sharp Cheddar
  cheese, at room temperature
One 8-ounce package cream
  cheese, at room temperature

One 4½-ounce can deviled ham
½ cup chopped pitted green olives
½ cup finely chopped pecans

In a small bowl, blend together the Cheddar and cream cheeses. Beat in the deviled ham, then stir in the olives.

Refrigerate the mixture for at least 2 hours so it's firm enough to slice.

Shape the cheese mixture into two 8-inch logs. Roll the cheese logs in chopped nuts. Serve with crackers.

Georgia Spiced Pecans

YIELDS 2½ CUPS

1 cup sugar
½ teaspoon cinnamon
⅓ cup evaporated milk

2 cups pecan halves
1 teaspoon vanilla extract

Combine the sugar, cinnamon, and milk in a medium-size saucepan. Bring to a boil and cook to the soft-ball stage (234–238 degrees on a candy thermometer). Add the pecans and vanilla and stir well. Using a slotted spoon, drop single pecans on a sheet of waxed paper; allow to cool.

Tangy Marinated Shrimp

YIELDS 26–30 SHRIMP

The marinade in this recipe also makes a wonderful salad dressing.

4 tablespoons olive oil
2 tablespoons white vinegar
1 teaspoon The Lady's House
  Seasoning
⅔ cup mayonnaise
2 scant tablespoons anchovy paste
2 tablespoons Creole or brown
  mustard

1 pound large cooked shrimp,
  peeled, with tails left on
1 red bell pepper, sliced into thin
  strips
4 green onions, chopped, using
  entire onion
2 tablespoons chopped fresh parsley
1 tablespoon fresh lemon juice

In a glass or ceramic bowl, beat together the oil, vinegar, and House Seasoning. Add the mayonnaise, anchovy paste, and mustard, and stir until well blended. Fold in the shrimp, bell pepper, onion, parsley, and lemon juice. Marinate overnight in the refrigerator. Serve cold or at room temperature.

Caviar Spread

YIELDS 3 CUPS

3 hard-boiled eggs
Salt and pepper
1 medium cucumber
Two 4-ounce jars caviar
One 8-ounce package cream cheese

1 small bunch green onions, finely
   sliced
¾ cup mayonnaise
Green onions, chopped, for garnish

Finely chop the eggs; season with salt and pepper to taste. Peel, seed and chop the cucumber. Blot with paper towels to remove excess moisture. Reserve ½ cup of caviar for the garnish.

In an 8-inch round serving dish, layer the ingredients in the following order: cream cheese, caviar, eggs, sliced green onions, cucumber, and mayonnaise. Garnish with chopped green onions and the reserved caviar; you can make a pretty pattern with the caviar. Serve with crackers.

Candied Dills

YIELDS 1 QUART

1 quart whole dill pickles
2¾ cups sugar

½ cup tarragon vinegar
2 tablespoons pickling spice

Drain the pickles, cut into ½-inch slices, and place them in a deep glass or ceramic bowl. Add the sugar and vinegar. Place the pickling spices in a small square of cheesecloth, tie it closed, and add to the bowl. Let stand at room temperature until the sugar is dissolved, about 4 hours. Pour the pickles into a 1-quart jar, cover, and refrigerate. These pickles taste best after 2 or 3 days. Remove the spice bag after one week.

"Boursin Cheese"

YIELDS 3 CUPS

The Boursin cheese sold in the grocery store is kind of on the pricey side, so just make your own and enjoy the savings.

1 pound cream cheese	¼ teaspoon dried basil
8 ounces whipped butter, at room	¼ teaspoon dried dill
temperature	¼ teaspoon dried marjoram
1 teaspoon garlic salt	¼ teaspoon black pepper
½ teaspoon dried oregano	¼ teaspoon dried thyme

Place the cream cheese and butter in the bowl of a food processor. With the machine running, add the seasonings, and process until smoothly blended. Line a medium-size crock or bowl with plastic wrap and fill it with the cheese mixture. Cover and refrigerate for up to 1 week. Serve with buttery crackers. This also makes a tasty spread for roast beef sandwiches.   ❦ ❦ ❦   **The Lady & Sons**

Herbed Cheese-and-Cracker Bits

SERVES 18–20

Two 10½-ounce boxes Ritz Cheese	1 heaping tablespoon dried dill
Bits (not peanut butter flavor)	1 teaspoon garlic powder
½ cup vegetable oil	1 teaspoon celery salt
One 1-ounce package Hidden	
Valley Original Ranch salad	
dressing mix	

Place the crackers in a large sealable freezer container. In a bowl, mix the oil, salad dressing mix, dill, garlic powder, and celery salt. Pour this mixture over the crackers, cover the container, and invert it to coat the crackers with seasoning. Refrigerate for at least 24 hours, turning the container every so often to keep the crackers coated. Let the mixture come to room temperature before serving. Store in the covered container in the refrigerator.

Party Eye-of-Round Steak

YIELDS 14–18

½ cup vegetable oil
½ cup bourbon
One 0.7-ounce package Italian
    salad dressing mix

2–3-pound eye-of-round beef steak
Salt
Coarsely ground black pepper

In a shallow glass dish, combine the oil, bourbon, and salad dressing mix. Add the beef and turn to coat it with the marinade. Cover and refrigerate overnight.

Preheat the oven to 325 degrees. Remove the meat from the marinade and blot it dry with a paper towel. Salt the meat, then coat it heavily with pepper. Roast uncovered until a meat thermometer registers your preferred doneness. Cool the beef, slice thin, and serve with assorted breads and spreads, including a variety of mustards.

Mexican Layered Dip

SERVES 20

3 ripe avocados, peeled and
    mashed
2 tablespoons fresh lemon juice
Pinch of garlic salt
Pinch of black pepper
Dash of hot sauce
1 cup sour cream
1 cup mayonnaise
One 1¼-ounce package taco
    seasoning
Four 9-ounce cans Frito-Lay bean
    dip
One 16-ounce jar picante sauce or
    drained salsa (optional)

1 cup chopped onion or green
    onions
3 tomatoes, chopped
One 6-ounce can pitted black
    olives, drained
Sliced jalapeño peppers (optional)
8 ounces sharp Cheddar cheese,
    grated
4 ounces Monterey Jack cheese,
    grated

In a bowl, stir together the avocado, lemon juice, garlic salt, black pepper, and hot sauce; set aside. In another bowl, mix the sour cream, mayonnaise, and taco seasoning; set aside. In a wide, shallow bowl, layer the bean dip, avocado mixture, sour-cream mixture, picante sauce, onions, tomatoes, olives, and jalapeño peppers to taste, and top with both cheeses. Serve with tortilla chips.

Salsa Chicken Salad

SERVES 4

1 pint sour cream
One 16-ounce jar chunky salsa
Half of a 1-ounce package
Hidden Valley Original Ranch
salad dressing mix
2 cups diced cooked chicken breast
or two 8-ounce cans premium
white-meat chicken

One 8-ounce can sliced water
chestnuts, drained
1 cup shredded pepper Jack cheese

In a large bowl, stir together the sour cream, salsa, and salad dressing mix. Fold in the chicken, water chestnuts, and cheese. Refrigerate until well chilled. Serve with chips, crackers, or flour tortillas.

Smoked Oyster Cheese Balls

SERVES 12

Two 8-ounce packages cream
  cheese, at room temperature
One 3 ¾-ounce can smoked oysters,
  drained
One 0.4-ounce package Hidden
  Valley Original Ranch
  Buttermilk Recipe salad
  dressing mix
1 tablespoon fresh lemon juice
1 heaping tablespoon Durkee
  Famous Sauce

COATING OPTIONS
Cracked black pepper
Chopped green onions
Cracker crumbs
Bacon bits
Chopped pecans
Chopped fresh parsley

In a large bowl, mix the cream cheese, oysters, salad dressing mix,
lemon juice, and Durkee Famous Sauce with a fork. Refrigerate the
mixture until workable, about 30 minutes. Place the cheese mixture on
a sheet of waxed paper and shape into ball. Roll the ball in one or more
of the suggested coatings (or create your own). I like to coat the cheese
ball with cracked pepper (2 tablespoons) and then with chopped green
onions (½–¾ cup).

Zesty Cheese Straws

YIELDS 5 DOZEN

½ cup (1 stick) butter, at room
  temperature
1 pound sharp Cheddar cheese,
  shredded, at room temperature

2 cups all-purpose flour
1 teaspoon salt
¼ teaspoon ground red pepper

Preheat the oven to 300 degrees. In a mixing bowl, cream the butter
until light and fluffy. Add the cheese and mix until blended. Add the
flour, salt, and red pepper, and mix to form a dough. Refrigerate for 30
minutes to firm up the dough, then place it in a cookie press, fitted

with a ridged tip. Pipe the dough in 2-inch strips onto a lightly greased cookie sheet. Bake for 10 to 15 minutes, or until lightly browned. Remove to racks to cool.

Stuffed French Bread

SERVES 12–15

3 small loaves French bread,
    approximately 6 inches long
Two 8-ounce packages cream
    cheese, at room temperature
1 cup mayonnaise
One 2-ounce jar pimento,
    drained and chopped

⅓ cup chopped fresh parsley
One 0.7-ounce package Italian
    salad dressing mix
One 2.25-ounce jar of chopped
    dried beef (optional)

Cut each loaf in half lengthwise to stuff. Remove some of the inside of the bread to make room for the stuffing. Combine the remaining ingredients and mix well. Fill the hollows in the bread with the mixture. Reassemble the bread into loaves. Wrap in plastic wrap and refrigerate until ready to serve, at least 3 hours. To serve, slice the loaves into 1-inch sections.

Egg Caviar Mold

SERVES 4–6

4 hard-boiled eggs
5 tablespoons butter, at room
    temperature
⅓ cup chopped green onions

⅓ cup mayonnaise
½ teaspoon fresh lemon juice
¼ cup sour cream
One 3.5-ounce jar caviar

In the bowl of a food processor, combine the eggs, butter, onions, mayonnaise, and lemon juice, and process until well blended. Fill a small greased mold with this mixture and refrigerate for at least 3 hours. Turn the mold out onto a platter. Spread sour cream over and then sprinkle caviar on top. Serve with butter crackers or toast points.

Soups and Salads

SOUPS

The Lady & Sons Beef Vegetable Soup

Poblano Chicken Chowder

Dian's Black Bean Soup

Vegetable Cheese Soup

Michele's Chicken Noodle Soup

Chef Jack's Corn Chowder

Susan's Caldo Soup

The Lady & Sons Crab Stew

Crab Bisque

Potato and Ham Soup

Senate Bean Soup

Chilled Zucchini Soup

BLT Soup

Mushroom Cloud Soup

Wayne's Award-Winning Maryland Crab Soup

Bean and Bacon Soup

Taco Soup

Homemade Dried Onion Soup Mix

SALADS

Hawaiian Chicken Salad

Nancy's Coleslaw

Pecan Cranberry Salad

Golda's Frozen Waldorf Salad

Feta Cheese and Tomato Salad

Chinese Salad

Gingersnap Pear Salad

Pickled Beets and Eggs

Spinach, Strawberry, and Hearts of Palm Salad

Blueberry Salad

Marinated Asparagus Salad

Fettuccine Chicken Salad

Colo Cucumber Salad

Thanksgiving Apple Salad

Fruit Salad with Honey Dressing

My Mother's Congealed Salad

Copper Pennies

Strawberry Mold

Fruit Bowl

Warm Apple and Goat Cheese Salad

Cherry Tomato and Mushroom Salad

Strawberry Pretzel Salad

Marinated Shrimp and Artichoke Hearts

The Lady & Sons Beef Vegetable Soup

YIELDS 8 QUARTS

Don't let the lengthy ingredient list scare you away. It's really not as bad as it looks. Even my brother, Bubba, can make it. On a cold winter's day it will make your tongue want to slap your brains out! This recipe serves two or three dozen people, but can easily be cut in half. It keeps for up to five days in the refrigerator or two months in the freezer.

2½–3 pounds beef short ribs or 2½–3-pound boneless chuck roast*

2 tablespoons vegetable oil (if using chuck roast)

4 quarts cold water

1 tablespoon dried Italian seasoning

3 tablespoons dried parsley

1 teaspoon garlic powder

1 tablespoon beef bouillon granules

1 tablespoon The Lady's House Seasoning

1 tablespoon The Lady's Seasoned Salt

2 bay leaves

½ teaspoon black pepper

1 teaspoon celery salt

1 tablespoon Worcestershire sauce

1½ cups chopped onion

One 28-ounce can diced tomatoes

1 cup thinly sliced carrots

1 cup diced celery

1 cup sliced green beans, fresh or canned

1 cup frozen black-eyed peas

1 cup frozen butter beans

1 cup cut okra, fresh or frozen

1 cup corn kernels, fresh or canned

1 cup diced potatoes

½ cup uncooked elbow macaroni

2 teaspoons Accent (optional)

If using chuck roast, heat the oil in a large skillet over medium heat. Place the roast in the skillet and cook until browned on both sides, about 5 minutes per side. Remove the roast from the skillet and cut it into 1½ to 2-inch cubes; discard the fat. Place the beef cubes in a large stockpot. (If using short ribs, you can put them right in the pot with no preparation.) Add the water, seasonings, onion, and tomatoes and bring to a boil over high heat. Cover the pot, reduce the heat so that the liquid simmers, and cook for 1½ to 2 hours, or until the meat is very

*The chuck roast will yield more meat, but the bones from the short ribs give the soup an incredible flavor.

tender. If using short ribs, remove them from the pot and cut the meat from the bones, discard the bones and fat, and return the meat to the pot. Add the remaining vegetables and the macaroni, and return the soup to a boil, stirring to distribute the ingredients. Reduce the heat and simmer for 45 minutes. Add Accent, if desired, and adjust the other seasonings to taste. To remove excess fat from the surface of the soup, swirl a lettuce leaf around the surface—it will pick up a lot of the fat.

❦ ❦ ❦ *The Lady & Sons*

Poblano Chicken Chowder

SERVES 12–16

¼ cup olive oil

3 large carrots, cut into ½-inch dice

2 large onions, cut into ½-inch dice

5 stalks celery, cut into ½-inch pieces

⅛ cup minced garlic

2–3 small poblano peppers, seeded and cut into ½-inch dice

1 teaspoon salt

½ teaspoon white pepper

¼ teaspoon cumin, or more to taste

¼ teaspoon dried thyme, or more to taste

1 tablespoon chicken bouillon granules

3 quarts chicken broth

½ bunch fresh cilantro, minced

3 cups diced (large pieces) grilled chicken

½ cup (1 stick) unsalted butter

1 cup all-purpose flour

½ teaspoon hot sauce, or more to taste

1 cup heavy cream

Heat the oil in a large stockpot over medium heat. Add the carrots, onions, celery, garlic, poblano peppers, salt, white pepper, cumin, and thyme. Sauté for 7 to 8 minutes, or until the vegetables begin to soften. Stir in the chicken bouillon. Add the chicken broth and cilantro, and cook for 10 to 12 minutes, or until the carrots are tender. Stir in the chicken and cook, stirring frequently, until the chowder is thick and the chicken is heated through. Shortly before the chowder is done, melt the butter in a large skillet over medium heat. Add the flour and stir to combine. Cook, stirring frequently, for 3 to 4 minutes to cook the flour. Do not allow the mixture to brown! Ladle 1 cup of the hot liquid from the stockpot into the skillet, whisking constantly.

When the first cup of liquid is incorporated, add another 2 cups of liquid, one at a time. Pour the mixture in the skillet into the stockpot, whisking to blend. Cook, stirring frequently, for 3 to 5 minutes longer, or until the mixture begins to thicken. Remove the pot from the heat. Stir in the hot sauce, then the cream, and serve.

Dian's Black Bean Soup

SERVES 12

1 pound dry black beans
1 tablespoon vegetable oil
2 cups chopped onions
1 cup finely chopped carrots
1 cup finely chopped celery
2 tablespoons minced garlic
2 teaspoons cumin
¼–½ teaspoon red pepper flakes
1 pound smoked ham hocks

Two 14½-ounce cans chicken broth
4 cups water
¼ teaspoon dried thyme
One 14½-ounce can Del Monte
    Mexican tomatoes
1½ teaspoons salt
Sour cream
Chopped green onions
Finely chopped crisp bacon

Place the beans in a large pot and add water to cover by 2 inches. Soak the beans overnight.

Drain the soaking liquid from the beans. Heat the oil in a Dutch oven over medium heat and add the onions, carrots, and celery; cook, stirring occasionally, until tender. Add the garlic, cumin, and pepper flakes, and cook for 30 seconds longer. Add the ham hocks, then stir in the beans, chicken broth, water, and thyme. Bring to a boil, reduce the heat, cover, and simmer for 1 hour. Stir in the tomatoes with their liquid, and the salt. Simmer, covered, until the beans are very tender, 1 to 2 hours longer. Remove the ham hock and cut the meat from the bones. Discard the skin and bones and return the meat to the pot. With a potato masher, mash some of the solids in the soup to thicken the broth. Ladle the soup into bowls and serve with a dollop of sour cream on top. Sprinkle with onions and bacon. ❦ ❦ ❦ *The Lady & Sons*

Vegetable Cheese Soup

SERVES 8–10

1 cup diced celery
1 cup diced onion
4 chicken bouillon cubes
4 cups water
3 cups cubed potatoes
1 cup shredded carrots
One 10-ounce package frozen
    creamed corn

One 10-ounce package frozen
    mixed vegetables
One 10¾-ounce can cream of
    chicken soup
1½-pound block Velveeta cheese
    product, cubed
Salt and pepper

In a large saucepan, bring the water to a boil, and add the celery, onion, and bouillon cubes. Reduce to medium heat. Cook for 20 minutes. Add the potatoes, carrots, corn, mixed vegetables, and soup, and cook until the vegetables are tender. Reduce the heat to low and add the cheese. Cook, stirring gently, until the cheese has melted and the soup is hot; do not boil. Add salt and pepper to taste.

Michele's Chicken Noodle Soup

SERVES 6–8

One whole 3–4 pound chicken with
    skin and fat removed
3 quarts water
3 onions, quartered
3 carrots, quartered
3 stalks celery, halved
6 whole dried Chinese black
    mushrooms (optional)

2 cloves garlic
4 sprigs fresh parsley
2 bay leaves
2 teaspoons salt
¼ teaspoon black pepper
5–7 ounces of your favorite egg
    noodles (I prefer dumpling
    style)

Place the chicken in a large stockpot. Add the water and place over medium-high heat. Add the vegetables, mushrooms (if using), garlic, parsley, bay leaves, salt, and pepper. Bring to a boil, reduce the heat, and simmer, partially covered, for 1½ hours. Remove the chicken from the pot. Remove the meat from the bones and cut into bite-size pieces; set aside. Remove the mushrooms, if using, and set aside. Remove and discard the bay leaves. With a slotted spoon, remove the rest of the solids from the stockpot and transfer them to a blender or large food processor. Purée the solids, adding some of the liquid from the stockpot if it is too thick to blend; set aside. Return the remaining stock to a boil, add the noodles, and cook until al dente—tender but still slightly firm. Reduce the heat, stir in the puréed vegetables, chicken, and mushrooms, and serve.

Chef Jack's Corn Chowder

SERVES 8–10

1 cup (2 sticks) butter
1 small onion, diced
1 small carrot, finely diced
1 small celery stalk, diced
1 clove garlic, minced
½ cup all-purpose flour

3 cups white corn kernels, fresh or
*   frozen*
3 cups chicken stock
2 cups half-and-half
Pinch of freshly grated nutmeg
Salt and pepper

Melt 1 stick of butter in a large skillet over medium heat. Add the onion, carrot, celery, and garlic, and sauté for 2 minutes. Add the flour and stir to make a roux. Cook until the roux is lightly browned; set aside to cool to room temperature. Meanwhile, combine the corn and chicken stock in a saucepan, and bring to a boil. Simmer for 10 minutes. Pour the boiling stock with the corn (a little at a time) into the skillet with the roux, whisking briskly so it doesn't lump. Return the skillet to the heat and bring to a boil. The mixture should become very thick. In a small saucepan, gently heat the half-and-half; stir it into the thick corn mixture. Add the nutmeg and salt and pepper to taste. Just before serving, cut the remaining stick of butter into large chunks. Add it to enrich the soup, stirring until the butter melts.

🍀 🍀 🍀 ***The Lady & Sons***

Susan's Caldo Soup

SERVES 4–6

½ pound Hillshire Farm Smoked
   Sausage
2 tablespoons butter
½ cup diced onion
Three 14½-ounce cans chicken
   broth

5 small new red potatoes,
   quartered
1 teaspoon The Lady's House
   Seasoning
One 10-ounce package frozen
   chopped collard greens

Cut the sausage into ¼-inch slices. Melt the butter over medium heat in a large saucepan; add the onion and sausage, and sauté until the onion is transparent, about 10 minutes. Add the chicken broth, potatoes, and House Seasoning. Bring to a boil, reduce the heat, cover, and cook for 10 minutes. Add the collard greens, cover, and cook for 20 minutes longer. Before serving, using a fork, mash some of the potatoes to thicken the soup. ❦ ❦ ❦ **The Lady & Sons**

The Lady & Sons Crab Stew

SERVES 10–12

4 tablespoons butter
3 tablespoons all-purpose flour
1 tablespoon minced garlic
2 cups heavy cream
2 cups half-and-half
2 Knorr fish-flavor bouillon cubes
1 pound crabmeat, picked free of
   any broken shells

¼ cup sherry
½ teaspoon white pepper
One 8-ounce bottle clam juice
   (optional)
Grated Parmesan and snipped
   chives, for garnish

Heat the butter in a large saucepan over medium heat. Add the flour, stirring to blend it in, then add the garlic. Gradually add the cream and half-and-half, stirring constantly. Add the bouillon cubes and stir well. As the mixture begins to thicken, add the crabmeat, then the sherry and pepper. If the stew seems too thick, thin it with clam juice, which will also add a lot of flavor. Serve in a mug, garnished with grated Parmesan and snipped chives.

.   ❧ ❧ ❧   *The Lady & Sons*

Crab Bisque

SERVES 4

One 10¾-ounce can cream of
   asparagus soup
One 10¾-ounce can cream of
   mushroom soup
¼ cup milk

¼ cup half-and-half
½ pound crabmeat, picked free of
   any broken shells
¼ cup dry sherry

Combine all the ingredients in a heavy saucepan and bring to a boil. Reduce the heat and simmer for 5 minutes.

   This delicate tasting soup can be frozen for up to 1 month.

Potato and Ham Soup

SERVES 10–12

5 pounds Russet baking potatoes,
   cut into 1-inch cubes
1 thick slice of cooked ham, cut
   into small pieces (not country
   ham, which is too salty)

½ cup (1 stick) butter
Salt and pepper
1 cup half-and-half
½ cup sour cream

Place the potatoes in a large pot and add enough water to just cover the potatoes (too much water will make the soup too thin). Cover and bring to a boil, then uncover and cook over medium-high heat for 20 minutes. Reduce the heat and add the ham and butter. Season with salt and pepper to taste. Over low heat, add the half-and-half and sour cream; keep warm over low heat until serving time. I promise that everyone will want the recipe (men more than women)!   ❧ ❧ ❧   *The Lady & Sons*

Senate Bean Soup

SERVES 12

Years ago, Mrs. Herman Talmadge, wife of our state senator, shared with us Georgia ladies the bean soup recipe that was served in the Senate dining room. It is quite wonderful.

2 pounds Michigan navy beans
4 quarts water
1½ pounds smoked ham hocks

¼ cup (½ stick) butter
1 medium onion, chopped
Salt and pepper

Rinse the beans in hot water until they are white. Place them in a stockpot, add the water, and bring to a boil. Reduce the heat and simmer for 3 hours. Meanwhile, simmer the ham hocks in a large pot of water for 3 hours. Heat the butter in a small skillet over medium heat. Sauté the onion until lightly browned. Add the onion to the pot of beans. Remove two cups of the bean mixture, purée in a blender, and return to the soup. Remove the ham hocks, and break down slightly with a knife. Add to soup mixture. Just before serving, season the soup with salt and pepper to taste. ❦ ❦ ❦ **The Lady & Sons**

Chilled Zucchini Soup

SERVES 4

2 cups chicken broth
2 large onions, chopped
3 medium zucchini, sliced
1 clove garlic, sliced
¼ teaspoon salt

1 cup mayonnaise
1 teaspoon fresh lemon juice
Half-and-half (optional)
Lemon slices

Combine the broth, onions, zucchini, garlic, and salt in a large saucepan and bring to a boil. Cook the vegetables for 5 to 8 minutes, or until tender. Let cool to room temperature, then transfer the mixture to a food processor, add the mayonnaise and lemon juice, and process until smooth. Refrigerate over-night. Thin with a little half-and-half if necessary. Serve cold, with lemon slices.

BLT Soup

SERVES 8

5 slices bacon, diced small
½ cup diced green onions
2 tablespoons butter
3½ cups iceberg lettuce, julienned
½ cup instant-blending flour
3½ cups fresh or canned chicken
    broth, heated to a simmer

1 cup diced fresh tomatoes
⅛ teaspoon grated fresh nutmeg
⅛ teaspoon ground red pepper
1 cup heavy cream
¼ cup mayonnaise
¼ cup sour cream
Crisp crumbled bacon

In a 3-quart pot, cook the bacon over medium heat till lightly browned. Add the onions and cook, stirring, until wilted. Add the butter and stir until melted. Add the lettuce and sauté for 2 minutes. Sprinkle the flour into the pot, then stir it in until well blended. Remove the pot from the heat and add the hot chicken broth, tomatoes, nutmeg, and pepper. Heat the soup to boiling, stirring constantly, then reduce the heat and simmer gently for 5 minutes. Add the cream and mix well. Mix together the mayonnaise and sour cream. Serve each portion of soup with a dollop of the mayonnaise mixture topped with crumbled bacon. ❧ ❧ ❧ **The Lady & Sons**

Mushroom Cloud Soup

SERVES 4

This is the perfect soup if you don't have much time. The whole thing's made in the microwave, and it's delicious.

¼ cup (½ stick) butter
½ pound sliced mushrooms
1 medium onion, chopped
1 cup lightly packed chopped fresh
    parsley

1 tablespoon all-purpose flour
One 14-ounce can beef broth
1 cup sour cream
Mushroom slices

In a 7 × 11-inch baking dish, heat the butter for 30 seconds in the microwave to melt it. Add the mushrooms, onion, and parsley, and microwave for 5 minutes, stirring once or twice. Stir in the flour and ½ cup of the beef broth. Cook, uncovered, for 1 to 2 minutes, or until bubbly. In a blender, working in batches, purée the mixture with the sour cream and the remaining beef broth. Return the soup to the baking dish and reheat for 3 minutes. If the soup is made ahead, cover and refrigerate. Serve cold, or reheat the soup, covered, in the microwave for 3 minutes. Ladle the soup into bowls and float mushroom slices on top.

Wayne's Award-Winning Maryland Crab Soup

YIELDS ABOUT 8 QUARTS

I've often spoken of all the interesting and wonderful people who cross my path. Well, Wayne Brokke is one of those people. Wayne had seen me on QVC several times, and when the opportunity arose for a trip to Savannah, he made a special point of coming in to meet me. We had a great time getting to know each other. Wayne is the owner of Wayne's Bar-B-Que in Baltimore, where he also does cooking segments for a local television station. When I mentioned to Wayne that I was writing another cookbook, he graciously offered to share a few of his recipes. They are Wayne's Cranberry Sauce, and the following recipe, which is a five-time winner of the Maryland Old Bay Soupstakes Critics and People's Choice Award. Thanks, Wayne, and continued good luck to you!

4 quarts water

2 tablespoons chicken bouillon
   granules

2 tablespoons beef bouillon
   granules

6 soup crabs, or three small live
   crabs, cleaned and rinsed

3 cups canned crushed tomatoes

¼ cup Worcestershire sauce

2 tablespoons Old Bay Seasoning,
   or more to taste

2 tablespoons sugar

1 teaspoon Tabasco sauce

2 bay leaves

1½ cups sliced carrots

1½ cups chopped celery

1½ cups corn kernels, fresh or
   frozen

1½ cups green beans, fresh or frozen

1½ cups lima beans, fresh or frozen

1 cup chopped cabbage

1 medium onion, chopped

2 cups cubed red potatoes, skins on

1 pound lump crabmeat, picked
   free of any broken shells

1 pound claw crabmeat, picked
   free of any broken shells

Salt and pepper

Bring the water to a boil in a stockpot, then add the chicken and beef bouillon granules and stir until dissolved. Cut the whole crabs in half, add them to the pot, and bring to a second boil. Skim any excess froth created by the crab parts. Add the tomatoes, Worcestershire sauce, Old Bay Seasoning, sugar, Tabasco, and bay leaves, and stir to combine. Add the carrots, celery, corn, green beans, lima beans, cabbage, and onion, bring to a low boil, and cook for 10 minutes. Add the potatoes and cook until tender. Add the crabmeat and cook for 10 minutes. Season with salt and pepper to taste.

Bean and Bacon Soup

SERVES 4

1 cup dry navy beans
6 slices bacon
1 carrot, diced
1 red bell pepper, diced
1 small onion, chopped
1 large clove garlic, minced

½ teaspoon paprika
2½ cups chicken broth
One 16-ounce can crushed tomatoes
1 bay leaf
The Lady's House Seasoning
Crumbled bacon

To quick-soak the beans, place them in a pot and add 2 cups of water. Bring to a boil, cover, and boil for 1 minute. Remove the pot from the heat and let the beans stand in the hot water for 1 hour. Meanwhile, fry the bacon in a Dutch oven until crisp. Remove the bacon and set aside. Add the carrot and bell pepper to the Dutch oven and sauté for 5 minutes. Add the onion and garlic and sauté for 5 minutes longer. Stir in the paprika. Cook, stirring, for a few minutes longer to develop the flavor of the paprika. Slowly add the chicken broth, then stir in the crushed tomatoes, bay leaf, and House Seasoning to taste. Drain the beans and discard the liquid. Add the beans to the soup, stir, and bring to a boil. Reduce the heat, cover, and simmer for 2 hours, or until the beans are as tender as you like. Thin the soup with the chicken broth. Remove and discard the bay leaf. Ladle the soup into bowls and sprinkle with bacon. 🌿 🌿 🌿 **The Lady & Sons**

Taco Soup

SERVES 12–16

2 pounds ground beef
2 cups chopped onions
Two 15½-ounce cans pink kidney
  beans
Two 15½-ounce cans pinto beans
One 15¼-ounce can niblet corn,
  drained
One 14½-ounce can Del Monte
  Mexican tomatoes
One 14½-ounce can diced
  tomatoes
One 14½-ounce can Del Monte
  tomatoes with chilies
Two 4½-ounce cans diced green
  chilies

1 small can black olives, drained
  and sliced (optional)
½ cup green olives, sliced (optional)
One 1¼-ounce package taco
  seasoning mix
One 1-ounce package Hidden
  Valley Original Ranch salad
  dressing mix
Corn chips
Sour cream
Grated cheese
Chopped onions

Brown the ground beef and onions in a large skillet; drain the excess fat, then transfer the browned beef and onions to a large crockpot or a stockpot. Add the beans, corn, tomatoes, chilies, olives, and seasonings, and cook on low setting all day (6 to 8 hours) if using a crockpot, or simmer over low heat for about 1 hour in a stockpot on the stove. To serve, place a few corn chips in each bowl and ladle soup over them. Top with sour cream, cheese, and onions.

Homemade Dried Onion Soup Mix

MAKES THE EQUIVALENT OF ONE ⅛-OUNCE PACKAGE
OF DRIED ONION SOUP MIX

½ teaspoon onion powder
½ teaspoon salt
¼ teaspoon sugar

¼ teaspoon Kitchen Bouquet
½ cup dehydrated onion

Combine the onion powder, salt, and sugar in a small bowl. Add the Kitchen Bouquet and stir until the mixture is uniformly brown. Add the onion and mix thoroughly until the color is again even (this step takes several minutes).

Hawaiian Chicken Salad

SERVES 8–10

This is wonderful served on croissants or on a bed of lettuce. It also makes a nice appetizer served in miniature phyllo shells.

4 cups cubed cooked chicken breast (4 large breasts)
2 cups diced celery
1 cup mayonnaise
1 cup sliced almonds
Two 11-ounce cans mandarin oranges, drained

One 20-ounce can pineapple tidbits, drained
1 pound seedless green grapes, cut in half

In a large bowl, combine the chicken, celery, mayonnaise, and almonds, and mix well. Gently fold in the oranges, pineapple, and grapes.

Nancy's Coleslaw

SERVES 8 OR MORE

1 medium onion, chopped
1 cup sugar
1 cup vegetable oil
½ cup cider vinegar
⅓ cup mayonnaise

1 teaspoon salt
½ teaspoon celery seed
1 medium green cabbage, cored and shredded

In a medium bowl, combine the onion and sugar and let stand for 30 minutes. In a separate bowl, combine the oil, vinegar, mayonnaise, salt, and celery seed and add to the onion mixture. Pour the mixture into a jar with a tight lid. Shake the jar to blend the dressing. Put the cabbage in a large serving bowl and add the onions, pour on the dressing, and toss well. Do not overdress.

Pecan Cranberry Salad

SERVES 12

One 15-ounce can crushed
  pineapple, drained, 1 cup of
  juice reserved
1 cup water
One 3-ounce package orange
  gelatin dessert mix
One 3-ounce package cherry
  gelatin dessert mix

One 16-ounce can whole-berry
  cranberry sauce
One 6-ounce can frozen orange
  juice concentrate
1 cup chopped pecans or walnuts
½ cup chopped celery (optional)

Combine the pineapple juice (from the can) and the water in a small saucepan; bring to a boil and remove from the heat. Pour the juice mixture into a large bowl and add the gelatin dessert mixes; stir until dissolved. Add the drained pineapple, cranberry sauce, orange juice concentrate, nuts, and celery, and mix well. Spray a 6-cup mold with nonstick cooking spray. Pour the gelatin mixture into the mold and refrigerate until firm.

Golda's Frozen Waldorf Salad

SERVES 8

½ cup sugar
½ cup pineapple juice
¼ cup fresh lemon juice
⅛ teaspoon salt
½ cup diced celery
½ cup miniature marshmallows
½ cup red seedless grapes, cut in half

½ cup crushed pineapple, drained
2 medium apples, diced, skins left
  on
½ cup broken walnuts or pecans
1⅓ cups heavy cream
8 fresh or maraschino cherries
Fresh mint leaves

In a saucepan, combine the sugar, pineapple juice, lemon juice, and salt. Cook over medium heat, stirring constantly, until thick. Let cool, then stir in the celery, marshmallows, grapes, pineapple, apples and nuts. Whip the cream and fold it into the fruit mixture. Spoon into an 8 × 8-inch pan and freeze.

Remove the salad from the freezer 5 minutes before serving and cut into squares. Garnish each serving with a fresh or maraschino cherry and fresh mint leaves.

Feta Cheese and Tomato Salad

SERVES 6–8

6 medium tomatoes (about 2½
   pounds), cut into wedges
1½ cups crumbled feta cheese
¼–½ cup chopped green onions
3 tablespoons olive oil

2 cloves garlic, minced
1 teaspoon dried oregano or
   1 tablespoon fresh
The Lady's House Seasoning
Boston lettuce leaves

In a large bowl, combine the tomatoes, cheese, onions, oil, garlic, and oregano. Toss gently and refrigerate at least 2 hours. At serving time, add House Seasoning to taste. Spoon the salad onto a bed of lettuce leaves. Serve with a good crusty bread.   ❦ ❦ ❦   **The Lady & Sons**

Chinese Salad

SERVES 12

2 heads Napa or Bok Choy
   cabbage
6 green onions
Two 3-ounce packages ramen
   noodles with seasoning packets
One 6-ounce package slivered
   almonds

2 tablespoons sesame seeds
1 cup vegetable oil
½ cup sugar
6 tablespoons white vinegar
½ teaspoon salt

Tear the cabbage into bite-size pieces and slice the onions. Combine them in a large salad bowl. Crumble the noodles into a broiler pan, add the almonds and sesame seeds, and broil for 2 minutes, being careful not to scorch the sesame seeds. In a jar with a tight lid, combine the oil, sugar, vinegar, and salt with the contents of the seasoning packets. Cover the jar and shake to blend the dressing. Just before serving, pour the dressing over the salad and toss to combine.

Gingersnap Pear Salad

SERVES 8

10 gingersnaps

One 3-ounce package cream cheese, at room temperature

1 tablespoon mayonnaise

8 canned pear halves, drained

Chilled crisp lettuce

Crush the gingersnaps to very fine crumbs. The easy way to do this is to put them in a plastic bag and crush them with a rolling pin. Put the cookie crumbs in a bowl, add the cream cheese and mayonnaise, and mix well. Place the pear halves on a bed of lettuce and fill the hollows with the cream cheese mixture.

Pickled Beets and Eggs

SERVES 6

One 15-ounce can whole beets, drained, juice reserved

¾ cup sugar

½ cup malt vinegar

½ teaspoon whole cloves

1 teaspoon salt

6 hard-boiled eggs, peeled and rinsed

Combine the reserved beet juice, sugar, vinegar, cloves, and salt in a saucepan and heat until the sugar has dissolved. Place the eggs in a large bowl, then add the beets. Pour in the juice, cover, and refrigerate overnight.

Spinach, Strawberry, and Hearts of Palm Salad

SERVES 12

⅓ cup cider vinegar
¾ cup sugar
2 tablespoons fresh lemon juice
1 teaspoon salt
1 cup vegetable oil
½ small red onion, grated
1½ tablespoons poppy seeds
1 teaspoon dry mustard

½ teaspoon paprika
1½ pounds fresh spinach, washed
 and torn into pieces
1 can hearts of palm, drained and
 chopped
2 cups strawberries, stemmed and
 sliced
1 cup chopped walnuts

For the dressing, combine the vinegar, sugar, lemon juice, and salt in a saucepan and heat until the sugar dissolves, stirring frequently. Cool to room temperature. Whisk in the oil, onion, poppy seeds, dry mustard, and paprika, and set aside. Combine the spinach, hearts of palm, strawberries, and walnuts in a salad bowl. Add a little of the dressing at serving time and toss gently. Serve the remaining dressing alongside, so guests may help themselves.

Blueberry Salad

SERVES 8–10

Two 3-ounce packages grape
 gelatin dessert mix
2 cups boiling water
One 21-ounce can blueberry pie
 filling
One 20-ounce can crushed
 pineapple

One 8-ounce package cream cheese,
 at room temperature
1 cup sour cream
1 cup pecan halves
1 teaspoon vanilla extract

In a large bowl, mix the gelatin dessert mix into the boiling water. When the powder has dissolved, stir in the blueberry pie filling and the pineapple with its juice. Pour into a 13 × 9-inch shallow baking dish.

Refrigerate for at least 4 hours, or overnight. Stir together the cream cheese, sour cream, pecans, and vanilla. Spread this mixture over the jelled salad. Chill for an additional hour.

Marinated Asparagus Salad

SERVES 10–12

2 bunches asparagus, trimmed and
   cooked, or three 15-ounce cans
   whole green asparagus spears
1 teaspoon dried tarragon leaves
Black pepper

1 teaspoon garlic salt
Two 0.7-ounce packages Italian
   salad dressing mix, prepared
   according to package directions
½ cup tarragon vinegar

Drain the asparagus and layer it in a shallow glass dish. Sprinkle each layer with some crumbled tarragon, pepper to taste, and garlic salt. Pour the salad dressing and vinegar over the asparagus, cover, and let stand overnight at room temperature. To serve, refrigerate until well chilled. Serve the asparagus on lettuce leaves, topped with a dollop of mayonnaise flavored with a little of the dressing.

Fettuccine Chicken Salad

SERVES 8

4 large boneless skinless chicken
   breast halves
2 teaspoons The Lady's House
   Seasoning
2 tablespoons chopped fresh
   thyme
3 tablespoons olive oil

Two 9-ounce packages fresh
   fettuccine
2 cups mayonnaise
½ cup chopped green onion tops
¼ cup chopped fresh parsley
¼ cup chopped fresh basil
1 teaspoon The Lady's Seasoned Salt

Slice the chicken breasts lengthwise into 1-inch wide strips. Sprinkle with 1 teaspoon of the House Seasoning and thyme, place on a baking sheet, and drizzle with olive oil. Bake at 350 degrees for 15 to 20 minutes or until cooked through but still juicy; do not overcook. While the chicken is cooking, cook the pasta according to package directions. Drain the pasta, rinse in cold water, and drain again. Pat excess moisture off the pasta with a paper towel if necessary.

Remove the chicken from the pan and set aside. Pour the juices from the pan into a bowl. Add the mayonnaise, green onions, parsley, basil, the remaining teaspoon of House Seasoning, and the Seasoned Salt. Pour the dressing over the pasta and toss gently. Place the chicken strips on top of the pasta. Garnish with tomato wedges and additional sliced green onion tops. You may make this dish the day before serving. ❦ ❦ ❦ *The Lady & Sons*

Colo Cucumber Salad

SERVES 4

2 cucumbers	*½ cup mayonnaise*
1 teaspoon salt	*¼ cup sour cream*
1 teaspoon vinegar	*1 tablespoon fresh dill*

Peel and slice the cucumbers and put them in a glass bowl. Sprinkle them with salt and vinegar. Cover and let stand for ½ hour. Pour off the excess liquid. Add the mayonnaise, sour cream, and dill, and mix well. Cover and refrigerate until serving time. ❦ ❦ ❦ *The Lady & Sons*

Thanksgiving Apple Salad

SERVES 8

¾ cup sugar	*¼ cup (½ stick) butter*
⅓ cup all-purpose flour	*3–4 large red apples, diced*
1 cup heavy cream	*1 cup chopped nuts*
One 20-ounce can crushed pineapple, drained	*½ cup halved maraschino cherries*

Stir together the sugar and flour. Whisk in the cream. Pour the cream mixture into a heavy nonaluminum saucepan. Continue mixing, add the pineapple, and cook over medium heat, whisking constantly, until the mixture thickens. Add the butter; remove the pan from the heat and let the mixture cool. When cooled, add the apples, nuts, and cherries, and mix well. Refrigerate until ready to serve.

❦ ❦ ❦ **The Lady & Sons**

Fruit Salad with Honey Dressing

SERVES 6

⅓ cup honey
¼ cup orange juice
¼ cup vegetable oil
½ teaspoon fresh lemon juice, plus the juice of 1 lemon
1½ teaspoons poppy seeds
¼ teaspoon salt
¼ teaspoon prepared mustard

1 apple, cored and diced
1 banana, sliced
1 avocado, peeled and sliced
One 11-ounce can mandarin oranges, drained
¼ cup raisins
¼ cup chopped walnuts or pecans

For the dressing, combine the honey, orange juice, oil, ½ teaspoon lemon juice, poppy seeds, salt, and mustard in a jar with a tight lid; cover and shake well. Toss the apple, banana, and avocado with juice from 1 lemon to prevent the fruit from turning brown. Combine the fruit, raisins, and nuts in a glass bowl. Add the dressing and stir gently. Serve on red leaf lettuce.

My Mother's Congealed Salad

SERVES 12–15

1½ cups water
One 3-ounce package lemon gelatin dessert mix
One 3-ounce package lime gelatin dessert mix

One 20-ounce can crushed pineapple, drained
½ cup orange juice
½ cup evaporated milk
1 tablespoon fresh lemon juice

1 cup mayonnaise

½ cup cottage cheese

½ cup chopped walnuts

½ cup cherries, cut in half

Prepared horseradish

Pinch of salt

Bring the water to a boil and stir in the gelatin mixes until dissolved. Let cool slightly, then add the pineapple, orange juice, evaporated milk, and lemon juice. Refrigerate until slightly thickened. Mix together the mayonnaise, cottage cheese, nuts, cherries, horseradish to taste, and salt. Stir this mixture into the gelatin. Pour into a lightly greased 13 × 9 × 2-inch pan and refrigerate until firm.

Copper Pennies

SERVES 12–15

1 cup sugar

¾ cup white vinegar

½ cup vegetable oil

1 teaspoon dry mustard

1 teaspoon Worcestershire sauce

1 teaspoon salt

¾ teaspoon coarsely ground black
pepper

One 10¾-ounce can tomato soup

2 pounds carrots, peeled, cooked,
and sliced

1 medium onion, sliced into rings

1 green bell pepper, coarsely
chopped

Combine the sugar, vinegar, oil, mustard, Worcestershire sauce, salt, and pepper in a saucepan over medium heat and bring to a boil. Remove from the heat and add the soup. Mix the carrots, onion, and bell pepper together in a large glass dish; pour the sauce over the vegetables, stir gently to combine, and refrigerate overnight. This salad will keep for up to 6 weeks in the refrigerator.   ❦ ❦ ❦ *The Lady & Sons*

Strawberry Mold

SERVES 12

Two 3-ounce packages strawberry
    gelatin dessert mix
1 cup boiling water
Two 10-ounce packages frozen
    strawberries

3 medium bananas, mashed
1 cup crushed canned pineapple,
    drained
1 cup chopped pecans
1 cup sour cream

Add the gelatin dessert mix to the boiling water and stir until dissolved. Add the strawberries, bananas, pineapple, and nuts. Pour half of the mixture into a 13 × 9-inch casserole; refrigerate until set. Cover with a layer of sour cream, then top with the remaining gelatin mixture. Refrigerate until firm; cut into squares to serve.

Fruit Bowl

SERVES 12–15

3 tablespoons orange Tang
    Breakfast Drink mix
One 15½-ounce can pineapple
    chunks, drained, juice reserved
One 3.4-ounce box instant lemon
    pudding mix
One 16-ounce can chunky mixed
    fruit, drained

One 11-ounce can mandarin
    oranges, drained
One 6-ounce jar maraschino
    cherries
3 large bananas

Stir the Tang into the pineapple juice. Add the lemon pudding mix and stir well. Combine the pineapple, mixed fruit, oranges, and cherries, then mix the fruit and pudding mixtures together; toss well. Refrigerate until ready to serve. Just before serving, slice and add the bananas.   🌿 🌿 🌿 *The Lady & Sons*

Warm Apple and Goat Cheese Salad

SERVES 4

2 tablespoons raspberry vinegar or
   red wine vinegar
½ teaspoon Dijon mustard
1 small clove garlic, minced
½ teaspoon salt
½ teaspoon pepper
⅓ cup olive oil
1 tablespoon chopped fresh parsley
3 Belgian endives, cored and
   separated into leaves

1 bunch watercress or spinach,
   washed
1 Granny Smith apple, sliced
4 ounces mild goat cheese, from a
   small log
¼ cup chopped walnuts

In a glass jar with a tight lid, combine the vinegar, mustard, garlic, salt, and pepper and shake to blend. Add the oil and parsley and shake again.

Arrange the endive leaves like spokes on 4 plates; arrange the watercress or spinach in the center. Preheat the broiler. Arrange the apple slices, slightly overlapping, in 4 fans in a broiler pan. Cut the cheese into 4 slices and top each fan of apples with a slice of cheese. Broil until golden, about 5 minutes. With a spatula, carefully place the apple slices and cheese on top of the endive. Drizzle dressing over the salads and sprinkle with walnuts. Serve at once.

Cherry Tomato
and Mushroom Salad

SERVES 8–10

1 pound cherry tomatoes
1 pound fresh mushrooms
¼ cup vegetable oil
½ cup cider vinegar

One 0.7-ounce package Italian
   salad dressing mix
Coarsely ground black pepper

Cut the cherry tomatoes in half. Halve any particularly large mushrooms. In a glass jar with a tight lid, combine the oil, vinegar, salad dressing mix, and pepper to taste. Combine the tomatoes and mushrooms in a salad bowl; pour on the dressing, and toss.

❧ ❧ ❧ *The Lady & Sons*

Strawberry Pretzel Salad

SERVES 8–10

2 cups crushed pretzels
¾ cup (1½ sticks) melted butter
3 tablespoons, plus ¾ cup sugar
One 8-ounce package cream cheese
One 8-ounce carton Cool Whip
Two 3-ounce packages strawberry
  gelatin dessert mix

2 cups boiling water
Two 10-ounce packages frozen
  strawberries
1 small can crushed pineapple

Preheat the oven to 400 degrees. For the crust, mix the pretzels, butter, and 3 tablespoons sugar. Press this mixture into a 9 × 13-inch pan. Bake for 7 minutes and set aside to cool. Beat together the cream cheese and ¾ cup sugar. Fold in the Cool Whip and spread over the cooled crust. Refrigerate until well chilled. Dissolve the gelatin dessert mix in the boiling water; cool slightly. Add the strawberries and pineapple, and pour over the cream-cheese mixture. Refrigerate until serving time.

Marinated Shrimp and Artichoke Hearts

SERVES 10–12

1 cup vegetable oil
½ cup red wine vinegar
⅓ cup dry white wine

1 tablespoon snipped fresh parsley
  or 1 teaspoon dry
1 teaspoon sugar

½ teaspoon salt
½ teaspoon paprika
¼ teaspoon whole black peppercorns
1 clove garlic, minced
2 pounds medium shrimp, cooked and peeled
Two 14-ounce cans artichoke hearts, drained and halved

One 8-ounce can sliced water chestnuts, drained
1 small red onion, thinly sliced into rings
Cherry tomatoes, for garnish

In a jar with a tight lid, combine the oil, vinegar, wine, parsley, sugar, salt, paprika, peppercorns, and garlic. Cover and shake well. In a 4-quart food-storage container, combine the shrimp, artichoke hearts, water chestnuts, and onion. Pour on the marinade, cover the container tightly, and shake it to coat the shrimp and vegetables with marinade. Refrigerate overnight, stirring occasionally. Serve this as a first course, garnished with cherry tomatoes.

Main Courses

FISH AND SHELLFISH

Shrimp and Rice Croquettes with Aioli

Shrimp and Grits with Marinara Sauce

Shrimp Gravy

Battered Fried Shrimp

Grilled Red Pepper Scallops

Beaufort Shrimp Pie

Stewed Salmon

The Lady's Bouillabaisse

Trey's Baked Grouper Parmigiano

Grouper Fromage

Wild Rice and Oyster Casserole

Can't-Miss Red Snapper

Easy Shrimp Bake

The Best Crab Casserole

Ginger Shrimp

Fiery Cajun Shrimp

Barbara's Mussels

Baked Shrimp-Crab Salad

Tuna Burgers

Nootsie's Chesapeake Bay Crab Cakes

MEAT

Brandied Prime Rib

Ron's Grilled Peanut Butter Ham

Bubba's Country-Fried Venison Steak

Prince Charles' Calf's Liver

Fried Veal

Perfect Eye-of-Round Roast

Spiced Beef with Dumplin's

Sunday Morning Casserole

Baked Pasta Florentine

Stuffed Red Peppers

The Lady & Sons Smoked Boston Butt Roast

Fried Spare Ribs

Duxelles-Stuffed Tenderloin

The Lady & Sons Pot Roast

Roast Pork with Plum Sauce

Baked Spaghetti

Pepper Steak

Venison Wellington with Oyster Pâté

Wayne's Beef Macaroni and Cheese

The Lady's Pork Stew

St. Paddy's Day Corned Beef and Cabbage

Sausage with Ravishing Rice

Dixieland Pork Chops

Barbecued Short Ribs

Texas-Style Chili

Ron's Tybee Island Sausage Pie
Steak Diane
Barbecue Meat Loaf
Perfect Char-Grilled Filet Mignon

POULTRY

Hot Savannah Chicken Salad Casserole
Mexican Chicken
Hurry-Up Chicken Pot Pie
Quail with Marsala Sauce
Chicken with Drop Dumplin's
Basil Grilled Chicken
Chicken Bog
Chicken Casserole
Fricasé de Pollo
Chicken Boudine
Chicken Florentine
Pat's Almond Chicken Casserole
Saucy Chicken and Asparagus Bake
Szechuan Chicken with Angelhair Pasta
Savannah Gumbo
Chicken and Wild Rice Casserole

Shrimp and Rice Croquettes with Aioli

SERVES 4

AIOLI
2 egg yolks
1 tablespoon prepared mustard
5 cloves garlic
¾ cup olive oil
1 tablespoon fresh lemon juice
½ teaspoon salt
½ teaspoon pepper

CROQUETTES
½ cup rice
1 tablespoon butter
2 cups minced cooked shrimp
½ cup finely chopped green onions
2 tablespoons fresh lemon juice
The Lady's House Seasoning
3 tablespoons all-purpose flour
2 eggs, lightly beaten
Breadcrumbs or cracker crumbs
1½ cups vegetable oil

For the aioli, combine the egg yolks, mustard, and garlic in the bowl of a food processor. Start the machine and add ½ cup of the oil in a fine stream. Add the lemon juice, salt, and pepper, then add the remaining oil, and process until thick and smooth. Refrigerate until needed.

For the croquettes, cook the rice in 1 cup boiling salted water for 20 minutes or until done. Add the butter while the rice is still hot. Add the shrimp, onions, lemon juice, and House Seasoning to taste. Stir in the flour and eggs. Refrigerate this mixture for 2 hours.

Shape the rice mixture into patties and coat with bread- or cracker crumbs. Heat the oil in a 10-inch cast-iron skillet. Oil should be hot but not smoking. Fry the croquettes over medium-high heat until nice and golden brown on both sides. Drain on paper towels. Serve with aioli.

Shrimp and Grits with Marinara Sauce

SERVES 4–6

2 medium Vidalia onions, coarsely
   chopped
1 large green bell pepper, seeded
   and coarsely chopped
2 tablespoons vegetable oil
1 pound large shrimp, peeled and
   deveined
Cayenne pepper
Chili powder

6 servings creamy white grits,
   cooked in milk or chicken broth
2–3 cups Marinara Sauce
   (recipe follows, or use store-
   bought)
¼ cup freshly grated Parmesan
¼ cup chopped fresh parsley or basil

Sauté the onions and bell pepper in oil until crisp-tender. Add the shrimp and sauté until pink, 2 to 3 minutes. Season with cayenne pepper and chili powder to taste. Add the cooked grits. Spoon grits into individual serving bowls, and ladle ½ cup Marinara Sauce over each serving. Sprinkle with the Parmesan and parsley or basil. Re-season, if necessary, with cayenne pepper and chili powder. Serve with crusty garlic bread.

MARINARA SAUCE

MAKES ABOUT 3 QUARTS

4 tablespoons olive oil
1 medium onion, diced
1 green bell pepper, diced
2 tablespoons minced garlic (4 or
   5 cloves)
1 tablespoon chopped fresh basil
1 tablespoon chopped fresh thyme

1 tablespoon chopped fresh oregano
½ cup red wine
Two 28-ounce cans diced tomatoes
Two 29-ounce cans tomato sauce
2 tablespoons sugar
2 teaspoons The Lady's House
   Seasoning

Heat the oil in a large, heavy pot over medium heat, then sauté the onions, bell pepper, and garlic until the onion is translucent (be careful not to burn the garlic). Stir often to keep the vegetables from sticking. Add the herbs and continue to stir for 1 minute. Add the wine (pour yourself a glass as well and enjoy) and cook, stirring for 1 minute longer. Add the diced tomatoes and stir for 2 minutes, then add the tomato sauce, sugar, and House Seasoning. Reduce the heat and simmer, stirring occasionally, for at least 2 hours. The longer it cooks, the thicker it gets. Freeze any extra.

Shrimp Gravy

SERVES 4

2 strips bacon
¼ cup chopped onion
2 cups uncooked shrimp, peeled and deveined (small ones preferred)

2 tablespoons all-purpose flour
¼ cup ketchup
1 teaspoon Worcestershire sauce
1½–2 cups water
The Lady's House Seasoning

Fry the bacon in a heavy skillet and remove from the pan; set aside. Sauté the onion in the bacon grease until soft. Add the shrimp and stir for a minute or two. Stir in the flour until the shrimp are coated. Add the ketchup and Worcestershire sauce, then slowly stir in 1½ to 2 cups of water—enough to make a good gravy. Add House Seasoning to taste. Serve with grits for breakfast or brunch.

Battered Fried Shrimp

SERVES 4–6

1 cup all-purpose flour
½ teaspoon sugar
½ teaspoon salt
1 cup ice water
1 egg

2 tablespoons melted fat or vegetable oil
2 pounds uncooked shrimp, peeled and deveined, tails left on
Vegetable oil for deep frying

In a large bowl stir together the flour, sugar, and salt. Beat in the ice water, egg, and 2 tablespoons fat or oil. Dry the shrimp thoroughly. Heat the oil for deep frying in a large, heavy pot until it registers 375 degrees. Holding the shrimp by the tails, dip them in batter. Carefully place them in the pot and fry until golden brown. Do *not* overcook; just a few minutes does the trick. Drain on paper towels and serve immediately.

Grilled Red Pepper Scallops

SERVES 6

1½ pounds large sea scallops
2 tablespoons olive oil
Zest of one lemon

Freshly ground black pepper
4 large red bell peppers

In a bowl, combine the scallops, olive oil, lemon zest, and black pepper to taste. Preheat the broiler or prepare coals for outdoor grilling. Cut the bell peppers in half lengthwise and remove the stems, seeds, and ribs. If cooking in a broiler, place the peppers cut-side down on a baking sheet.

Broil or grill the peppers until blackened, 6 to 10 minutes. Transfer to a paper bag, close the top and let steam for 10 minutes. Remove the charred skins and cut the peppers lengthwise into ¾-inch strips. Wrap a pepper strip around each scallop to cover completely, overlapping the pepper ends. Secure the strips by running a 10-inch metal skewer through the scallop and pepper. Use 6 skewers; add scallops to each skewer until filled. Grill skewers over a medium-hot fire, turning once, until scallops are almost firm to the touch, 1 to 2 minutes on each side. Alternatively, cook under the broiler for about 3 minutes per side. Serve immediately.

Beaufort Shrimp Pie

SERVES 6–8

In the Carolina Sea Islands, a "pie" does not necessarily have a crust. This shrimp casserole is a superb luncheon dish and is one of these pies.

½ cup chopped onion
¼ cup chopped green bell pepper
2 tablespoons butter
3 cups cooked and peeled shrimp
2 cups soft breadcrumbs

2 cups milk
2 eggs
Salt and pepper
3 strips bacon

Sauté the onion and bell pepper in butter until soft. In a casserole, make layers of the shrimp, breadcrumbs, and the onions and peppers. Beat together the milk, eggs, and salt and pepper to taste, and pour over the shrimp. Cut each strip of bacon into 4 pieces. Lay bacon on top of the casserole and bake at 325 degrees until the filling is set and the bacon is brown.   ❦ ❦ ❦   *The Lady & Sons*

Stewed Salmon

SERVES 3–4

We sometimes serve this on our buffet, if the staff doesn't eat it all first!

1 medium onion, diced
4 tablespoons butter
One 14¾-ounce can salmon
1½ cups water

1 teaspoon The Lady's House
   Seasoning
½ teaspoon Accent (optional)

In a large skillet, sauté the onion in butter until tender. Turn the salmon out of the can, saving the liquid. Pick the salmon free of bones (some folks like the bones, and I am one of them). Add the salmon and its liquid, along with the water, to the skillet. Add the House Seasoning and Accent, if using, and simmer for 10 minutes. Serve hot over grits or rice.   ❦ ❦ ❦   *The Lady & Sons*

The Lady's Bouillabaisse

SERVES 8

This dish is a specialty of the South of France, but living or visiting on the coast of Georgia you are quite likely to see it offered on menus. I hope you enjoy The Lady & Sons' version of this wonderful French dish. Feel free to add any of your favorite shellfish to the pot.

2 pounds mussels
2 cups water
2 pounds firm fresh fish fillets such as grouper or striped bass (ask your local fishmonger for additional suggestions)
¾ cup olive oil
1½ tablespoons finely chopped garlic
1½ cups chopped onions
5 Roma tomatoes, peeled and sliced, or 2 cups canned Italian tomatoes

2 teaspoons fennel seed
¼ teaspoon saffron
1 tablespoon, plus ½ teaspoon kosher salt
1½ teaspoons freshly ground pepper
5 cups boiling water
One 8-ounce bottle clam juice
4 whole crabs, cut in half
1 pound unpeeled shrimp
1 loaf French bread
Butter

Wash and scrub the mussels in cold water. Bring 2 cups of water to a boil in a large, heavy pot. Add the mussels and cover the pot. Steam for 6 to 8 minutes, or until the mussels open. Discard any mussels that didn't open. Remove from the heat and set aside. Cut the fish into 1-inch thick slices. Heat the oil in a large pot. Add the garlic, onions, tomatoes, fennel, saffron, salt, and pepper. Add the boiling water and clam juice. Bring to a rolling boil, add the crabs and fish, and continue to boil for 6 to 8 minutes. Add the mussels and their broth to the pot along with the shrimp, and boil for an additional 5 minutes.

Slice the French bread, butter it, and toast lightly. Serve the bouillabaisse in large individual bowls lined with toasted French bread; pile in the seafood and ladle the broth over it. Top each bowl with 1 tablespoon of butter. Pass the remaining bread at the table. If you like a spicier soup you may add a couple of whole hot peppers to the pot at the start of cooking.　　❧ ❧ ❧　**The Lady & Sons**

Trey's Baked Grouper Parmigiano

SERVES 2

We have many good local seafood suppliers here on the coast, but one that has consistently been there to serve me with good, fresh seafood, day in and day out, is Mathews Seafood. This business was started years ago by Louis Mathews. Today, his three sons, Chris, Trey, and John, carry on in their father's footsteps. I can always count on these young men to guide us in selecting the best they have to offer. Thanks, guys!

Butter	*3 teaspoons fresh lemon juice*
Two 8-ounce grouper fillets	*1 tablespoon minced fresh dill*
½ cup mayonnaise	*Black pepper*
¼ cup freshly grated Parmesan	*½ teaspoon paprika*

Preheat the oven to 350 degrees. Butter a baking dish. Place the grouper fillets in the dish. In a small bowl, whisk together the mayonnaise, Parmesan, lemon juice, dill, and pepper to taste, and spread this over the fish. Sprinkle with paprika and bake for 10 minutes, or until just cooked through.

Grouper Fromage

SERVES 4

Rance, the young man who has the large task of managing our kitchen, still finds time to prepare this all-time favorite dish for our dinner guests. We love you, Rance!

1 cup mayonnaise	*1 teaspoon The Lady's House*
2 cups shredded Monterey Jack	*Seasoning*
cheese	*4 grouper fillets, about 8 ounces*
½ cup sautéed chopped onion	*each*
1 teaspoon Texas Pete Hot Sauce	*1 lemon*
1 teaspoon ground red pepper	

Mix together the mayonnaise, cheese, onion, hot sauce, red pepper, and ½ teaspoon House Seasoning; set aside.

Preheat the oven to 350 degrees. Grease a 13 × 9 × 2-inch baking dish. Add just enough water to come to a depth of ¼ inch. Sprinkle the fish with the remaining ½ teaspoon of House Seasoning. Place the fish in the baking dish and squeeze the juice of the lemon over it. Bake for 10 to 20 minutes; the time will depend on the thickness of your fish. When the fish is almost done, remove the dish from the oven and cover each fillet with ½ cup of the cheese mixture. Return to the oven and continue to bake for 8 to 10 minutes longer.　　❧ ❧ ❧　***The Lady & Sons***

Wild Rice and Oyster Casserole

SERVES 10–12

One 10¾-ounce can beef broth
2½ cups water
2 cups raw Mahatma Long Grain
　and Wild Rice with Seasoning
¾ cup (1½ sticks) butter
2 quarts oysters, very well drained
4 dashes Texas Pete Hot Sauce

Salt and pepper
One 10¾-ounce can cream of
　mushroom soup
1 cup half-and-half
1½ teaspoons onion powder
½ teaspoon garlic salt
½ cup finely minced fresh parsley

Preheat the oven to 350 degrees. In a saucepan, bring the beef broth and water to a boil. Add the rice, bring to a boil again, reduce heat, and simmer covered for 25 minutes. Drain any liquid remaining. Add ½ cup of the butter and stir; fluff with a fork.

Sauté the drained oysters in ¼ cup of the butter over medium-high heat until the edges curl, approximately 3 to 5 minutes. Remove the oysters with a slotted spoon; set aside. Place half of the rice in a greased 13 × 9 × 2-inch baking dish. Cover it with oysters and sprinkle with hot sauce and salt and pepper to taste. Top with the remaining rice.

In a saucepan, heat the mushroom soup over medium heat. Add the half-and-half, onion powder, and garlic salt. Pour over the oyster mixture. Bake for 35 to 40 minutes, until golden brown and bubbling. Garnish with parsley.

Can't-Miss Red Snapper

SERVES 4

Four 8-ounce red snapper fillets,
  ½ inch thick
1 teaspoon salt
½ teaspoon pepper
1 tablespoon Worcestershire sauce

1 cup chopped onions
1 chopped green bell pepper
½ cup (1 stick) butter
1 cup freshly grated Parmesan

Season the fish with the salt, pepper, and Worcestershire sauce. Spread the onions and pepper in a 13 × 9 × 2-inch metal baking pan and place the fish on top. Dot the fish with butter. Bake in a 350-degree oven for 8 minutes, then baste with the pan juices. Cook for 8 minutes longer, basting again. Bake for a final 8 minutes, continuing to baste with the juices. Cover the fish with Parmesan and place under the broiler until the cheese browns. To serve, spoon the vegetables over the fish.

Easy Shrimp Bake

SERVES 6

1 cup sliced fresh mushrooms
4 green onions, chopped
2 tablespoons butter
2 cups cooked and peeled shrimp
6–8 slices of day-old bread,
  trimmed, buttered, and cubed
½ pound sharp cheese, grated

3 eggs
½ teaspoon salt
½ teaspoon dry mustard
Pinch of pepper
Pinch of paprika
1½ cups milk

In a skillet, sauté the mushrooms and onions in butter. Grease a 2-quart casserole. Put the shrimp, the mushrooms, the onions, half of the bread cubes, and half of the cheese in the casserole, and stir gently. Top with rest of the cheese and bread cubes. Lightly beat the eggs with the salt, mustard, pepper, and paprika. Stir in the milk and pour into the casserole. If making this dish the day before serving, cover and refrigerate. Bake at 325 degrees for 40 to 50 minutes, or until set and golden brown.   ❦ ❦ ❦   **The Lady & Sons**

The Best Crab Casserole

SERVES 4–6

One 6½-ounce can crabmeat,
    drained
1 cup mayonnaise
1 cup soft breadcrumbs
¾ cup half-and-half
6 hard-boiled eggs, finely chopped
½ cup chopped onion

¼ cup sliced stuffed green olives
2 tablespoons chopped fresh parsley
¾ teaspoon salt
Pinch of pepper
½ cup buttered soft breadcrumbs
Olive slices, for garnish

In a large bowl, break up the crabmeat in chunks. Add the mayonnaise, soft breadcrumbs, half-and-half, eggs, onion, olives, parsley, salt, and pepper, and fold together. Divide the mixture among greased individual bakers or spoon it into a 1-quart casserole dish. Top with the buttered crumbs and bake at 350 degrees for 20 to 25 minutes. Garnish with olive slices.   ❦ ❦ ❦   **The Lady & Sons**

Ginger Shrimp

SERVES 4

1 tablespoon vegetable oil
1½ pounds shrimp, peeled and
    deveined
2 tablespoons grated fresh ginger

1 cup chopped green onions (about 5)
1½ cups chicken broth
2 tablespoons cold water
1 tablespoon cornstarch

Heat 1½ teaspoons of oil in a large nonstick skillet and sauté the shrimp until they turn a light pink, about 4 minutes. Remove the shrimp and set aside. Heat the remaining oil over medium-low heat, add the ginger and onions, and sauté until onions are tender. Add the chicken broth and bring to a boil. Mix together the water and cornstarch and stir the mixture into the skillet; the sauce will thicken in about 1 minute. Return the shrimp to the skillet and bring the sauce to a boil. Serve over your favorite rice.

Fiery Cajun Shrimp

SERVES 8

2 cups (4 sticks) melted butter
½ cup Worcestershire sauce
¼ cup fresh lemon juice
¼ cup ground pepper
2 teaspoons Texas Pete Hot Sauce

4 cloves garlic, minced
2 teaspoons salt
5 pounds unpeeled medium shrimp
2 lemons, thinly sliced

Stir together the butter, Worcestershire sauce, lemon juice, pepper, hot sauce, garlic, and salt. Pour half this mixture into a large heatproof dish. Layer half the shrimp and half the lemon slices in the dish; then form a second layer with the remaining shrimp and lemon slices, and pour remaining sauce into the dish. Bake, uncovered, at 400 degrees for 20 minutes, or until the shrimp are pink, stirring twice. Pour off the sauce into individual serving dishes. Serve the shrimp with plenty of French bread for dipping in the spicy butter sauce.

Barbara's Mussels

SERVES 4

This can be done with mussels and clams mixed, and you can also add shrimp at the end if you like variety.

2 pounds mussels*
2 cups wine (Chardonnay or
   Cabernet)
One 14½-ounce can Italian-style
   chopped tomatoes
½ cup (1 stick) butter, cut into
   quarters

½ cup fresh or 1 cup minced garlic
   from a jar**
1-ounce bunch fresh basil, chopped
2 shallots, chopped

Rinse and scrub the mussels in cold water. Fill a large pot 1-inch deep with water and bring to a boil. Add the mussels and boil gently until the shells just open, 5 to 7 minutes. Pour off half the liquid and keep rest of the liquid in the pot with the mussels. Discard any mussels that did not open. Add the wine, tomatoes, butter, garlic, basil, and shallots, and cook slowly on low heat (keep stirring occasionally) for about 20 minutes. Serve the mussels in a large bowl with hot crusty bread and salad.

*For plumper, more succulent mussels, place the mussels in a pot of cold water and stir in ½ cup flour; refrigerate for 4 hours or overnight. Drain the mussels and rinse in cold water.
**This may sound like too much garlic but it really isn't.

Baked Shrimp-Crab Salad

SERVES 6–8

1 green bell pepper, chopped
1 onion, chopped
1 cup finely chopped celery
One 6-ounce can crabmeat, picked
   free of any broken shells
One 4-ounce can medium shrimp

¾ cup mayonnaise
½ teaspoon salt
¼ teaspoon pepper
1 teaspoon Worcestershire sauce
1 cup buttered cracker crumbs or
   breadcrumbs

In a large bowl, combine the bell pepper, onion, and celery. Add the crabmeat and shrimp, then the mayonnaise and seasonings. Spoon the mixture into a buttered casserole, cover with buttered crumbs, and bake at 350 degrees until golden brown, about 30 minutes.

🌿 🌿 🌿   *The Lady & Sons*

Tuna Burgers

SERVES 4

Two 6-ounce cans solid white
   tuna, drained
½ cup breadcrumbs
2 large eggs, lightly beaten
½ cup finely chopped onion
½ cup finely chopped celery
1 tablespoon chopped pimento
   (optional)

1 tablespoon fresh lemon juice
1½ teaspoons prepared horseradish
1 clove garlic, minced
¼ teaspoon pepper
1 tablespoon vegetable oil

In a large bowl, combine the tuna, breadcrumbs, and egg, and stir lightly. Add the onion, celery, pimento (if using), lemon juice, horseradish, garlic, and pepper, and mix again. Form the mixture into four patties. Heat the oil in a nonstick skillet over medium heat and cook the patties, covered, until golden brown. Carefully flip the patties and cook the other side for 5 minutes.

Nootsie's Chesapeake Bay Crab Cakes

SERVES 4–6

½ cup peanut oil
1 pound crabmeat, picked free of
   any broken shells
1 egg
¼ cup dry breadcrumbs
4½ teaspoons heavy cream
2 tablespoons melted butter
2 tablespoons cracker crumbs

2 tablespoons chopped fresh parsley
2 tablespoons minced onion
1 teaspoon fresh lemon juice
½ teaspoon red pepper
½ teaspoon dry mustard
½ teaspoon salt
½ teaspoon Worcestershire sauce
¼ teaspoon black pepper

Pour the peanut oil into a large skillet and set aside. Combine all of the remaining ingredients and shape into 10 crab cakes. Heat the oil over medium-high heat, add the crab cakes (in batches), and fry until browned, 3 to 5 minutes. Flip the cakes and panfry the other side until golden brown.

Brandied Prime Rib

SERVES 6–8

8-pound standing rib roast
4–6 cloves garlic, slivered
¼ cup soy sauce
1 tablespoon freshly ground pepper

Fresh oregano and thyme sprigs
1 cup brandy
1 cup beef broth
Salt and pepper

Using a sharp knife, make 1-inch-deep slits, evenly spaced, over the entire surface of the roast; press the slivered garlic into the slits. Place in a roasting pan. Brush the outside of the roast with soy sauce, sprinkle with pepper and oregano and thyme sprigs, and let roast stand at room temperature for 1 hour.

Preheat the oven to 350 degrees. Cook the roast to the preferred doneness: For medium rare, roast the beef 14 minutes per pound or until meat thermometer inserted into the center reads 125 degrees. For medium, roast 15 minutes per pound or until temperature reaches

135 degrees. While cooking, baste every 10 minutes with brandy. When the roast is done, transfer it to a warmed platter and let stand for 15 minutes before carving.

Skim and discard the fat from the roasting pan. Place the pan on the stove over medium heat and pour in the broth. Deglaze the pan by stirring to dislodge any browned bits. Simmer the sauce for a few minutes, then season with salt and pepper to taste. Carve the roast and spoon the sauce over the meat.

Ron's Grilled Peanut Butter Ham

SERVES 8–10

1 cup chicken broth
½ cup peanut butter
¼ cup honey
1 small onion, grated
1 clove garlic, chopped

2 teaspoons soy sauce
1 teaspoon Kitchen Bouquet
¼ teaspoon black pepper
2 center-cut ham slices (1½ inches
thick)

In a blender, combine the broth, peanut butter, honey, onion, garlic, soy sauce, Kitchen Bouquet, and pepper. Put the ham in a shallow glass dish, pour the marinade over it, and marinate for 3 to 4 hours in the refrigerator.

Prepare a charcoal fire. Cook approximately 15 minutes per side over glowing coals. Carve into 1-inch-thick slices. This sauce is also excellent with lamb or pork chops.

Bubba's Country-Fried Venison Steak

SERVES 4

You may substitute beef round steak (have butcher run through cubing machine to tenderize) for venison if you like.

1½ cups, plus 2 tablespoons all-
    purpose flour
½ teaspoon black pepper
Eight 4-ounce venison steaks, cubed
1 teaspoon The Lady's House
    Seasoning
1 teaspoon The Lady's Seasoned
    Salt

¾ cup vegetable oil
1½ teaspoons salt
4 cups hot water
½ teaspoon Accent (optional)
1 bunch green onions, or 1
    medium yellow onion, sliced

Combine 1½ cups flour and ¼ teaspoon of the black pepper. Sprinkle one side of meat with the House Seasoning and the other side with the Seasoned Salt. Dredge the meat in the flour mixture. Heat ½ cup oil in a heavy skillet over medium-high heat, add two of the venison steaks, and fry until nice and brown, 5 to 6 minutes per side. Repeat with the remaining steaks, adding up to ¼ cup oil, as needed.

When all the steaks are cooked, make the gravy: Add the 2 tablespoons of flour to the pan drippings; stir in the remaining ¼ teaspoon pepper, and the salt. Stir until the flour is medium brown and the mixture is bubbly. Slowly add the water and the Accent (if using), stirring constantly. Return the steaks to the skillet and bring to a boil; reduce the heat, place the onions on top of the steaks, cover, and simmer for 30 minutes.

Prince Charles' Calf's Liver

SERVES 4–6

Charles Polite is in charge of producing our evening buffet at The Lady &
Sons. I hold him in high esteem and therefore nicknamed him my "Prince
Charles." Our guests always enjoy his liver and onions. We hope you do as well.

1 cup (2 sticks) butter
1 jumbo onion, sliced
1½ pounds calf's liver
2 teaspoons The Lady's House
   Seasoning

2 teaspoons The Lady's Seasoned
   Salt
½ cup vegetable oil

In a large skillet, melt the butter over medium-high heat. Add the
onion and sauté until tender. Remove the onion and set aside; leave the
butter in the skillet. With a meat mallet, lightly pound the liver to tenderize it. Season the liver with House Seasoning and Seasoned Salt.
Add the oil to the skillet and heat until the oil crackles. Sear the liver
quickly on both sides. The liver is done when the surface is no longer
pink. Serve the liver topped with the onions.

❦ ❦ ❦   *The Lady & Sons*

Fried Veal

SERVES 4–6

2 pounds veal shoulder-blade steak
   (remove any bone and trim the
   fat)
¼ cup all-purpose flour
½ teaspoon salt
½ teaspoon garlic powder

¼ teaspoon pepper
2 eggs, lightly beaten
¾ cup seasoned breadcrumbs
4 tablespoons olive oil
1 cup water
½ pound sliced provolone cheese

Cut the veal into 8 individual size pieces. Dredge the meat in flour and
pound it with a meat mallet to half its original thickness. Sprinkle salt,

garlic powder, and pepper on both sides of the veal. Dip each piece into the beaten eggs, then into the breadcrumbs. Heat the oil in a large non-stick skillet over medium-high heat. Cook the veal pieces in batches until golden brown. Add the water, cover, and simmer for 45 minutes. Check the water level in the pan occasionally and add a little more water if necessary. Just before serving, place a slice of cheese on each piece of veal, cover the skillet, and serve as soon as the cheese melts.

Perfect Eye-of-Round Roast

SERVES 6–8

1 beef eye-of-round roast, 2½–3
    pounds
1 tablespoon vegetable oil
1 teaspoon The Lady's Seasoned
    Salt
1 teaspoon paprika

½ teaspoon sugar
½ teaspoon pepper
½ teaspoon garlic powder
¼ teaspoon dried oregano
¼ teaspoon ground ginger

Preheat the oven to 500 degrees. Rub the roast with oil. Mix all of the remaining ingredients in a small bowl. Completely coat all sides of roast with the seasonings. Place roast in a 12- to 15-inch iron skillet. Put the roast in the oven and immediately reduce the oven temperature to 350 degrees. Roast the beef for 20 minutes per pound. You may use a meat thermometer and cook to 125 degrees for medium-rare beef or 135–140 degrees for medium. Cool for 15 minutes before carving. Cut into thin slices across the grain of meat.

Spiced Beef with Dumplin's

SERVES 6–8

One 3-pound boneless chuck roast
2 tablespoons vegetable oil
One 16-ounce can tomatoes
1½ cups water

¼ cup red wine
2 teaspoons beef bouillon granules
1 teaspoon salt
¼ teaspoon pepper

2 cloves garlic, minced
6 whole cloves
1 package (8 count) refrigerated
 biscuits

1 tablespoon minced fresh parsley
¼ cup cold water
2 tablespoons cornstarch

Trim the excess fat from the roast. Heat the oil in a large Dutch oven over medium heat. Brown the roast on all sides. Add the tomatoes, water, wine, bouillon granules, salt, pepper, garlic, and cloves, cover, and cook slowly for 2 to 2½ hours, or until tender. Place the biscuits on the roast and sprinkle with parsley. Cover tightly and steam the dumplings for 15 minutes, giving the pot an occasional little shake. Remove the meat and dumplings to a platter. Make the gravy by mixing the water and cornstarch. Stir into the boiling broth, continuing to stir until the gravy is thick. (If the broth doesn't need thickening, you can serve it as is.)   ❦ ❦ ❦ *The Lady & Sons*

Sunday Morning Casserole

SERVES 6

2 slices white bread
1 pound ground mild sausage
6 eggs, beaten
2 cups milk
1 teaspoon dry mustard
½ teaspoon salt

Pinch of pepper
1½ cups thinly sliced, cooked,
 unpeeled red potatoes
1½ cups combined grated Cheddar
 and Monterey Jack cheeses

Cube the bread and place it in a buttered 8 × 11 × 2-inch casserole. Fry the sausage until it's almost done; drain off the fat. Mix the eggs, milk, dry mustard, salt, and pepper. Layer the sausage over the bread, and top with a layer of potatoes. Sprinkle the cheese on top. Pour the egg mixture over the casserole. Cover and refrigerate overnight. In the morning, bake the casserole at 350 degrees for 30 minutes or until set.

Baked Pasta Florentine

SERVES 8

One 10-ounce package frozen
   chopped spinach
1 tablespoon, plus ½ cup vegetable
   oil
1½ pounds ground beef
1 medium onion, chopped
1 clove garlic, minced
One 15½-ounce jar pasta sauce
   with mushrooms

One 8-ounce can tomato sauce
One 6-ounce can tomato paste
½ teaspoon salt
Pinch of pepper
1 8-ounce package seashell
   macaroni
1 cup shredded sharp cheese
½ cup breadcrumbs
2 eggs, well beaten

Cook the spinach according to package directions; drain, reserving the liquid and adding enough water to measure 1 cup; set aside. In a large, heavy pot, heat the 1 tablespoon of oil over medium heat. Brown the ground beef, onion, and garlic in the oil, stirring well to crumble the beef. Drain off the fat. Stir the spinach liquid, pasta sauce, tomato sauce, tomato paste, salt, and pepper into the meat mixture. Simmer for 10 minutes, then cover and set aside. Cook the macaroni according to package directions; drain and return the macaroni to the pot. Add the spinach, cheese, breadcrumbs, eggs, and the ½ cup of oil; stir gently to mix well. Spread the mixture evenly in a lightly greased 13½ × 8¾-inch baking dish. Top with the meat sauce and bake at 350 degrees for 30 minutes.   🌿 🌿 🌿   *The Lady & Sons*

Stuffed Red Peppers

SERVES 6–8

4 large red bell peppers, preferably
   with stems
¾ pound ground chuck
½ pound ground pork

1 medium onion, chopped
2 cloves garlic, minced
2 teaspoons beef bouillon
   granules

2 teaspoons The Lady's House
  Seasoning
1 cup cooked rice ·
½ cup jarred Old El Paso Cheese
  and Salsa

½ cup sour cream
1 cup diced tomatoes
½ cup chopped green onion tops
1 tablespoon soy sauce
1 cup hot water

Cut the peppers in half lengthwise, leaving the stems intact and halving them also. Remove the seeds and ribs. Sauté the beef and pork, the onion, garlic, 1 teaspoon of the bouillon granules, and the House Seasoning together, scrambling well, until the onion is transparent. Drain off the fat. Add the rice, cheese, sour cream, tomatoes, green onion tops, and soy sauce. Mix well. Stuff this mixture into peppers. Mix the hot water and the remaining 1 teaspoon bouillon granules. Pour this into a shallow casserole large enough to hold all the peppers. Place the stuffed peppers in the dish. (The water in the dish allows the peppers to steam while retaining some of their crispness.) Cover the casserole with foil and bake at 350 degrees for 25 to 35 minutes. Remove the foil and spoon a little juice over the peppers; bake for an additional 10 to 15 minutes.   ❧ ❧ ❧ **The Lady & Sons**

The Lady & Sons Smoked Boston Butt Roast

SERVES 12–15

The secret to this recipe is rubbing your seasonings into the meat thoroughly.

One 8-pound pork butt roast
4 tablespoons The Lady's House
  Seasoning
2 tablespoons The Lady's Seasoned
  Salt

4 tablespoons liquid smoke
1 medium onion, sliced
1 cup water
3 bay leaves

Sprinkle one side of the roast with 2 tablespoons of the House Seasoning, rubbing well. Flip the roast over and sprinkle with the remaining House Seasoning, rubbing well. Repeat the process with the Seasoned Salt and the liquid smoke. Place the meat in a large roaster pan; add the onion, water, and bay leaves. Cover and cook at 350 degrees for 2½ to

3 hours, or until a meat thermometer registers 170 degrees. Let cool slightly for easier slicing. Serve with a good barbecue sauce. Leftovers make wonderful chopped barbecue sandwiches.

❧ ❧ ❧   *The Lady & Sons*

Fried Spare Ribs

SERVES 4

When we serve fried ribs at the restaurant, the reaction is always the same: "Fried ribs, we've never heard of those!" Well, they really are very good. We all love fried pork chops, so why wouldn't we love fried ribs?

2 teaspoons The Lady's House Seasoning	1 small slab pork ribs, 4–5 pounds (have the butcher crack them)
½ teaspoon The Lady's Seasoned Salt	1 cup all-purpose flour
	6 cups vegetable oil

Sprinkle the seasonings on both sides of the ribs, rubbing them thoroughly into the meat. Cut the slab into individual ribs. Roll each rib into flour, and shake off the excess. Drop the ribs, a few at a time, into hot, deep oil (350 degrees), and cook for 14 to 15 minutes. Drain on paper towels. Serve with barbecue sauce for dipping.

❧ ❧ ❧   *The Lady & Sons*

Duxelles-Stuffed Tenderloin

SERVES 8–12 AS AN ENTRÉE, 20–30 AS AN APPETIZER

DUXELLES
3 cups minced mushrooms
4 tablespoons butter
¼ cup-white wine
1 or 2 shallots, finely chopped
½ teaspoon salt
½ teaspoon pepper

MEAT
2 cups spinach
One 4–6-pound beef tenderloin, butterflied (ask the butcher to do this, or do it yourself)
1 tablespoon kosher salt
1 tablespoon minced garlic

6 ounces Gruyère cheese	*½ pound thinly sliced prosciutto*
2 teaspoons pepper	*2 tablespoons olive oil*

For the duxelles, combine the mushrooms, butter, wine, shallots, salt, and pepper in a saucepan. Cook over medium-low heat until the mushrooms cook down and the liquid is completely evaporated. The duxelles can be made well in advance and refrigerated.

Place the spinach in a saucepan; sprinkle it with a few drops of water, cover, and cook over low heat just until the spinach is barely wilted. Drain and set aside.

Lay the beef on a flat surface and sprinkle it with 1½ teaspoons of the kosher salt; rub the garlic into the meat. Slice the cheese fairly thin and lay it on top of the meat, leaving a 2-inch border all around. Place the spinach on top of the cheese, followed by the duxelles, forming the filling into a long, narrow mound. Bring the sides of the meat together, overlapping the sides. Continue to shape and form the tenderloin to create a nice tight loaf. Sprinkle with the pepper and the remaining 1½ teaspoons kosher salt. Lay out the prosciutto on a large flat surface lined with waxed paper, forming a rectangle of prosciutto to accommodate the tenderloin. Lay the tenderloin on one end of the prosciutto slices and roll, using the waxed paper to help you. Roll until the prosciutto is snugly wrapped around the beef. Using 4 feet of cotton kitchen twine, tie one end of the tenderloin, then tie the meat much as you would lace your tennis shoes. Tie this on the snug side to allow for a little shrinkage of the meat. Drizzle olive oil over the meat, gently rubbing it over the entire roast. Bake in a preheated 450-degree oven for 45 minutes, or until a meat thermometer registers 140 degrees for medium-rare, 160 degrees for medium, and 170 degrees for well-done.

❧ ❧ ❧ *The Lady & Sons*

The Lady & Sons Pot Roast

SERVES 8

Before I give you this recipe, I must tell you a story. It is about a tall, handsome, talented young man who walked into our restaurant one hot Saturday afternoon. This beautiful young man had an equally beautiful and charming young woman on his arm. I could hear the wait staff just a'buzzing. Being ever watchful, I came out into the dining room to make sure all was well. I saw that our hostess had seated the couple, so I walked over and introduced myself and welcomed them to our home. That hot afternoon I had the pleasure of getting to know Harry Connick, Jr., and his lovely wife, Jill. I have Harry and Jill to thank for one of the most memorable nights of my life. Harry was performing that night at the Johnny Mercer Theater, but much to my dismay I had been too busy to get tickets. I laughingly told Harry that with the exception of him, just about everyone I cared to see in concert was dead, and because of my lack of organization I was going to miss this opportunity. With a sweet smile and a twinkle in his eye he said, "Well, I'm just not going on tonight if you're not going to be there." I repeated that I didn't have a ticket. Harry and Jill just smiled and said, "Yes you do. We'll have five tickets waiting at the box office for you and your two sons and their dates. Be there at 7:30." Shortly before show time Harry called the restaurant to see what was cooking. Well, every Saturday night we serve our wonderful Southern Pot Roast and Mashed Potatoes on the buffet. Harry's instructions were to put as much pot roast and mashed potatoes on one plate as we could, and to fill another plate with Jill's favorite, the collard greens. I was home getting ready to attend the concert when our manager, Renee, called to ask if I could pick the plates up on my way to the concert. I agreed, and said, "While you're fixing Harry's and Jill's plates, how about a platter of fried chicken and biscuits for the band members?" So my sons, their dates, and I, loaded down with food, took off for the concert. We had the pleasure of feeding the Connicks for a second time on that steaming hot day of August 21, 1999. The concert was wonderful! Harry left me speechless in the middle of his performance by recounting our meeting and describing the meals that he and Jill had enjoyed that day. Just when I thought he couldn't be sweeter, Harry dedicated his next song to me. The song was "Sensational." Needless to say, I was a puddle in my chair! Thank you, Harry and Jill, for a wonderful night. How proud your parents must be to have raised such gracious, thoughtful, considerate people. This one's for you, Harry!

One 3–4-pound boneless chuck
   roast
1 teaspoon The Lady's House
   Seasoning
1 teaspoon The Lady's Seasoned
   Salt
½ teaspoon black pepper
2 tablespoons vegetable oil

1 tablespoon beef bouillon granules
1 cup thinly sliced onion wedges
3 cloves garlic, crushed
2 bay leaves
One 10¾-ounce can cream of
   mushroom soup
¼ cup red wine
2 tablespoons Worcestershire sauce

Preheat the oven to 350 degrees. Rub the roast with House Seasoning, Seasoned Salt, and pepper. Heat the oil in a large skillet and brown the roast, searing it on both sides. Place the meat in a roaster pan. Sprinkle the bouillon granules over the meat, and cover it with onions, garlic, and bay leaves. Combine the mushroom soup, wine, Worcestershire sauce, and half a soup can of water, and pour this over the roast. Cover and bake for 2 to 2½ hours, or until tender. Remove and discard the bay leaves. If the gravy is not thick enough, remove the meat from the pan and pour the gravy into a saucepan. Bring it to a boil and thicken it by adding 2 tablespoons of cornstarch mixed with ¼ cup cold water, stirring constantly.   ❧ ❧ ❧ *The Lady & Sons*

Roast Pork with Plum Sauce

SERVES 10

PLUM SAUCE
2 tablespoons butter
¾ cup chopped onions
1 cup plum preserves
⅔ cup water
½ cup packed brown sugar
⅓ cup chili sauce
¼ cup soy sauce
2 tablespoons prepared mustard
3 drops Tabasco sauce
2 tablespoons fresh lemon juice
Garlic salt to taste

ROAST
One 5-pound pork loin roast
2 cloves garlic, slivered
2 teaspoons salt
2 teaspoons dried or fresh rosemary
1½ teaspoons dried oregano
1½ teaspoons dried thyme
1½ teaspoons rubbed sage
¼ teaspoon pepper
¼ teaspoon freshly grated nutmeg

To make the saucce, melt the butter in a saucepan; add the onions and sauté until tender. Add the remaining ingredients and simmer for 15 minutes. Set aside.

Preheat the oven to 325 degrees. Moisten the roast with a damp paper towel to help hold the seasonings. In a small bowl, stir together the garlic, salt, herbs, and spices. With a sharp knife make ½-inch-deep slits in the top of the roast. Press the seasoning mixture into the slits, and rub the remainder over the entire roast. Place the roast in a roaster pan and pour ½ cup plum sauce over it. Cover and bake for 2½ hours. Uncover the roast and baste it with additional plum sauce; bake for 30 minutes longer, basting 2 or 3 times, until the roast is nicely browned. Serve the remaining plum sauce on the side for dipping.

Baked Spaghetti

SERVES 10

Dora Charles—my head cook, my soul sister, and my friend—really puts her big toe in this dish. In fact, **Fodor's Travel Guide** *called it "The Best Baked Spaghetti in the South." Go, Dora! (P.S. Dora doesn't really put her toe in this, that's just a Southern expression we use when someone has done a dish just right!)*

2 cups canned diced tomatoes
2 cups tomato sauce
1 cup water
½ cup diced onions
½ cup diced green bell peppers
2 cloves garlic, chopped
¼ cup chopped fresh parsley
1½ teaspoons Italian seasoning
1½ teaspoons The Lady's House Seasoning

1½ teaspoon The Lady's Seasoned Salt
1½ teaspoons sugar
2 small bay leaves
1½ pounds ground beef
8 ounces uncooked angelhair pasta
1 cup grated Cheddar cheese
1 cup grated Monterey Jack cheese

To make the sauce, in a stockpot, combine the tomatoes, tomato sauce, water, onions, peppers, garlic, parsley, seasoning mixtures, sugar, and bay leaves. Bring to a boil, then reduce the heat and simmer, covered, for 1 hour. Crumble the ground beef in a saucepan. Cook until no pink remains, then drain off the fat. Add the ground beef to the stockpot. Simmer for another 20 minutes. While the sauce simmers, cook the pasta according to the package directions. Cover the bottom of a 13 × 9 × 2-inch pan with sauce. Add a layer of pasta, then half of the cheese; repeat the layers, ending with the sauce. Bake at 350 degrees for 30 minutes. Top with the remaining cheese, return to the oven, and continue to cook until the cheese is melted and bubbly. Cut into squares before serving. ❦ ❦ ❦ **The Lady & Sons**

Pepper Steak

SERVES 4–6

¼ cup vegetable oil
1½ pounds round steak, trimmed
   of fat and cut in strips
1 cup water
1 medium onion, sliced
½ teaspoon garlic salt
¼ teaspoon ground ginger

2 medium green bell peppers, cut
   into strips
2 tablespoons soy sauce
2–3 teaspoons sugar
1 tablespoon cornstarch
2 tomatoes, cut into wedges

Heat the oil in a large, heavy pot. Add the meat and brown for 5 minutes. Stir in the water, onion, garlic salt, and ginger. Bring to a boil, cover, reduce the heat, and simmer for 15 minutes. After 10 minutes, add the peppers. Stir together the soy sauce, sugar, and cornstarch. Pour this into the pot and stir until the liquid thickens. Place tomato wedges on top of the meat and bring to a boil. Simmer for 5 minutes longer. Serve over rice.   🦋 🦋 🦋   *The Lady & Sons*

Venison Wellington with Oyster Pâté

SERVES 4

1½–2 pounds venison tenderloin
   (backstrap works, too)
Salt and pepper
Vegetable oil
1 tablespoon butter
2 ounces peeled shallots, finely
   chopped
1 clove garlic, finely chopped
4 ounces mushrooms, finely
   chopped

12 ounces shucked May River
   Oysters (or the best oysters
   available in your area),
   drained of liquor and picked
   free of any broken shells
1 tablespoon dry sherry
2 tablespoons fresh breadcrumbs
Sour Cream Pastry (recipe
   follows)
1 egg, beaten with 1 teaspoon
   water

Preheat the oven to 450 degrees. Rub the tenderloin with salt and pepper and brush it lightly with oil. Heat a skillet over medium-high heat and lightly sear all surfaces of the meat, including the ends. Remove the meat from the pan and set aside. Melt the butter over high heat; add the shallots and garlic and sauté for 2 to 3 minutes. Add the mushrooms and sauté for 2 to 3 minutes longer. Add the oysters and sherry, and cook until the oysters are opaque. Remove from the heat and allow to cool slightly. Drain off any liquid and combine the mixture with the breadcrumbs in the bowl of a food processor. Process until well blended and nearly smooth. Line a colander with several layers of cheesecloth and spoon the pâté into it. Allow to drain for 10 to 15 minutes. If the pâté seems too wet, pick up the edge of the cheesecloth, twist it together, and wring out the excess liquid.

Roll the pastry dough out on a lightly floured surface to form a rectangle less than ¼ inch thick. Spoon some pâté into the center of the dough and spread it to form a shape similar to that of the tenderloin. Place the venison on the pâté, then cover the top and sides of the meat with the remaining pâté. Wrap the pastry around the venison, overlapping the edges to form a seam. Moisten the edges with water and pinch lightly to seal. Trim the top layer of pastry from both ends and fold the ends up over the sides of the venison, sealing as before. Carefully turn over the pastry-wrapped tenderloin and place seam-side down on a lightly greased baking sheet. Brush with the beaten egg. Decorate the top with designs cut from the pastry scraps. Brush the cutouts with beaten egg. Bake the tenderloin for 15 to 20 minutes, or until the pastry is golden brown. Remove from the oven and let stand in a warm place for 10 minutes before carving.

VARIATIONS: For those who don't care for oysters, a mushroom duxelles may be used instead of pâté. Substitute 8 ounces of finely chopped fresh mushrooms (any kind will do) for the oysters, and follow the above procedure. You may also substitute a beef tenderloin for the venison.

SOUR CREAM PASTRY

1½ cups all-purpose flour　　　　*½ cup sour cream*
½ teaspoon salt
¾ cup (1½ sticks) unsalted butter,
chilled

Combine the flour and salt in a food processor and pulse once or twice
to mix. Cut the butter into chunks and add it to the processor. Process
until the mixture resembles coarse cornmeal. Add the sour cream and
pulse until the dough forms a ball. Remove the dough and knead it a
few times. Wrap the dough in waxed paper and refrigerate for at least
1 hour. The dough can be frozen for up to 1 month; allow it to thaw
partially before rolling.

Wayne's Beef Macaroni and Cheese

SERVES 8–10

One 1-pound box elbow macaroni　　*3 cups canned crushed tomatoes*
2 tablespoons vegetable oil　　　　*Salt and pepper*
2 cups chopped green bell pepper　　*1 teaspoon each dried basil,*
2 cups chopped onion　　　　　　　　*cumin, and dried oregano*
1 tablespoon chopped garlic　　　　*2–3 cups grated Cheddar cheese*
2 pounds lean ground beef

Cook the macaroni according to package directions; drain and set
aside. Heat the oil in a skillet; add the peppers, onion, and garlic, and
sauté until soft. Add the ground beef and sauté until browned. Add the
tomatoes, salt and pepper to taste, and the basil, cumin, and oregano.
In a large bowl, combine the macaroni and the beef mixture. Spread
this mixture in a 9 × 13-inch baking dish. Top with the cheese and
bake at 350 degrees for 20 to 25 minutes, or until the cheese is lightly
browned and bubbly. Ground turkey or chicken can be used in place of
beef, if desired.

The Lady's Pork Stew

SERVES 8–10

One 3-pound Boston butt roast,
    trimmed of exterior fat
2 tablespoons Dale's Steak
    Seasoning
1½ teaspoons The Lady's House
    Seasoning
1½ teaspoons The Lady's Seasoned
    Salt
1 teaspoon garlic salt
2 tablespoons vegetable oil
6 cups water

1 medium onion, cut into wedges
2 bay leaves
Salt and pepper
1½ cups sliced carrots
3 medium turnips, skin on, cut
    into wedges
3 medium red potatoes, skin on,
    cut into wedges
3 tablespoons cornstarch
⅓ cup cold water

Rub the meat well with the Dale's Seasoning, House Seasoning, Seasoned Salt, and garlic salt—in that order. If time allows, let the roast sit for 1 hour at room temperature. Heat the oil in a Dutch oven. Cook the roast on all sides until browned. Add the 6 cups of water, the onion, and the bay leaves. Bring to a boil, reduce the heat, cover, and simmer for 1½ to 2 hours. Remove the meat from the pot and allow to cool. Cut the pork into chunks. While meat is cooling, taste the stock and add salt and pepper, if necessary. Add the carrots, turnips, and potatoes to the Dutch oven and return to a boil. Cover, reduce the heat, and cook for 15 minutes or until the vegetables are tender. Stir the cornstarch into the ⅓ cup water. Pour this into the pot and stir until the liquid thickens. Return the pork to the pot and simmer for 10 to 15 minutes longer.   ❦ ❦ ❦ *The Lady & Sons*

St. Paddy's Day Corned Beef and Cabbage

SERVES 8

Savannah holds the second largest St. Patrick's Day celebration in the United States. It is quite a sight to see: Our city turns green and corned beef and cabbage is everyone's favorite dish for the day.

One 3-pound corned beef brisket
1 large head green cabbage*
4–6 tablespoons butter

1–2 teaspoons The Lady's House
   Seasoning

Place the corned beef in a large stockpot and cover it with cold water to nearly fill pot. Some corned beef comes with a sealed packet of seasoning. If yours does, add it to the pot. Bring to a boil, reduce the heat, cover, and simmer for 2½ to 3 hours, or until the beef is firm but tender to the fork. Remove the beef from the pot. When the corned beef is almost done, chop the cabbage. (If it has a lot of outside dark green leaves, chop them separately and set aside. These leaves add beautiful color to the dish, but they are tougher and require a little more cooking time, so put them in the pot about 10 minutes before you add the remaining cabbage.) Place the cabbage in a colander and rinse it with cool water. When you are ready to add the cabbage, in a separate pot, melt the butter over medium-high heat. Immediately add the cabbage to the pot, leaving as much water as possible on the leaves. Cook, stirring until the cabbage is well coated with butter. Sprinkle with the House Seasoning. Cover the pot and simmer until the cabbage is tender but still somewhat crisp, 7 to 10 minutes.

Slice the corned beef thinly across the grain. Place the cabbage in a serving dish and place the sliced corned beef on top. You can drizzle a spoonful or two of stock from the pot over the corned beef and cabbage, if you like. Serve with mashed potatoes and Corny Corn Muffins (see page 320). Leftover corned beef makes wonderful sandwiches.

❦ ❦ ❦ *The Lady & Sons*

*When we're serving cabbage without the corned beef, we season the pot with a little bacon along with the butter: Fry 2 to 3 strips of cut-up bacon along with the butter until the bacon is about half done, then proceed with the recipe.

Sausage with Ravishing Rice

SERVES 10–12

1 pound fresh sausage
5 cups water
1 cup raw long-grain white rice
2 packages dry chicken noodle soup
* mix from a 4.2-ounce box*
1 cup chopped onion
1 large green bell pepper, chopped
1 cup finely chopped celery

¼ cup (½ stick) butter
½ teaspoon The Lady's Seasoned
* Salt*
1 teaspoon The Lady's House
* Seasoning*
¼ cup chopped fresh parsley
¼ cup slivered almonds
⅛ teaspoon paprika

Preheat the oven to 350 degrees. Crumble the sausage and cook in a skillet over medium heat until nicely browned; drain well and set aside. In a large, heavy pot, bring the water to a boil, add the rice and soup mix, and cook for 10 minutes, stirring occasionally. Add the sausage, onion, bell pepper, celery, butter, seasonings, and parsley. Pour into a greased 2-quart casserole, top with almonds, and sprinkle with paprika. Bake the casserole for 40 to 50 minutes, or until all liquid is absorbed.

Dixieland Pork Chops

SERVES 4–8

1½–2 pounds thin pork chops (8
* chops)*
½ cup all-purpose flour
3 tablespoons vegetable oil
½ cup chopped onions
1 clove garlic, minced
One 10¾-ounce can Cheddar
* cheese soup*

One 7-ounce can broiled
* mushrooms with broth*
1 tablespoon Worcestershire sauce
1 teaspoon The Lady's House
* Seasoning*

Dredge the pork chops in the flour. Reserve the excess flour. Heat the oil in a large skillet, add two or three chops, and brown them on both sides until half done. Repeat with the remaining chops. Remove the meat from the skillet and add the onions and garlic (if necessary, add a little more oil to the pan). Sauté until the onions are golden. Sprinkle the reserved flour over the onions and stir until blended. Add the soup, mushrooms, Worcestershire sauce, and House Seasoning. Simmer, stirring, until the sauce is hot and bubbly. Place a layer of pork chops in a $13 \times 9 \times 2$-inch casserole; pour half the sauce over the chops, then add another layer of chops, and top with the remaining sauce. Bake at 275 degrees for an hour and a half, until the pork chops are tender. Serve over hot creamy grits, white rice, or egg noodles.

❦ ❦ ❦ *The Lady & Sons*

Barbecued Short Ribs

SERVES 4

*2 pounds short ribs, cut in 2-inch
    pieces
Salt
¼ cup minced onion
½ cup ketchup
¼ cup water*

*2 tablespoons fresh lemon juice
2 tablespoons brown sugar
1 tablespoon prepared mustard
⅛ teaspoon salt
1 tablespoon Worcestershire sauce*

Trim the top layer of fat from the short ribs. Place several pieces of this fat in a Dutch oven, and cook over medium heat until the bottom is lightly coated with fat. Remove the pot from the heat. Sprinkle the short ribs with salt, then brown them on all sides, removing pieces as they are done. Add the onion and sauté until lightly browned. Return the short ribs to the pot and add the ketchup, water, lemon juice, sugar, mustard, salt, and Worcestershire sauce. Cover the pot and cook over low heat for 2 hours, or until tender, stirring occasionally. Or, you may finish cooking the short ribs in the covered pot in a 300-degree oven.

Texas-Style Chili

YIELDS ABOUT 5 QUARTS

3 pounds ground chuck
1 pound hot bulk sausage
3 medium onions, chopped
4 cloves garlic, minced
¼ cup chili powder
2 tablespoons all-purpose flour
1 tablespoon sugar

1 tablespoon dried oregano
1 teaspoon salt
Two 28-ounce cans whole tomatoes,
    chopped, with their juice
Three 16-ounce cans kidney beans,
    or Bush's hot chili beans,
    drained

Combine the ground chuck, sausage, onions, and garlic in a Dutch oven. Cook over medium heat until the meat is browned; stir the meat to break it up as it cooks. Drain off the pan drippings. Stir in chili powder, flour, sugar, oregano, and salt, and stir well to mix. Cover, and simmer for 1 hour, stirring occasionally. Add the tomatoes, beans, and simmer for 20 minutes longer. ❦ ❦ ❦ *The Lady & Sons*

Ron's Tybee Island Sausage Pie

SERVES 6

1 pound ground sausage
1 tablespoon butter
⅓ cup chopped onion
¾ cup milk
One 3-ounce package cream cheese
3 eggs
1 cup shredded Cheddar cheese

½ teaspoon Worcestershire sauce
½ teaspoon salt (use less if the
    sausage is salty)
⅛ teaspoon pepper
One 9-inch deep-dish pie crust,
    partially baked and cooled

Preheat the oven to 375 degrees. In a heavy skillet over medium heat, crumble the sausage with a fork. Sauté the sausage until completely cooked. Drain off the fat, remove the sausage, and set aside. Melt the butter in another skillet over medium heat. Sauté the onions in the butter until tender. Add the milk and heat until steam rises, but do not boil the milk. Cut the cream cheese into small pieces, add it to the onion mixture, and remove the pan from the heat. In a large bowl, beat the eggs, then add the Cheddar, the onion mixture, the Worcestershire, salt, and pepper. Mix thoroughly and pour this into the pie crust. Top with cooked sausage, and bake for 30 minutes, or until set.

Steak Diane

SERVES 4

6 tablespoons butter
½ cup sliced mushrooms
2 tablespoons minced onion
1 clove garlic, crushed
1 teaspoon fresh lemon juice

1 teaspoon Worcestershire sauce
⅛ teaspoon salt
2 tablespoons snipped fresh parsley
1 pound beef tenderloin, cut into 8
   slices

Melt 4 tablespoons of the butter in a large skillet over medium heat. Add the mushrooms, onions, garlic, lemon juice, Worcestershire sauce, and salt, and cook, stirring, until the mushrooms are tender. Stir in the parsley; pour the sauce into a small metal bowl or saucepan, cover, and keep warm. Melt the remaining 2 tablespoons of butter in the skillet. Cook the steaks over medium-high heat, turning them once, for 3 to 4 minutes on each side for medium. Serve the steaks with the mushroom sauce.

Barbecue Meat Loaf

SERVES 6

1½ pounds ground beef
1 cup fresh breadcrumbs
1 onion, chopped
1 egg, lightly beaten
1½ teaspoons salt
½ teaspoon pepper

Two 8-ounce cans tomato sauce
½ cup water
3 tablespoons vinegar
3 tablespoons brown sugar
2 tablespoons prepared mustard
2 tablespoons Worcestershire sauce

Mix together the beef, breadcrumbs, onion, egg, salt, pepper, and ½ cup of the tomato sauce. Form this mixture into a loaf and place it in a shallow pan. Stir together the remaining tomato sauce, the water, vinegar, sugar, mustard, and Worcestershire. Pour this sauce over the meatloaf. Bake at 350 degrees for 1 hour, basting occasionally with the pan juices. ❦ ❦ ❦ **The Lady & Sons**

Perfect Char-Grilled Filet Mignon

SERVES 2

One 8-ounce bottle zesty Italian
   salad dressing
2 beef tenderloin fillets,
   1½–2 inches thick

2 slices bacon
2 tablespoons Lea and Perrins
   Steak Sauce
2 teaspoons water

Pour the salad dressing into a shallow pan, place the steaks in the pan, and let them marinate for 3 to 4 hours.

Prepare a fire in a charcoal grill. Wrap a strip of bacon around each steak, securing it with a toothpick. Grill the steaks over hot coals for about 8 minutes per side (5 minutes per side for rare). Baste with a mixture of steak sauce and water. For perfect steaks, turn them only once.

Hot Savannah Chicken Salad Casserole

SERVES 8–10

Two 10¾-ounce cans condensed
   cream of chicken soup
1½ cups mayonnaise
1 tablespoon prepared mustard
1 tablespoon Worcestershire sauce
One 10-ounce bag potato chips,
   crushed

½ cup slivered almonds
4 cups cubed cooked chicken
2 cups diced celery
¼ cup finely chopped onion
4 hard-boiled eggs, sliced

Lightly butter a $13 \times 9 \times 2$-inch casserole. Stir together the soup, mayonnaise, mustard, and Worcestershire sauce. In a medium bowl, reserve 1 cup of the potato chips and 2 tablespoons of the almonds for the topping. Place half of the remaining potato chips in the casserole, spreading them evenly. Place half each of the chicken, celery, onion, eggs, and remaining almonds in the casserole, then spread half of the soup mixture on top. Repeat the layers, ending with the reserved potato chips and almonds. Bake at 350 degrees for 30 to 40 minutes, or until heated through.

Mexican Chicken

SERVES 8

One 10¾-ounce can cream of
  chicken soup
One 10¾-ounce can Cheddar
  cheese soup
One 10¾-ounce can cream of
  mushroom soup
One 10-ounce can Ro-Tel
  tomatoes

1 whole chicken, cooked, boned,
  and chopped, or 4 cups leftover
  cooked chicken
One 11½-ounce package flour
  tortillas
2 cups shredded Cheddar cheese

In a large bowl, stir together the three kinds of soup and the tomatoes. Stir in the chicken. In a greased 13×9-inch pan, layer the tortillas and the chicken mixture, beginning and ending with tortillas. Sprinkle the cheese over the casserole and bake at 350 degrees for 30 minutes.

❧ ❧ ❧ *The Lady & Sons*

Hurry-Up Chicken Pot Pie

SERVES 4–6

This casual dish is a shortcut version of the lavish Chicken Pot Pie on our dinner menu.

2 cups chopped cooked chicken
  breast
2 hard-boiled eggs, sliced
½ cup thinly sliced carrots
½ cup frozen green peas
1 cup chicken broth

One 10¾-ounce can cream of
  chicken soup
Salt and pepper (optional)
1 cup Lady & Sons Biscuit Mix
1 cup milk
½ cup (1 stick) melted butter

In a greased 2-quart casserole, layer the chicken, eggs, carrots, and peas. Mix the broth with the soup, and season with salt and pepper, if desired. Pour over the layers. Stir together the Biscuit Mix and milk, and pour this over the casserole. Drizzle butter over the topping. Bake at 350 degrees until the topping is golden brown, 30 to 40 minutes.

❦ ❦ ❦ *The Lady & Sons*

Quail with Marsala Sauce

SERVES 8 AS AN APPETIZER, 4 AS A MAIN DISH

4 slices bacon
4–8 dressed quail
Salt and pepper
1 tablespoon olive oil
1 tablespoon butter
8 ounces fresh mushrooms, sliced
2 ounces shallots, minced

1 clove garlic, minced
1 tablespoon all-purpose flour
1¼ cups chicken broth
3 ounces Marsala
½ cup sour cream
1½ cups cooked white rice
1½ cups cooked wild rice

In a large skillet, cook the bacon over medium heat until crisp; crumble the bacon and set aside. Drain all but 1 tablespoon bacon fat from the pan. Rub the quail with salt and pepper, and brown them on all sides in the skillet over medium-high heat. Place the quail in a single layer in a 13 × 9-inch casserole. Add the oil and butter to the pan. Over medium heat, add the mushrooms, shallots, and garlic; sauté until the mushrooms begin to release their liquid. Remove the mushrooms from the pan with a slotted spoon and put them in the casserole. Stir the flour into the hot fat in the pan and cook, stirring until the roux begins to bubble and brown (take care not to burn it). Add the broth and Marsala; when the mixture begins to thicken, remove the pan from the heat and whisk in the sour cream. Pour the sauce over the quail and mushrooms. Bake in a 350-degree oven until the sauce is bubbly and quail has cooked through, 15 to 20 minutes. Combine the white rice and wild rice in a bowl and keep warm. Serve the quail on a bed of rice with the Marsala sauce and mushrooms spooned on top.

Chicken with Drop Dumplin's

SERVES 6–8

One 3–4-pound chicken, cut up
2 stalks celery, diced
2 tablespoons chicken bouillon
   granules
1 bay leaf
8 cups water
2 cups all-purpose flour
4 teaspoons baking powder
1 teaspoon salt

¾ cup milk
½ cup green onion tops, chopped
Pinch of cayenne pepper
½ cup chopped fresh parsley
¼ teaspoon freshly grated nutmeg
One 10¾-ounce can cream of
   chicken soup
Salt and pepper

Place the chicken pieces, celery, bouillon granules, and bay leaf in a stockpot. Add the water and bring to a boil over medium-high heat. Reduce the heat and cook for 45 minutes to 1 hour, or until the chicken is tender. Remove the chicken and let it cool slightly. Pick the meat off of the bones, discarding the bones and skin; set aside.

Sift the flour, baking powder, and salt into a large bowl. Add the milk and mix well. Add the onions and cayenne, and mix. Drop the batter by tablespoons into the boiling broth until all the batter is used up. Gently shake the pot. (Never stir dumplings with a spoon, as this will tear them up.) Add the parsley and nutmeg, and shake the pot again. Cover, reduce the heat, and simmer gently for about 15 minutes without lifting the lid.

While the dumplings are cooking, heat the soup with 1 can of water in a small saucepan. When the dumplings are done, carefully pour the soup into the dumpling pot. Shake the pot gently. Return the chicken to the pot and again shake the pot, this time in a rotating motion. Season to taste with salt and pepper.

❦ ❦ ❦   The Lady & Sons

Basil Grilled Chicken

SERVES 4

¾ teaspoon coarsely ground black pepper
4 skinned chicken breast halves
¼ cup chopped fresh basil, plus 2 tablespoons minced fresh basil
⅓ cup (5 tablespoons) butter, melted, plus ½ cup (1 stick) butter, at room temperature

1 tablespoon grated Parmesan
¼ teaspoon garlic powder
⅛ teaspoon salt
⅛ teaspoon pepper
Fresh basil sprigs (optional)

Prepare a fire in a charcoal grill. Press the coarsely ground pepper into the meaty side of the chicken breast halves. Stir the chopped basil into the melted butter. Brush the chicken lightly with this mixture. In a small bowl, combine the softened butter, minced basil, Parmesan, garlic powder, salt, and pepper. Beat at low speed with an electric mixer until smoothly blended. Transfer to a small serving bowl; set aside.

Grill the chicken over medium coals for 8 to 10 minutes on each side, basting frequently with the remaining melted butter mixture.

Serve the grilled chicken with the basil-butter mixture. Garnish with fresh basil sprigs if desired.

Chicken Bog

SERVES 10–12

One 3-pound chicken, quartered
1 pound smoked link sausage
1 cup chopped onion
½ cup (1 stick) butter

2 teaspoons The Lady's Seasoned Salt
2 teaspoons The Lady's House Seasoning

1 teaspoon ground red pepper

1 teaspoon ground black pepper

3 bay leaves

8 cups water

3 cups raw white rice

Slice the sausage into ½-inch pieces. In a stockpot, combine the chicken, sausage, onion, butter, and seasonings. Add the water, bring to a boil, cover, and cook at a low boil for 40 minutes. Remove the chicken from the pot and let cool slightly. Pick the meat from the bones, discarding the bones and skin. Add the rice to the pot and bring to a boil, stirring well. Boil for 10 minutes, then reduce the heat, cover the pot, and simmer for 10 minutes, or until the rice is done. Remove the bay leaves, and return the chicken to the pot.

❧ ❧ ❧ **The Lady & Sons**

Chicken Casserole

Fair decent sauce

SERVES 6

2 cups cubed cooked chicken

2 cups breadcrumbs

1 cup cooked rice

1 cup milk

One 2-ounce jar pimentos, finely chopped

1½ teaspoons salt

Pinch of cayenne pepper

4 eggs, well beaten

One 10¾-ounce can cream of mushroom soup

1 cup heavy cream

In a large bowl, combine the chicken, breadcrumbs, rice, milk, pimentos, salt, and cayenne. Stir in the eggs. Pour the mixture into a buttered 2-quart baking dish and bake at 325 degrees for 1 hour. For the sauce, in a small saucepan stir together the soup and cream and heat until bubbly. Serve the sauce on the side.

❧ ❧ ❧ **The Lady & Sons**

Fricasé de Pollo

SERVES 4

4 boneless chicken breast halves
1 large tomato, peeled and diced
2 cloves garlic, minced
2 bay leaves
1 teaspoon dried oregano
¼ teaspoon black pepper
½ cup white wine
One 8-ounce can tomato sauce

1 medium onion, diced
12 pitted green olives
1 tablespoon capers
1½ teaspoons olive oil
1 green bell pepper, sliced
Salt
One 2-ounce jar pimentos

Put all the ingredients except the pimentos in a Dutch oven on top of the stove. Over medium heat, bring to a boil. Reduce the heat and cook until the chicken is tender. Stir in the pimentos. Serve the fricasé over rice.

Chicken Boudine

SERVES 8–10

2 cups freshly cooked egg noodles
Two 10¾-ounce cans cream of
   mushroom soup
½ cup chicken broth
¼ cup dry sherry
4 cups chopped cooked chicken
3 cups grated sharp cheese

One 2¼-ounce package slivered
   almonds, toasted
½ cup drained, chopped pimentos
One 4-ounce can sliced
   mushrooms, drained
Salt and pepper

In a large bowl, toss together the noodles, soup, broth, and sherry. Add the chicken, 2 cups of the cheese, the almonds, pimento, mushrooms, and salt and pepper to taste, and toss gently to combine. Transfer the mixture to a greased 13 × 9 × 2-inch casserole and top with the remaining cup of cheese.

Bake at 350 degrees for 30 minutes, or until bubbly.

Chicken Florentine

SERVES 6–8

Two 10-ounce packages frozen
  spinach (or chopped broccoli)
Two 10¾-ounce cans cream of
  mushroom soup
1 cup mayonnaise
1 cup sour cream
1 cup grated sharp Cheddar cheese
¼ cup white wine or sherry

1 tablespoon fresh lemon juice
1 teaspoon curry powder
Salt and pepper
6 cooked chicken breast halves,
  shredded
½ cup grated Parmesan
½ cup breadcrumbs

Cook and drain the spinach; set aside. In a large bowl, mix together
the soup, mayonnaise, sour cream, Cheddar, wine, lemon juice, curry
powder, and salt and pepper to taste. Spread the chicken in a greased
13 × 9-inch casserole. Cover the chicken with spinach, then pour the
soup mixture over the spinach. Combine the Parmesan and breadcrumbs and sprinkle this over the casserole. Bake at 350 degrees for 30
minutes.

Pat's Almond Chicken Casserole

SERVES 8–10

*This casserole can be prepared in advance and refrigerated or frozen. Thaw
the frozen casserole in the refrigerator overnight before baking.*

8 boneless chicken breast halves
One 2¼-ounce package sliced
  almonds
One 10¾-ounce can cream of
  celery soup
One 10¾-ounce can cream of
  chicken soup

One 10¾-ounce can cream of
  mushroom soup
1 cup sour cream
½ cup chopped celery
3 tubes Ritz Crackers, crushed
¾ cup (1½ sticks) melted butter

Place the chicken in a large, deep skillet and add water to cover. Cook over medium heat for 30 minutes, or until tender.

Meanwhile, place the almonds in a shallow pan and toast in a 300-degree oven for 5 minutes, or until pale golden brown. Watch closely—almonds can scorch quickly. Tip the almonds into a plate and set aside.

Drain and cool the chicken and tear it into bite-size pieces. Put the chicken in a large bowl and add the three cans of soup, the sour cream, and the celery; mix well. Spread the chicken mixture in a greased 13 × 9-inch pan. Mix the crackers and butter, and cover the casserole with the crumbs. Bake at 350 degrees for 30 minutes, or until bubbly.

Saucy Chicken and Asparagus Bake

SERVES 4

1½ pounds fresh asparagus spears, trimmed and halved
2 tablespoons vegetable oil
4 boneless chicken breast halves
½ teaspoon salt
¼ teaspoon pepper

One 10¾-ounce can cream of chicken soup
½ cup mayonnaise
1 teaspoon fresh lemon juice
1 cup shredded Cheddar cheese

If the asparagus spears are thick or seem tough, cook them in boiling water for 2 minutes; drain. Place the asparagus in a greased 9 × 9-inch baking dish. Heat the oil in a skillet over medium heat; add the chicken and brown on both sides; season with salt and pepper. Arrange the chicken over the asparagus. In a bowl, mix the soup, mayonnaise, and lemon juice; pour this over the chicken. Cover and bake at 375 degrees for 40 minutes, or until the chicken is tender and its juices run clear. Sprinkle the dish with the cheese and let stand for 5 minutes so the cheese melts. 🌿 🌿 🌿 **The Lady & Sons**

Szechuan Chicken with Angelhair Pasta

SERVES 4

1 tablespoon dark sesame oil
¼ cup chili-garlic sauce (found in the Asian section of your grocery store)
4 boneless chicken breast halves
1 pound angelhair pasta
1½ pounds broccoli crowns, cut into florets

1 red bell pepper, cut into ½-inch strips
1 yellow bell pepper, cut into ½-inch strips
12 green onions
2 cloves garlic, minced
¼ cup soy sauce
1½ teaspoons minced fresh ginger

Heat the oil and 2 tablespoons of the chili-garlic sauce in a large skillet over medium heat; add the chicken, and cook for 4 minutes on each side, or until cooked through. Meanwhile bring a large pot of water to a boil for pasta. Add pasta to boiling water, cook as directed on package, and drain. Remove the chicken from the pan and cut it into strips. Add the broccoli, bell peppers, green onions, garlic, remaining chili-garlic sauce, soy sauce, and ginger to the skillet. Cook the vegetables, stirring until they are crisp-tender. Add the chicken strips and cook until heated through. Serve over the pasta.

Savannah Gumbo

SERVES 10–12

2 tablespoons all-purpose flour
2 tablespoons butter
1 onion, chopped
1 green bell pepper, chopped
1 tablespoon chopped garlic (2–3 cloves)
2 cups diced or sliced smoked sausage
4 large boneless chicken breasts, diced

4 cups chicken broth
One 28-ounce can diced tomatoes
2 cups cut okra
1 teaspoon dried thyme
2 bay leaves
½ teaspoon cayenne pepper
1 teaspoon filé powder
Salt and pepper

In a 5-quart pot combine the flour and butter and cook over medium heat, stirring constantly, until the roux has browned to a light chocolate color. Add the onion, pepper, and garlic, and sauté for 2 minutes. Add the sausage, chicken, broth, tomatoes, okra, thyme, bay leaves, and cayenne, and simmer over low heat for 45 to 50 minutes. Add the filé powder and salt and pepper to taste. Remove and discard the bay leaves. Serve the gumbo over rice. For an extra special pot of gumbo, throw in some peeled shrimp before adding the filé.

❦ ❦ ❦ *The Lady & Sons*

Chicken and Wild Rice Casserole

SERVES 8

One 6-ounce package long-grain and wild rice, cooked according to directions
4 cups diced cooked chicken breast
Two 10¾-ounce cans cream of chicken soup

1 cup mayonnaise
2 teaspoons curry powder, or to taste
One 8-ounce package Pepperidge Farm Cornbread Dressing Mix
¼ cup (½ stick) butter

Put the rice in a greased 2-quart casserole. Layer the chicken on top of the rice. Mix the soup, mayonnaise, and curry powder, and pour this over the chicken. Sprinkle the dressing mix over the casserole and dot with butter. Bake at 350 degrees for 30 minutes or until bubbly.

Vegetables and Side Dishes

Fancy Green Beans

Sweet Potato Casserole

Southern-Style Black-Eyed Peas

Tomato Casserole

Saturday Night Vidalia Onions

Corn Casserole

Jelly Roll's Crab Fried Rice

Oven-Roasted Red Potatoes with Rosemary and Garlic

Tomato Grits

Swiss Broccoli Casserole

Sweet Potato Yams

Turnips in Dijon Sauce

Green Rice Casserole

Squash Casserole

Sweet Potato Balls

Mushroom Rice Casserole

Vidalia Onion Casserole

Sweet Stewed Tomatoes

Curry-Crusted Bananas

Mixed Vegetable Casserole

Crunchy New Potatoes

Snow Peas with Grand Marnier

Oven-Fried Potato Wedges

Fried Green Tomatoes with Dijon Pepper Dippin' Sauce

Crème Fraîche Mashed Potatoes

Spicy Tomato Red Rice

Okra Fritters

Sausage-Almond Rice

Crockpot Pinto Beans

Mashed Potato Bake

Cheese Noodles

Italian Potatoes

Noodle Casserole

Corn Chive Pudding

Half-Baked Potato

Cottage Potatoes

Vegetable Pancakes

Hash Brown Potato Casserole

Asparagus Casserole

Pimento Cheese Tomato Bake

Roasted Onions

Green Bean Casserole

Baked Wild Rice

Bo's Eggplant Supreme

Fancy Green Beans

SERVES 6–8

2 tablespoons teriyaki sauce
1 tablespoon honey
1 tablespoon butter
1 tablespoon fresh lemon juice
1½ pounds fresh green beans,
    preferably thin ones, trimmed

2 slices bacon
½ cup red bell pepper, cut into
    strips
½ cup thin onion wedges
½ cup whole cashews

In a small bowl, stir together the teriyaki sauce, honey, and butter. Fill a bowl with cold water and ice cubes. Bring a large pot of water to a boil and add the lemon juice. Drop in the beans and cook for 4 to 5 minutes, or until the beans are bright green. Drain the beans in a colander, then plunge them into ice water; drain again and set aside (this may be done in advance). In a skillet, cook the bacon until very crisp; crumble and set aside. Sauté the bell pepper and onion in the hot bacon fat for 2 minutes. Add the beans, cashews, and bacon to the skillet. Add the teriyaki-honey sauce and toss gently.

Sweet Potato Casserole

SERVES 6–8

1 cup packed brown sugar
1 cup chopped pecans
½ cup self-rising flour
½ cup (1 stick) melted butter
3 cups mashed cooked sweet
    potatoes

1 cup granulated sugar
1 cup coconut flakes
½ cup raisins
2 eggs, lightly beaten
1 teaspoon vanilla extract
¼ cup heavy cream (optional)

For the topping, in a bowl combine the brown sugar, nuts, flour, and ¼ cup of the melted butter, and stir together with a fork; set aside. Mix with a fork. In a large bowl, stir together the sweet potatoes, sugar, coconut, raisins, eggs, and vanilla. If the mixture seems too thick, stir in up to ¼ cup heavy cream. Spoon into a large greased casserole. Spread the topping over the sweet potatoes and bake at 350 degrees for 20 to 30 minutes, or until the topping is golden brown.

❦ ❦ ❦ *The Lady & Sons*

Southern-Style Black-Eyed Peas

SERVES 4–6

1 ham hock, about ½ pound (break it down with a knife, if possible)
2 quarts water
One 16-ounce package frozen black-eyed peas, or fresh black-eyed peas
2 tablespoons butter

½ teaspoon The Lady's House Seasoning
¼ teaspoon The Lady's Seasoned Salt
½ teaspoon Texas Pete Hot Sauce, or 1 small hot pepper (fresh or dried)

Put the ham hock in a stockpot and add the water. Bring to a boil, cover, reduce heat to a simmer, and cook for 1 to 1½ hours. The longer you cook the hock, the stronger your stock will be. When the meat is done you may find that you need to add more water (sometimes I need 2 cups more). Add the peas, butter, House Seasoning, Seasoned Salt, and hot sauce, and return the liquid to a boil. Reduce the heat, cover, and cook over low heat for 20 to 30 minutes, or until the peas are done to your liking. Use this same formula for butter beans, butter peas, crowder peas, or any of their cousins. To make your peas extra special, drop pods of fresh or frozen okra in the pot for the last 10 to 15 minutes of cooking time.

Tomato Casserole

SERVES 6–8

3 tablespoons butter
½ cup chopped onion

½ cup chopped green bell pepper
½ cup chopped celery

One 28-ounce can diced tomatoes
½ cup sugar
2–3 tablespoons chopped fresh basil
Salt and pepper

2 tablespoons cornstarch
2 teaspoons vinegar
2 teaspoons water
1½ cups buttered breadcrumbs

Melt the butter in a large skillet. Add the onion, peppers, and celery, and sauté 3 to 5 minutes, until tender. Add the tomatoes, sugar, basil, and salt and pepper to taste, and bring to a boil. Mix the cornstarch with the vinegar and water, and stir into the skillet. Pour the mixture into a greased casserole and sprinkle with the buttered crumbs. Bake at 350 degrees for 30 to 40 minutes. ❦ ❦ ❦ **The Lady & Sons**

Saturday Night Vidalia Onions

When I was first married, back in the late sixties and early seventies, going out to eat was reserved for very special occasions. Because of our tight budgets and young children, our social lives consisted of cooking out with our friends on Saturday nights. When the steaks and Vidalia onions were piled on our plates and we took our first bites, I think for a short while we all forgot that we were as poor as church mice, because we were eating like kings. What fond memories these Vidalia onions bring back!

1 large Vidalia onion, or a com-
    parable sweet onion, per person
1 tablespoon butter per onion

1 beef bouillon cube per onion
Pepper

Prepare a fire in a charcoal grill. Trim a slice from the top of each onion, and peel the onion without cutting off the root end. With a potato peeler, cut a small cone-shaped section from the center of the onion. Cut the onion into quarters from the top down, stopping within a half inch of the root end. Place a bouillon cube in the center, slip slivers of butter in between the sections, and sprinkle with pepper. Wrap each onion in a double thickness of heavy-duty foil. Place the onions directly onto the hot coals and cook for 45 minutes, turning every so often. These can also be baked in a 350-degree oven for 45 minutes, but I still say they're better grilled over charcoal. Serve in individual bowls because they produce a lot of broth, which tastes like French onion soup.

Too sweet

Corn Casserole

NO

SERVES 6–8

One 15¼-ounce can whole kernel
  corn, drained
One 14¾-ounce can cream-style
  corn

One 8-ounce package Jiffy corn
  muffin mix
1 cup sour cream
½ cup (1 stick) melted butter

+ salt + dash pepper

In a large bowl, stir together the two cans of corn, corn muffin mix, sour cream, and butter. Pour into a greased casserole. Bake at 350 degrees for 45 to 60 minutes, or until golden brown.

❦ ❦ ❦ *The Lady & Sons*

Jelly Roll's Crab Fried Rice

SERVES 6–8

This dish is delicious served alongside a nice fresh fish or stuffed inside a fish fillet.

½ cup (1 stick) butter
1 medium onion, diced
1 medium green bell pepper, diced
1 pound claw crabmeat, picked
  free of any broken shells
2 cups cooked white rice

1 teaspoon The Lady's House
  Seasoning
1 teaspoon Accent (optional)
¼ cup chopped fresh parsley

Melt the butter in a large skillet. Add the onions and green pepper and sauté until tender, about 5 minutes. Add the crabmeat, rice, House Seasoning, and Accent, and mix well. Stir in the parsley and simmer over low heat for 15 minutes.

❦ ❦ ❦ *The Lady & Sons*

Oven-Roasted Red Potatoes with Rosemary and Garlic

SERVES 6

1½ pounds small new red potatoes (about 15), scrubbed and dried
¼ cup extra-virgin olive oil

4–6 cloves garlic, crushed
1 tablespoon fresh or 1 teaspoon dried rosemary

Pare a narrow strip of peel from the middle of each potato. In a large bowl mix the oil, garlic, and rosemary; add the potatoes and toss well. Transfer the potatoes to a shallow baking pan and roast at 350 degrees until the potatoes are tender when tested with the tip of a knife. Serve hot. These can also be chilled and served with fried chicken or ham.

Tomato Grits

SERVES 8–10

2 cups water
1¼ cups milk
1 teaspoon salt
1 cup quick-cooking grits
½ cup (1 stick), plus 1 tablespoon butter
⅓ cup diced green onions

One 6-ounce Kraft Garlic Cheese Roll
2½ cups shredded Cheddar cheese
One 10-ounce can Ro-Tel diced tomatoes and green chilies
2 eggs, lightly beaten

Preheat the oven to 350 degrees. In a saucepan, bring the water and milk to a boil. Add the salt. Slowly add the grits and return to a boil; stir for 1 full minute. (The secret to preparing good grits is the initial stirring of the pot.) Reduce the heat, cover, and cook for 3 minutes. Stir the grits and add 1 stick of butter, stirring until it has melted. Cover and cook for 3 to 5 minutes, or until the grits are thick and creamy. Remove from the heat and set aside. Sauté the onions in the remaining 1 tablespoon butter for 1 minute. Add the garlic cheese, 1½ cups Cheddar, and onions to the grits, and stir until the cheese is melted. Add the tomatoes and mix well; stir in the beaten eggs. Pour the grits into a greased 8 × 11 × 2-inch casserole. Bake the casserole for 40 minutes. Sprinkle the remaining cheese over the casserole for the last 5 minutes of cooking time.   ❦ ❦ ❦   *The Lady & Sons*

Swiss Broccoli Casserole

SERVES 6

Two 10-ounce packages frozen broccoli spears, cooked and drained
3 hard-boiled eggs, sliced
2 cups french-fried onion rings

½ cup shredded Swiss cheese
One 10¾-ounce can of cream of celery soup
⅔ cup milk

Preheat the oven to 350 degrees. Arrange the broccoli in a shallow 2-quart baking dish. Layer the eggs, 1 cup of the onion rings, and then the cheese over the broccoli. Combine the soup and milk, mixing well. Pour this over the cheese and bake for 25 minutes. Top with the remaining onion rings and bake for 5 minutes longer.

Sweet Potato Yams

SERVES 4

3 large sweet potatoes
3 cups water
1½ cups sugar
1 teaspoon vanilla extract

4 tablespoons butter
½–1 teaspoon cinnamon
¼ teaspoon freshly grated nutmeg

Wash and dry the sweet potatoes. Bake at 400 degrees for 1 hour, or until the potatoes are soft to the touch. Remove from the oven and let cool slightly. Reduce the oven heat to 350 degrees. While the potatoes are baking, combine the remaining ingredients in a saucepan; bring to a boil, then reduce the heat and simmer for 30 minutes, or until the sauce is slightly thickened. Slice the potatoes ½ inch thick into a medium casserole, pour the sauce over them, and return to the oven for 15 minutes, or until hot.   ❧ ❧ ❧ *The Lady & Sons*

Turnips in Dijon Sauce

SERVES 4–6

*2 medium turnips, peeled and
    sliced
1 medium potato, peeled and
    diced
1 carrot, diced
1 onion, diced*

*1 stalk celery, diced
½ cup mayonnaise
1 tablespoon Dijon mustard
1 tablespoon fresh lemon juice
Freshly ground pepper*

Steam the vegetables for 10 minutes, or until tender. Combine the mayonnaise, mustard, lemon juice, and pepper in a small saucepan and heat gently. Add the vegetables to the sauce and stir to coat the vegetables. Serve immediately.

Green Rice Casserole

SERVES 6–8

*One 10-ounce package frozen
    chopped broccoli
2 cups cooked rice
One 10 ¾-ounce can cream of
    mushroom soup*

*½ cup (1 stick) butter, at room
    temperature
One 8-ounce jar Cheez-Wiz*

Cook the broccoli according to package directions; drain well. In a large bowl, combine the broccoli, rice, soup, and butter. Reserving a small amount for the top of the casserole, add the Cheez-Wiz. Stir until the butter and Cheez-Wiz are blended in. Transfer to a greased casserole and top with remaining Cheez-Wiz. Bake at 325 degrees for 30 minutes, or until the top starts to bubble.

❧ ❧ ❧ *The Lady & Sons*

Squash Casserole

SERVES 4

2 cups cooked mashed yellow squash
2 cups Ritz Cracker crumbs
1 cup evaporated milk
1 cup shredded cheese, such as
   Cheddar or Swiss
1 cup chopped onion

2 eggs, lightly beaten
1 teaspoon salt
1 teaspoon pepper
Pinch of sugar
6 tablespoons butter

Place the squash in a large bowl. Add the cracker crumbs, milk, cheese, and onion, and stir well. Stir in the eggs, salt, pepper, sugar, and butter, and pour into a greased 1-quart casserole. Bake at 350 degrees for 40 minutes.   🌿 🌿 🌿 *The Lady & Sons*

Sweet Potato Balls

SERVES 4–6

4 large sweet potatoes
⅔ cup packed brown sugar
2 tablespoons orange juice
1 teaspoon orange zest
½ teaspoon freshly grated nutmeg

2 cups shredded coconut
½ cup granulated sugar
1 teaspoon cinnamon
8 large marshmallows

Bake the potatoes until tender, then peel and mash them (the potatoes can be baked the day before). Stir in the sugar, orange juice, zest, and nutmeg. Toss the coconut with the sugar and cinnamon. Press mashed potatoes around each marshmallow, then roll the balls in the coconut mixture. Bake at 350 degrees for 15 to 20 minutes. Watch carefully for the last few minutes of cooking; the expanding marshmallows can cause the potato balls to burst open. These are wonderful served with turkey or ham.

Mushroom Rice Casserole

SERVES 4–6

5 tablespoons butter
1 cup sliced fresh mushrooms
1 cup chopped onion
1 cup raw long-grain rice

One 10¾-ounce can cream of
mushroom soup
One 10¾-ounce can beef consommé

Heat the butter in a skillet. Sauté the mushrooms and onions for 3 to 5 minutes, then stir in the rice and sauté for 3 minutes longer, stirring constantly. Stir in the soup and consommé. Pour the mixture into a greased casserole, cover, and bake at 350 degrees for 45 to 60 minutes. Check the rice after 30 minutes; if it is drying out, add a little boiling water. 🐾 🐾 🐾 **The Lady & Sons**

Vidalia Onion Casserole

SERVES 4–6

4 large Vidalia onions, quartered
7 tablespoons butter
3 eggs
One 5-ounce can evaporated milk

1 tube Ritz Crackers, crushed
1½ cups grated Cheddar cheese
Salt and pepper

Boil the onions until tender; drain. Heat 4 tablespoons of the butter in a skillet and sauté the onions. Beat the eggs and milk together. Add the onions, half the cracker crumbs, the cheese, and salt and pepper to taste. Bake in a buttered casserole at 375 degrees for 35 minutes. Melt the remaining 3 tablespoons butter and stir it into the remaining cracker crumbs. Top the casserole with the buttered crumbs and bake for 15 minutes longer. 🐾 🐾 🐾 **The Lady & Sons**

Sweet Stewed Tomatoes

SERVES 6

During the winter months I recommend using canned tomatoes, but in the summer, don't miss the chance to use vine-ripened fresh tomatoes.

5 large fresh tomatoes, or 4 cups
    canned diced tomatoes
4 tablespoons bacon drippings or
    butter
1 cup diced onions
2 cloves garlic, minced
1 teaspoon The Lady's House
    Seasoning

3 tablespoons sugar
2 tablespoons chopped fresh parsley
1 tablespoon cornstarch
3 tablespoons milk
¼ cup grated Parmesan (optional)

If using fresh tomatoes, peel and dice them. Heat the drippings in a skillet and sauté the onions and garlic, stirring to prevent the garlic from burning. Add the House Seasoning and tomatoes, cover the pan, and cook over medium-low heat for 35 minutes. Add the sugar and parsley. Mix the cornstarch and milk until smooth. Bring the tomatoes to a boil and pour in the cornstarch mixture, stirring constantly. Add the Parmesan, if using, and stir well. The stewed tomatoes are wonderful served over rice. 🌺 🌺 🌺 *The Lady & Sons*

Curry-Crusted Bananas

SERVES 8

These bananas—crispy on the outside and soft on the inside—are wonderful served with baked ham, pork chops, or lamb.

4 firm bananas, peeled
6 tablespoons melted butter
1 teaspoon curry powder

2 cups crushed cornflakes
Sugar for sprinkling (optional)

Preheat the oven to 450 degrees. Halve the bananas lengthwise, then crosswise. In a bowl, mix the butter and curry powder. Dip the bananas in butter, coating well. Roll the bananas in the cornflakes until completely coated and sprinkle with sugar, if desired. Place the bananas in a greased baking dish and bake for 10 minutes. ❦ ❦ ❦ *The Lady & Sons*

Mixed Vegetable Casserole

SERVES 6

One 15-ounce can Veg-All, drained
One 8-ounce can sliced water chestnuts, drained
1 cup grated sharp cheese

1 cup chopped celery
¾ cup mayonnaise
1 small onion, chopped
20 Ritz Crackers, crushed
2 tablespoons melted butter

In a large bowl, mix the Veg-All, water chestnuts, cheese, celery, mayonnaise, and onion; transfer to a greased casserole. Bake at 350 degrees for 30 minutes.

Meanwhile, combine the cracker crumbs and butter. When the casserole has baked for 30 minutes, sprinkle it with the buttered crumbs and return it to the oven to brown. ❦ ❦ ❦ *The Lady & Sons*

Crunchy New Potatoes

SERVES 4

12 small new red potatoes
One 0.4-ounce package Hidden Valley Original Ranch Buttermilk Recipe mix

2 cups crushed cornflakes
½ cup (1 stick) melted butter

Cook the potatoes in boiling water until tender, 20 to 25 minutes. Preheat the oven to 400 degrees. Drain the potatoes and let cool slightly, then peel them. Mix dressing mix and the cornflakes in a bowl. Dip the potatoes in melted butter, then roll them in the cornflake mixture. Place the potatoes in a greased baking dish and bake for 20 to 25 minutes, or until golden brown. ❦ ❦ ❦ *The Lady & Sons*

Snow Peas with Grand Marnier

SERVES 8

1 cup water
1 teaspoon sugar
Three 10-ounce packages frozen
   snow peas
One 8-ounce can sliced water
   chestnuts, drained

¼ cup Grand Marnier
5 tablespoons butter
1 tablespoon chopped fresh mint, or
   1½ tablespoons dried mint
1 teaspoon salt

Bring 1 cup of water to a boil and add the sugar. Drop in the snow peas and cook until barely tender, drain, and return to pan. Add the water chestnuts, Grand Marnier, butter, mint, and salt. Cook over medium-low heat until heated through.

Oven-Fried Potato Wedges

SERVES 6

3 large baking potatoes
½ cup mayonnaise
½ teaspoon Texas Pete Hot Sauce
¼ teaspoon onion salt

¼ teaspoon The Lady's Seasoned Salt
⅛ teaspoon black pepper
2 cups Pepperidge Farm
   Cornbread Dressing Mix

Preheat the oven to 375 degrees. Wash the potatoes and cut into thick wedges (each potato should yield six wedges). Mix the mayonnaise with the hot sauce, onion salt, Seasoned Salt, and pepper. Coat the potato wedges with the mayonnaise mixture and roll them in the dressing mix. Place in a greased baking dish and bake for 45 to 50 minutes, or until the potatoes are tender. Goes great with a good ol' char-grilled hamburger.

Fried Green Tomatoes with Dijon Pepper Dippin' Sauce

SERVES 6

This recipe is a new twist on one in **The Lady & Sons Savannah Country Cookbook.** *Dip into the Dijon sauce with care—it's a little on the hot side. We like to put a small dollop of roasted red pepper vinaigrette on each tomato slice.*

3 or 4 large firm green tomatoes	*1 cup buttermilk*
Salt	*2 cups self-rising flour*
2 cups vegetable or peanut oil for deep-frying	*Dijon Pepper Dippin' Sauce (recipe follows)*

Slice the tomatoes ¼ inch thick. Lay them out in a shallow baking pan and sprinkle with salt. Place the tomato slices in a colander and allow time for the salt to pull the water out of the tomatoes (30 minutes should do it).

In a skillet heat the oil for deep-frying over medium-high heat.

Dip the tomatoes into buttermilk, then dredge them in flour. Deep-fry until golden brown.   ❦ ❦ ❦   *The Lady & Sons*

DIJON PEPPER DIPPIN' SAUCE

MAKES 2 CUPS

1 cup Dijon mustard	*½ cup vegetable oil*
½ cup mayonnaise	*1 tablespoon red pepper flakes*
2 tablespoons balsamic vinegar	*1 tablespoon whole peppercorns*
1 tablespoon white pepper	
4 tablespoons coarsely ground black pepper	

In the bowl of a food processor, combine the mustard, mayonnaise, balsamic vinegar, white pepper, and 1 tablespoon of the black pepper, and beat until just blended; set aside.

In a small saucepan combine the oil, the remaining 3 tablespoons of black pepper, the red pepper flakes, and the whole peppercorns. Heat the oil until hot, then reduce the heat to low and simmer for 20 minutes. Allow to cool, then strain. With the food processor running, drizzle the oil into the mayonnaise mixture. Continue processing for 2 minutes.

ং ং ং   *The Lady & Sons*

Crème Fraîche Mashed Potatoes

SERVES 8

1 cup, plus 2 tablespoons heavy
  cream
¾ cup sour cream
2 pounds small red potatoes
1 teaspoon salt
One 8-ounce package cream cheese,
  at room temperature
2 teaspoons roasted garlic (from a
  jar, or homemade)

1 teaspoon The Lady's House
  Seasoning
1 teaspoon The Lady's Seasoned
  Salt
4 tablespoons butter, slivered
¼ cup sliced green onions
1 tablespoon chopped fresh chives

Prepare the crème fraîche ahead of time by combining 1 cup of the heavy cream with ½ cup of the sour cream. Cover with plastic wrap and let stand at room temperature for 12 to 24 hours, or until thick. Stir well and refrigerate for at least 4 hours. Crème fraîche will keep for up to 2 weeks.

Put the potatoes in a pot and cover with cold water. Add the salt and bring to a boil. Cook until the potatoes are tender, 20 to 25 minutes; drain. Preheat the oven to 350 degrees. With an electric mixer, beat the potatoes with the cream cheese, the remaining ¼ cup sour cream, and the 2 tablespoons of heavy cream, the garlic, House Seasoning, and Seasoned Salt. Stir in the butter and onions. Place the mashed potatoes in a lightly greased 2-quart round casserole. Spoon the crème fraîche on top and sprinkle with chives. Bake until the potatoes are hot, 20 to 30 minutes.

ং ং ং   *The Lady & Sons*

Spicy Tomato Red Rice

SERVES 4

4 strips bacon
1 medium onion
1 small green bell pepper
1 cup raw rice
One 14½-ounce can whole
tomatoes, with liquid

1 cup water
One 6-ounce can tomato paste
1 teaspoon sugar
1 teaspoon salt
1 teaspoon hot sauce

Fry the bacon in a heavy saucepan; remove the bacon from the pan and set aside. Sauté the onion and bell pepper in the bacon fat. Add the rice and stir until it is coated with fat; crumble in the bacon. Add the tomatoes, water, tomato paste, sugar, salt, and hot sauce, and bring to a boil. Cook covered over low heat for 20 minutes. Remove from the heat and let stand for 20 minutes longer. *Do not peek!*

❧ ❧ ❧ ***The Lady & Sons***

Okra Fritters

SERVES 4–6

1½ cups all-purpose flour
1 tablespoon The Lady's House
Seasoning
⅓ cup buttermilk

4 cups cut okra, fresh or frozen
(thawed if frozen)
6 cups vegetable oil (for deep-frying)

Mix the flour and House Seasoning. Pour the buttermilk over the okra and toss to coat. Place the okra in the flour mixture and toss; shake off any excess flour. Heat the oil in a cast-iron Dutch oven. When it registers 350 degrees, add the okra and fry until golden brown, 13 to 15 minutes.

❧ ❧ ❧ ***The Lady & Sons***

Sausage-Almond Rice

SERVES 6

3 cups water
One 2.1-ounce package chicken
   noodle soup
1 pound ground pork sausage
1 cup raw rice

1 cup chopped celery
½ cup chopped onion
½ cup chopped green bell pepper
¼ cup sliced almonds

Preheat the oven to 350 degrees. Combine the water and soup mix in a saucepan and simmer for 10 minutes. Meanwhile, brown the sausage and rice in a large skillet. Add the celery, onions, and bell pepper, and mix well. Combine the rice mixture with the soup, add the almonds, and pour into a greased casserole; cover and bake for 1 hour.

Crockpot Pinto Beans

SERVES 8

1 pound dry pinto beans
¼ pound streak o' lean, or
   ½ pound ham hocks*
4 cups water

1 onion, chopped
1 teaspoon chili powder
½ teaspoon dried oregano
The Lady's House Seasoning

Wash the beans and place in a large pot. Add enough cold water to cover and soak overnight.

Drain the beans. If using streak o' lean, cut it into cubes, brown in a skillet, and place the meat and any rendered fat in the crockpot. Add the water, onion, chili powder, and oregano. Add the drained beans and stir well.

Season to taste with House Seasoning, cover the pot, and cook on high for 5 hours.

*If using ham hocks, try to break them down some, using a sharp knife.

Mashed Potato Bake

SERVES 8

5 cups water
4 cups frozen hash brown potatoes
One 7.6-ounce package Betty
  Crocker Butter and Herb
  Mashed Potatoes mix
½ cup (1 stick) butter
4 ounces cream cheese

1 cup Monterey Jack cheese
½ cup sour cream
½ teaspoon garlic salt
½ teaspoon salt
½ teaspoon pepper
2 cups canned french-fried onion
  rings

Preheat the oven to 350 degrees. Bring the water to a boil, add the hash browns, and cook for 5 minutes; drain. Prepare the mashed-potato mix according to package directions. Soften the butter and cream cheese together in the microwave. In a large bowl, mix together the hash browns, mashed potatoes, butter and cream cheese, Jack cheese, sour cream, garlic salt, salt, and pepper. Place in a greased 2-quart casserole. Bake for 25 to 35 minutes, or until golden on top. Sprinkle the onion rings over the casserole and bake for about 5 to 8 minutes longer, or until onions are golden brown.   ❦ ❦ ❦   *The Lady & Sons*

Cheese Noodles

SERVES 6–8

1 cup cottage cheese
1 cup sour cream
One 6-ounce package fine-cut
  noodles, cooked and drained

2 tablespoons grated onion
1 teaspoon Worcestershire sauce
½–¾ teaspoon garlic salt
½ cup grated Parmesan

Stir together the cottage cheese and sour cream, and add this to the noodles. Add the onion, Worcestershire sauce, and garlic salt to taste, and place in a greased casserole. Sprinkle the Parmesan over the casserole and bake at 350 degrees for 45 minutes.

❦ ❦ ❦   *The Lady & Sons*

Italian Potatoes

SERVES 16

14 or 15 large red potatoes (about
     5 pounds)
½ cup chopped fresh parsley
½ cup chopped green onions
3 large cloves garlic, thinly sliced
1 heaping teaspoon salt

½ teaspoon dry mustard
1 scant tablespoon sugar
1 tablespoon Worcestershire sauce
1 cup olive oil
½ cup tarragon vinegar

Boil the potatoes until tender. When done peel and cut in 1-inch chunks. Sprinkle parsley and green onions over the potatoes. Make the sauce by mixing the rest of the ingredients; then pour over the potatoes. Stir well. Let it stand all day (or at least 4 hours). Stir every hour. Do not refrigerate.   ❦ ❦ ❦   **The Lady & Sons**

Noodle Casserole

SERVES 4

¼ cup (½ stick) butter
One 8-ounce can sliced
     mushrooms, drained, or 1 cup
     sliced fresh mushrooms
¼ cup finely chopped onion
¼ cup finely sliced blanched
     almonds

1 clove garlic, minced, or ¼
     teaspoon garlic purée
1 tablespoon fresh lemon juice
One 10¾-ounce can French onion
     soup
2 cups fine-cut noodles, uncooked

Melt the butter in a large skillet. Add the mushrooms, onions, almonds, garlic, and lemon juice, and sauté gently for about 10 minutes. Stir in the soup and bring to a boil. Add the noodles; reduce the heat, cover, and simmer for about 5 minutes. This is very good served with chicken or beef.   ❦ ❦ ❦   **The Lady & Sons**

Corn Chive Pudding

SERVES 8

Two 10-ounce packages frozen
   corn, thawed
¼ cup sugar
1¼ teaspoons salt
4 large eggs
2 cups milk

¼ cup (½ stick) melted unsalted
   butter, cooled
¼ cup chopped fresh chives
3 tablespoons all-purpose flour
1 teaspoon vanilla extract
Pinch of freshly grated nutmeg

Preheat the oven to 350 degrees. Butter a 1½-quart baking dish. In a food processor, pulse half of the corn until coarsely chopped; transfer to a mixing bowl. Add the remaining corn and sprinkle with the sugar and salt; stir to combine. Whisk together the eggs, milk, butter, chives, flour, and vanilla, and combine with the corn. Pour into the baking dish and sprinkle with nutmeg. Bake in the center of the oven until the center of the pudding is just set, about 45 minutes.

Half-Baked Potato

SERVES 1

This recipe is for one person—you can expand it as necessary.

1 large baking potato
2 tablespoons olive oil or melted
   butter

¼ cup grated Parmesan
¼ teaspoon paprika

Cut the potato in half lengthwise. Brush the cut sides with olive oil or butter. Mix Parmesan and paprika together. Dip the cut sides in the Parmesan and paprika mix. Place the potato, cut sides down, on a greased pan, and bake at 350 degrees for 1 hour.

❧ ❧ ❧   *The Lady & Sons*

Cottage Potatoes

SERVES 4

3 large Idaho potatoes
¼ cup (½ stick) butter
1 cup cottage cheese

½ onion, diced
Salt and pepper
Paprika

Scrub the potatoes, slice them, and put in a pot with water to cover. Boil the potatoes until tender, then drain and mash them with 2 tablespoons of the butter. Add the cottage cheese, onion, and salt and pepper to taste. Stir the mixture gently, then put it in a greased casserole. Dot with the remaining 2 tablespoons of butter and sprinkle with paprika. Bake, uncovered, at 350 degrees for 30 minutes.

🌸 🌸 🌸 *The Lady & Sons*

Vegetable Pancakes

SERVES 8

These pancakes are delicious with a dollop of sour cream.

½ cup all-purpose flour
½ teaspoon baking powder
½ teaspoon salt
¼ teaspoon pepper
1 egg
¼ cup milk

1 cup grated carrots (about 2
    carrots)
1 cup grated zucchini (1 medium
    zucchini)
2 green onions, sliced
2 tablespoons vegetable oil

In a mixing bowl, stir together the flour, baking powder, salt, and pepper. In another bowl, beat together the egg, milk, carrots, zucchini, and onions. Add this to the dry ingredients and stir until just combined. Heat 1 tablespoon of the oil in a large skillet over medium heat. Pour the batter by tablespoonfuls into the pan, making a few pancakes at a time. Cook until golden, about 2 minutes on each side. Add the remaining oil to the pan as needed. Serve at once.

Hash Brown Potato Casserole

SERVES 10–12

2 pounds frozen hash brown
  potatoes
4 cups grated Cheddar cheese
One 10¾-ounce can cream of
  chicken or cream of mushroom
  soup

2 cups sour cream
½ cup (1 stick) melted butter
1 medium onion, chopped
2 teaspoons The Lady's House
  Seasoning

Preheat the oven to 350 degrees. In a large bowl, combine the potatoes, 2 cups of the Cheddar, the soup, sour cream, butter, onion, and House Seasoning. Place in a buttered 13 × 9 × 2-inch pan and bake for 35 minutes. Remove from the oven and top with the remaining Cheddar. Return to the oven and bake for 10 minutes longer.

VARIATION: Instead of topping the casserole with cheese, you may use 2 cups crushed Ritz Crackers mixed with a ½ cup melted butter.

❧ ❧ ❧ **The Lady & Sons**

Asparagus Casserole

SERVES 6

2 tablespoons butter
2 tablespoons all-purpose flour
2 cups milk
Two 15-ounce cans asparagus
  spears, drained

1 cup grated Cheddar cheese
4 hard-boiled eggs, sliced
Salt and pepper
1 cup breadcrumbs

To make the sauce, heat the butter in a skillet; stir in the flour, mixing well, then add the milk all at once. Cook over medium heat, stirring constantly, until thick and creamy; set aside. Arrange half of the asparagus in the bottom of a buttered 2-quart casserole. Top with half of the Cheddar and half of the egg slices. Sprinkle with salt and pepper to taste. Pour half of the sauce on top. Repeat the layers beginning with the remaining asparagus. Top with the breadcrumbs and bake at 350 degrees for 30 minutes.   🍃 🍃 🍃   **The Lady & Sons**

Pimento Cheese Tomato Bake

SERVES 8–10

1 cup grated sharp Cheddar cheese
1 cup grated Monterey Jack cheese
½ cup mayonnaise
One 3-ounce package cream cheese, at room temperature
3 tablespoons mashed pimentos
½ teaspoon The Lady's House Seasoning, plus more to taste
1 teaspoon grated onion

Cracked pepper
12 slices white bread, trimmed of crusts
2 or 3 ripe tomatoes, sliced
2 teaspoons chopped fresh oregano, or 1 teaspoon dried oregano
One 10-ounce can Ro-Tel diced tomatoes with green chilies

Preheat the oven to 350 degrees. Using an electric mixer, beat together the Cheddar and Jack cheeses, the mayonnaise, cream cheese, pimentos, House Seasoning, onion, and cracked pepper to taste. Spread the pimento cheese mixture on one side of each slice of bread. Roll each slice up jelly-roll style. Place the fresh tomato slices in an 8 × 11 × 2-inch baking dish, covering the entire bottom. Sprinkle the tomatoes with half of the oregano and House Seasoning to taste. Place the rolls on top of the sliced tomatoes, pour the canned tomatoes evenly over them, and sprinkle with the remaining oregano. Bake for 30 minutes.   🍃 🍃 🍃   **The Lady & Sons**

Roasted Onions

SERVES 4–6

2 or 3 large Vidalia onions
½ cup chopped fresh mint
3 tablespoons extra-virgin olive oil
2 tablespoons chopped garlic

1 teaspoon salt, or to taste
½ teaspoon freshly ground black pepper, or to taste
¼ cup balsamic vinegar

Peel and trim the onions. Cut each one in half through the stem and root end. In a medium bowl, stir together the mint, oil, garlic, salt, and pepper. With your hands, coat the onions with this mixture and place the onions in a roasting pan. Bake at 350 degrees for 30 minutes. Baste the onions with the juices and continue roasting for 15 minutes longer, or until the onions are soft when pierced with a knife. Remove the pan from the oven and drizzle the vinegar over the onions. Arrange the onions on a platter. 🍀 🍀 🍀 *The Lady & Sons*

Green Bean Casserole

SERVES 6

3 tablespoons butter
½ cup diced onions
½ cup sliced fresh mushrooms
2 cups cooked sliced green beans,
  drained
One 10 ¾-ounce can cream of
  mushroom soup

One 2.8-ounce can french-fried
  onion rings
The Lady's House Seasoning
1 cup grated Cheddar cheese

Preheat the oven to 350 degrees. Melt the butter in a large skillet. Sauté the onions and mushrooms in the butter. Add the green beans, mushroom soup, onion rings, and House Seasoning to taste. Stir well. Pour into a greased 1½-quart baking dish. Bake for 20 minutes, then top the casserole with the Cheddar and bake for 10 minutes longer, or until the casserole is hot and cheese is melted.

🍀 🍀 🍀 *The Lady & Sons*

Baked Wild Rice

SERVES 6

½ pound raw wild rice
1 cup (2 sticks) butter
1 pound fresh mushrooms
1 medium white onion, chopped

2 teaspoons all-purpose flour
1 cup heavy cream
½ cup sherry
½ cup buttered breadcrumbs

Cook the rice according to package directions. Drain and return the pot to the heat briefly to steam the rice dry. Melt the butter in a large skillet. Sauté the mushrooms and onion, then push them to one side of the pan and add the flour. Stir until the mushrooms are coated with butter. Add the cream, stirring constantly. Add the sherry and stir until smooth. Fold in the cooked rice. Pour into a greased casserole and top with breadcrumbs. Bake at 350 degrees for about 30 minutes, or until the top is brown.

Bo's Eggplant Supreme

SERVES 4–6

1 large eggplant
1 teaspoon The Lady's House
   Seasoning
5 tablespoons butter

One 10-ounce can minced clams,
   drained, juice reserved
1 cup cracker crumbs
½ cup half-and-half

Peel the eggplant and cut it into thin rounds. Bring a pot of water to boil. Add the House Seasoning, then the eggplant, and cook for 10 to 15 minutes, or until tender. Drain the eggplant well and mash it with 2 tablespoons of the butter. In a greased casserole, layer the mashed eggplant, the clams, and the cracker crumbs. Dot with the remaining 3 tablespoons of butter. Blend the half-and-half with the reserved clam juice. Taste, and add salt, if needed. Pour this mixture over the casserole and bake at 350 degrees for 30 minutes.

Breads

Plantation Skillet Cake

Currant and Oat Scones

Popovers

Cheese Muffins

Easy Yeast Rolls

Crunchy Peanut Butter Muffins

The Lady & Sons Onion-Cheese Bread

Riz Biscuits

Blackberry Muffins

Easy Herb Rolls

Pineapple Upside-Down Biscuits

Green Muffins

Sour Cream Butter Biscuits

Old-Time Spoon Bread

Sweet Potato Biscuits

Hush Puppies

Apple Raisin Muffins

Gorilla Bread

Nutty Orange Coffee Cake

Cheesy French Bread

Corny Corn Muffins

Banana Bread

Plantation Skillet Cake

SERVES 4–6

This is a delicious breakfast dish, very easily prepared and quick to cook. It is something like Yorkshire pudding.

3 eggs
½ cup all-purpose flour
¼ teaspoon salt

½ cup milk
2 tablespoons vegetable oil

Preheat the oven to 400 degrees. Beat the eggs well, then add the flour and salt and beat again. Slowly add the milk, then the oil, beating constantly. Butter an 8-inch cast-iron skillet generously and pour in the batter. Bake for about 20 minutes, or until the cake is puffed and brown at the edges. Cut the cake in wedges and serve it with warm applesauce and brown sugar.

Currant and Oat Scones

YIELDS 12 SCONES

1½ cups all-purpose flour
1¼ cups rolled oats
¼ cup, plus 1 teaspoon sugar
1 tablespoon baking powder
¼ teaspoon salt

⅓ cup margarine
1 cup dried currants
½ cup milk
1 egg, lightly beaten
⅛ teaspoon cinnamon

Preheat the oven to 375 degrees. In a mixing bowl, combine the flour, oats, ¼ cup of the sugar, the baking powder, and salt. Cut in the margarine until the mixture resembles course crumbs. Stir in the currants. In a small bowl, combine the milk and egg. Add the milk mixture to the flour mixture and stir until just moistened. Shape the dough into a ball. Working on a lightly floured surface, knead the dough gently 6 times. On a lightly greased baking sheet, pat out the dough to form an

8-inch circle. Using a sharp knife, score the round into 12 wedges. Stir together the remaining 1 teaspoon sugar and the cinnamon. Sprinkle this over the dough and bake for 20 to 25 minutes, or until golden brown. Break apart the wedges. Serve warm.

Popovers

YIELDS 12 POPOVERS

These popovers are so good it's hard to believe they are so simple to make. The secret is starting with a cold oven. And don't peek for the full 30 minutes.

4 eggs	*2 cups all-purpose flour*
2 cups milk	*1 teaspoon salt*

Grease 12 large muffin-tin cups or 12 custard cups. If using custard cups, place them in a shallow pan. Break the eggs into a bowl; beat well with a fork or whisk. Add the milk, flour, and salt, and beat until just blended. Fill the muffin tins or custard cups three-quarters full with the batter. Place the pan on a rack in the center of the oven. Set the oven at 450 degrees and turn it on. Bake for 30 minutes without opening the oven door. Serve the popovers hot with plenty of butter, jam, syrup, or honey.

Cheese Muffins

YIELDS ABOUT 12 MUFFINS

These delectable muffins are so rich they can be served with nothing more than a large green salad for a luncheon.

1½ cups all-purpose flour	*1 egg*
1 tablespoon sugar	*1 cup milk*
2½ teaspoons baking powder	*¼ cup (½ stick) melted butter*
½ teaspoon salt	
3 cups coarsely grated Cheddar cheese	

Preheat the oven to 350 degrees. Sift together the flour, sugar, baking powder, and salt. Stir the Cheddar into the dry ingredients until all the particles of cheese are coated with flour. Beat the egg with the milk and stir this into the flour mixture until just blended, then add the butter. Bake the batter in greased muffin tins for 20 minutes.

Easy Yeast Rolls

YIELDS 15 ROLLS

One ¼-ounce package dry yeast
¾ cup warm water (105–115
    degrees)
2½ cups, plus ½–1 cup The Lady
    & Sons Biscuit Mix, or any
    prepared biscuit mix

1 teaspoon sugar
¼ cup (½ stick) melted butter

Preheat the oven to 400 degrees. Dissolve the yeast in the water. Put the 2½ cups of Biscuit Mix in a large bowl; stir in the sugar. Add the yeast mixture, stirring vigorously. Sprinkle the work surface generously with the remaining ½–1 cup Biscuit Mix. Turn the dough out onto the surface and knead well 15 to 20 times. Shape the dough as desired. (I shape heaping tablespoons of dough into balls.) Place on a lightly greased baking sheet, cover with a damp cloth, and let rise in a warm place for 1 hour. Bake for 12 to 15 minutes, or until golden brown. Brush the rolls with melted butter while they're hot.

Crunchy Peanut Butter Muffins

YIELDS 15 MUFFINS

MUFFINS
2 cups all-purpose flour
4 teaspoons baking powder
2 teaspoons cinnamon
¾ teaspoon salt
¼ cup peanut butter (crunchy or smooth)
¼ cup peanut oil
¾ cup packed light brown sugar
1 very ripe banana, mashed

¾ cup milk
1 egg

TOPPING
½ teaspoon cinnamon
¼ cup packed light brown sugar
2 tablespoons butter
1 cup unsalted roasted peanuts, chopped

Preheat the oven to 400 degrees. For the muffins, stir the flour with the baking powder, cinnamon, and salt until well blended; set aside. In a separate bowl, beat the peanut butter with the peanut oil, sugar, and banana. Add in the milk and egg and beat until smooth. Pour this mixture into the center of the dry ingredients and stir with a large spoon until just moistened. Line 2½-inch muffin tins with paper or foil liners and fill the cups two-thirds full with batter.

For the topping, stir the cinnamon into the sugar. Using a pastry blender or two knives, cut the butter into the sugar until the mixture is crumbly. Lightly stir in the peanuts; set aside. Sprinkle the topping evenly over each batter-filled cup.

Bake for 18 to 20 minutes, or until the muffins spring back if lightly pressed in their centers.

The Lady & Sons Onion-Cheese Bread

YIELDS 8 WEDGES

This bread is wonderful served along with our Baked Spaghetti (see page 260) and a fresh salad.

1 tablespoon vegetable oil
¾ cup finely diced onion
½ cup milk
1 egg, beaten
1½ cups The Lady & Sons Biscuit
    Mix

1 cup shredded sharp Cheddar
    cheese
½ teaspoon onion salt
2 tablespoons melted butter
1 tablespoon chopped fresh chives or
    parsley

Preheat the oven to 400 degrees. In a small skillet, heat the oil; sauté the onions until tender, about 2 minutes. Combine the milk and egg, and add to the Biscuit Mix along with the sautéed onions and ½ cup of the cheese. Stir only until the dry ingredients are just moistened. Spread the dough into a greased 8-inch round cake pan. Stir the onion salt into the butter. Drizzle this over the dough, and sprinkle with chives or parsley. Bake for 15 minutes, then sprinkle the dough with the remaining ½ cup cheese and return to the oven to bake for 5 minutes longer, or until golden brown. Cut the bread into wedges and serve hot with butter.

        ❦ ❦ ❦   **The Lady & Sons**

Riz Biscuits

YIELDS 18–24 BISCUITS

One ¼-ounce package dry yeast
1 cup warm buttermilk
½ teaspoon baking soda
2½ cups all-purpose flour
1 tablespoon sugar

1 teaspoon baking powder
¾ teaspoon salt
½ cup vegetable shortening
Melted butter

Dissolve the yeast in the milk; add the baking soda. Sift together the flour, sugar, baking powder, and salt. Cut the shortening into the flour with a fork. Stir the yeast mixture into the flour mixture with a spoon. Dust a rolling pin with additional flour and roll the dough out thin; brush with melted butter. Fold the dough over into a double thickness and brush the top with melted butter. Cut into rounds with a small biscuit cutter. Place the rounds of dough on a greased baking sheet and let rise for 1 hour. Preheat the oven to 425 degrees. Bake the biscuits for 10 to 12 minutes, or until lightly browned.

Blackberry Muffins

YIELDS 18 MUFFINS

½ cup (1 stick) melted butter
½ cup milk
2 large eggs, at room temperature
2 cups all-purpose flour
1¼ cups, plus 4 teaspoons sugar

2 teaspoons baking powder
½ teaspoon salt
2 cups fresh blackberries, or frozen
   blackberries, thawed and
   drained

Preheat the oven to 350 degrees. Grease eighteen 2½-inch muffin tins or line them with paper or foil liners. In a bowl, stir together the butter, milk, and eggs. In a mixing bowl, sift together the flour, 1¼ cups of the sugar, the baking powder, and the salt. Make a well in the center and pour in the milk mixture all at once; stir until blended. The batter will be lumpy: Do not overmix. Fold in the berries. Divide the batter among the prepared cups and sprinkle the remaining 4 teaspoons of sugar over the batter. Bake for about 25 minutes, or until golden.

Easy Herb Rolls

SERVES 6–8

One 12-ounce package
   refrigerated buttermilk biscuits
   (10 count)

¼ cup (½ stick) melted butter
2 tablespoons crumbled blue cheese
2 teaspoons dried parsley

1 teaspoon minced garlic
1 teaspoon minced chives
1 tablespoon onion flakes

1 teaspoon dried tarragon
½ teaspoon dried oregano
½ teaspoon celery seeds

Preheat oven to 375 degrees. Cut the biscuits into quarters. On a greased baking sheet arrange the biscuit pieces into an 11-inch-long loaf. It should resemble a loaf of French bread. In a small bowl, stir together the butter, blue cheese, parsley, garlic, chives, onion flakes, tarragon, oregano, and celery seeds. Spread the herbed butter over the loaf and bake for 18 to 20 minutes, or until golden.

Pineapple Upside-Down Biscuits

YIELDS 10 BISCUITS

One 10-ounce can crushed
 pineapple, drained, juice
 reserved
½ cup packed light brown sugar
¼ cup (½ stick) butter, at room
 temperature

10 maraschino cherries
One 12-ounce package
 refrigerated buttermilk biscuits
 (10 count)

Preheat the oven to 400 degrees. Grease 10 cups of a muffin tin. Combine the pineapple, sugar, and butter, and mix well. Divide the pineapple mixture among the muffin cups. Place a cherry in the center of each muffin cup. Place one biscuit in each cup on top of sugar and pineapple mixture. Spoon 1 teaspoon pineapple juice over each biscuit. Bake for 12 to 15 minutes, or until golden. Cool for 2 minutes. Invert the pan onto a plate to release the biscuits. Serve warm.

Green Muffins

YIELDS ABOUT 8 MUFFINS

Never miss the opportunity to make these when you have turnip greens left over from a previous meal.

1 cup self-rising cornmeal
½ cup self-rising flour
2 eggs
½ cup cooked turnip greens,
  chopped and drained, ½ cup pot
  liquor reserved

¼ cup vegetable oil
¼ cup sour cream

Preheat the oven to 350 degrees. Generously grease an 8-cup muffin tin and put it the oven to heat. In a mixing bowl, stir together the cornmeal and flour. Add the eggs, the greens and pot liquor, the oil, and sour cream. Divide the batter among the hot muffin cups. Bake for about 20 minutes. Serve the muffins hot with butter and a cup of pot liquor for dipping.

Sour Cream Butter Biscuits *very very good very easy*

YIELDS ABOUT 3 DOZEN MINIATURE BISCUITS

These biscuits take me back to my days at The Bag Lady. I would put a couple of these in each lunch container for an extra treat! They are wonderful.

fragile but good looking

2 cups self-rising flour
1 cup (2 sticks) butter, at room
  temperature

1 cup sour cream

Preheat the oven to 400 degrees. Mix the flour and butter together; add the sour cream, and blend well. Place spoonfuls of the batter in greased miniature muffin pans. Bake for 8 to 10 *12+* minutes, or until golden.

Old-Time Spoon Bread

SERVES 4–6

1½ cups water
1 teaspoon salt
1 cup cornmeal

3 tablespoons butter
2 eggs, separated
1 cup milk

Preheat the oven to 350 degrees. Bring the water to a boil and add the salt. Stir in the cornmeal and butter, then the egg yolks. Gradually stir in the milk. Beat the egg whites until stiff. Fold the egg whites into the cornmeal mixture. Pour the batter into a greased 2-quart casserole. Bake for 30 to 45 minutes, or until golden brown. Serve hot with gravy or butter.

Sweet Potato Biscuits

YIELDS 15–18 BISCUITS

¾ cup mashed cooked sweet
potatoes
¼ cup milk
¼ cup (½ stick) butter

1¼ cups all-purpose flour
4 tablespoons baking powder
2 heaping tablespoons sugar
½ teaspoon salt

Preheat the oven to 450 degrees. In a large bowl, mix the potatoes, milk, and butter. In another bowl, sift together the flour, baking powder, sugar, and salt. Add the flour mixture to the potato mixture and combine to make a soft dough. Turn the dough out onto a floured board and toss lightly until the outside of the dough looks smooth. Roll the dough out to one-half inch thick and cut with a biscuit cutter. Place the biscuits on a greased pan and bake for about 15 minutes. (Watch your oven: If the biscuits are browning too fast, lower the temperature.)

Hush Puppies

YIELDS ABOUT 35 HUSH PUPPIES

6 cups vegetable oil
1½ cups self-rising cornmeal
½ cup self-rising flour
½ teaspoon baking soda

½ teaspoon salt
1 small onion, chopped
1 cup buttermilk
1 egg, lightly beaten

Prepare the oil for frying in a skillet. Preheat it to 350 degrees. In a mixing bowl, stir together the cornmeal, flour, baking soda, and salt. Stir in the onion. In a small bowl, stir together the buttermilk and egg. Pour the buttermilk mixture into the dry ingredients and mix until blended—don't worry if there are a few lumps. Drop the batter, one teaspoon at a time, into the oil. Dip the spoon in a glass of water after each hush puppy is dropped. Fry until golden brown, turning the hush puppies and during the cooking process.

VARIATION: For a sweet hush puppy, add 2 tablespoons sugar.

Apple Raisin Muffins

YIELDS ABOUT 5 DOZEN MINIATURE MUFFINS

2 cups water
2 cups sugar
2 cups grated apples
2 cups raisins
1 cup (2 sticks) butter
2 teaspoons cinnamon

2 teaspoons freshly grated nutmeg
½ teaspoon ground cloves
1 cup chopped walnuts
2 teaspoons baking soda
3½ cups all-purpose flour

Preheat the oven to 350 degrees. Combine the water, sugar, apples, raisins, butter, cinnamon, nutmeg, and cloves in a saucepan; bring to a boil. Remove the pan from the heat and cool completely.

In a large bowl, stir the nuts and baking soda into the flour. Add the cooled mixture to the bowl, and stir until blended. Fill greased miniature muffin tins with batter to the top. Bake for 15 minutes.

Gorilla Bread

SERVES 12–15

This bread kicks traditional monkey bread's butt! It's the best.

½ *cup granulated sugar*	*One 8-ounce package cream cheese*
3 teaspoons cinnamon	*Two 12-ounce cans refrigerated*
½ *cup (1 stick) butter*	*biscuits (10 count)*
1 cup packed brown sugar	*1½ cups coarsely chopped walnuts*

Preheat the oven to 350 degrees. Spray a bundt pan with nonstick cooking spray. Mix the granulated sugar and cinnamon. In a saucepan, melt the butter and brown sugar over low heat, stirring well; set aside. Cut the cream cheese into 20 equal cubes. Press the biscuits out with your fingers and sprinkle each with ½ teaspoon of cinnamon sugar. Place a cube of cream cheese in the center of each biscuit, wrapping and sealing the dough around the cream cheese. Sprinkle ½ cup of the nuts into the bottom of the bundt pan. Place half of the prepared biscuits in the pan. Sprinkle with cinnamon sugar, pour half of the melted butter mixture over the biscuits, and sprinkle on ½ cup of nuts. Layer the remaining biscuits on top, sprinkle with the remaining cinnamon sugar, pour the remaining butter mixture over the biscuits, and sprinkle with the remaining ½ cup of nuts. Bake for 30 minutes. Remove from the oven and cool for 5 minutes. Place a plate on top and invert.

Nutty Orange Coffee Cake

SERVES 10–12

¾ *cup granulated sugar*	*One 8-ounce package cream cheese*
½ *cup chopped pecans*	½ *cup (1 stick) melted butter*
2 teaspoons orange zest	*1 cup sifted confectioners' sugar*
Two 12-ounce cans refrigerated	*2 tablespoons fresh orange juice*
buttermilk biscuits (10 count)	

Preheat the oven to 350 degrees. In a small bowl, combine the granulated sugar, pecans, and zest; set aside. Separate the biscuits. Place about ¾ teaspoon cream cheese in the center of each biscuit. Fold each biscuit in half over the cheese, pressing the edges to seal. Dip the biscuits in melted butter, then dredge in the granulated sugar mixture. Place the biscuits, curved-side down, in a single layer in the hollows of a lightly greased 12-cup bundt pan, spacing them evenly (do not stack). Place any remaining biscuits around the tube, filling in any gaps. Drizzle any remaining butter over the biscuits, and sprinkle with any remaining sugar mixture. Bake for 35 to 40 minutes, until golden brown. Immediately invert the cake onto a serving platter. Combine the confectioners' sugar and orange juice, stirring well; drizzle the glaze over the warm cake. Serve warm.

Cheesy French Bread

SERVES 6–8

One 8-ounce package shredded
  sharp Cheddar cheese or
  Mexican cheese blend
¾ cup mayonnaise

1½ teaspoons dried parsley flakes
⅛ teaspoon garlic powder
One 16-ounce loaf French bread,
  cut in half lengthwise

Combine the cheese, mayonnaise, parsley, and garlic powder, stirring well. Spread this mixture on the cut sides of the bread. Place the bread on a baking sheet and bake at 350 degrees for 15 to 20 minutes, or until the topping is melted and lightly browned.

Corny Corn Muffins

YIELDS 12 MUFFINS

In the restaurant, we serve our guests hot cheese biscuits and hoecake cornbread at lunchtime, but at dinner we swap out the hoecakes for these wonderful melt-in-your-mouth corn muffins.

1 cup self-rising cornmeal mix
¾ cup self-rising flour
½ cup vegetable oil
1 cup white creamed corn, fresh if
   possible, or frozen

2 eggs
1 cup sour cream
2 tablespoons sugar

Preheat oven to 375 degrees and grease a 12-cup muffin tin. (If you like a crispy edge around your muffins, preheat the tin in the oven until the grease is very hot.) Combine all ingredients and stir until moistened. Fill the muffin cups with batter and bake for 20 minutes or until golden brown. ❦ ❦ ❦ *The Lady & Sons*

Banana Bread

YIELDS 1 LOAF

No electric mixer needed here—just mix in a bowl by hand.

½ cup (1 stick) butter, at room
   temperature
1 cup sugar
½ teaspoon salt
2 eggs

1 teaspoon vanilla extract
1½ cups all-purpose flour, sifted
1 teaspoon baking soda
1 teaspoon baking powder
3 ripe bananas, mashed

Preheat the oven to 350 degrees. Grease a 9 × 5-inch loaf pan. In a mixing bowl, combine the butter and sugar; mix well. Add the salt, eggs, vanilla, flour, baking soda, baking powder, and bananas, and mix well. Pour the batter into the prepared pan and bake for 50 minutes.

Sauces, Dressings, and Marinades

Southern Spice Rub

House Seasoning

Sweet-and-Sour Sauce

Wayne's Cranberry Sauce

Easy Homemade Blender Mayonnaise

Berry Steak Sauce

White Sauce

Mushroom Sauce

Tarragon Butter

Auntie's Peanut Sauce

Easy Hollandaise

Jezebel Sauce

Raspberry Sauce

Mocha Sauce

Peanut Butter Chocolate Sauce

Lime Vinaigrette

Warm Brie Salad Dressing

Balsamic Vinaigrette

Roasted Red Pepper Vinaigrette

Greek Salad Dressing

Southern Spice Rub

YIELDS ⅔ CUP

2 tablespoons ground cumin
2 tablespoons chili powder
1 tablespoon ground coriander
1 tablespoon kosher salt

2 teaspoons freshly ground pepper
½ teaspoon ground cinnamon
½ teaspoon red pepper flakes

Mix all of the ingredients in a small bowl. Sprinkle and rub the mixture on both sides of steaks just before grilling. Watch the meat while grilling: The spice rub should darken, but you don't want it to burn.

House Seasoning

YIELDS 1½ CUPS

1 cup salt
¼ cup black pepper

¼ cup garlic powder

Stir the ingredients together. Keep the seasoning in a shaker near the stove for convenience. ❦ ❦ ❦ *The Lady & Sons*

Sweet-and-Sour Sauce

YIELDS ABOUT 1¾ CUPS

1 cup sugar
½ cup white vinegar
½ cup, plus 1 tablespoon water
1 tablespoon chopped green bell
  pepper

1 tablespoon chopped pimentos
½ teaspoon salt
2 teaspoons cornstarch
1 teaspoon paprika

In a saucepan combine the sugar, vinegar, the ½ cup of water, bell pepper, pimento, and salt; simmer for 5 minutes. Stir together the cornstarch and the remaining 1 tablespoon water. Add this to the vinegar mixture; remove the pan from the heat and stir until thick. Add the paprika and let cool completely. Serve with fried shrimp, fried chicken bites, or pork bites.

Wayne's Cranberry Sauce

YIELDS 4–5 CUPS

1 cup sugar
1 cup water
One 16-ounce bag fresh
  cranberries
1 cup chopped apple
1 cup chopped walnuts

½ cup raisins
¼ cup Grand Marnier
Juice of ½ orange
Juice of ½ lemon
1 teaspoon cinnamon
1 teaspoon freshly grated nutmeg

Combine the sugar and water in a large saucepan and bring to a boil. Add the cranberries and return to a boil, then lower the heat so that the liquid simmers. Add the apple, walnuts, raisins, Grand Marnier, orange and lemon juices, cinnamon, and nutmeg, and cook for 10 to 15 minutes. Remove the pan from the heat and let the sauce cool.

Easy Homemade Blender Mayonnaise

YIELDS 1 CUP

1 cup vegetable oil
1 egg
3 teaspoons fresh lemon juice

¾ teaspoon salt
½ teaspoon dry mustard
1 tablespoon hot water

In the container of a blender, combine ¼ cup of the oil, the egg, lemon juice, salt, and mustard, and blend for just a few seconds. With the blender running, drizzle in the remaining ¾ cup oil. Blend in the hot water.

Berry Steak Sauce

YIELDS 2 CUPS

One 16-ounce can jellied
  cranberry sauce
⅓ cup bottled steak sauce

1 tablespoon brown sugar
1 tablespoon vegetable oil
2 teaspoons prepared mustard

Combine all the ingredients in a mixing bowl and beat with an electric mixer until smooth. Serve hot or cold, with pork, beef, or chicken.

White Sauce

YIELDS 1 CUP

To make a tasty cheese sauce for vegetables, add ½ cup shredded cheese.

2 tablespoons butter
2 tablespoons all-purpose flour
¼ teaspoon salt

Pinch of white pepper
1 cup milk

Melt the butter in a saucepan over medium heat. Whisk in the flour, salt, and pepper. Add the milk all at once, and cook quickly, stirring constantly, until the sauce is thick and creamy.

Mushroom Sauce

YIELDS ABOUT 2 CUPS

3 tablespoons butter
½ pound fresh mushrooms,
    trimmed and sliced
1 tablespoon all-purpose flour

1 teaspoon soy sauce
¾ cup half-and-half
The Lady's House Seasoning

Melt the butter in a skillet. Add the mushrooms, sprinkle in the flour, and stir well. Cook over medium heat for 8 to 10 minutes, stirring as needed. Add the soy sauce, then slowly stir in the half-and-half. Cook and stir until the sauce thickens. Season to taste with House Seasoning. This sauce is delicious with steak.

Tarragon Butter

YIELDS 1 STICK (½ CUP)

½ cup (1 stick) butter, at room
    temperature
1 tablespoon minced fresh
    tarragon

1 teaspoon fresh lemon juice

Beat the butter with an electric mixer until fluffy, then stir in the tarragon and lemon juice. Using waxed paper, shape the butter into a log. (If you want to pipe the butter into decorative shapes, spoon it into a pastry bag fitted with a star tip.) Chill. Slice the butter log and place a few slices on top of grilled steak or fish.

Auntie's Peanut Sauce

YIELDS 1¾ CUPS

This is excellent on char-grilled chicken or pork. Swab or brush the sauce on the meat for the last 15 minutes of grilling time. Turn often, continuing to baste, to prevent burning.

½ cup (1 stick) butter
2 large cloves garlic, crushed
1 cup Worcestershire sauce

¼ cup crunchy peanut butter
Juice of 2 lemons
½ teaspoon black pepper

Heat the butter in a skillet. Add the garlic and sauté, being careful not to burn the garlic. Add the Worcestershire sauce, peanut butter, lemon juice, and pepper, and blend well. Simmer for 10 minutes.

🐾 🐾 🐾 **The Lady & Sons**

Easy Hollandaise

YIELDS ⅔ CUP

½ cup (1 stick) butter
3 egg yolks

3 tablespoons fresh lemon juice

Combine the ingredients in a small saucepan and let stand at room temperature until the butter is soft (45 to 60 minutes). Five minutes before serving time, place the saucepan over low heat, and stir constantly until the sauce thickens.

Jezebel Sauce

YIELDS 3½ CUPS

One 12-ounce bag frozen
 cranberries
½ cup, plus 2 tablespoons prepared
 horseradish

3 tablespoons dry mustard
1 tablespoon coarsely ground
 pepper

Combine all the ingredients in a large bowl and stir well. Pour the sauce into an airtight container and store in the refrigerator. Serve with crackers and cream cheese, as an appetizer, or along with chicken, pork, or beef.   ❦ ❦ ❦ **The Lady & Sons**

Raspberry Sauce

YIELDS ABOUT 2½ CUPS

This sauce makes something special out of plain cake or vanilla ice cream.

One 10-ounce package frozen
 raspberries, thawed
½ cup currant jelly

1 tablespoon cornstarch
1 tablespoon butter
¾ cup fresh orange juice

In a saucepan, mix ¾ cup of the raspberries with the jelly and bring to a boil. Reduce the heat. Stir the cornstarch into the remaining raspberries and add this to the saucepan; cook, stirring constantly, until thickened. Remove the pan from the heat and stir in the butter. Cool. Stir in the orange juice and refrigerate until chilled.

Mocha Sauce

YIELDS 1 CUP

This sauce is wonderful on pound cake, ice cream, and many other desserts.

½ *cup unsweetened cocoa powder*   ½ *cup honey*
½ *cup strong brewed coffee*   ¼ *cup heavy cream*

In a small saucepan, combine all the ingredients and cook over medium heat, stirring constantly, until the mixture is smooth and slightly thickened. Cool.

Peanut Butter Chocolate Sauce

YIELDS 2⅔ CUPS

One 13-ounce can evaporated milk   ½ *cup creamy peanut butter*
2 cups sugar   *1 teaspoon vanilla extract*
3 squares (3 ounces) unsweetened
   chocolate

In a medium saucepan, combine the milk, sugar, and chocolate. Bring to a boil over low heat, stirring until the sugar is dissolved and chocolate is melted. Boil gently, stirring occasionally, for 15 minutes. Remove the pan from the heat and stir in the peanut butter and vanilla; beat until blended. Serve warm. This sauce keeps well in the refrigerator, but it will thicken when chilled. To serve, spoon the desired amount of sauce into a saucepan; place over low heat and stir until warm and pourable.

Lime Vinaigrette

YIELDS 2⅓ CUPS

¾ cup olive oil
¾ cup vegetable oil
½ cup red wine vinegar
1½ tablespoons Dijon mustard
1½ tablespoons fresh lime juice
1½ tablespoons crushed garlic
1½ tablespoons soy sauce

Pinch of dried thyme
Pinch of dried basil
Pinch of dried oregano
Pinch of dried dillweed
Pinch of salt
Pinch of pepper

Combine all the ingredients in the container of a blender and blend until thick and smooth. This dressing may be stored in the refrigerator in a tightly closed jar for up to 2 weeks.

Warm Brie Salad Dressing

YIELDS ABOUT 1¼ CUPS

Pour this dressing over mixed greens such as Romaine, Boston, and one or two types of bitter greens.

2 tablespoons olive oil
1 green onion, finely chopped
½ pound Brie
2 tablespoons coarse Dijon
   mustard

3 tablespoons sherry vinegar or
   raspberry vinegar
1 tablespoon capers (optional)
Salt and pepper

Heat the oil in a saucepan over low heat. Add the onion and cook until softened. Meanwhile, use a paring knife to remove the rind from the Brie. Add the mustard to the suacepan, then the vinegar, and stir well. Add the Brie and mix until smooth; let cool slightly, then add the capers, if using. Add salt and pepper to taste.

Balsamic Vinaigrette

YIELDS 1⅓ CUPS

This dressing is especially good on tossed greens with tomatoes, red onion, and crumbled blue cheese.

1 cup olive oil
¼ cup balsamic vinegar
2 tablespoons sugar

2 large cloves garlic, crushed
1 teaspoon salt
½ teaspoon pepper

Combine all the ingredients in a jar with a tight-fitting lid and shake well. Let stand for at least ½ hour before using.

Roasted Red Pepper Vinaigrette

YIELDS 2–2½ CUPS

This is great over salad greens and excellent with fish; you can also use it as a light veggie dip. I recommend roasting fresh red bell peppers, but if time doesn't allow, substitute a 14-ounce jar of roasted red peppers, drained, adding 1 teaspoon of sugar to ensure sweetness.

4 red bell peppers
¼ cup balsamic vinegar
1 tablespoon minced garlic

¾ cup olive oil
Salt and pepper

Roast the bell peppers under the broiler, or bake them on a baking sheet in a 500-degree oven for 10 to 12 minutes, or until the skins are blackened. Place the charred peppers in a paper bag, close the top, and let the peppers cool for 10 minutes. When the peppers are cool, rub off the charred skin and rinse under cold water. Stem and seed the peppers. In a food processor or blender, purée the peppers to a fine consistency. Add the vinegar and garlic and process on low speed, slowly drizzling in the oil. Add salt and pepper to taste.

❦ ❦ ❦ **The Lady & Sons**

Greek Salad Dressing

YIELDS 1 CUP

¼ cup balsamic vinegar
3 tablespoons water
One 0.7-ounce package Good
 Seasons Italian Salad Dressing
 Mix

1 teaspoon anchovy paste (from a
 tube)
½ cup extra-virgin olive oil

Whisk together the vinegar, water, dressing mix, and anchovy paste.
Add the oil and whisk until blended.

And from My Peers . . .

HERB TRAUB AND THE PIRATES' HOUSE

Ring Tum Ditty

Gussie's Fried Chicken with Pecan-Honey Glaze

Green Beans with Onions

THE GRANITE STEPS INN

French Toast Stuffed with Bananas and Walnuts

Lemon-Pecan Sunburst Coffee Cake

Oven-Baked Dutch Apple Pancakes

DAMON LEE FOWLER

Turnips Stuffed with Winter Greens

Asparagus with Leeks and New Potatoes

Watermelon Salad

MARTHA GIDDENS NESBIT

Mosaic Chicken Terrine

Crab Cakes with Lemon Dill Sauce

Mrs. Sullivan's Benne Wafers

THE GASTONIAN

Traditional Raisin Scones
Strawberry Soup
Pesto Cheese Blossom

MRS. WILKES' BOARDING HOUSE

Mrs. Wilkes' Boarding House–Style Biscuits
Baked Bean Casserole
Beef Stew Casserole

ELIZABETH ON 37TH

Fried Grits Cakes with Sausage
Shrimp Bel Vedere
Blueberry Raspberry Pecan Crisp

THE JOHNNY HARRIS RESTAURANT

Steak au Poivre
Baked Flounder
Pasta Puttanesca Sauce

LUCILE WRIGHT

Lucile Wright's Tomato Sandwiches
Lucile Wright's Oyster Bisque

JOHN BERENDT

Fresh Cabbage and Sweet Sausages
Lemon Hollandaise Sauce
Pots de Crème

THERE ARE so many things of interest here in our beautiful city of Savannah—too many to mention in just one book. Our city is full of restaurants, old and new, offering a variety of cuisines. She has more than two dozen antique-filled inns gracing the historic district, and literally wraps her arms around us with rich history and great beauty.

In this chapter I have included recipes from two inns located near my home, four restaurants that have brought pleasure to their guests for years, two local (and very successful) cookbook authors, and one caterer.

Thank you all so much for your contributions to this book. They are truly the icing on the cake.

Herb Traub and the Pirates' House

For years Herb Traub was known as one of the most hospitable and gracious hosts in Savannah. He was the proprietor of the legendary Pirates' House, located in one of the most historic spots in Georgia, on the site of the Trustees' Garden, the first public experimental garden in America.

When General James Edward Oglethorpe arrived here from England in 1733, he established this large garden on what was then the edge of the city, and he named it in honor of his fellow Englishmen who were the Trustees of the infant colony of Georgia. By the middle of the eighteenth century, the need for the garden no longer existed, and it soon became the site of some of Savannah's earliest construction. Located just yards from the Savannah River, it was a natural spot for an inn for visiting sailors. The inn soon became a rendezvous for bloodthirsty pirates from around the world. It is said that Old Cap'n Flint died in one of the rooms upstairs, and on moonless nights his ghost still haunts the grounds of the Pirates' House.

Today the inn is home to a bustling restaurant—a meandering maze of twenty-three dining rooms in nine connected old buildings. Upstairs is one of Savannah's favorite nightspots, Hannah's East, where Savannah's own Ben Tucker pours out a healthy helping of jazz. Hannah's East is also where our dear, sweet "Miss" Emma Kelley, "The Lady of 6,000 Songs," can be found stroking the ivories and singing some of my favorite tunes.

Herb published *The Pirates' House Cookbook* in 1982, and while he is no longer involved in the restaurant, his cookbook has remained ever so popular. He always has a smile and I can just hear him saying, "What foods these morsels be."

Thank you for your contribution to my cookbook, Herb!

Ring Tum Ditty

SERVES 4 HOGOLETTOS (OR 6 NORMAL PEOPLE)

12 ounces bacon, chopped
2 cups chopped onions
Two 16-ounce cans whole tomatoes,
 juice reserved
One 16-ounce can whole kernel
 corn

Dried basil
Salt and pepper
3 cups (¾ pound) grated extra-
 sharp Cheddar cheese
4–6 baking potatoes, baked

Sauté the bacon and onions in a heavy pot until the bacon is crisp and the onion is translucent. Drain off the fat. Drain the tomato juice into the pot; squish the tomatoes through your fingers into the pot. Add the corn, and basil, salt, and pepper to taste, and simmer the mixture for 10 to 15 minutes or until desired thickness. Add the cheese and stir until melted. Spoon the Ring Tum Ditty over the halved potatoes and wait for the compliments.

Gussie's Fried Chicken
with Pecan-Honey Glaze

SERVES 4

They use deep-fat fryers at the Pirates' House. If you have one at home, by all means use it.

3–3½ pounds frying chicken, cut
 up, or your favorite chicken parts
2 eggs
Salt and pepper
Garlic powder
Vegetable shortening or vegetable
 oil

2 cups self-rising flour
1 cup (2 sticks) butter
½ cup honey
½ cup coarsely chopped pecans

Rinse the chicken and pat it dry. Beat the eggs in a 9 × 13-inch dish. Lay the chicken pieces in the dish, and sprinkle with salt, pepper, and garlic powder to taste. Turn the chicken and season the other side, then slosh the chicken parts around in the egg until well coated. Place enough shortening or oil in a cast-iron skillet or electric skillet to come just over halfway up the sides of the chicken parts. Heat just until smoking (375 degrees). Place the flour in a paper bag, add the chicken pieces, a few at a time, and shake to coat well. Remove the chicken with tongs and place it in the hot fat. Cover the pan, leaving a crack for steam to escape, lower the heat (to 325 degrees for electric skillet), and cook for 10 minutes. Turn the chicken with tongs, cover again (leaving the lid open just a crack), and cook for 10 minutes longer. Very large pieces may need to be cooked a little longer. Drain the chicken on paper towels and transfer to a platter.

To make the glaze, melt the butter in a saucepan over low heat. Whisk in the honey until well blended. Bring to a simmer and add the pecans. Simmer for 15 minutes, stirring occasionally. Ladle the glaze over the hot fried chicken and serve.

Green Beans with Onions

SERVES 6

2½–3 pounds string beans
4 slices thick bacon or 4 tablespoons
bacon fat
1 tablespoon sugar

1 small onion, peeled and cut into
thin wedges
Salt and pepper

With a paring knife or peeler, trim the edges off the beans to remove the strings. Do not omit this step—you can do it while watching TV or chatting with a friend. Place the bacon in a heavy Dutch oven and cook over low heat to render some of the fat; do not brown. (If using bacon fat, just melt it.) Meanwhile, wash the beans. Then hold a handful at a time under vigorously running cold water and drop the wet beans directly into the Dutch oven. Sprinkle the beans with sugar; do not add water. Bring to a boil, cover the pot, and immediately reduce the heat to low. Cook until the beans are tender, 45 to 60 minutes. Add a little more water if necessary. During the last 30 minutes of cooking, place the onions around the edge of the pot. When the beans are done, season to taste with salt and pepper. (Do not add salt at the beginning, or the beans may be too salty.)

The Granite Steps Inn

This beautiful mansion is located at 126 East Gaston Street. The Granite Steps Mansion was a private residence until 1998, making it one of the "newest" old bed-and-breakfasts in Savannah. The innkeeper, Donna Panoz Sparks, and I became fast friends. Donna and her mother, Nancy Panoz, are two of the most genial ladies you could ever meet. These two are no strangers to seeing to the comfort of others. They have a proven recipe for true "quality of life" in their winery and resort, the Chateau Élan, located in the hills of northern Georgia. The Chateau offers a welcoming refuge rich in old-world tradition and warm hospitality—qualities that also characterize the Granite Steps Inn.

Along with some favorite recipes served at the Inn, Donna sends this message to everyone: "It is an unbelievable honor to be able to establish a bed-and-breakfast inn in Savannah. Apart from being the most beautiful city in the United States, Savannah has welcomed us with open arms. In return, we want to provide Savannah with one of the finest bed-and-breakfast inns available anywhere. The Granite Steps has provided the perfect backdrop for this. It is a grand and elegant house that beckons people to come inside. However, once they are inside, we hope to provide our guests with the kind of warm hospitality that is the essence of Savannah. We like to call it 'white-glove service without the white gloves.'"

French Toast Stuffed with Bananas and Walnuts

SERVES 4

Sandwiching two slices of bread with a mixture of bananas and walnuts results in French toast with a surprise filling. Try other favorite nuts in place of the walnuts, if you like. Accompany the French toast with bacon, ham, or sausage.

6 eggs
¼ cup milk
4 very ripe bananas
¼ cup (1 ounce) coarsely chopped
   walnuts

⅛ teaspoon freshly grated nutmeg
8 slices egg bread
4 tablespoons (½ stick) unsalted
   butter
Confectioners' sugar, for dusting

In a large, shallow bowl, using a fork, beat the eggs until lightly frothy. Stir in the milk; set aside. Peel the bananas into a small bowl and mash them with a fork. Stir in the walnuts and nutmeg. Spread the banana-walnut mixture evenly over half the bread slices, leaving a ¼-inch border uncovered on all edges. Top with the remaining bread slices and press down gently to seal. Place 2 sandwiches in the egg mixture and press down gently. Turn gently and let soak for a moment, until evenly saturated on both sides. Remove from the bowl and repeat with the remaining 2 sandwiches. In a frying pan or on a griddle large enough to hold all the sandwiches at once, melt 2 tablespoons of the butter over medium heat. Add the sandwiches and fry until the undersides are golden brown, about 2 minutes. Cut the remaining 2 tablespoons butter into several pieces and dot them around the pan. Flip the sandwiches with a spatula and fry until the second side is browned, about 2 minutes longer. Place the French toast on warmed individual plates. Using a small, fine sieve, lightly dust the tops with confectioners' sugar. Serve hot, with jam or maple syrup.

Lemon-Pecan Sunburst Coffee Cake

SERVES 8

One 17.3-ounce can refrigerated
   Pillsbury Grands Flaky Biscuits
¼ cup finely chopped pecans
¼ cup granulated sugar
2 teaspoons grated lemon zest

2 tablespoons melted butter
½ cup confectioners' sugar
1½ ounces cream cheese, at room
   temperature
2½–3 teaspoons fresh lemon juice

Preheat the oven to 375 degrees. Grease a 9- or 8-inch round cake pan. Separate the biscuit dough into 8 biscuits. Place one biscuit in the center of the pan. Cut the remaining biscuits in half, forming 14 half-circles. Arrange these pieces around the center biscuit in a sunburst pattern, with all the cut sides facing in the same direction. In a small bowl, combine the pecans, granulated sugar, and lemon zest, and mix well. Brush the tops of the biscuits with the melted butter and sprinkle with the pecan mixture. Bake for 20 to 25 minutes, or until golden brown. Meanwhile, in a small bowl, combine the confectioners' sugar, cream cheese, and enough lemon juice to make a pourable glaze; beat until smooth. Drizzle the glaze over the warm coffee cake. Let stand for 10 minutes, or just until the glaze is set. Serve warm.

Oven-Baked Dutch Apple Pancakes

SERVES 4–6

2 cans apple pie filling
2 tablespoons butter
1 teaspoon cinnamon
3 eggs
½ cup milk

½ cup all-purpose flour
1 tablespoon sour cream
1 teaspoon lemon zest
¼ teaspoon salt
Confectioners' sugar, for dusting

Preheat the oven to 350 degrees. In a 10-inch cast-iron skillet, warm the apple pie filling, butter, and cinnamon. In a bowl, beat the eggs until frothy. Add the milk, flour, sour cream, lemon zest, and salt. Beat just until the batter is smooth. Pour over the hot apple mixture in the skillet, and immediately put the pan in the oven. Bake for 20 to 25 minutes, or until the pancake is puffed and golden brown. Using a small, fine sieve, lightly dust the top of the pancake with confectioners' sugar. Serve warm.

Damon Lee Fowler

My friend Damon is a nationally recognized authority on Southern cooking and its history. He received a master's degree in architecture from Clemson University, after which he practiced as an architect for more than a decade before turning to his true loves: food writing, teaching, and culinary history. I always enjoy my time spent with Damon; he's so knowledgeable, and funny as all get-out.

Damon has authored three cookbooks. His first, *Classical Southern Cooking: A Celebration of the Cuisine of the Old South,* was nominated for two Julia Child Cookbook Awards and a James Beard Foundation Award. His second book, *Beans, Greens, and Sweet Georgia Peaches,* explores Southern fruit and vegetable cookery. His last was simply called *Fried Chicken.*

He has shared with us three recipes from his book *Beans, Greens, and Sweet Georgia Peaches.* I hope you enjoy them.

Turnips Stuffed with Winter Greens

SERVES 4

4 large turnips (about 2 pounds)
4 tablespoons (½ stick) unsalted
   butter, plus more for greasing
1 pound kale or young collards
½ cup dry breadcrumbs

Grated zest of 1 lemon
4 green onions, thinly sliced
Salt and freshly ground black
   pepper

Position a rack in the upper third of the oven and preheat the oven to 400 degrees. Trim most of the taproots and green tops from the turnips, but leave a little of both attached. Scrub the turnips well under cold running water and pat dry. Rub them with a little butter, wrap them in foil, and put them on a baking sheet. Place the baking sheet on the upper rack of the oven and bake until the turnips yield slightly when pressed with a finger, about 1 hour.

Meanwhile, stem the greens and cut them into 1-inch-wide strips. Wash them thoroughly and drain them, leaving some moisture clinging to the leaves. Put the greens in a large skillet, cover, and cook over medium-high heat until the greens are wilted but still bright green, about 4 minutes. Turn the greens out onto a platter and spread them out to cool.

Melt 2 tablespoons of the butter in a small pan over medium heat. Add the breadcrumbs and lemon zest, and thoroughly mix them with the butter. Transfer the mixture to a bowl and set aside.

When the turnips are tender, unwrap them and let them stand until cool enough to handle. Slice off the tops; then, with a melon baller or a small spoon, scoop out the inner flesh, leaving a ½-inch-thick shell. Set aside the inner flesh for another use. Put the shells on a lightly greased baking sheet and set aside.

Put the onions and the remaining 2 tablespoons of butter in the skillet used to cook the greens, and place over medium-high heat. Sauté until the onions are softened, about 2 minutes. Add the greens, a liberal pinch of salt, and a few grindings of pepper, and toss well. Fill the turnips with the greens, sprinkle them with the crumb mixture, and bake until the crumbs are golden and the turnips and greens are heated through, about 20 minutes.

Asparagus with Leeks and New Potatoes

SERVES 4

1½ pounds fresh asparagus, peeled and trimmed

Green tops of 2 large leeks, washed and trimmed

½ pound small new red potatoes, cooked but not peeled

4 tablespoons (½ stick) unsalted butter

Salt and freshly ground pepper

Cut the asparagus crosswise into 1-inch lengths, keeping the tips separate from the stems; set aside. Slice the leek tops crosswise about ¼ inch thick. Slice the potatoes into ¼-inch-thick rounds.

In a skillet or sauté pan that will comfortably hold all the ingredients, melt the butter over medium-high heat. Add the potatoes and the asparagus stems. Sauté, shaking the pan frequently, until the potatoes are beginning to turn golden, about 3 minutes.

Add the leek greens and asparagus tips, a healthy pinch of salt, and a liberal grinding of pepper. Sauté, shaking the pan and tossing the ingredients frequently, until the asparagus is tender and beginning to brown a little. It should still be firm and bright green. Taste and correct the seasonings, and serve at once.

Watermelon Salad

SERVES 6

Here, watermelon gives up its usual place at the table as a fruit and goes to work in a role usually occupied by its cousin, the cucumber. The melon is a lovely foil for the salty feta, tangy onion, and tart vinegar. It makes a refreshing and unusual salad for any summer brunch, luncheon, or dinner.

½ small watermelon (about 5 pounds)
1 medium Vidalia or other sweet onion
¼ cup red wine vinegar
Salt and freshly ground black pepper

½ cup extra-virgin olive oil
2 tablespoons chopped fresh mint
4 ounces feta cheese, crumbled
6 whole mint sprigs, for garnish

Cut the flesh from the melon and cut it into bite-size pieces, removing and discarding the seeds as you go; set aside. Peel and slice the onion into thin rings.

In a bowl, combine the vinegar, a large pinch of salt, and a few liberal grindings of pepper, and whisk until the salt is dissolved. Slowly whisk in the oil, a few drops at a time. Stir in the chopped mint, taste, and correct the seasonings.

Combine the melon, onion, and feta in a bowl, pour the dressing over them, and toss gently until they are coated and evenly mixed. Garnish with the mint sprigs, or divide the salad among individual salad plates and garnish each serving. Serve at once.

Martha Giddens Nesbit

Since her graduation twenty-five years ago, Martha has worked in various capacities at the Savannah *Morning News*—as columnist, food editor, and lifestyle editor. She writes regularly for the Accent/Food section, and is a regular contributor to *Savannah Magazine*. Martha has been the recipient of many national awards for fashion and nutrition reporting.

In 1986 Martha self-published a cookbook called *Savannah Collection,* five years later she wrote *Savannah, Crown of the Colonial Coast,* and last but not least, in 1996 she came out with *Savannah Entertains.*

Over the years my respect for Martha has grown with everything she's done. I know everyone will enjoy the recipes that she has contributed from her own cookbooks. Thanks, Martha!

Mosaic Chicken Terrine

SERVES 12–14

2 eggs, lightly beaten
½ teaspoon lemon pepper
½ teaspoon Lawry's Seasoned Salt
1½ pounds boneless chicken breast
    halves
2 cups grated Parmesan
One 14 ½-ounce can artichoke
    hearts, drained and cut in half
6 slices mortadella, salami, or
    prosciutto

12–16 large fresh basil leaves, or
    8 spinach leaves
1 cup mayonnaise
½ clove garlic, minced
1 teaspoon fresh dillweed, or
    ½ teaspoon dried
1 teaspoon chopped fresh parsley

Beat the eggs in a small bowl and add the lemon pepper and Seasoned Salt. Dip the chicken breasts into the eggs, then into the Parmesan. Dip the artichoke hearts into the eggs, then into the Parmesan.

Line a large loaf pan with parchment paper. Place one layer of chicken breasts on the bottom of the pan (this will use about 2½ breasts). Cover the chicken with a layer of mortadella, salami, or prosciutto. Cover the ham with a layer of artichoke hearts, then cover with the basil leaves, using all the leaves. Repeat the layers of chicken, ham, and artichoke hearts. Cover the top of the terrine with parchment paper or foil. During baking, the terrine must be weighted with something heavy to compress the layers. A clean brick wrapped in foil works nicely and fits nicely in loaf pan. Put the loaf pan in a larger baking pan, and pour in water to a depth of 1½ inches. Bake at 350 degrees for 1 hour and 20 minutes.

Let the terrine cool completely at room temperature, then refrigerate in the loaf pan for several hours, or overnight. In a bowl, blend the mayonnaise, garlic, dillweed, and parsley with a spoon; chill. To serve, carefully turn the terrine out of the pan onto a platter and cut ¾-inch slices. Serve with mayonnaise mixture and good buttery crackers.

Crab Cakes with Lemon Dill Sauce

SERVES 4

3 tablespoons butter
1 green onion, finely chopped
2 tablespoons finely chopped red
   bell pepper
1 clove garlic, minced
3 tablespoons heavy cream
1 tablespoon Dijon mustard
Cayenne pepper

1 cup breadcrumbs
1 egg
½ teaspoon minced fresh parsley
1 pound white or claw crabmeat,
   picked free of any bits of shell
¼ cup grated Parmesan
2 tablespoons vegetable oil

Melt 1 tablespoon of the butter in a heavy skillet over medium heat. Sauté the onion, bell pepper, and garlic in the butter until the pepper is limp, about 3 minutes. Add the cream, mustard, and cayenne to taste, and mix well. Add ½ cup of the breadcrumbs, the egg, and the parsley, and mix well. Gently fold in the crabmeat.

Form the mixture into 8 patties, about ½ inch thick. Combine the remaining ½ cup breadcrumbs and the Parmesan in a bowl; pat this topping onto both sides of the patties. Refrigerate until firm, about 2 hours.

Combine the oil and the remaining 2 tablespoons of butter in the skillet. Sauté the crab cakes in the hot oil-butter mixture for about 3 minutes on each side, or until golden brown. Or, place the crab cakes on a baking sheet, drizzle with the oil and butter mixture, and bake at 400 degrees for 7 to 10 minutes, turning once.

Spoon a dollop of Lemon Dill Sauce alongside each crab cake, and serve the remaining sauce separately.

LEMON DILL SAUCE

YIELDS ABOUT 1½ CUPS

1 cup mayonnaise
¼ cup buttermilk
2 tablespoons chopped fresh dill
1 tablespoon minced fresh parsley

1 tablespoon grated lemon zest
2 teaspoons fresh lemon juice
1 small garlic clove, minced

Combine all the ingredients in a bowl and stir well. Refrigerate until chilled; the sauce will thicken as it chills.

Mrs. Sullivan's Benne Wafers

YIELDS ABOUT 12 DOZEN WAFERS

1½ cups sesame seeds, toasted
2 cups all-purpose flour
1 teaspoon baking powder
¼ teaspoon salt

1½ cups (3 sticks) butter
1 pound light brown sugar
2 eggs
2 teaspoons vanilla extract

Line some baking sheets with waxed paper. Preheat the oven to 350 degrees. To toast the sesame seeds, spread them in a shallow baking pan. Bake for about 5 minutes, watching carefully. The seeds should just begin to lightly brown. Immediately tip the seeds into a shallow dish and set aside to cool. Reduce the oven temperature to 300 degrees.

Sift together the flour, baking powder, and salt. In a mixing bowl, cream together the butter and sugar. Beat in the eggs. Stir in the flour mixture until combined, then add the vanilla. Stir in the sesame seeds. Drop by ½ teaspoons on the prepared baking sheets.

Bake until brown, 14 to 16 minutes. The cookies should be very brown, but not burned around the edges. Let the cookies cool completely on the waxed paper, then lift them off. Store the wafers in an airtight container. These freeze well in tins.

The Gastonian

The Gastonian is located at 220 East Gaston Street in Savannah's beautiful historic district. Anne Landers, owner and innkeeper, has a gift for making people feel welcome in this breathtaking 1868 Regency-Italianate-style home.

This beautiful inn has been the recipient of many awards, among them being named one of the top inns and bed-and-breakfasts in the United States by the Zagat survey.

The Gastonian was selected as one of the twelve most romantic inns on the East Coast by *The Discerning Traveler* and also boasts the prestigious AAA "Four Diamond Award."

Anne, along with her full-time pastry chef, Laura Steele, has been gracious enough to share a few of their sumptuous recipes. The recipes that Anne and Laura selected for us are prepared and served at High Tea every afternoon at the inn. Thank you, ladies, for your generosity.

Traditional Raisin Scones

YIELDS 1 DOZEN SCONES

3 cups all-purpose flour
1 tablespoon baking powder
1 cup (2 sticks) unsalted butter, at
  room temperature

¼ cup, plus 2 tablespoons sugar
3 large eggs
⅓ cup buttermilk
½ cup raisins

Preheat the oven to 350 degrees. Sift together the flour and baking powder. In a separate bowl, beat the butter until creamy. Add the ¼ cup sugar, beating until pale and fluffy. Add the eggs, one at a time, then add the flour mixture and the buttermilk. Sprinkle the raisins over the dough and gently fold them in. Using an ice-cream scoop, place mounds of dough on a baking sheet and sprinkle with the remaining sugar. Bake for 30 minutes. Serve the scones warm, with softened butter and preserves.

Strawberry Soup

SERVES 6–8

1 quart strawberries, hulled
4 cups buttermilk
¾ cup sugar

⅔ cup sour cream
3 tablespoons peach schnapps
Fresh mint sprigs

In the bowl of a food processor, combine the strawberries, 1 cup of the buttermilk, and the sugar. Process until blended and set aside. Combine the remaining 3 cups of buttermilk, the sour cream, and schnapps in a large bowl. Pour the strawberry mixture into the sour cream mixture and stir to combine. Cover and refrigerate until well chilled. Serve the soup chilled in small cups, garnished with mint sprigs.

Pesto Cheese Blossom

SERVES 15–20

One 8-ounce package sliced
   provolone cheese
Two 8-ounce packages cream
   cheese, at room temperature
20 pistachios, shelled
2 cloves garlic
½ cup fresh basil leaves

½ cup fresh parsley leaves
½ cup pine nuts
¼ teaspoon salt
¼ teaspoon freshly ground pepper
2 tablespoons extra-virgin olive oil
3 ounces oil-packed sun-dried
   tomatoes*

Line a medium bowl with plastic wrap, leaving enough overhang to cover the top. Reserving 3 slices of the provolone, line the bottom and sides of the bowl with the remaining provolone, overlapping the slices. For the cream cheese layer, process the cream cheese, pistachios, and 1 of the garlic cloves in a food processor until blended; scrape the mixture into a bowl and set aside. For the pesto layer, process the basil, parsley, pine nuts, and the remaining garlic clove in the food processor

*If you can't get oil-packed sun-dried tomatoes, use the dry-packed kind. Reconstitute them by placing the tomatoes in a small saucepan, adding a little olive oil and water, and cooking, covered, for 3 minutes.

until blended. Dissolve the salt and pepper in the olive oil and mix well. With the machine running, add the oil in a fine stream. Scrape this mixture into a second bowl and set aside. For the tomato layer, drain the tomatoes, reserving the oil. Purée the tomatoes with a small amount of the reserved oil in a food processor. Spread some of the cream cheese mixture over the cheese slices lining the bowl. Layer the pesto mixture, half of the remaining cream cheese mixture, the sun-dried tomato mixture, and then remaining cream cheese mixture in the bowl. Cover with the remaining provolone cheese. Bring the edges of the plastic wrap together over the top and secure with a twist tie. Freeze until firm.

Remove the plastic wrap and invert the mold onto a serving platter. Serve with party crackers. This will keep in the refrigerator for up to 3 months.

Mrs. Wilkes' Boarding House

Although Mrs. Sema Wilkes and my grandmother Irene Paul never met, they had a lot in common. Mrs. Wilkes is, and my grandmother was, a wonderful Southern cook. They both began their businesses in the early 1940s, before it was fashionable for women to be in the business world. Today, fifty-seven years later, Mrs. Wilkes' Boarding House involves four generations of the family. They have traveled to New York, Brussels, and Tokyo promoting Southern food and hospitality for the state of Georgia.

Savannah is proud to be home to such a popular and long-lived establishment. Mrs. Wilkes and Grandmother Paul are definitely my two true heroes.

Mrs. Wilkes and her family send warm regards, and hope that you enjoy the following recipes from the cookbook *Famous Recipes from Mrs. Wilkes' Boarding House.*

Mrs. Wilkes' Boarding House–Style Biscuits

YIELDS ABOUT 16 BISCUITS

2 cups self-rising flour
½ teaspoon baking powder
1 tablespoon vegetable shortening

2 tablespoons margarine
⅓ cup buttermilk
⅓ cup milk

Preheat the oven to 450 degrees. Sift the flour and baking powder into a mixing bowl and make a well in the center. Cut in the shortening and margarine until the mixture resembles coarse cornmeal. Pour the buttermilk and milk into a measuring cup and add enough water to make ¾ cup. Pour this into the dry ingredients. Mix lightly and quickly with your hands to form a dough moist enough to leave the sides of the bowl. Turn the dough onto a lightly floured surface. Knead by turning the dough away from you, pressing down with palms of hands, and pushing the dough away. Repeat 6 or 7 times. Work the dough into a large ball while kneading; keep your fingers dry by dipping them into dry flour frequently. Pinch off portions of dough and place them on a well-greased baking sheet. Press lightly to flatten the biscuits slightly. Bake for 12 to 15 minutes, or until golden brown on top.

Baked Bean Casserole

SERVES 8

2 tablespoons bacon fat or vegetable oil	1 cup diced cooked ham
1 cup sliced onions	1 tablespoon prepared mustard
Two 1-pound cans Boston-style baked beans	2 tomatoes, peeled and sliced
	2 teaspoons brown sugar
	1 teaspoon salt

Preheat the oven to 400 degrees. Heat the fat in a heavy skillet, add the onions, and sauté until tender. Combine the beans, ham, and mustard; arrange half this mixture in a 2-quart casserole. Place half of the onions and tomatoes over the beans; sprinkle with half of the sugar and salt. Repeat with the remaining ingredients. Bake, covered, for 30 minutes. Uncover the casserole and bake for 5 minutes longer.

Beef Stew Casserole

SERVES 6

2 pounds beef stew meat	2 medium unpeeled cooking apples, sliced
1 teaspoon salt	3 carrots, cut into long, narrow strips
Pinch of pepper	1 cup diced celery
1/3 cup all-purpose flour	1 bay leaf
2 tablespoons vegetable shortening	1/4 teaspoon dried oregano
1 large onion, quartered	
1 cup apple juice	

Sprinkle the meat with salt and pepper, then dredge it in the flour. Heat the shortening in a heavy skillet. Add the meat and cook until browned on all sides. Add the onion. Pour in the apple juice and bring to a boil. Cover and simmer for about 1½ hours, or until the meat is tender. Place the apples, carrots, and celery in a casserole, then pour the stew into the casserole. Add the bay leaf and oregano and bake at 350 degrees for 30 minutes. Remove and discard the bay leaf. Serve the stew over mashed potatoes or rice.

Elizabeth on 37th

Elizabeth on 37th opened in Savannah in May 1981, as the creation of chef Elizabeth Terry and her husband, Michael. The simple elegance of their turn-of-the-century Southern mansion sets the perfect tone for her stunning regional cooking.

Chef Terry is devoted to classic Southern cooking, and she has extensively researched Savannah cooking of the eighteenth and nineteenth centuries. She has combined traditional cooking methods with a modern interest in fresh, health-conscious menus.

Elizabeth Terry's reputation as an innovator and leader in the cuisine of the "New South" is well established. Her awards have been many.

We hope that you enjoy the recipes from Elizabeth's cookbook *Savannah Seasons: Food and Stories from Elizabeth on 37th*.

Fried Grits Cakes with Sausage

SERVES 6

1 pound hot bulk sausage
2 tablespoons grated orange zest
4 cups chicken broth

1 cup stone-ground yellow grits
Vegetable oil

In a large skillet over medium heat, combine the sausage and orange zest, stirring to break up the sausage. Sauté until browned and then drain; set aside.

In a large saucepan over medium heat, bring the chicken broth to a boil. Slowly stir in the grits. Reduce the heat, cover, and simmer for 20 minutes, stirring occasionally. Stir the sausage into the grits. Spread the mixture in a 13 × 9-inch baking pan to cool, then refrigerate until well chilled. Cut the chilled grits into squares and sauté in vegetable oil until crisp and browned on both sides.

Shrimp Bel Vedere

SERVES 6

2 cups new potatoes, cut into
  ½-inch dice
1 cup water
½ cup (1 stick) butter
2 pounds medium shrimp, peeled
  and deveined, tossed with
  1 tablespoon cornstarch
1¼ cups fresh corn kernels
  (from 3 ears)
3 green or poblano peppers, seeded
  and slivered

1 cup julienned Vidalia or other
  sweet onion
2 cups diced fresh tomatoes
18 whole small okra
2 bay leaves
¼ teaspoon cayenne pepper
½ teaspoon paprika
½ teaspoon salt

Put the potatoes and water in a large stockpot and bring to a boil over high heat. Lower the heat to medium and cook for 15 minutes, or until the potatoes are soft and the water almost gone. Stir in the butter and cook for 3 minutes longer, then stir in the shrimp, vegetables, bay leaves, cayenne, paprika, and salt, increase the heat to high, and cook, stirring occasionally, until the shrimp are just pink, about 5 minutes. Discard the bay leaves and serve immediately.

Blueberry Raspberry Pecan Crisp

SERVES 4

⅔ cup all-purpose flour
2 tablespoons rolled oats
⅓ cup packed brown sugar
½ teaspoon cinnamon
¼ cup (½ stick) cold butter, cubed
½ cup pecans, toasted

1 cup fresh raspberries or
  blackberries
½ cup granulated sugar
1 tablespoon cornstarch
4 cups fresh blueberries
2 tablespoons honey

Preheat the oven to 375 degrees.

For the topping, in the bowl of a food processor, combine the flour, oats, brown sugar, and cinnamon, and process briefly to mince the oats. Add the butter and process until the mixture looks moist and begins to stick together. Stir in the pecans. Transfer to a small bowl and refrigerate.

In a large saucepan over high heat, stir together the raspberries, granulated sugar, and cornstarch. Bring to a boil and cook, stirring, until the mixture is slightly thick and shiny, about 3 minutes. Stir in the blueberries and pour into a baking dish. Crumble the topping over the berries and bake for 30 minutes, or until golden. Remove the dish from the oven, drizzle the honey over the topping, and return to the oven for 5 minutes. Cool for at least 15 minutes before serving. Serve warm.

The Johnny Harris Restaurant

The Johnny Harris Restaurant is truly a Savannah institution. Located at 1651 East Victory Drive, it began life in 1936. Some say it had the first air-conditioned dining room in the South. Phil Donaldson, the owner, has worked in the restaurant in various capacities since the age of seven. Over the years Phil has had the privilege of meeting and feeding hundreds of thousands of people from all walks of life. When Jackie Gleason's train rumbled through Savannah it would stop long enough to send out for Johnny Harris's succulent spareribs.

Renowned songwriter Johnny Mercer, a Savannah native, always ate fried chicken in the restaurant's kitchen when he was in town. It's said that many nights, just before closing, he would place orders for fried chicken for his late evening card games. The list goes on and on, from Robert Mitchum to Bob Hope to John Berendt, who wrote in *Midnight in the Garden of Good and Evil* that while incarcerated Jim Williams would get supper from Johnny Harris's one night and Elizabeth on 37th the next.

I think, however, that what might please the gentlemanly Phil Donaldson the most is the multiple generations of hometown folks who continue to carry on the tradition of enjoying wonderful meals from Johnny Harris's.

Thanks ever so much for sharing with us, Phil—your food, your hospitality, and your recipes.

Steak au Poivre

SERVES 4

⅓ cup black peppercorns
Four ¾- to 1-inch thick strip steaks
5 tablespoons olive oil

2 tablespoons, plus 1 teaspoon butter
¼ cup minced shallots
¼ cup Cognac or brandy

½ cup rich beef broth

Salt and pepper

4 tablespoons chopped fresh
   tarragon

Crack the peppercorns by crushing them against a cutting board with the side of a heavy knife or the bottom of a pan. Press the peppercorns into both sides of the steaks. Heat the oil and 2 tablespoons of the butter in a heavy skillet. Cook the steaks to the desired doneness. Remove them from the pan and keep warm while you prepare the sauce. Add the shallots to the hot skillet and sauté until translucent. For the next step, be very careful as the Cognac will create a large flame. Add the Cognac or brandy to the pan. Light a match and touch flame to liquid. Stepping back, shake the pan above the burner until the flame dies out; add the broth and cook over very high heat. Whisk in the remaining teaspoon of butter and the tarragon. Season with salt and pepper to taste. Serve the sauce over the steaks.

Baked Flounder

SERVES 3–4

1½ pounds flounder fillets*

1½ cups (2 sticks) melted butter

Salt and pepper

2 cups breadcrumbs

3 ounces sherry

Preheat the oven to 375 degrees. Lay the flounder fillets in a buttered 13 × 9 × 2-inch baking dish. Season with salt and pepper to taste.

Pour the sherry over the fish, then pour on half of the butter. Cover the fish with breadcrumbs and pour the remaining butter over the crumbs. Bake for 15 minutes.

*Cooked lobster meat or raw scallops may be substituted for flounder.

Pasta Puttanesca Sauce

SERVES 4–6

Phil Donaldson writes: "This Italian sauce is probably the best-tasting spaghetti sauce we have ever tasted. However, it is not very well-known. The name means 'prostitute's sauce,' and the story goes that the ladies would prepare the sauce and put it on their windowsills, and the smell was so fabulous that it attracted clients for them."

¼ cup olive oil
4 cloves garlic, crushed
Two 14½-ounce cans Italian plum tomatoes, coarsely chopped, juice reserved
½ cup sliced black olives
¼ cup dry red wine

¼ cup drained capers
8 anchovy fillets, minced
¼ cup chopped fresh Italian parsley or basil
1½ teaspoons dried oregano
½ teaspoon dried rosemary
⅛ teaspoon red pepper flakes

Heat the olive oil in a heavy skillet over medium heat. Sauté the garlic until translucent. Add the tomatoes and their reserved juice, then stir in the olives, wine, capers, anchovies, parsley, dried herbs, and pepper flakes.

Bring to a boil, cover, and reduce to a slow simmer. Simmer for 45 minutes. Serve over pasta.

Lucile Wright

This chapter would not be complete without a sampling of recipes from Mrs. Lucile Wright. Mrs. Wright just celebrated her ninety-first birthday and is no longer active in the food-service business, but to native Savannahians she remains a sweet memory of bygone days.

Miss Lucile was the most sought-after caterer in Savannah. Her food was in such high demand that parties were sometimes rescheduled to suit her availability. Firmly established as a local legend, Miss Lucile was made even more famous by the book *Midnight in the Garden of Good and Evil*. Page 8 in "The Book" will acquaint you with Mrs. Wright even more. Jim Williams loved to entertain and entertain he did, always quite lavishly. His Christmas party was the highlight of Savannah's social season, and the party would not be complete if the tables were not groaning with delectable bites provided by Miss Lucile. I wish to thank the Savannah *News Press* for supplying me with two of her famous recipes from the "Inside Close-ups" column.

Lucile Wright's Tomato Sandwiches

Bread: Use thin slices, whole wheat on the bottom, white on the top. Cut the bread into circles with a biscuit cutter, and remove the circle of bread. Prepare the bread a day ahead, if you like.

Spread: Mix a little grated onion (too much makes it bitter), black pepper, and Accent into Hellman's mayonnaise. No measurements here. Make it to taste. Spread the bread a day ahead. Cover and refrigerate.

Tomatoes: Peel, slice, and drain thoroughly between layers of paper towels. (Soggy tomatoes make soggy sandwiches.) Sprinkle the tomatoes with Lawry's Seasoned Salt before assembling the sandwiches. You may prepare the sandwiches several hours before a party. Cover with a damp tea towel and refrigerate.

Lucile Wright's Oyster Bisque

YIELDS 2½ QUARTS

1 quart oysters (extra pint optional)
Salt and black pepper
4 stalks celery, cut in medium-size pieces
1 medium onion, chopped
4 cups milk
2 cups heavy cream
4 tablespoons butter

4 tablespoons all-purpose flour
Freshly grated nutmeg
Curry powder
Accent
1 tablespoon fresh lemon juice
1 tablespoon Worcestershire sauce
Cayenne pepper
Paprika
Chopped fresh parsley

Pick over the oysters for shells. Simmer the oysters in a covered pot over low heat with a little salt and black pepper. Stir occasionally until the edges of the oysters curl. Lift the oysters out of the stock with a slotted spoon and put them in a colander with a bowl underneath to catch the pot liquor. Pour the stock from the pot into the bowl, being careful to discard any oyster dregs. Set the stock aside.

Cook the celery and onion in a little water until tender; drain, reserving the broth. Add the broth to the oyster stock (should measure about 2 cups), then add the milk and cream (reserve a little cream to whip for garnish).

Heat the butter, then whisk in the flour to make a roux. Add the stock mixture to the roux, and stir briskly until thickened and smooth. Add a little nutmeg, a pinch of curry powder, a pinch of Accent, the lemon juice, Worcestershire, and cayenne. Correct the seasonings. Mash the oysters with the celery and onions and mix well; add to oyster stock. Keep warm over hot water until time to serve. Whip the reserved cream. Pour bisque into individual bowls. Swirl an even portion of whipped cream into each bowl. Add a little paprika and chopped parsley to garnish. Offer sherry separately, if desired.

John Berendt

All of the people and places included in the Peers chapter of this book live in Savannah, with the exception of one. This person could not be more a part of this city if he had lived here a hundred years—and do tell, dearie, he's a Yankee! The man I'm talking about is noted author John Berendt, who brought fame to himself and Savannah with his highly acclaimed *Midnight in the Garden of Good and Evil*. If you haven't read "The Book," as we refer to it here in Savannah, by all means treat yourself to the talent of John's storytelling ability. I promise, you won't be disappointed.

John wrote the wonderful Introduction to my first book, *The Lady & Sons Savannah Country Cookbook,* for which I will always be grateful. It seems only fitting that I take this opportunity to formally thank you, John, for the support you gave me. Thank you from the bottom of my heart!

I felt this project wouldn't be complete without some of John's favorite recipes, so naturally I turned to his mother, Carol Berendt, who I knew was filled with love and pride for the son she affectionately calls Johnny. So, here we go, three of Johnny's and his mother's favorite recipes.

Fresh Cabbage and Sweet Sausages

SERVES 2

4 Italian-style sweet sausages, or 4 unseasoned fresh pork sausages
2 potatoes, peeled and quartered

4 cups finely sliced green cabbage
½ cup water

Put sausages in a skillet, place potatoes between them, cover with cabbage, and add water. Cover and cook over very low heat, and forget about it until suppertime. It won't burn, but it will brown by itself. Serve with mustard and vinegar.

Lemon Hollandaise Sauce

YIELDS ½ CUP

John and his mother serve this wonderful sauce over roasted chicken breasts to make a delicious lemon chicken.

2 egg yolks
4 tablespoons cream
2 large tablespoons butter
Juice of ½ lemon

Pinch of salt
Pinch of sugar
Chicken broth (optional)

Combine all ingredients in the top of a double boiler, over boiling water. Stir until thick, approximately 3 minutes; set aside until ready to use. Do not reheat or cover the pot. Mrs. Berendt suggests thinning this out with a little chicken broth, if needed.

Pots de Crème

6 ounces semisweet chocolate chips
2 eggs
1 tablespoon sugar

1 tablespoon brandy
Pinch of salt
¾ cup milk

Put all ingredients except the milk in a blender. In a saucepan, over medium heat, heat the milk until very hot but not boiling. Add the milk to the blender and blend 20 seconds. Pour the mixture into 6 ramekins or demitasse cups and chill for at least 4 hours. Serve with whipped cream, if desired, or try using it as the filling in a pie, using a prebaked crust.

Desserts

CAKES AND PIES

Pear-Licious Cake

Chocolate Torte

Green Tomato Cake

Fourth-Generation Blackberry Jam Cake

Double-Dutch Chocolate Fudge Upside-Down Cake

Milky Way Cake

Sour Cream Caramel Cake

Texas Sheet Cake

Cheesecake with Praline Sauce

Caramel-Nut Pound Cake

Hummingbird Cake

Coconut Cream Cake

Mississippi Mud Cake

Orange Blossoms

Chocolate Chip Pound Cake

Red Velvet Pound Cake

Orange Slice Cake

Volcano Cake

Caramel Apple Cheesecake

Italian Love Cake

Coconut White Fruit Cake

Grandgirl's Fresh Apple Cake from Georgia

Pig Pickin' Cake

Turtle Cheesecake

Pecan Pudding Cake

Blueberry Cream Pie

Peanut Butter Pie

Lisa's Southern Pecan Pie

Cherry Cream Cheese Pie

Chocolate Cream Pie

Apple Crisp

Ritz Cracker Pie

Lemon Meringue Pie

Old-Fashioned Sweet Potato Pie

Key Lime Pie

Shaver's Chocolate Pecan Pie

Half-Million-Dollar Pie

Fried Apple Pies

Our Pear Cobbler

Old-Fashioned Fudge Pie

PUDDINGS AND CUSTARDS

Pumpkin Gingerbread Trifle

Old-Fashioned Rice Pudding

Crème Brûlée

Strawberry Cream Shortcake

Chocolate Trifle

English Trifle

Mexican Flan

Compote Clouds

Butterscotch Delight

Heavenly Banana Delight

Chocolate Bread Pudding

COOKIES AND BROWNIES

Sugar Cookies

Oatmeal Cookies

Hidden Kisses

Brown Sugar Cookies

Swedish Countess Cookies

Magical Peanut Butter Cookies

Brenda's Kahlúa Brownies

Pecan Pie Squares

Lemon Bars

Glazed Honey Bars

Chocolate Mound Brownies

Pear-Licious Cake

SERVES 16–20

CAKE

1¼ cups vegetable oil
2 cups granulated sugar
3 eggs
3 cups all-purpose flour
1 teaspoon salt
1 teaspoon baking soda
1 teaspoon cinnamon
1 teaspoon vanilla extract
2 cups chopped canned Bartlett
   pears in syrup, well drained
   (reserve syrup for glaze)
1 cup chopped pecans

GLAZE

1 tablespoon butter, at room
   temperature
1½ cups confectioners' sugar
2–3 tablespoons syrup from canned
   pears

Preheat the oven to 325 degrees. In a mixing bowl, combine the oil, sugar, and eggs, and beat well. Sift together the flour, salt, baking soda, and cinnamon. Add this to the creamed mixture and stir until blended. Stir in the vanilla. Fold in the pears and pecans. Grease and flour a 10-inch tube pan or Bundt pan, and spoon in the batter. Bake for 1 hour and 20 minutes, or until the cake tests done. Let the cake cool for 20 minutes, then turn it out onto a cake rack to cool completely. While the cake cools, make the glaze. Blend the butter and confectioners' sugar with enough of the reserved pear syrup to make a smooth, slightly runny glaze. Drizzle the glaze over the cake top, letting some run down the sides. ❦ ❦ ❦ *The Lady & Sons*

Chocolate Torte

SERVES 8

One 6-ounce package chocolate
    chips
¼ cup (½ stick) butter
¼ cup hot water
4 egg yolks
8 tablespoons cold water

8 tablespoons Kahlúa, sweet sherry,
    or amaretto
2 packages ladyfingers
1½ cups heavy cream
⅓ cup sugar

Combine the chocolate, butter, and hot water in the top of a double boiler. Place the pan over medium-high heat and cook until the chocolate and butter are melted. Add the egg yolks one at a time, stirring well after each; continue to stir for 2 minutes. Remove the pan from the heat. Combine the cold water and liqueur in a small bowl, and quickly dip the ladyfingers in this mixture. Line the bottom of a 9 × 5 × 3-inch loaf pan with ladyfingers, and pour half of the chocolate cream over them.

Add another layer of ladyfingers, the remaining chocolate cream, and another layer of ladyfingers. Refrigerate for at least 2 hours. Just before serving, whip the cream with the sugar until stiff. Unmold the torte onto a platter and frost it with the whipped cream.

Green Tomato Cake

SERVES 15–20

2¼ cups sugar
1 cup melted vegetable shortening
3 eggs
2 teaspoons vanilla extract
3 cups all-purpose flour
1 teaspoon salt
1 teaspoon baking soda

1 teaspoon cinnamon
½ teaspoon freshly grated nutmeg
1 cup chopped walnuts
1 cup raisins
2½ cups diced green tomatoes
1 small can Angel Flake coconut

Preheat the oven to 350 degrees. In a mixing bowl, cream the sugar, shortening, eggs, and vanilla until smooth.

Add the flour, salt, soda, and spices, and stir to blend. Stir in the nuts, raisins, and tomatoes. Grease a 9 × 13-inch pan. Pour the batter into the pan and sprinkle the coconut on top. Bake for 1 hour.

❦ ❦ ❦   *The Lady & Sons*

Fourth-Generation Blackberry Jam Cake

SERVES 15–18

CAKE
1 cup vegetable shortening
1⅓ cups granulated sugar
4 eggs
4 cups all-purpose flour
1 teaspoon baking powder
1 teaspoon baking soda
1 teaspoon salt
1 teaspoon ground allspice
1 teaspoon cinnamon
1 teaspoon freshly grated nutmeg

1 cup buttermilk
1 cup chopped pecans
1 cup raisins
2 cups blackberry jam

CARAMEL ICING
½ cup (1 stick) butter
1 cup packed brown sugar
¼ cup milk
2 cups confectioners' sugar, sifted

Preheat the oven to 350 degrees. Grease and flour two 10-inch round cake pans.

For the cake, in a mixing bowl, cream the shortening and granulated sugar until fluffy. Add the eggs one at a time, mixing well after each. Sift the flour with the baking powder, baking soda, salt, and spices. Add the flour mixture alternately with the buttermilk, beginning and ending with the flour. Stir in the nuts and raisins, then stir in the jam.

Pour the batter into the prepared pans and bake for 30 to 40 minutes, or until the cake pulls away from the pan. Cool the cakes in the pans for 10 minutes, the turn them out onto cake racks to cool completely.

While the cake cools, make the icing. Melt the butter in a saucepan, add the brown sugar, and bring to a boil. Boil over low heat for 2 minutes, stirring constantly. Add the milk and continue stirring until the mixture returns to a boil. Remove the pan from the heat and scrape the mixture into a mixing bowl. Let cool. Add the confectioners' sugar a little at a time, beating well after each addition, until the icing is thick enough to spread. Fill and ice the cake.

VARIATION: You may prefer to bake this cake in a tube pan: Pour the batter into the greased and floured pan and bake for 15 minutes, then reduce the heat to 300 degrees and bake for about 1 hour 15 minutes, or until the cake tests done. Cool as directed for the 10-inch layers.

Double-Dutch Chocolate Fudge Upside-Down Cake

SERVES 8–10

1 cup all-purpose flour
1 cup granulated sugar
2 tablespoons, plus ¼ cup cocoa
    powder
2 teaspoons baking powder
¼ teaspoon salt
½ cup milk

2 tablespoons vegetable oil or
    melted butter
1½ teaspoons vanilla extract
½ cup chopped walnuts (optional)
1 cup packed brown sugar
1½ cups boiling water
1 cup heavy cream

Preheat the oven to 350 degrees.

In a mixing bowl, stir together the flour, ¾ cup of the granulated sugar, 2 tablespoons of the cocoa powder, the baking powder, and the salt. Add the milk, the oil, and 1 teaspoon of the vanilla, and stir until blended. Stir in the nuts, if using. Pour the batter into a greased 9 × 13-inch pan.

In a small bowl, combine the brown sugar with the ¼ cup cocoa powder; stir well. Spread this mixture over the batter in the pan. Using a large spoon, drizzle the boiling water over the cake; do not stir. Bake for 40 to 45 minutes, or until the top of the cake is firm. Let the cake cool slightly. Meanwhile, whip the cream with the remaining ¼ cup granulated sugar and ½ teaspoon vanilla. Cut the cake into squares and place them upside down (gooey side up) on dessert plates. Spoon a dollop of whipped cream onto each piece of cake.

Milky Way Cake

SERVES 16–20

CAKE

Confectioners' sugar, for dusting
   pans
Eight 1¾-ounce Milky Way bars
1½ cups (3 sticks) butter
2 cups granulated sugar
4 eggs, well beaten
2½ cups all-purpose flour
¼ teaspoon baking soda
1¼ cups buttermilk
1 cup chopped pecans
1 teaspoon vanilla extract

ICING

2½ cups granulated sugar
1 cup evaporated milk
1 cup marshmallow cream
½ cup (1 stick) butter
6-ounces chocolate chips
1 cup chopped pecans

Preheat the oven to 325 degrees. Grease three 9-inch cake pans and dust them with confectioners' sugar. To make the cake, melt the Milky Way bars with 1 stick of butter. Remove from the heat and let cool. Cream the remaining 2 sticks of butter with the granulated sugar. Add the beaten eggs and the cooled chocolate mixture. Sift the flour and the baking soda together. Alternately add the flour and buttermilk to the batter, blending well. Add the nuts and vanilla. Divide the batter among the prepared pans and bake for 30 to 40 minutes, or until the cake is firm to the touch. Cool for 5 minutes, remove from the pans, and place on cooling racks. While the cake cools, prepare the icing: Combine the sugar and milk in a heavy saucepan. Cook to the soft-ball stage (234 degrees on a candy thermometer). Remove the pan from the heat and add the marshmallow cream, butter, and chocolate chips, stirring until melted. Add the pecans. When the cake has cooled completely, frost each layer, sides, and the top of the Milky Way Cake.

❦ ❦ ❦ **The Lady & Sons**

Sour Cream Caramel Cake

SERVES 15–20

CAKE
1 cup (2 sticks) butter
3 cups granulated sugar
6 eggs
2⅔ cups all-purpose flour
1 teaspoon salt
¼ teaspoon baking soda
1 cup sour cream
1 tablespoon vanilla extract

EASY CARAMEL ICING
2 cups packed dark brown sugar
1 cup (2 sticks) butter
½ cup evaporated milk
½ teaspoon vanilla extract
4 cups confectioners' sugar

Preheat the oven to 350 degrees. Grease and flour three 9-inch round cake pans or one 13 × 9-inch pan. For the cake, cream the butter and granulated sugar until fluffy. Add the eggs one at a time, beating after each addition. Sift the flour, salt, and baking soda together. Alternately add the flour mixture and the sour cream to the batter, stirring well. Stir in the vanilla. Pour the batter into the prepared pans and bake for 25 to 35 minutes or until firm to the touch if using round pans, 45 minutes if using the rectangular pan. Let the cakes cool in the pans for a few minutes, then turn them out onto cake racks to cool completely.

While the cakes cool, make the icing: In a large, heavy saucepan, combine the brown sugar, butter, and milk. Cook over low heat until the butter melts. Increase the heat to medium and cook, stirring constantly, for 2 minutes longer. Remove the pan from the heat and stir in the vanilla. Gradually mix in the confectioners' sugar. Let the icing cool slightly, then frost the cooled cake.   ❧ ❧ ❧ **The Lady & Sons**

Texas Sheet Cake

SERVES 20–24

CAKE

1 cup (2 sticks) butter
1 cup water
4 tablespoons cocoa powder
2 cups all-purpose flour
2 cups granulated sugar
1 teaspoon baking soda
½ teaspoon salt
2 eggs
½ cup sour cream

ICING

½ cup (1 stick) butter
6 tablespoons milk
4 tablespoons cocoa powder
*1 pound confectioners' sugar,
  sifted*
1 teaspoon vanilla extract
1 cup chopped pecans (optional)

Preheat the oven to 350 degrees. For the cake, combine the butter, water, and cocoa in a saucepan, and bring to a boil. Remove from the heat. In a mixing bowl, mix together the flour, granulated sugar, baking soda, and salt. Add the butter mixture all at once, and stir to blend. Whisk the eggs and sour cream together; add to the batter and mix well. Pour the batter into an 18 × 12 × 1-inch pan and bake for 20 minutes.

Just before the cake is done, make the icing: Combine the butter, milk, and cocoa in a large, heavy saucepan and bring to a boil. Add the confectioners' sugar and vanilla, and mix well. Ice the cake while it is still warm, and top with nuts if desired. ❦ ❦ ❦ *The Lady & Sons*

Cheesecake with Praline Sauce

SERVES 12

CRUST

1½ cups graham cracker crumbs
4 tablespoons granulated sugar
¼ cup (½ stick) melted butter

TOPPING

1½ cups sour cream
4 tablespoons granulated sugar
1 teaspoon vanilla extract

FILLING

Three 8-ounce packages cream
  cheese, at room temperature
1 cup granulated sugar
5 eggs
1 tablespoon vanilla extract

PRALINE SAUCE

2 tablespoons light brown sugar
2 tablespoons cornstarch
1 cup dark corn syrup
½ cup chopped pecans
1 teaspoon vanilla extract

Preheat the oven to 350 degrees.

For the crust, stir together the graham cracker crumbs, sugar, and butter. Pat this mixture into the bottom and sides of a 9-inch spring-form pan.

Make the filling: In a large bowl, beat together the cream cheese and granulated sugar. Beat in the eggs, one a time, then beat in the vanilla. Pour the filling into the crust and bake for 1 hour. Remove the cake from the oven and cool for 10 minutes.

Meanwhile, make the topping: In a bowl, mix the sour cream, sugar, and vanilla until well blended. Spread this mixture over the warm cake and return to the oven for 5 minutes. Let the cake cool to room temperature in the pan, then cover with plastic wrap and refrigerate for at least 4 hours, or overnight.

At serving time, use a table knife to loosen the cake from the pan. Remove the sides of the pan and place the cake on a platter, leaving it on pan bottom. To make the praline sauce, in a small heavy saucepan stir together the brown sugar and cornstarch. Stir in the corn syrup and cook over medium heat, stirring constantly, until thick. Remove the pan from the heat and stir in the nuts and vanilla. Cool slightly.

Serve the cheesecake, passing the sauce in a bowl with a small ladle. Store any leftovers in the refrigerator.   ❧ ❧ ❧ **The Lady & Sons**

Caramel-Nut Pound Cake

SERVES 16–20

1 cup (2 sticks) butter
½ cup vegetable shortening
1 pound light brown sugar
1 cup granulated sugar
5 large eggs
3 cups all-purpose flour

½ teaspoon baking powder
½ teaspoon salt
1 cup milk
1 cup chopped pecans
1 tablespoon vanilla extract

Preheat the oven to 325 degrees. In a mixing bowl, cream the butter and shortening. Beat in the brown sugar a little at a time. Add the granulated sugar and beat until light and fluffy. Add the eggs one at a time, beating well after each addition. Sift the flour with the baking powder and salt. Alternately add the flour mixture and the milk to the batter, blending well. Stir in the nuts and vanilla.

Bake in a greased and floured tube pan for 1½ hours. Cool for 10 to 15 minutes and invert onto serving platter. ❦ ❦ ❦ **The Lady & Sons**

Hummingbird Cake

SERVES 18–20

CAKE
3 cups all-purpose flour
2 cups granulated sugar
1 teaspoon baking soda
1 teaspoon cinnamon
½ teaspoon salt
3 eggs, beaten
¾ cup vegetable oil
1¾ cups mashed bananas
One 8-ounce can crushed
    pineapple, with juice
1 cup chopped pecans
1½ teaspoons vanilla extract

FROSTING
One 8-ounce package cream cheese,
    at room temperature
½ cup (1 stick) butter, at room
    temperature
1 pound confectioners' sugar,
    sifted
1 teaspoon vanilla extract
½ cup chopped pecans

Preheat the oven to 350 degrees. Grease and flour three 9-inch round cake pans. For the cake, in a mixing bowl, stir together the flour, sugar, baking soda, cinnamon, and salt. Add the eggs and oil and stir just until the dry ingredients are moistened. Do *not* beat. Stir in the banana, the pineapple and its juice, the pecans, and the vanilla. Divide the batter among the prepared pans and bake for 23 to 28 minutes, or until a wooden pick inserted in the center comes out clean. Cool the cake layers in the pans for 10 minutes, then turn them out onto a rack to cool completely.

While the cake cools, make the frosting: In a bowl, blend together the cream cheese and butter. Gradually add the confectioners' sugar, beating until light and fluffy. Beat in the vanilla. Stir in the pecans, or reserve them to sprinkle over the frosted cake. Fill and frost the cake.

❦ ❦ ❦ *The Lady & Sons*

Coconut Cream Cake

SERVES 20

This cake is worth the wait. The longer it sits the better it tastes.

CAKE
1 cup (2 sticks) butter, at room
   temperature
2 cups granulated sugar
5 eggs
3½ cups all-purpose flour
3 teaspoons baking powder
1 cup milk
2 teaspoons vanilla extract

FILLING
1 cup chilled heavy cream
2 cups sour cream
2 cups confectioners' sugar
1 teaspoon vanilla extract
3 cups shredded coconut, plus more
   for topping
One 12-ounce container Cool
   Whip (optional)

Preheat the oven to 350 degrees. Grease and flour three 9-inch round pans. For the cake, cream the butter and granulated sugar until light and fluffy. Add the eggs one at a time, beating well after each addition. Combine the flour and baking powder; add to the creamed mixture alternately with the milk, beginning and ending with flour. Stir in the vanilla. Divide the batter among the prepared pans and bake for 25 to

30 minutes, or until firm to the touch. Cool the cakes for 10 minutes in the pans, then turn them out to cool completely.

While the cakes cool, make the filling: In a large chilled bowl, whip the heavy cream until stiff. Fold in the sour cream, then gradually add the confectioners' sugar. Stir in the vanilla, then fold in the coconut.

To serve, split each cake layer in half horizontally. Spread the filling between the layers and on top of the cake. Place the cake in an airtight container and refrigerate for 3 days before serving. When ready to serve, remove from refrigerator and sprinkle with coconut. If desired, frost with Cool Whip. ❦ ❦ ❦ *The Lady & Sons*

Mississippi Mud Cake

SERVES 15–20

CAKE
2 cups granulated sugar
1 cup vegetable shortening
4 eggs
1½ cups all-purpose flour
⅓ cup cocoa powder
1¼ teaspoons salt
1 cup chopped walnuts
3 teaspoons vanilla extract
One 10½-ounce package
   miniature marshmallows

ICING
¾ cup (1½ sticks) butter, at room
   temperature
1 pound confectioners' sugar
⅓ cup cocoa powder
½ cup evaporated milk
1 cup chopped walnuts
1 teaspoon vanilla extract

Preheat the oven to 300 degrees. For the cake, in a mixing bowl, cream the granulated sugar and shortening well. Add the eggs and beat well. Sift the flour, cocoa powder, and salt together. Stir the flour mixture into the creamed mixture. Add the nuts and vanilla. Pour the batter into a greased 9 × 13-inch pan and bake for 30 minutes. Remove from the oven and cover the top of the cake with the marshmallows. Return the cake to the oven and bake for about 10 minutes longer, or until the marshmallows melt. While the cake is baking, make the icing: Beat the butter, confectioners' sugar, and cocoa, until creamy. Slowly beat in the milk. Stir in the nuts and vanilla. Ice the cake while it is still warm.

❦ ❦ ❦ *The Lady & Sons*

Orange Blossoms

YIELDS 7–8 DOZEN

CAKES

1 package yellow cake mix

One 3.4-ounce package instant
    lemon pudding mix

4 eggs

¾ cup cold water

¾ cup vegetable oil

GLAZE

3 cups confectioners' sugar

½ cup frozen orange juice
    concentrate, thawed

3 tablespoons melted butter

3 tablespoons water

Preheat the oven to 325 degrees. Grease one or two miniature muffin pans. For the cakes, in a mixing bowl, combine the cake mix, pudding mix, eggs, water, and oil, and beat well. Fill the prepared muffin pans, using about 1 tablespoon of batter for each cake. Bake for 10 to 12 minutes, or until the cakes spring back when touched.

For the glaze, mix the confectioners' sugar, orange juice, butter, and water until smooth; set aside.

Dip the blossoms in the glaze immediately after removing them from the oven. Drain on waxed paper.

Chocolate Chip Pound Cake

SERVES 16

4 eggs

1½ cups water

1 teaspoon vanilla extract

1 package butter recipe cake mix

One 3.4-ounce package instant
    vanilla pudding mix

One 3.4-ounce package instant
    chocolate pudding mix

½ cup (1 stick) melted butter

¼ cup vegetable oil

6-ounces chocolate chips

Confectioners' sugar, for dusting

Preheat the oven to 350 degrees. Grease and flour a tube pan or bundt pan. In a mixing bowl, beat the eggs, water, and vanilla by hand. Stir in the cake mix and pudding mixes. Slowly add the butter and oil, and mix well. Stir in the chocolate chips. Pour into the prepared pan.

Bake for 50 to 60 minutes. Cool for 10 minutes, then invert onto a cake plate. Sift confectioners' sugar over the cake, or drizzle chocolate sauce over it, if desired. ❀❀❀ ***The Lady & Sons***

Red Velvet Pound Cake

SERVES 16

CAKE

1 cup (2 sticks) butter, at room temperature
½ cup vegetable shortening
3 cups granulated sugar
7 eggs
One 1-ounce bottle red food coloring
2 teaspoons vanilla extract
3 cups cake flour
¼ teaspoon salt
1 cup milk

FROSTING

Two 3-ounce packages cream cheese, at room temperature
½ cup (1 stick) butter, at room temperature
1 teaspoon vanilla extract
One 1-pound package confectioners' sugar, sifted
1–2 tablespoons milk, if needed

Preheat the oven to 325 degrees. Grease and flour a 10-inch tube pan. For the cake, in a mixing bowl, combine the butter, shortening, and sugar, and cream until light and fluffy. Add the eggs one at a time, beating well after each addition. Stir in the food coloring and vanilla. Stir together the flour and salt; add this to the creamed mixture alternately with the milk, beating well. Pour the batter into the prepared pan. Bake 1 hour and 20 minutes, or until a toothpick inserted in the center comes out clean. Cool the cake in the pan for 10 minutes, then turn it out onto a rack to cool completely.

While the cake cools, make the frosting: Combine the cream cheese and butter and blend until smooth. Stir in the vanilla, mixing well. Gradually add the sugar, beating until creamy. If necessary, add a little milk to achieve a spreading consistency.

Frost the cake.

Orange Slice Cake

SERVES 15–20

CAKE

4 cups all-purpose flour
½ teaspoon baking soda
1 pound candy orange slices
One 8-ounce package pitted dates
2 cups chopped pecans
1 cup shredded coconut
1 cup (2 sticks) butter
2 cups granulated sugar

4 eggs
1 teaspoon baking soda
½ cup buttermilk

GLAZE

1 cup confectioners' sugar
2 tablespoons orange juice
1 teaspoon grated orange zest

Preheat the oven to 300 degrees. Grease a 10-inch tube pan. For the cake, sift together 3½ cups of the flour and the baking soda. Cut the orange slices and dates into small pieces and add them with the remaining ½ cup flour. Add the nuts and coconut; set aside. Cream the butter and sugar. Add the eggs and beat well. Stir the baking soda into the buttermilk. Alternately add the flour and the buttermilk mixture, beginning and ending with flour. Fold in the candy mixture. Pour the batter into the prepared pan and bake for 1¾ to 2 hours, or until a wooden pick inserted in the center comes out clean. Cool the cake in the pan for 10 minutes, then turn the cake out of the pan onto a rack.

To make the glaze, stir together the confectioners' sugar, orange juice, and zest.

Drizzle the glaze over the warm cake.   ❦ ❦ ❦   *The Lady & Sons*

Volcano Cake

SERVES 12–16

1 cup shredded coconut
1 cup chopped walnuts or pecans

1 package German chocolate cake
  mix

10 bite-size Almond Joy candy
  bars, chopped
One 8-ounce package cream cheese,
  at room temperature
½ cup (1 stick butter), at room
  temperature
2 cups confectioners' sugar

Preheat the oven to 350 degrees. Spray a 13 × 9 × 2-inch pan with nonstick cooking spray. Mix the coconut and nuts and spread them evenly in the pan. Prepare the cake mix as directed on the box. Stir in the chopped candy bars. Pour the batter over the coconut and nuts. Combine the cream cheese, butter, and sugar. Randomly drop tablespoonfuls of this on top of the batter; do not spread them. Bake for 40 to 50 minutes, or until sides of the cake pull away from the pan.

This cake is wonderful served warm or cool with a dollop of whipped cream.   🍀 🍀 🍀   *The Lady & Sons*

Caramel Apple Cheesecake

SERVES 8

One 21-ounce can apple pie filling
One 9-inch graham cracker crust
Two 8-ounce packages cream
  cheese, at room temperature
½ cup sugar
¼ teaspoon vanilla extract
2 eggs
¼ cup caramel topping
12 pecan halves, plus 2 tablespoons
  chopped pecans

Preheat the oven to 350 degrees. Reserve ¾ cup of the apple filling; set aside. Spoon the remaining filling into the crust. Beat together the cream cheese, sugar, and vanilla until smooth. Add the eggs and mix well. Pour this over the pie filling. Bake for 35 minutes, or until the center of the cake is set. Cool to room temperature. Mix the reserved pie filling and caramel topping in a small saucepan and heat for about 1 minute, or until spreadable. Spoon the apple-caramel mixture over the top of the cheesecake and spread evenly. Decorate the edge of the cake with pecan halves and sprinkle with chopped pecans. Refrigerate the cake until ready to serve.

Italian Love Cake

SERVES 15–20

CAKE

2 pounds ricotta cheese
4 eggs
¾ cup sugar
1 teaspoon vanilla extract
1 package fudge marble cake mix

ICING

One 5.1-ounce package instant
    chocolate pudding mix
1 cup cold milk
8 ounces Cool Whip

Preheat the oven to 350 degrees. Grease and flour a 13 × 9-inch pan. For the cake, mix the ricotta, eggs, sugar, and vanilla; set aside. Prepare the cake mix according to package directions and pour it into the prepared pan. Immediately spread the ricotta mixture directly on top of the batter. Bake for 1 hour. Remove from the oven and let cool completely in the pan.

For the icing, stir the pudding mix into the milk, then fold in the Cool Whip. Spread the icing on the cake in the pan and refrigerate overnight. 🌢 🌢 🌢 *The Lady & Sons*

Coconut White Fruit Cake

SERVES 16–20

7 egg whites
1 cup candied cherries
1 cup candied pineapple
1 pound golden raisins
4 cups pecans, chopped
2 cups all-purpose flour
½ teaspoon salt

1 cup (2 sticks) butter, at room
    temperature
2 cups sugar
One 6-ounce package frozen
    grated coconut
1 teaspoon vanilla extract

Preheat the oven to 325 degrees. Line the bottom of a tube or loaf pan with brown paper and grease the paper. In a large bowl, beat the egg whites until stiff peaks form, and set aside. In another large bowl, combine the candied fruits, raisins, and nuts. Add the flour and salt, and toss to mix; set aside. Cream the butter and sugar. Add the beaten egg whites, then the coconut and vanilla. Add the fruit to the coconut mixture. Pour the batter into the prepared pan and bake for 2¼ hours.

Grandgirl's Fresh Apple Cake from Georgia

SERVES 16–20

CAKE
2 cups sugar
3 eggs
1½ cups vegetable oil
¼ cup orange juice
3 cups all-purpose flour
1 teaspoon baking soda
¼ teaspoon salt
1 tablespoon cinnamon
1 tablespoon vanilla extract

3 cups peeled and finely chopped apples
1 cup shredded coconut
1 cup chopped pecans

SAUCE
½ cup (1 stick) butter
1 cup sugar
½ cup buttermilk
½ teaspoon baking soda

Preheat the oven to 325 degrees. Generously grease a tube pan. For the cake, combine all the cake ingredients in a large bowl in the order given and mix well. Pour the batter into the prepared pan and bake for 1½ hours.

Shortly before the cake is done, make the sauce: Melt the butter in a large saucepan, stir in the sugar, buttermilk, and baking soda, and bring to a good rolling boil, stirring constantly. Boil for 1 minute. Pour the sauce over the hot cake in the pan as soon as you remove it from the oven. Let stand 1 hour, then turn out.

Pig Pickin' Cake

SERVES 16–20

CAKE
1 box yellow cake mix
One 11-ounce can mandarin
    oranges, with juice
4 eggs
¼ cup vegetable oil

FROSTING
One 16-ounce can crushed
    pineapple, drained
One 3.4-ounce package instant
    vanilla pudding mix
Two 8-ounce containers Cool
    Whip, or 1 quart heavy cream,
    whipped and sweetened with 1
    cup sugar

Preheat the oven to 350 degrees. Grease and flour three 8-inch round pans. Mix together the cake mix, the oranges with their juice, eggs, and oil. Divide the batter among the prepared pans; layers will be thin. Bake for 15 to 20 minutes, or until the cake tests done. Cool the layers on wire racks.

While the cake cools, make the frosting: Mix the drained pineapple with the pudding mix and fold this mixture into the Cool Whip. Fill and frost the cooled cake layers. Refrigerate until ready to serve.

❀ ❀ ❀ *The Lady & Sons*

Turtle Cheesecake

SERVES 12

CRUST
3 cups chocolate wafer crumbs
¼ cup sugar
⅓ cup melted butter

FILLING
Three 8-ounce packages cream
    cheese, at room temperature
1¼ cups sugar
4 large eggs

1 cup sour cream
1 tablespoon vanilla extract

TOPPING
¼ cup (½ stick) butter
6 ounces chocolate chips
One 12-ounce jar caramel topping
    (Smucker's makes a good one)
1 cup chopped pecans

Preheat the oven to 325 degrees. Lightly grease a 9-inch springform pan. In a bowl, combine the wafer crumbs, sugar, and butter; stir well. Firmly press the mixture on the bottom and 1 inch up the sides of the prepared pan. Bake for 10 minutes. Cool on a wire rack.

For the filling, beat the cream cheese with an electric mixer on medium speed until creamy. Gradually add the sugar, beating well. Add the eggs one at a time, beating well after each addition and scraping the sides and bottom of the bowl as needed. Stir in the sour cream and vanilla. Pour the batter into the prepared crust. Bake for 1 hour and 5 minutes. (Center of cake will not be completely set.) Turn the oven off and partially open the oven door. Leave the cheesecake in the oven for 1 hour. Remove to a wire rack to cool completely. Cover the cake and refrigerate for at least 8 hours. Carefully remove the sides of the pan and transfer the cake to a platter.

For the topping, melt the butter in a small heavy saucepan. Add the chocolate chips and stir over low heat just until the chocolate melts and blends with the butter. Spread the warm chocolate mixture over the cheesecake; refrigerate for 15 minutes.

Combine the caramel topping and pecans in a small saucepan. Bring to a boil, over medium heat, stirring constantly, and boil for 2 minutes. Remove from the heat and cool for 5 minutes, then spread over the chocolate and cool completely. Serve right away, or cover and chill. Refrigerate any leftovers. ❀ ❀ ❀ ***The Lady & Sons***

Pecan Pudding Cake

SERVES 15–20

CAKE

1 package yellow cake mix
1 cup milk
4 eggs
⅓ cup vegetable oil
1 cup chopped pecans

TOPPING

2 cups cold milk
One 3.4-ounce package instant vanilla pudding mix
One 8-ounce package cream cheese, at room temperature
2 cups heavy cream
6 tablespoons sugar
One 26-ounce can crushed pineapple, with juice
½ cup chopped pecans
½ cup coconut flakes

Preheat the oven to 350 degrees. Grease and flour a 13 × 9 × 2-inch pan. In a bowl, combine the cake mix, milk, eggs, oil, and pecans, and blend just until moistened; then beat at medium speed for two minutes. Pour the batter into the prepared pan and bake for 30 to 35 minutes, or until a wooden pick comes out clean.

While the cake is baking, make the topping: Stir together the milk and the pudding, then beat in the cream cheese, a few small pieces at a time; set aside. Whip the cream with the sugar until stiff.

When the cake is done, prick the top with a fork. Pour the pineapple and juice over the hot cake. Spread the cream cheese mixture over the pineapple, then cover the cake with the whipped cream. Garnish the cake with the pecans and coconut. Refrigerate for a while. The longer the cake is refrigerated the better it tastes. This cake freezes well.

Blueberry Cream Pie

SERVES 6–8

¾ cup chopped pecans or walnuts
One 9-inch deep-dish pie crust
 (thawed if frozen)
Two 3-ounce packages cream
 cheese, at room temperature

1 cup confectioners' sugar
1 cup heavy cream
¼ cup granulated sugar
One 21-ounce can blueberry pie
 filling

Press the chopped nuts into the bottom of the pie crust. Bake as directed on the package and let cool. Beat the cream cheese with the confectioners' sugar. Beat the heavy cream with the granulated sugar until it forms soft peaks. Fold the whipped cream into the cream cheese mixture. Spoon this mixture into the cooled pie shell and top with blueberry pie filling. Refrigerate until well chilled. ❦ ❦ ❦ **The Lady & Sons**

Peanut Butter Pie

SERVES 6

One 3-ounce package cream cheese
1 cup confectioners' sugar
½ cup peanut butter
¼ cup evaporated milk

1½ cups Cool Whip
One 8-inch graham cracker crust
⅓ cup chopped peanuts

Whip the cream cheese until fluffy, then beat in the sugar and peanut butter. Slowly add the milk, blending well. Fold the Cool Whip into the cream cheese mixture and spoon this into the pie crust. Sprinkle with peanuts. ❦ ❦ ❦ *The Lady & Sons*

Lisa's Southern Pecan Pie

SERVES 6–8

Lisa, our head chef and night kitchen manager, whips these pies up fresh daily for our guests in the restaurant. They go great with our homemade vanilla ice cream.

4 tablespoons butter
¾ cup packed brown sugar
1 tablespoon all-purpose flour
¼ teaspoon salt
¾ cup cane syrup

3 eggs
1 teaspoon vanilla extract
1 cup pecan halves
One 9-inch pie crust

Preheat the oven to 325 degrees. Cream the butter, sugar, flour, and salt until smooth. Add the syrup, eggs, and vanilla, then fold in the pecans. Pour the filling into the pie crust and bake for 45 to 50 minutes or until firm to the touch.

Serve the pie warm or cool. ❦ ❦ ❦ *The Lady & Sons*

Cherry Cream Cheese Pie

SERVES 6–8

One 8-ounce package cream cheese,
    at room temperature
One 14-ounce can sweetened
    condensed milk
½ cup fresh lemon juice

1 teaspoon vanilla extract
One 9-inch graham cracker crust
One 21-ounce can cherry pie
    filling, chilled

In a mixing bowl, beat the cream cheese until light and fluffy. Gradually add the milk; stir until well blended. Stir in the lemon juice and vanilla. Pour the filling into the crust and refrigerate for 2 to 3 hours. Top with the pie filling before serving.   ❦ ❦ ❦   *The Lady & Sons*

Chocolate Cream Pie

SERVES 6–8

FILLING
1 cup sugar
3 tablespoons cocoa powder
2 tablespoons all-purpose flour
Pinch of salt
3 egg yolks, beaten
2 cups milk
1 tablespoon butter

1 teaspoon vanilla extract
One 9-inch baked pie crust

MERINGUE
3 egg whites
¼ teaspoon cream of tartar
4 tablespoons sugar

For the filling, in a saucepan, stir together the sugar, cocoa, flour, and salt. Slowly stir in the beaten yolks and the milk. Cook over low heat, stirring constantly, until the mixture thickens. Remove from the heat and stir in the butter and vanilla. Pour the filling into a bowl to cool. Pat waxed paper onto the surface of the filling to prevent a crust from forming. When cool, pour the filling into the pie crust.

Preheat the oven to 350 degrees. Make the meringue: Beat the egg whites with the cream of tartar until they form soft peaks. Add 1 tablespoon of sugar at a time, beating constantly, until the whites form stiff peaks. Spoon the meringue over the pie filling, spreading it out to touch the crust all around. Bake until brown, 10 to 12 minutes.

Apple Crisp

SERVES 8

6 large apples (about 2½ pounds), peeled, cored, and thinly sliced
¼ cup water
Juice of 1 lemon
2 cups rolled oats

2 cups all-purpose flour
2 cups packed brown sugar
2 tablespoons cinnamon
1¼ cups (2½ sticks) melted butter

Preheat the oven to 350 degrees. Combine the apples, water, and lemon juice in an 8 × 8-inch baking pan. In a bowl, combine the oats, flour, sugar, and cinnamon. Pour in the butter and stir to make a crumbly mixture. Spread the topping in an even layer over the apples and bake for 45 to 55 minutes, or until the topping is crisp and browned.

Ritz Cracker Pie

SERVES 6–8

This is an old family recipe. It really is a pie—as it bakes, it makes its own crust.

3 egg whites
1 teaspoon baking powder
1½ cups sugar
20 Ritz Crackers, crumbled

1½ cups chopped pecans
1 teaspoon vanilla extract
2 cups heavy cream

Preheat the oven to 325 degrees. Grease a 9-inch pie pan. Beat the egg whites with the baking powder until stiff. Blend in 1 cup of the sugar, then add the cracker crumbs, pecans, and vanilla. Pour into the prepared pie pan and bake for 30 minutes. Meanwhile, whip the cream with the remaining ½ cup sugar until thick and spreadable. When the pie is done, place it on a rack to cool completely. Spread the whipped cream over the cooled pie.

Lemon Meringue Pie

SERVES 6

1½ cups sugar
Pinch of salt
3 tablespoons cornstarch
1½ cups cold water
4 egg yolks, lightly beaten
Grated zest of 1 lemon

½ cup fresh lemon juice
1 tablespoon butter
One 9-inch prebaked pie crust
4 egg whites
½ teaspoon cream of tartar

Preheat the oven to 350 degrees. For the filling, in a 2-quart saucepan, stir together 1 cup of the sugar, the salt, and cornstarch. Gradually stir in the water until smooth. Add the egg yolks, stirring constantly. Bring to a boil over medium heat and boil for 1 minute. Remove from the heat. Stir in the lemon zest, lemon juice, and butter, and set aside to cool. Turn the filling into the pie crust.

For the meringue, in a small bowl, with an electric mixer on high speed, beat the egg whites and cream of tartar until foamy. Add the remaining ½ cup of sugar 1 tablespoon at a time, beating well after each addition. Continue beating until stiff peaks form.

Spread some meringue around the edge of the filling first, touching the crust all around. Then fill the center with meringue. Bake for 15 to 20 minutes or until the meringue is lightly browned. Cool the pie at room temperature away from drafts.

Old-Fashioned Sweet Potato Pie

SERVES 6-8

2 cups peeled, cooked, mashed sweet
 potatoes*

1¼ cups sugar
¼ cup (½ stick) melted butter

*Mash the sweet potatoes with an electric mixer. This will produce a smooth, creamy pie with no lumps.

2 eggs
1 teaspoon vanilla extract, or
   1–2 tablespoons bourbon
¼ teaspoon salt
¼ teaspoon cinnamon

¼ teaspoon ground ginger
1 cup milk
One 9-inch unbaked pie crust
3 egg whites

Preheat the oven to 350 degrees. For the filling, in a large bowl, combine the potatoes, 1 cup of the sugar, the butter, eggs, vanilla, salt, and spices. Mix thoroughly. Add the milk, stirring well. Pour the mixture into the pie crust and bake for 40 to 50 minutes, or until a knife inserted in the center comes out clean. Place the pie on a rack and cool to room temperature before covering with meringue.

For the meringue, using an electric mixer, beat the egg whites until soft peaks form; beat in the remaining ¼ cup sugar 1 tablespoon at a time. Continue beating until the sugar dissolves and the mixture is glossy and stiff, but not dry. With a rubber spatula, spoon the meringue onto the pie, forming peaks. Make sure the meringue touches the crust all around. Sprinkle with a pinch of granulated sugar. Bake for 5 to 10 minutes, or until delicately browned. Cool and serve.

Key Lime Pie

SERVES 6

A true Key lime pie should not be green!

One 14-ounce can sweetened
   condensed milk
½ cup Key lime juice
1 teaspoon grated lime zest
3 eggs, separated

One 8-inch prebaked pie crust or
   graham cracker crust
¼ teaspoon cream of tartar
¼ cup sugar

Preheat the oven to 325 degrees. In a medium bowl, combine the milk, lime juice, and zest; blend in the egg yolks. Pour the filling into the crust. For the meringue, beat the egg whites with the cream of tartar until soft peaks form. Gradually beat in the sugar until the mixture is stiff. Spread the meringue over the filling; spread it to touch the edge of the crust all around. Bake for 12 to 15 minutes, or until the meringue is golden brown.

Shaver's Chocolate Pecan Pie

SERVES 6–8

½ cup (1 stick) butter
2 squares (2 ounces) semisweet
  chocolate
2 eggs, well beaten
½ cup sugar
½ cup light corn syrup

¼ cup all-purpose flour
1 teaspoon vanilla extract
⅛ teaspoon salt
¾ cup chopped or whole pecans
  (depending on your preference)
One 9-inch unbaked pie crust

Preheat the oven to 325 degrees. Melt the butter and chocolate in a double boiler over hot water. Pour this into a bowl and add the beaten eggs, then stir in the sugar, corn syrup, flour, vanilla, and salt. Fold in the pecans. Pour the filling into the crust and bake for about 30 minutes. Watch carefully and do not take the pie out of the oven until the top looks dry. You can make up to 4 pies at one time. They freeze beautifully. Serve with whipped cream or vanilla ice cream on top, if you like.

Half-Million-Dollar Pie

SERVES 16–20

One 14-ounce can sweetened
  condensed milk
¼ cup fresh lemon juice
One 11-ounce can mandarin
  oranges, drained and chopped

One 8-ounce can crushed
  pineapple, drained
1 cup chopped pecans
One 16-ounce carton Cool Whip
2 graham cracker pie crusts

In a bowl, mix the milk and lemon juice. Stir in the oranges, pineapple, and pecans. Fold the Cool Whip into the fruit mixture. Divide the filling between the pie crusts. Cover and refrigerate. Refrigerated, the pies will keep for up to 8 days.

Fried Apple Pies

YIELDS 8 PIES

My grandmother Irene Paul taught me to make fried pies years ago. She made the pastry dough from scratch in the early days, but later in life she began to take advantage of modern conveniences. So here's the recipe for Grand-mother's updated but old-fashioned fried pies. *

One 5-ounce package dried apples
  (or any other dried fruit)
2 cups water
½ cup sugar
2 tablespoons butter
½ teaspoon cinnamon

One 15-ounce package
  refrigerated pie crust (found in
  dairy section)
1½ cups vegetable oil, or more as
  needed

Cook the apples with the water in a covered pot over medium-low heat for about 1 hour, or until all liquid has been absorbed. Stir occasionally. Add the sugar, butter, and cinnamon, mixing well; set aside to cool. Unfold the pie crust and break into 8 equal pieces like pie slices. Place 1 heaping tablespoon of fruit on each round of dough, leaving a ½-inch border all around. Dip your finger in water and moisten the edges of the crust, then place a second round on top of the filling and press the edges to seal. Dip the tines of a dinner fork in flour and crimp the edges to ensure a proper seal.

Pour the oil into a cast-iron skillet to a depth of a little less than ½ inch. (This would be 1½ cups oil in a 10-inch skillet.) Heat over medium-high heat. When the oil is hot, place 3 to 4 pies in the skillet and cook for about 2 minutes on each side, or until golden brown. Drain on paper towels. Repeat until all the pies are cooked, or wrap and freeze some of the uncooked pies for another day.

Sprinkle the pies with granulated sugar while they're hot.

*For super-quick fried pies, use canned apple pie filling and canned biscuits that have been rolled out into a 5- or 6-inch round. Shape and cook pies as directed.

Our Pear Cobbler

SERVES 8

This cobbler is sooo good and sooo easy. It's unbeatable topped with vanilla ice cream. You can substitute peaches or pineapple tidbits for the pears.

½ cup (1 stick) butter
1 cup sugar
¾ cup self-rising flour

¾ cup milk
One 29-ounce can pear halves in
   heavy syrup

Place the butter in a baking dish and place in a 350-degree oven until the butter has melted. Leave the oven on. Stir together the sugar and flour; slowly stir in the milk and mix well. Pour the batter over the melted butter in the pan. *Do not stir.* Break the pears in half and place them on top of the batter; gently pour the syrup from the pears over the cobbler. *Do not stir.* Bake the cobbler for 30 minutes.

❀ ❀ ❀ **The Lady & Sons**

Old-Fashioned Fudge Pie

SERVES 6–8

2 squares (2 ounces) semisweet
   chocolate
½ cup (1 stick) butter

1 cup sugar
2 eggs, beaten
One 9-inch unbaked pie crust

Preheat the oven to 375 degrees. Melt the chocolate and butter together in a heavy saucepan over low heat. Remove the pan from the heat and add the sugar, then the eggs; beat well. Pour the filling into the pie crust and bake for 25 minutes. Serve warm or cold, with ice cream or whipped cream.

Pumpkin Gingerbread Trifle

SERVES 20

Two 14-ounce packages
  gingerbread mix
One 5.1-ounce package cook-and-
  serve vanilla pudding mix
One 30-ounce can pumpkin pie
  filling

½ cup packed brown sugar
⅓ teaspoon ground cardamom or
  cinnamon
One 12-ounce carton Cool Whip
½ cup gingersnaps (optional)

Bake the gingerbread according to the package directions; cool completely. Meanwhile, prepare the pudding and set aside to cool. Stir the pumpkin pie filling, sugar, and cardamom into the pudding.

Crumble one batch of gingerbread into the bottom of a large, pretty bowl. Pour ½ the pudding mixture over the gingerbread, then add a layer of Cool Whip. Repeat with the remaining gingerbread, pudding, and Cool Whip. Sprinkle the top with crushed gingersnaps if desired. Refrigerate overnight. Can be layered in a punch bowl.

❦ ❦ ❦ *The Lady & Sons*

Old-Fashioned Rice Pudding

SERVES 8–10

My friend Damon Fowler, chef and author, taught me the importance of using freshly grated nutmeg. The difference is remarkable, so please don't substitute ground nutmeg from a jar. Grate the nutmeg on the fine side of your grater, being careful that you don't include a little knuckle! Fresh nutmeg can be found right next to the ground nutmeg in your local supermarket.

1 cup sugar

2 tablespoons all-purpose flour

½ teaspoon salt

2 cups milk

3 egg yolks

2⅓ cups cooked white rice

⅓ cup raisins

¼ cup (½ stick) butter

2 teaspoons vanilla extract

2 teaspoons fresh lemon juice

¼ teaspoon freshly grated nutmeg

3 egg whites, at room temperature

¼ teaspoon cream of tartar

4 tablespoons sugar

Preheat the oven to 350 degrees. In a saucepan, mix the sugar, flour, and salt. Slowly stir in the milk. Cook over medium-low heat, stirring constantly, until thickened. Beat the egg yolks lightly, then stir in about ½ cup of the hot custard to temper the eggs. Add the egg mixture to the custard and cook for 2 minutes longer, stirring constantly.

Remove from the heat and stir in the rice, raisins, butter, vanilla, lemon juice, and nutmeg. Pour into a greased 1½-quart casserole and bake for 20 to 25 minutes. Five minutes before the pudding is done, make the meringue: Beat the egg whites and cream of tartar in a deep, narrow bowl until the egg whites form soft peaks. Add 1 tablespoon of sugar at a time, beating well after each addition.

Remove the pudding from the oven and top with the meringue, swirling it into peaks. Bake for 12 to 15 minutes longer, or until browned.   ❦ ❦ ❦ **The Lady & Sons**

Crème Brûlée

SERVES 4

2 cups heavy cream

1 vanilla bean, split lengthwise

4 large egg yolks

¼ cup, plus 1 tablespoon
   granulated sugar

⅓–½ cup white granulated or light
   brown sugar

Preheat the oven to 300 degrees. In a heavy-bottomed medium nonreactive saucepan, heat the cream with the vanilla bean for 15 minutes, stirring to ensure it does not burn. Remove from the heat and let steep for 15 minutes. Remove and discard the vanilla bean. Strain the cream. Meanwhile, in a medium bowl, beat the egg yolks with an electric mixer on high speed for 5 minutes, or until they are light and fluffy. Gradually beat in the granulated sugar. Add about half the cream mixture, a little at a time, to the egg mixture, whisking until well blended. Then pour the egg mixture into the remaining cream mixture. Stir until completely blended.

Pour the custard into four 8-ounce ramekins or custard cups. Place the dishes in large baking pan. Pour enough hot water into the pan to come halfway up the sides of the ramekins. Bake for 35 to 40 minutes or until the mixture is set in the center (it should still wiggle when shaken). Remove the dishes from the baking pan. Let cool completely at room temperature, then refrigerate for at least 2 or up to 24 hours.

Let the ramekins stand at room temperature 20 minutes before serving. Spoon the ⅓ to ½ cup white or light brown sugar in a thin, even layer over each portion of custard, covering it completely. To caramelize the sugar, light a propane torch and hold it so the flame just touches the surface. Start at the center and spiral out toward the edges of the ramekins. If the sugar begins to burn, pull the torch away and blow on the sugar to extinguish the flame.

VARIATIONS: Finely grate orange zest or bittersweet chocolate over the crème before adding the sugar for caramelizing. A propane torch can be bought at your local hardware store. If you don't have one, caramelize the topping under the broiler, watching carefully so as not to burn it.

Strawberry Cream Shortcake

SERVES 8–10

1 large Sara Lee Pound Cake
One 5.1-ounce package vanilla
   instant pudding mix
1½ cups water
1 cup sweetened condensed milk

1 teaspoon vanilla extract
One 12-ounce container Cool
   Whip
2 cups strawberries, hulled and
   sliced

Slice the cake very thin and lay half the slices in a 13 × 9-inch glass baking dish. In a bowl, combine the pudding mix, water, milk, and vanilla with an electric mixer. Fold in the Cool Whip. Pour half of this over the cake and lay half of the strawberries on top. Repeat to make a second layer.

Refrigerate until well chilled.

Chocolate Trifle

SERVES 20–25

This recipe evolved quite by accident in the restaurant kitchen on a particularly harried day. The baker had put a pan of blond brownies in the oven, and in the rush had left them in too long. When I looked at them, and then at her, our faces fell—the brownies were burned. But we had to have that dessert. "Don't worry," I told her, "I'll think of something." I knew I had to act quickly to get the desserts to the table. So I cut the brownies into pieces and carefully trimmed off the burned edges. I crumbled up the good part, sprinkled it with sherry, covered it with chocolate pudding and topped it with fresh whipped cream—and our Chocolate Trifle was born. Today it is one of our most requested desserts. Hope y'all enjoy. Oh, by the way, you really don't have to go to the trouble of burning the brownies!

3 eggs
½ cup (1 stick) butter
1 pound light brown sugar
2 cups self-rising flour

1 tablespoon vanilla extract
2 cups chopped almonds
6 ounces chocolate chips

1 cup shredded coconut (optional)
Two 3.4-ounce packages cook-and-
  serve chocolate pudding mix

¼ cup sherry
2 cups heavy cream
½ cup granulated sugar

Preheat the oven to 375 degrees. Grease and flour a 13 × 9 × 2-inch pan. In a bowl, beat the eggs and butter together; add the brown sugar, then gradually add the flour and mix well. Stir in the vanilla. Fold in the nuts, chocolate chips, and coconut (if using). Spread the batter in the prepared pan and bake for 25 to 30 minutes. Cool and cut into squares.

Prepare the pudding according to the package directions. Let cool slightly. Crumble the brownies into chunks, put them back into the glass dish, and sprinkle with sherry. Spoon the pudding over the brownies. Beat the cream with the granulated sugar until stiff. Spoon the whipped cream onto the completely cooled trifle. Refrigerate until serving time.   🌸 🌸 🌸 ***The Lady & Sons***

English Trifle

SERVES 12

CUSTARD
6 egg yolks
⅔ cup sugar
4 tablespoons cornstarch
2 cups milk
2 teaspoons vanilla extract

FRUIT MIXTURE
1 pineapple, peeled, cored, and cut
2 cups strawberries, hulled and
  sliced

2 bananas, peeled and sliced
2 kiwifruit, peeled and sliced
½ cup Triple Sec
6 ladyfingers
3 tablespoons raspberry jam

WHIPPED CREAM
1 cup heavy cream
1¼ cups sugar

First, make the custard: In a bowl, beat the egg yolks and sugar until light. Stir in the cornstarch. In a saucepan, scald the milk (do not boil it). Whisk the hot milk into the yolk mixture, then pour this back into the pan. Cook, stirring, over low heat until the custard thickens. Remove the pan from the heat and stir in the vanilla. Pour the custard into a bowl and set aside to cool completely.

While the custard cools, combine the cut-up fruit with the Triple Sec. Set aside to macerate for 30 minutes.

Spread the flat sides of the ladyfingers with jam, and place them in the bottom of a pretty glass bowl. Spoon the fruit and any liquid over the ladyfingers. Pour the cooled custard over the fruit. Refrigerate, covered, until the custard has set.

Beat the cream with the sugar until it holds a fairly stiff peak. Spread the whipped cream over the chilled custard, reserving some of the cream to pipe decoratively through a pastry tube, if desired.

Mexican Flan

SERVES 8

8 eggs
⅔ cup granulated sugar
¼ teaspoon salt
Two 12-ounce cans evaporated
   milk

1 teaspoon vanilla extract or
   brandy
½ cup packed brown sugar

Preheat the oven to 350 degrees. In a large bowl, beat the eggs well until fluffy. Beat in the sugar and salt, then beat in the milk. Stir in the vanilla. Sift the brown sugar into the bottom of a 5 × 9-inch loaf pan, covering the entire bottom. Carefully pour the custard into the pan. Place the loaf pan in a 13 × 9 × 2-inch pan and pour in enough hot water to reach halfway up the sides of the pan. Bake for 1 hour, or until a knife blade inserted in the center comes out clean. Let cool, then refrigerate overnight. Unmold the flan onto a platter.

Compote Clouds

SERVES 8

One 8-ounce package cream cheese,
   at room temperature
7 tablespoons sugar
One 8-ounce can crushed
   pineapple, drained, juice
   reserved

1 cup heavy cream
½ cup slivered almonds, toasted
½ cup fresh blueberries
¼ cup drained maraschino cherry
   halves

Beat the cream cheese with 3 tablespoons of the sugar until fluffy. Gradually add ¼ cup of the reserved pineapple juice and continue to beat until smooth. In another bowl, beat the cream with the remaining 4 tablespoons of sugar until it forms stiff peaks. Fold the whipped cream into the cream cheese mixture along with the pineapple, almonds, blueberries, and cherries. Refrigerate for 2 to 3 hours, or until well chilled. For a very pretty dessert, spoon the "clouds" into a stemmed glass compote.

Butterscotch Delight

SERVES ABOUT 15

2 cups graham cracker crumbs
½ cup (1 stick) melted butter
⅓ cup, plus ¾ cup granulated
   sugar
One 8-ounce package cream cheese,
   at room temperature
1 cup confectioners' sugar

3 cups heavy cream
Two 3.4-ounce packages
   butterscotch instant pudding
   mix
3 cups milk
Chopped peanuts (optional)

Preheat the oven to 350 degrees. For the crust, in a bowl, mix the graham cracker crumbs, butter, and ⅓ cup of the granulated sugar. Press this into the bottom of a 13 × 9 × 2-inch pan. Bake for 10 minutes; let cool. Beat the cream cheese with the confectioners' sugar. In another bowl, whip the cream with the remaining ¾ cup granulated sugar until it forms stiff peaks.

Prepare the pudding according to the package directions, using the 3 cups of milk.

Fold 1 cup of the whipped cream into the cream cheese mixture and spread this over the crust. Spread the pudding over the cream cheese layer.

Cover the pudding with the remaining whipped cream. Garnish with chopped peanuts, if desired. 🍀 🍀 🍀 *The Lady & Sons*

Heavenly Banana Delight

SERVES 10–12

One 3½-ounce package vanilla
  instant pudding mix
One 14-ounce can sweetened
  condensed milk
1 cup milk

1 cup heavy cream
1 cup sour cream
One 12-ounce box vanilla wafers
3 or 4 bananas, sliced
3 tablespoons chocolate syrup

In a large mixing bowl, combine the pudding mix, condensed milk, and milk, and beat for 2 minutes, or until well blended. Refrigerate for 10 minutes. In another bowl, whip the heavy cream. Add the whipped cream and sour cream to the pudding mixture. Place half the vanilla wafers in the bottom of a 13 × 9 × 2-inch dish. Top with half the sliced bananas, half the pudding mixture, and a drizzle of chocolate syrup. Repeat each layer and decorate the top with the remaining chocolate syrup. 🍀 🍀 🍀 *The Lady & Sons*

Chocolate Bread Pudding

SERVES 10–12

This simple, old-fashioned dessert is for chocolate lovers everywhere! Serve it warm or cold, with whipped cream or a dessert sauce.

One 1-pound loaf French or
   Italian bread, cut into cubes
   (about 15 cups)
3 cups milk
¼ cup heavy cream
½ cup coffee-flavored liqueur, such
   as Kahlúa
1 cup granulated sugar

1 cup packed light brown sugar
¼ cup Hershey cocoa powder
1 tablespoon vanilla extract
2 teaspoons pure almond extract
1½ teaspoons cinnamon
6 large eggs, lightly beaten
8 ounces semisweet chocolate,
   grated

Preheat the oven to 325 degrees. Lightly grease a 13 × 9-inch baking dish. Place the bread in the baking dish.

In a large bowl, whisk together the milk, cream, and liqueur. In another bowl, combine the granulated and brown sugars with the cocoa powder and mix well. Add this to the milk mixture and whisk to combine. Add the vanilla and almond extracts and the cinnamon to the beaten eggs. Combine the egg mixture with the milk mixture and mix well.

Stir in the grated chocolate. Pour the mixture evenly over the bread cubes; let stand, stirring occasionally, for at least 20 minutes, or until the bread has absorbed most of the milk mixture.

Bake the pudding for 1 hour, or until set; a knife inserted into the center of the pudding should come out clean.

Serve the pudding warm, or refrigerate it and serve chilled.

Sugar Cookies

YIELDS 5 DOZEN COOKIES

1½ cups confectioners' sugar, sifted
1 cup (2 sticks) butter
1 egg
1 teaspoon vanilla extract

1 teaspoon pure almond extract
2½ cups all-purpose flour
1 teaspoon baking soda
1 teaspoon cream of tartar

In a bowl, cream together the sugar and butter, then mix in the egg and the vanilla and almond extracts. In another bowl, stir together the flour, baking soda, and cream of tartar; mix the dry ingredients into the creamed mixture, then cover and refrigerate for 2 to 3 hours, or overnight.

Preheat the oven to 375 degrees. Divide the chilled dough in half and roll it out on a lightly floured pastry cloth to a ¼-inch thickness. Lightly grease some baking sheets. Cut the dough with a floured cookie cutter; sprinkle with sugar. Transfer the cookies to the prepared sheets and bake for 9 minutes.

Oatmeal Cookies

YIELDS ABOUT 45 LARGE COOKIES

*1 cup (2 sticks) butter, at room
  temperature*
1 cup granulated sugar
1 cup packed light brown sugar
2 eggs
1 teaspoon vanilla extract
2 cups all-purpose flour
1 teaspoon baking soda

½ teaspoon baking powder
¼ teaspoon salt
*½ teaspoon freshly grated nutmeg
  (optional) ***
2½ cups quick-cooking oats
1½ cups chopped walnuts
1 cup raisins

Preheat the oven to 375 degrees. Lightly grease some baking sheets. In a large bowl, cream the butter with the granulated and brown sugars until light and fluffy. Add the eggs, one at a time, beating well. Stir in the vanilla. In another bowl, mix the flour, baking soda, baking powder, salt, and nutmeg, if using. Beat the flour mixture into the creamed mixture. Stir in the oats, nuts, and raisins. Drop the dough by heaping tablespoons 2 inches apart on the prepared baking sheets. Bake for 10 to 12 minutes, or until golden brown.

*Do not substitute ground nutmeg for freshly grated. Omit if not available.

Hidden Kisses

YIELDS 3½–4½ DOZEN COOKIES

1 cup (2 sticks) butter, at room
temperature
⅔ cup sugar
½ teaspoon vanilla extract
¼ teaspoon pure almond extract

1¾ cups all-purpose flour
¾ cup finely chopped pecans
One 9-ounce package Hershey's
Kisses
1½ cups confectioners' sugar

In a large bowl, cream the butter, sugar, and vanilla and almond extracts. Stir in the flour and blend well. Add the pecans and blend well. Cover the bowl and refrigerate the dough for 1 hour. Preheat the oven to 375 degrees.

Unwrap the Hershey's Kisses. Press a scant tablespoon of dough around each Kiss, covering it completely; shape into balls.

Place the cookies on ungreased cookie sheets and bake for 10 minutes. Cool slightly, then transfer to a rack to cool completely. Roll the cookies in confectioners' sugar.

Brown Sugar Cookies

YIELDS ABOUT 4½ DOZEN COOKIES

1 cup (2 sticks) butter, at room
temperature
2 cups packed brown sugar
2 tablespoons vanilla extract

2 eggs
2 cups self-rising flour
2 cups chopped walnuts or pecans

Preheat the oven to 375 degrees. In a bowl, cream the butter and sugar, then beat in the vanilla. Add the eggs one at a time, beating well. Add the flour ½ cup at a time, continuing to beat. Stir in the nuts.

Drop the dough by heaping tablespoon onto ungreased cookie sheets. Bake for 10 to 12 minutes, until golden brown.

VARIATION: For variety you may want to add chocolate chips or coconut flakes. Sometimes I add both, depending on my mood.

Swedish Countess Cookies

YIELDS 30–40 COOKIES

This recipe was found in a handwritten Swedish cookbook, dated about 1864, belonging to Countess Frida Af Trampe. This was said to be her favorite cookie. Ingrid Albertzon Parker, who is Swedish, took the time to translate this recipe into American measurements. I had the pleasure of having Ingrid come into my kitchen one afternoon to teach me the art of making these buttery little morsels. They are really very simple to make. The optional Cognac and shaved chocolate were added by Ingrid.

10 tablespoons (1¼ sticks) butter
¾ cup sugar
1¼ cups all-purpose flour

1 tablespoon Cognac (optional)
Shaved chocolate (optional)

Preheat the oven to 350 degrees. Grease some baking sheets. Using an electric mixer, cream the butter until fluffy and white (about 5 minutes). Add the sugar and continue to beat. Add the flour a little at a time. Add the Cognac, if using, and mix well. Pinch off a piece of dough about the size of an egg. If the dough is sticky, sprinkle the work surface with a little flour. Place the piece of dough on the work surface. With your palms, roll the dough back and forth to form a rope of dough about as thick as your finger. Using your fingers, start at one end and flatten the dough to form a strip about 1¼ inches wide. Cut the dough on the diagonal into 2½-inch-long strips. They should be roughly diamond-shaped. Slip a knife blade under the dough and transfer to a greased baking sheet. Repeat until all the dough is used. Sprinkle a little shaved chocolate over each cookie, if desired. Bake for 8 to 10 minutes. These cookies should not brown, but should remain an off-white color.

Magical Peanut Butter Cookies

YIELDS 18 COOKIES

You won't believe how good this easy cookie is. For a change, press a Hershey's Kiss down into the center of each ball of dough. Omit the crisscross design.

1 cup peanut butter, creamy or
   crunchy
1⅓ cups sugar

1 egg
1 teaspoon vanilla extract

Preheat the oven to 350 degrees. Grease a large baking sheet. In a mixing bowl, combine the peanut butter, 1 cup of the sugar, the egg, and vanilla, and stir well with a spoon. Roll the dough into balls the size of walnuts. Place the balls on the prepared baking sheet. With a fork, press a crisscross design on each cookie. Bake for 12 minutes, remove from the oven, and sprinkle the cookies with some of the remaining sugar. Cool slightly before removing from pan.

Brenda's Kahlúa Brownies

YIELDS 2 DOZEN BROWNIES

⅔ cup butter
3 squares (3 ounces) unsweetened
   chocolate
1½ cups all-purpose flour, sifted
½ teaspoon baking powder

½ teaspoon salt
3 large eggs
2 cups sugar
½ cup, plus 1 tablespoon Kahlúa
¾ cup chopped walnuts or pecans

Preheat the oven to 350 degrees. Grease a 9 × 9-inch baking pan. Melt the butter and chocolate in the top of a double boiler over boiling water. Let cool slightly. Sift together the flour, baking powder, and salt; set aside. Beat the eggs with the sugar until light. Stir in the chocolate mixture and ½ cup of the Kahlúa, then add the flour mixture and blend. Stir in the nuts. Turn the batter into the prepared pan and bake for 30 minutes. When the brownies have cooled, brush the top with the remaining 1 tablespoon of Kahlúa.

Pecan Pie Squares

YIELDS 3 DOZEN BARS

1 box yellow cake mix
½ cup (1 stick) melted butter
4 eggs
1½ cups light corn syrup

½ cup packed dark brown sugar
1 teaspoon vanilla extract
2 cups chopped pecans

Preheat the oven to 350 degrees. Grease a 13 × 9-inch pan. For the crust, in a bowl mix the cake mix, butter, and 1 egg. Measure out ⅔ cup of this mixture and reserve it for the topping. Pat the remaining mixture into the bottom of the prepared pan and bake for 15 minutes.

Meanwhile, stir together the reserved crust mixture, the remaining 3 eggs, the corn syrup, sugar, and vanilla. Stir in the pecans. Pour this mixture over the partially baked crust. Increase the oven heat to 375 degrees and bake for 30 minutes, or until the cake is set. Let cool, then cut into bars. ❦ ❦ ❦ ***The Lady & Sons***

Lemon Bars

YIELDS 24 BARS

CRUST
2 cups all-purpose flour
1 cup confectioners' sugar
Pinch of salt
1 cup (2 sticks) butter, at room temperature

FILLING
4 eggs
2 cups granulated sugar
6 tablespoons all-purpose flour
6 tablespoons fresh lemon juice

Preheat the oven to 350 degrees. Lightly grease a 13 × 9 × 2-inch pan. Make the crust: Combine the flour, confectioners' sugar, and salt in a large bowl. Cut in the butter to make a crumbly mixture. Press the mixture into the prepared pan. You may need to dip your fingers into a little flour or confectioners' sugar to keep the dough from sticking to your fingers. Bake for 20 minutes. Meanwhile, make the filling: Mix the eggs, granulated sugar, flour, and lemon juice. Pour this over the baked crust and bake for 25 minutes longer. Sprinkle with confectioners' sugar, if desired, when the bars are done.   ❧ ❧ ❧   **The Lady & Sons**

Glazed Honey Bars

YIELDS ABOUT 2 DOZEN BARS

¾ cup vegetable oil
¼ cup honey
1 cup granulated sugar
1 egg
1 teaspoon cinnamon
2 cups self-rising flour

1 cup chopped walnuts
1 cup confectioners' sugar
1 tablespoon mayonnaise
1 tablespoon milk
1 teaspoon vanilla extract

Preheat the oven to 350 degrees. Lightly grease a $13 \times 9 \times 2$-inch pan. In a mixing bowl, beat the oil, honey, granulated sugar, and egg. Stir the cinnamon into the flour. Stir this into the sugar mixture and mix well. Stir in the nuts. Spread the batter in the prepared pan and bake for 30 minutes. Remove from the oven and let stand a few moments while you make the glaze: In a bowl, stir together the confectioners' sugar, mayonnaise, milk, and vanilla. Pour the glaze over the cake and spread it with a metal spatula. Let cool, then cut into bars.   ❧ ❧ ❧   **The Lady & Sons**

Chocolate Mound Brownies

SERVES 15–20

4 squares (4 ounces) unsweetened
   chocolate
1 cup (2 sticks) butter
4 eggs, beaten
2 cups sugar
2 teaspoons vanilla extract

1 cup all-purpose flour
1 teaspoon baking powder
¼ teaspoon salt
2 cups chopped pecans
1 cup shredded coconut

Preheat the oven to 350 degrees. Grease a 13 × 9-inch baking dish. In a large saucepan, or in the microwave, melt the chocolate and butter. Add the eggs, sugar, and vanilla, and stir well. Stir in the flour, baking powder, and salt, then add the pecans and coconut and stir until well blended. Pour the batter into the prepared baking dish and bake for 30 minutes. Cut into squares to serve. ❦ ❦ ❦ *The Lady & Sons*

Weights and Measures

All measurements given are level, unless otherwise specified.

1 cup—½ pint
2 cups—1 pint—1 pound
2 pints—1 quart—2 pounds
4 quarts—1 gallon—8 pounds
16 ounces—1 pound
1 fluid ounce—2 tablespoons
16 fluid ounces—1 pint
1 teaspoon—⅓ tablespoon
1 tablespoon—3 teaspoons
4 tablespoons—¼ cup
8 tablespoons—½ cup
1 quart—2 pints
8 quarts—1 peck
4 pecks—1 bushel
2 tablespoons butter—
    1 ounce
2 cups butter—1 pound
1 stick butter—½ cup

1 square baking chocolate—
    1 ounce
1 cup grated cheese—4 ounces
4 cups coarsely chopped nuts—
    1 pound
2⅓ cups uncooked rice—
    1 pound
1 cup uncooked rice—3½ cups
    cooked
2 cups granulated sugar—
    1 pound
2¼ cups packed brown sugar—
    1 pound
3½ cups sifted confectioners'
    sugar—1 pound
1 pound raw ground meat—
    2 cups
1 tablespoon liquid—½ ounce

Acknowledgments

To all my family, friends, staff, and guests who have given their invaluable help in making this book and restaurant a reality. My most heartfelt thanks go out to each and every one of you: John and Carol Berendt, Jack H. Biel, Travis Blackshear, John Brown, Dian Brownfield, Sharon Bruggeman, Lori Burnett, Lisa Calcaine, Bobbi I. Cappelli, Dora Charles, Tracy Clark, Sandra Cowan, Roger Crews, Stephanie Crystal, Carolyn Cundiff, Peggy Deen, Phil Donaldson, Lawrence Duncan, Susan Dupuy, Ann G. Fisch, Rodney Floyd, Damon Lee Fowler, Levita and Ron Garner, Rick Gnann, Steve Green, Lori Greenlee, Tracey Gribbon, Anne Hanson, Bubba Hiers, James Hodges, Patricia Hoisington, Brenda B. Hollis, Angie Hopper, Jeanne Hungerpillar, Bunny Hutchins, Rance Jackson, Ineata Jones, Virgil Kummero, Anne Landers, Audanta Lewis, John Lucas, Jude Mathews, Louis (Trey) Mathews III, Barbara McChesney, Laura Miller, Marilyn Milson, Renee Mincey, Donna Mobley, Delonzo Moody, Jackie Mullins, Catherine Nadeau, Stacey Nelson, Martha Gidden Nesbit, Zeide Nuss, Kelly Ort, Peggy Ort, Patrick Otis, Ingrid Parker, Donna Pichard, Ginger Pitts, Robert Pleasanton, Mary H. Plyler, Byron Polite, Charles Polite, Helen Rooks, Barbara Russell, Bruce and Carolyn Ryder, Vickie Sepielli, Esther Shaver, Michelle and Bruce Shelar, Kristen Short, Martha (Betty) Smith, Donna Sparks, Amanda Stephens, Cathy Stephens, Jeffery Stevens, Polly Powers Stramm, Bobbie Strong, Elizabeth Terry, Herb Traub, Donald Wade, Suzette Wagner, Dustin Walls, Tom Walsh, Doris Warren, Serna Wilkes, and Lucile Wright.

I would especially like to express thanks for the wonderful care and consideration Random House has given me in transforming what started off as a collection of local recipes into a national cookbook—it has been a dream come true. Since discovering The Lady & Sons on a business trip, my editor, Pamela Cannon, has worked tirelessly on the books' behalf, for which I thank her a thousand times over. I would also like to express my gratitude to: Beth Pearson, Janet Wygal, Vicki Wong, Stacy Rockwood, Kathy Rosenbloom, Krista Vossen, and Christina Figel.

Index

A

Aioli, Shrimp and Rice Croquettes with, 235
almond(s):
  Chocolate Almond Pie, 147–48
  Pat's Almond Chicken Casserole, 277–78
  Sausage-Almond Rice, 298
  Sour Cream Cake, xxi–xxii
Almond Joy candy:
  Volcano Cake, 386–87
Angelhair Pasta, Szechuan Chicken with, 279
appetizers:
  cold, 9–10, 18–23, 185–86, 193–201
    Black Bean Salsa, 23
    Bobby's Pimento Cheese, 23
    "Boursin Cheese," 197
    Candied Dills, 196
    Caviar Spread, 196
    Creamy Roquefort Dip, 22
    Devilish Cheese Logs, 194–95
    Egg Caviar Mold, 201
    Garlic Cheese Spread, 21
    Georgia Spiced Pecans, 195
    Herbed Cheese and Cracker Bits, 197
    Herbed Cream Cheese Round, 20
    Italian Roasted Red Peppers, 19
    Mexican Layered Dip, 198–99
    Party Eye-of-Round Steak, 198
    Pesto Cheese Blossom, 353–54
    Pickled Okra Sandwiches, 20
    Quick Guacamole-Spinach Dip, 21
    Salsa Chicken Salad, 199
    Shrimp Butter, 18
    Smoked Oyster Cheese Balls, 200
    Southwestern Dip, 19–20
    Strawberry Cheese Ring, 22
    Stuffed French Bread, 201
    Tangy Marinated Shrimp, 195–96
    Zesty Cheese Straws, 200–201
  hot, 9, 11–18, 185, 187–93
    Artichoke and Spinach Dip, 18
    Artichoke Frittata, 192
    Bacon Wraps, 17
    Baked Cheese Spread, 187
    Black Bean Dip, 193
    Brie en Croûte #1, 15–16
    Brie en Croûte #2, 16
    Cheese-Stuffed Mushrooms, 14
    Chicken Nuggets, 192–93
    Collard Green Wontons, xix
    Duxelles-Stuffed Tenderloin, 256–57
    Georgia Sugared Peanuts, 11
    Hot Asparagus Dip, 12
    Hot Crab Canapé, 12
    Hot Crab Dip, 187
    Italian Chicken Sticks, 189
    Mini Onion Quiches, 13
    Mushroom Canapés, 191
    Oysters in the Patty Shell, 15
    Pecan-Stuffed Dates, 11
    Polynesian Chicken Wings, 188
    Quail with Marsala Sauce, 272–73
    Sausage Balls, 13
    Sesame Chicken Strips, 14–15

appetizers: hot (*cont'd*)
    Shore Is Good Seafood Dip, 190
    Shrimp Mold, 193–94
    South Georgia "Caviar," 194
    South of the Border Mason-Dixon
       Dip, 17
    Spinach and Shrimp Dip, 188–89
    Sugar-and-Nut Glazed Brie, 190
    Tomato Canapés, 191
apple(s):
    Applesauce Bread, 109
    Applesauce Cupcakes, 142
    Baked, 161–62
    Caramel Apple Cake with Caramel
       Topping, 127
    Caramel Apple Cheesecake, 387
    Crisp, 395
    Fried Apple Pies, 399
    Fritters, 106
    Fruit Salad with Honey Dressing, 224
    Golda's Frozen Waldorf Salad, 218–19
    Grandgirl's Fresh Apple Cake from
       Georgia, 389
    Oven-Baked Dutch Apple Pancakes, 344
    Piggy Pudding, 67
    Raisin Muffins, 318
    Thanksgiving Apple Salad, 223–24
    Warm Apple and Goat Cheese Salad,
       227
Applesauce Bread, 109
Applesauce Cupcakes, 142
artichoke(s):
    Cream of Artichoke Soup, 33
    Frittata, 192
    Marinated Shrimp and Artichoke Hearts,
       228–29
    Mosaic Chicken Terrine, 348–49
    Shrimp and Artichoke Bake, 56–57
    and Spinach Dip, 18
asparagus:
    Casserole, 303–4
    Egg and Lemon Sauce, 117
    Hot Asparagus Dip, 12
    with Leeks and New Potatoes, 346–47
    Marinated Asparagus Salad, 222
    Saucy Chicken and Asparagus Bake, 278
Aunt Glennis's Blonde Brownies, 159
Auntie's Peanut Sauce, 329
Aunt Peggy's Italian Dressing, 119
avocado(s):
    Black Bean Salsa, 23

Chicken Salad, 40–41
    Dressing, 41
    Fruit Salad with Honey Dressing, 224
    Mexican Layered Dip, 198–99
    Sherried Avocado Bouillon, 30
    Southwestern Dip, 19–20

B
bacon:
    Bean and Bacon Soup, 215
    BLT Soup, 213
    Broccoli Salad, 42
    Cornucopia Salad, 41
    Pecan-Stuffed Dates, 11
    Ring Tum Ditty, 340
    Southern Baked Beans, 92
    Wraps, 17
Baked Apples, 161–62
Baked Bean Casserole, 356
Baked Beans, Southern, 92
Baked Cheese Spread, 187
Baked Flounder, 362
Baked Grits, 83
Baked Hen and Dressing, 70–71
Baked Pasta Florentine, 254
Baked Shrimp-Crab Salad, 246–47
Baked Spaghetti, 260
Baked Wild Rice, 306
Balsamic Vinaigrette, 333
banana(s):
    Bread, 321
    Cornucopia Salad, 41
    Cream Pie, 150
    Curry-Crusted, 292–93
    English Trifle, 405–6
    French Toast Stuffed with Bananas and
       Walnuts, 342–43
    Fritters, 106
    Fruit Bowl, 226
    Fruit Salad with Honey Dressing, 224
    Heavenly Banana Delight, 408
    Hummingbird Cake, 381–82
    Nut Bread, 103
    Nut Cake, xx–xxi
    Pudding, 164–65
    Punch Bowl Cake, 141
    Split Cake, 138
    Strawberry Mold, 162, 226
Barbara's Mussels, 246
Barbecued Short Ribs, 266–67
Barbecue Meat Loaf, 269–70

barbecue sauces:
The Lady's, 116
Spicy, 116
Barbecue-Style Pork Chops, 59
bars, *see* brownies and bars
Basic Biscuits, 105
Basic Meat Loaf, 58–59
basil:
Grilled Chicken, 274
Pesto Cheese Blossom, 353–54
Battered Fried Shrimp, 237–38
bean(s):
and Bacon Soup, 215
Baked Bean Casserole, 356
Black Bean Dip, 193
Black Bean Salsa, 23
Black-Eyed Pea Salad, 39
Confederate Bean Soup, 33
Crockpot Pinto Beans, 298
Dian's Black Bean Soup, 207
Duxelles-Stuffed Tenderloin, 256–57
Hoppin' John, 98
Mexican Layered Dip, 198–99
Senate Bean Soup, 212
Southern Baked, 92
Southern-Style Black-Eyed Peas, 284
South Georgia "Caviar," 194
South of the Border Mason-Dixon Dip,
17
Southwestern Dip, 19–20
Taco Soup, 216
Texas-Style Chili, 268
White Bean Chili, 29
see also green bean(s)
Beaufort Shrimp Pie, 239
beef:
Baked Pasta Florentine, 254
Baked Spaghetti, 260
Barbecued Short Ribs, 266–67
Barbecue Meat Loaf, 269–70
Basic Meat Loaf, 58–59
Bourbon Beef Tenderloin, 57–58
Brandied Prime Rib, 248–49
Burgundy Beef Roast, 60–61
Cheeseburger Meat Loaf and Sauce, 62
Duxelles-Stuffed Tenderloin, 256–57
Foolproof Standing Rib Roast, 63
The Lady & Sons Beef Vegetable Soup,
205–6
The Lady & Sons Pot Roast, 257–59
Lemon Butter for Steak, 118

Old-Time Beef Stew, 58
Oriental Marinade, 115
Party Eye-of-Round Steak, 198
Pepper Steak, 60, 261
Perfect Char-Grilled Filet Mignon, 270
Perfect Eye-of-Round Roast, 252
Pot Roast, 59–60
Prince Charles' Calf's Liver, 251
St. Paddy's Day Corned Beef and
Cabbage, 265
Sherried Avocado Bouillon, 30
Spiced Beef with Dumplin's, 252–53
Steak and Greens, 65–66
Steak au Poivre, 361–62
Steak Diane, 269
Stew Casserole, 356–57
Stroganoff, 61–62
Stuffed Red Peppers, 254–55
Swiss Steak, 64
Taco Soup, 216
Texas-Style Chili, 268
Wayne's Beef Macaroni and Cheese, 263
beer:
Bubba's Beer Biscuits, 109
beet(s):
Pickled Beets and Eggs, 220
Roasted Beet Salad, 42
Benne Wafers, Mrs. Sullivan's, 350–51
Berendt, John, recipes from, 366–67
Fresh Cabbage and Sweet Sausages, 366
Lemon Hollandaise Sauce, 367
Pots de Crème, 367
berry(ies):
Berry Steak Sauce, 327
Blackberry Muffins, 314
Blueberry Cream Pie, 392
Blueberry Raspberry Pecan Crisp,
359–60
Blueberry Salad, 221–22
Chocolate Strawberry Shortcake, 129
Cranberry Salad, 39
English Trifle, 405–6
Fourth-Generation Blackberry Jam Cake,
375–76
Jezebel Sauce, 330
Pecan Cranberry Salad, 218
Punch Bowl Cake, 141
Raspberry Sauce, 330
Spinach, Strawberry, and Hearts of Palm
Salad, 221
Strawberry and Cream Pie, 148

berry(ies): (cont'd)
　Strawberry Cheese Ring, 22
　Strawberry Cream Shortcake, 404
　Strawberry Fig Preserves, 121
　Strawberry Mold, 162, 226
　Strawberry Pretzel Salad, 228
　Strawberry Soup, 353
　Wayne's Cranberry Sauce, 326
Best Crab Casserole, 244
Better Than Sex? Yes!, 140
biscuits:
　Basic, 105
　Bubba's Beer, 109
　Cheese, 107–8
　Mrs. Wilkes' Boarding House–Style,
　　355–56
　Pineapple Upside-Down, 315
　Riz, 313–14
　Sour Cream Butter, 316
　Sweet Potato, 317
bisques:
　Crab, 211
　Lucile Wright's Oyster, 365
　Shrimp, 29
　Shrimp or Lobster, 32
Bisquick:
　Bubba's Beer Biscuits, 109
　Pineapple Cake, 136–37
　Sausage Balls, 13
black bean(s):
　Dian's Black Bean Soup, 207
　Dip, 193
　Salsa, 23
blackberry(ies):
　Fourth-Generation Blackberry Jam Cake,
　　375–76
　Muffins, 314
black-eyed pea(s):
　Hoppin' John, 98
　Salad, 39
　Southern-Style, 284
　South Georgia "Caviar," 194
Black Pepper Shrimp, 47–48
Blonde Brownies, Aunt Glennis's, 159
BLT Soup, 213
blueberry(ies):
　Cream Pie, 392
　Raspberry Pecan Crisp, 359–60
　Salad, 221–22
Bobby's Pimento Cheese, 23
Bo's Eggplant Supreme, 306

Boston butt:
　The Lady & Sons Smoked Boston Butt
　　Roast, 255–56
Bouillabaisse, The Lady's, 240
Bouillon, Sherried Avocado, 30
bourbon:
　Beef Tenderloin, 57–58
　Mint Julep Jelly, 120–21
"Boursin Cheese," 197
Boursin Cheese Potatoes, 91
Brandied Prime Rib, 248–49
bread(s), 101–11, 307–21
　Applesauce, 109
　Banana, 321
　Banana Nut, 103
　biscuits
　　Basic, 105
　　Bubba's Beer, 109
　　Cheese, 107–8
　　Mrs. Wilkes' Boarding House–Style,
　　　355–56
　　Pineapple Upside-Down, 315
　　Riz, 313–14
　　Sour Cream Butter, 316
　　Sweet Potato, 317
　Cheesy French, 320
　Chocolate Bread Pudding, 409
　corn bread
　　Corn Bread (recipe), 70
　　Corny, 106
　　Cracklin', 108
　　Herb, 110
　　Piggy Pudding, 67
　　Southern Corn Bread Stuffing, 70–71
　Currant and Oat Scones, 309–10
　Dutch, 108–9
　French Toast Stuffed with Bananas and
　　Walnuts, 342–43
　Gorilla, 319
　Hoecakes, 105
　Hush Puppies, 318
　The Lady & Sons Onion-Cheese, 313
　Lucile Wright's Tomato Sandwiches, 364
　muffins
　　Apple Raisin, 318
　　Blackberry, 314
　　Cheese, 310–11
　　Corny Corn, 320–21
　　Crunchy Peanut Butter, 312
　　Green, 316
　　Orange Blossoms, 384

Nutty Orange Coffee Cake, 319–20
Old-Time Spoon, 317
Peanut Butter, 110
Pear Fritters, 106
Pineapple Cheese, 110–11
Plantation Skillet Cake, 309
Popovers, 310
Pumpkin, 104
rolls
    Easy, 104
    Easy Herb, 314–15
    Easy Yeast, 311
    Mother's, 107
Stuffed French, 201
Traditional Raisin Scones, 352
Zucchini, 103
breadsticks:
Bacon Wraps, 17
breakfast and brunch:
Easy Coffee Cake, 142
French Toast Stuffed with Bananas and
    Walnuts, 342–43
Fried Grits Cakes with Sausage, 358
Lemon-Pecan Sunburst Coffee Cake,
    343–44
muffins
    Apple Raisin, 318
    Blackberry, 314
    Cheese, 310–11
    Corny Corn, 320–21
    Crunchy Peanut Butter, 312
    Green, 316
    Orange Blossoms, 384
Nutty Orange Coffee Cake, 319–20
Oven-Baked Dutch Apple Pancakes, 344
Plantation Skillet Cake, 309
Shrimp Gravy, 237
Sunday Morning Casserole, 253
Traditional Raisin Scones, 352
Brenda's Kahlúa Brownies, 413
Brie:
Brie en Croûte #1, 15–16
Brie en Croûte #2, 16
Sugar-and-Nut Glazed, 190
Walnut Praline Brie with Fruit, 163
Warm Brie Salad Dressing, 332
broccoli:
Casserole, 95
Cheesy Broccoli Bake, 83
Egg and Lemon Sauce, 117
Green Rice, 289

Salad, 42
Soufflé, 90
Swiss Broccoli Casserole, 288
Brokke, Wayne, 214
brownies and bars, 124–25, 156–59, 371,
    413–16
Aunt Glennis's Blonde Brownies, 159
Brenda's Kahlúa Brownies, 413
Chocolate Mound Brownies, 415–16
Cream Cheese Brownies, 158
Glazed Honey Bars, 415
Glazed Spice Bars, 413
Grandma's Iced Georgia Squares,
    156–57
Lady Brownies, 157–58
Lemon Bars, 414–15
Peanut Butter Bars, 158
Pecan Pie Squares, 414
Brown Sugar Cookies, 411
brunch, *see* breakfast and brunch
Brunswick Stew, Chicken, 69–70
Bubba's Country-Fried Venison Steak,
    250
Burgers, Tuna, 247
Burgundy Beef Roast, 60–61
butter:
Cookies, 156
Fingers, 154
Garlic, 108
Gooey Butter Cakes, 133–34
Honey, 122
Lemon Butter for Fish, 118
Lemon Butter for Steak, 118
Shrimp, 18
Sour Cream Butter Biscuits, 316
Tarragon, 328
Buttermilk Dressing, 120
butterscotch:
Delight, 407–8
Fudgie Scotch Ring, 157
Pie, 145

C
cabbage:
Chinese Salad, 219–20
Esther's Dill Coleslaw, 40
Fresh Cabbage and Sweet Sausages, 366
The Lady's Coleslaw, 37
Nancy's Coleslaw, 217
St. Paddy's Day Corned Beef and, 265
Cajun Shrimp, Fiery, 245

cakes, 123–24, 127–44, 367–68, 373–92
  Almond Sour Cream, xxi–xxii
  Applesauce Cupcakes, 142
  Banana Nut, xx–xxi
  Banana Split, 138
  Better Than Sex? Yes!, 140
  Caramel Apple Cake with Caramel
      Topping, 127
  cheesecakes
      Caramel Apple, 387
      Cheesecake (recipe), 135–36
      Luscious Lime, 132–33
      with Praline Sauce, 380
      Turtle, 390–91
  Chocolate Chip Nut, 132
  Chocolate Damnation, 143
  Chocolate Sheet, 137–38
  Chocolate Strawberry Shortcake, 129
  Chocolate Torte, 374
  Coconut, 128–29
  Coconut Cream, 382–83
  Coconut White Fruit, 388–89
  Double-Dutch Chocolate Fudge Upside-
      Down, 376–77
  Easy Coffee Cake, 142
  Fourth-Generation Blackberry Jam,
      375–76
  Gooey Butter, 133–34
  Grandgirl's Fresh Apple Cake from
      Georgia, 389
  Grandmama Hiers's Carrot, 138–39
  Grandmother Paul's Red Velvet, 134–35
  Green Tomato, 374–75
  Hummingbird, 381–82
  Italian Love, 388
  Lemon-Pecan Sunburst Coffee Cake,
      343–44
  Low-Fat Peach, 129–30
  Milky Way, 377
  Mississippi Mud, 383
  Nutty Orange Coffee Cake, 319–20
  Old-Time Lemon "Cheesecake,"
      139–40
  Orange Blossoms, 384
  Orange Slice, 386
  Peanut Butter, 144
  Pear-Licious, 373
  Pecan Pudding, 391–92
  Pig Pickin', 390
  Pineapple, 136–37
  Plantation Skillet, 309

  pound
      Caramel-Nut, 381
      Chocolate, 141
      Chocolate Chip, 384–85
      Grandmother Paul's Sour Cream, 133
      Mama's, 131
      Red Velvet, 385
  Punch Bowl, 141
  Rum, 127–28
  Savannah Chocolate Cake with Hot
      Fudge Sauce, 130–31
  Sour Cream Caramel, 378
  Strawberry Cream Shortcake, 404
  Texas Sheet, 379
  Tunnel of Fudge, 139
  Volcano, 386–87
Caldo Soup, Susan's, 210
Calf's Liver, Prince Charles', 251
canapés:
  Hot Crab, 12
  Mushroom, 191
  Tomato, 191
Candied Dills, 196
Can't-Miss Red Snapper, 243
caramel:
  Apple Cake with Caramel Topping, 127
  Apple Cheesecake, 387
  Crème Caramel, 163
  Easy Caramel Icing, 378
  Icing, 375–76
  Nut Pound Cake, 381
  Sauce, 162
  Sour Cream Caramel Cake, 378
  Turtle Cheesecake, 390–91
carrot(s):
  Copper Pennies, 225
  Grandmama Hiers's Carrot Cake,
      138–39
  Vegetable Pancakes, 302
Carter, Jimmy, 22
Carter, Rosalynn, 22
casseroles:
  Asparagus, 303–4
  Baked Bean, 356
  Baked Grits, 83
  Beaufort Shrimp Pie, 239
  Beef Stew, 356–57
  Best Crab, 244
  Bo's Eggplant Supreme, 306
  Boursin Cheese Potatoes, 91
  Broccoli, 95

Broccoli Soufflé, 90
Cheesy Broccoli Bake, 83
Chicken, 79, 275
Chicken and Rice, 75
Chicken and Wild Rice, 280
Chicken Boudine, 276
Chicken Florentine, 277
Corn, 286
Deviled Seafood, 51
Easy Shrimp Bake, 243–44
Eggplant, 89
Fresh Corn Scallop, 94
Green Bean, 305
Green Rice, 289
Hash Brown Potato, 303
Hot Savannah Chicken Salad, 270–71
The Lady's Cheesy Mac, 86
Mexican Chicken, 271
Mixed Vegetable, 293
Mushroom Rice, 291
Noodle, 300
Pat's Almond Chicken, 277–78
Pattypan Summer Squash, 97
Pineapple, 98–99
Potato, 96
Saucy Chicken and Asparagus Bake, 278
Sausage-Rice, 61
Sausage with Ravishing Rice, 266
Savannah Red Rice, 88
Savory Rice, 93
Shrimp and Mushroom, 55
Shrimp Gumbo, 54
Shrimp with Rice, 53
Southern Baked Beans, 92
Spicy Shrimp and Pasta, 49–50
Squash, 84, 290
Sunday Morning, 253
Sweet Potato, 283–84
Sweet Potato Bake, 94
Swiss Broccoli, 288
Tomato, 284–85
Vidalia Onion, 291
Wayne's Beef Macaroni and Cheese, 263
Wild Rice and Oyster, 242
Zucchini and Corn, 92
cauliflower:
Egg and Lemon Sauce, 117
caviar:
Egg Caviar Mold, 201
Spread, 196
"Caviar," South Georgia, 194

Cheddar cheese:
Artichoke Frittata, 192
Asparagus Casserole, 303–4
Baked Grits, 83
Bobby's Pimento Cheese, 23
Broccoli Salad, 42
Cheese Biscuits, 107–8
Cheeseburger Meat Loaf and Sauce, 62
Cheesy Broccoli Bake, 83
Cheesy French Bread, 320
Cornucopia Salad, 41
Corny Corn Bread, 106
Creamy Cheddar Soup, 31
The Lady & Sons Onion-Cheese Bread,
    313
The Lady's Cheesy Mac, 86
Mexican Chicken, 271
Muffins, 310–11
Pineapple Casserole, 98–99
Pineapple Cheese Bread, 110–11
Potato Casserole, 96
Ring Tum Ditty, 340
Ron's Tybee Island Sausage Pie, 268–69
Sausage and Grits, 67
Sausage Balls, 13
Shrimp with Rice, 53
South of the Border Mason-Dixon Dip,
    17
Squash Casserole, 84
Strawberry Cheese Ring, 22
Sunday Morning Casserole, 253
Tomato Grits, 287–88
Tomato Pie, 95
Wayne's Beef Macaroni and, 263
Zesty Cheese Straws, 200–201
cheese:
Artichoke and Spinach Dip, 18
Artichoke Frittata, 192
Asparagus Casserole, 303–4
Bacon Wraps, 17
Baked Cheese Spread, 187
Baked Grits, 83
Biscuits, 107–8
Bobby's Pimento, 23
"Boursin Cheese," 197
Boursin Cheese Potatoes, 91
Brie en Croûte #1, 15–16
Brie en Croûte #2, 16
Broccoli Salad, 42
Cheeseburger Meat Loaf and Sauce, 62
Cheese-Stuffed Mushrooms, 14

cheese: (*cont'd*)
Cheesy Broccoli Bake, 83
Cheesy French Bread, 320
Cherry Cream Cheese Pie, 394
Chicken and Rice Casserole, 75–76
Chicken Boudine, 276
Chicken Georgia, 73
Collard Green Wontons, xix
Cornucopia Salad, 41
Corny Corn Bread, 106
Cottage Potatoes, 302
Creamy Cheddar Soup, 31
Creamy Roquefort Dip, 22
Devilish Cheese Logs, 194–95
Eggplant Casserole, 89
Feta Cheese and Tomato Salad, 219
Garlic Cheese Spread, 21
Grouper Fromage, 241–42
Herbed Cheese-and-Cracker Bits, 197
Herbed Cream Cheese Round, 20
Herbed Stuffed Chicken Breasts, 73–74
Italian Love Cake, 388
The Lady & Sons Onion-Cheese Bread,
    313
The Lady's Cheesy Mac, 86
Mexican Chicken, 271
Mexican Layered Dip, 198–99
Mini Onion Quiches, 13
Mixed Vegetable Casserole, 293
Muffins, 310–11
Noodles, 299
Pesto Cheese Blossom, 353–54
Pimento Cheese Tomato Bake, 304
Pineapple Casserole, 98–99
Pineapple Cheese Bread, 110–11
Potato Casserole, 96
Ring Tum Ditty, 340
Roasted Beet Salad, 42
Ron's Tybee Island Sausage Pie, 268–69
Salsa Chicken Salad, 199
Sausage and Grits, 67
Sausage Balls, 13
Scallops Charleston, 50
Shrimp and Artichoke Bake, 56–57
Shrimp with Rice, 53
Smoked Oyster Cheese Balls, 200
South of the Border Mason-Dixon Dip,
    17
Spicy Shrimp and Pasta Casserole, 49–50
Squash Casserole, 84, 290
Strawberry Cheese Ring, 22

Sugar-and-Nut Glazed Brie, 190
Sunday Morning Casserole, 253
Swiss Broccoli Casserole, 288
Tomato Grits, 287–88
Tomato Pie, 95
Trey's Baked Grouper Parmigiano, 241
Vegetable Cheese Soup, 208
Walnut Praline Brie with Fruit, 163
Warm Apple and Goat Cheese Salad, 227
Warm Brie Salad Dressing, 332
Watermelon Salad, 347
Wayne's Beef Macaroni and, 263
Zesty Cheese Straws, 200–201
Cheeseburger Meat Loaf and Sauce, 62
"Cheesecake," Old-Time Lemon, 139–40
cheesecakes:
Caramel Apple, 387
Cheesecake (recipe), 135–36
Luscious Lime, 132–33
with Praline Sauce, 380
Turtle, 390–91
Cheesy Broccoli Bake, 83
Cheesy French Bread, 320
Chef Jack's Corn Chowder, 209
cherry(ies):
Coconut White Fruit Cake, 388–89
Cream Cheese Pie, 394
Cherry Tomato and Mushroom Salad,
    227–28
Chesapeake Bay Crab Cakes, Nootsie's, 248
Chess Pie, Mama's, 149
Chewy Pecan Cookies, 151
chicken:
Avocado Chicken Salad, 40–41
Baked Hen and Dressing, 70
Basil Grilled, 274
Bog, 274–75
Boudine, 276
Breasts in Sour Cream Sauce, 78
Brunswick Stew, 69–70
Casserole, 79, 275
with Drop Dumplin's, 273–74
and Dumplings, 76–77
Fettuccine Chicken Salad, 222–23
Florentine, 277
Fricasé de Pollo, 276
Georgia, 73
Giblet Gravy, 71
Gussie's Fried Chicken with Pecan-
    Honey Glaze, 340–41
Hawaiian Chicken Salad, 217

Herb-Baked, 77–78
Herbed Stuffed Chicken Breasts, 73–74
Hot Savannah Chicken Salad Casserole, 270–71
Hurry-Up Chicken Pot Pie, 271–72
Italian Chicken Sticks, 189
Jamie's Chicken Salad, 35
The Lady's Chicken Noodle Soup, 30–31
Marinade, 115–16
Mexican, 271
Michele's Chicken Noodle Soup, 208–9
Mini Handle Sandwiches, xviii–xix
Mosaic Chicken Terrine, 348–49
Nuggets, 192–93
Oriental Chicken Salad, 37–38
Oriental Marinade, 115
Paprika, 72–73
Pat's Almond Chicken Casserole, 277–78
Pecan, 75
Poblano Chicken Chowder, 206–7
Polynesian Chicken Wings, 188
Pot Pie, 68–69
and Rice Casserole, 75
Salsa Chicken Salad, 199
Saucy Chicken and Asparagus Bake, 278
Savannah Gumbo, 279–80
Savory Grilled Chicken Sauce, 117–18
Sesame Chicken Strips, 14–15
Southern Fried, 68
Szechuan Chicken with Angelhair Pasta, 279
and Wild Rice Casserole, 280
in Wine Sauce, 72
chili:
South of the Border Mason-Dixon Dip, 17
Texas-Style, 268
White Bean, 29
Chilled Zucchini Soup, 212
Chinese Salad, 219–20
Chips, Sweet Potato, 90
chive(s):
Corn Chive Pudding, 301
chocolate:
Almond Pie, 147–48
Aunt Glennis's Blonde Brownies, 159
Better Than Sex? Yes!, 140
Bread Pudding, 409
Brenda's Kahlúa Brownies, 413

Chocolate Chip Nut Cake, 132
Chocolate Chip Pie, 147
Chocolate Chip Pound Cake, 384–85
Corrie's Kentucky Pie, 145–46
Cream Cheese Brownies, 158
Cream Pie, 394–95
Damnation, 143
Double-Dutch Chocolate Fudge Upside-Down Cake, 376–77
Five-Minute Fudge, 161
Fudgie Scotch Ring, 157
Glaze, 143
Hidden Kisses, 411
Hot Fudge Sauce, 131
Italian Love Cake, 388
Lady Brownies, 157–58
Milky Way Cake, 377
Million-Dollar Pie, 150–51
Mississippi Mud Cake, 383
Mocha Sauce, 331
Mound Brownies, 415–16
Old-Fashioned Fudge Pie, 400
Old-Time Chocolate Fudge, 160–61
Peanut Butter Buckeyes, 159
Peanut Butter Chocolate Sauce, 331
Pecan Clusters, 160
Pots de Crème, 367
Pound Cake, 141
Savannah Chocolate Cake with Hot Fudge Sauce, 130–31
Shaver's Chocolate Pecan Pie, 398
Sheet Cake, 137–38
Strawberry Shortcake, 129
Torte, 374
Trifle, 404–5
Tunnel of Fudge Cake, 139
Turtle Cheesecake, 390–91
Volcano Cake, 386–87
chowders:
Chef Jack's Corn, 209
Poblano Chicken, 206–7
cinnamon:
Snickerdoodles, 152
clams:
Bo's Eggplant Supreme, 306
cobblers:
Our Pear, 400
Peach, 166
coconut:
Aunt Glennis's Blonde Brownies, 159
Cake, 128–29

coconut: (*cont'd*)
  Chocolate Mound Brownies, 415–16
  Cream Cake, 382–83
  French Coconut Pie, 144–45
  Grandgirl's Fresh Apple Cake from
    Georgia, 389
  Low Country Cookies, 155
  Orange Slice Cake, 386
  Sweet Potato Balls, 290
  Sweet Potato Casserole, 283–84
  Volcano Cake, 386–87
  White Fruit Cake, 388–89
coffee:
  Brenda's Kahlúa Brownies, 413
  Mocha Sauce, 331
coffee cakes:
  Easy, 142
  Lemon-Pecan Sunburst, 343–44
  Nutty Orange, 319–20
Colby cheese:
  Baked Cheese Spread, 187
coleslaw:
  Esther's Dill, 40
  The Lady's, 37
  Nancy's, 217
collard green(s):
  Collard Greens (recipe), 88–89
  Susan's Caldo Soup, 210
  Wontons, xix
Colo Cucumber Salad, 223
Compote Clouds, 407
condiments, 113–22, 323–34
  Candied Dills, 196
  Chicken or Shrimp Marinade, 115–16
  Crème Fraîche, 52
  Garlic Butter, 108
  Honey Butter, 122
  House Seasoning, 325
  Mint Julep Jelly, 120–21
  Oriental Marinade, 115
  Pear Honey, 120
  Pepper Jelly, 121–22
  Port Wine Jelly, 121
  Southern Spice Rub, 325
  Strawberry Fig Preserves, 121
  Tarragon Butter, 328
  see also dressings; sauces
confections, 125, 159–61
  Five-Minute Fudge, 161
  Fudgie Scotch Ring, 157
  Old-Time Chocolate Fudge, 160–61

  Peanut Butter Balls, 160
  Peanut Butter Buckeyes, 159
  Pecan Clusters, 160
Confederate Bean Soup, 33
Congealed Salad, My Mother's, 224–25
cookies, 124–25, 151–56, 371, 409–13
  Brown Sugar, 411
  Butter, 156
  Butter Fingers, 154
  Chewy Pecan, 151
  Goodies, 154
  Hidden Kisses, 411
  Lady Lock, 152–53
  Low Country, 155
  Magical Peanut Butter, 412–13
  Mrs. Sullivan's Benne Wafers, 350–51
  Oatmeal, 410
  Sliced Nut, 153–54
  Snickerdoodles, 152
  Southern Tea Cakes, 153
  Sugar, 409–10
  Swedish Countess, 412
  Thumb Print, 155–56
  see also brownies and bars
cooking tips, 167–68, 181–83
Copper Pennies, 225
corn:
  Black Bean Salsa, 23
  Casserole, 286
  Chef Jack's Corn Chowder, 209
  Chive Pudding, 301
  Corny Corn Bread, 106
  Corny Corn Muffins, 320–21
  Creamed, 97
  Fresh Corn Scallop, 94
  Low Country Boil, 47
  South Georgia "Caviar," 194
  Zucchini and Corn Casserole, 92
corn bread:
  Corn Bread (recipe), 70
  Corny, 106
  Cracklin', 108
  Herb, 110
  Piggy Pudding, 67
  Southern Corn Bread Stuffing, 70–71
corned beef:
  St. Paddy's Day Corned Beef and
    Cabbage, 265
Cornish game hens:
  Honey Game Hens, 74
  Marinated Cornish Hens, 77

cornmeal:
Corn Bread, 70
Corny Corn Bread, 106
Corny Corn Muffins, 320–21
Cracklin' Corn Bread, 108
Green Muffins, 316
Herb Corn Bread, 110
Hoecakes, 105
Hush Puppies, 318
Old-Time Spoon Bread, 317
Turnip Greens with Cornmeal
Dumplings, 85
Cornucopia Salad, 41
Corny Corn Bread, 106
Corny Corn Muffins, 320–21
Corrie's Kentucky Pie, 145–46
Cottage Potatoes, 302
Country-Fried Venison Steak, Bubba's, 250
crab:
Baked Shrimp-Crab Salad, 246–47
Best Crab Casserole, 244
Bisque, 211
Cakes with Lemon Dill Sauce, 349–50
Hot Crab Canapé, 12
Hot Crab Dip, 187
Jelly Roll's Crab Fried Rice, 286
The Lady & Sons Crab Stew, 210–11
The Lady's Bouillabaisse, 240
Nootsie's Chesapeake Bay Crab Cakes,
248
Red Snapper Stuffed with Crabmeat, 56
Savannah Crab Cakes, 48–49
She Crab Soup, 27
Shore Is Good Seafood Dip, 190
Wayne's Award-Winning Maryland Crab
Soup, 214–15
cracker(s):
Georgia Cracker Salad, 36
Herbed Cheese-and-Cracker Bits, 197
Ritz Cracker Pie, 395–96
Cracklin' Corn Bread, 108
cranberry(ies):
Berry Steak Sauce, 327
Jezebel Sauce, 330
Pecan Cranberry Salad, 218
Salad, 39
Wayne's Cranberry Sauce, 326
cream:
of Artichoke Soup, 33
Banana Cream Pie, 150
Blueberry Cream Pie, 392

Chocolate Cream Pie, 394–95
Coconut Cream Cake, 382–83
Crème Brûlée, 402–3
Crème Fraîche Mashed Potatoes, 296
Horseradish, 58
Pots de Crème, 367
Strawberry and Cream Pie, 148
Strawberry Cream Shortcake, 404
see also sour cream
cream cheese:
"Boursin Cheese," 197
Brownies, 158
Cherry Cream Cheese Pie, 394
Herbed Cream Cheese Round, 20
Creamed Corn, 97
Creamy Cheddar Soup, 31
Creamy Roquefort Dip, 22
Crème Brûlée, 402–3
Crème Caramel, 163
Crème Fraîche, 52
Crème Fraîche Mashed Potatoes, 296
crisps:
Apple, 395
Blueberry Raspberry Pecan, 359–60
Crockpot Pinto Beans, 298
croquettes:
Shrimp and Rice Croquettes with Aioli,
235
Crunchy New Potatoes, 293
Crunchy Peanut Butter Muffins, 312
cucumber:
Colo Cucumber Salad, 223
Cupcakes, Applesauce, 142
Currant and Oat Scones, 309–10
Curry-Crusted Bananas, 292–93
custards and puddings:
savory
Corn Chive Pudding, 301
Piggy Pudding, 67
Zucchini Custard Bake, 99
sweet, 163–65
Banana Pudding, 164–65
Butterscotch Delight, 407–8
Chocolate Bread Pudding, 409
Chocolate Trifle, 404–5
Compote Clouds, 407
Crème Brûlée, 402–3
Crème Caramel, 163
English Trifle, 405–6
Heavenly Banana Delight, 408
Mexican Flan, 406

custards and puddings: sweet (*cont'd*)
    Old-Fashioned Rice Pudding, 401–2
    Pecan Pudding Cake, 391–92
    Pots de Crème, 367
    Pumpkin Gingerbread Trifle, 401
    Rice Pudding, 164
    Savannah "Tiramisu," 165
    Strawberry Cream Shortcake, 404

D

Daddy's Tangy Grilling Sauce, 115
Dates, Pecan-Stuffed, 11
desserts, 123–66, 369–416
  Apple Crisp, 395
  Baked Apples, 161–62
  Blueberry Raspberry Pecan Crisp,
    359–60
  Five-Minute Fudge, 161
  Fudgie Scotch Ring, 157
  Old-Time Chocolate Fudge, 160–61
  Our Pear Cobbler, 400
  Peach Cobbler, 166
  Peanut Butter Balls, 160
  Peanut Butter Buckeyes, 159
  Pecan Clusters, 160
  Savannah "Tiramisu," 165
  Strawberry Mold, 162
  Walnut Praline Brie with Fruit, 163
  see also brownies and bars; cakes; cookies;
    custards and puddings; pies
Deviled Seafood Casserole, 51
Devilish Cheese Logs, 194–95
Dian's Black Bean Soup, 207
Dijon:
  Pepper Dippin' Sauce, 295–96
  Turnips in Dijon Sauce, 289
dill:
  Esther's Dill Coleslaw, 40
  Lemon Dill Sauce, 350
  Tomato Dill Soup, 34
Dills, Candied, 196
dips:
  Artichoke and Spinach, 18
  Black Bean, 193
  Black Bean Salsa, 23
  Creamy Roquefort, 22
  Hot Asparagus, 12
  Hot Crab, 187
  Mexican Layered, 198–99
  Quick Guacamole-Spinach, 21
  Shore Is Good Seafood, 190

South Georgia "Caviar," 194
South of the Border Mason-Dixon, 17
Southwestern, 19–20
Spinach and Shrimp, 188–89
see also spreads
Dixieland Pork Chops, 266–67
Donaldson, Phil, 361
Double-Dutch Chocolate Fudge Upside-
    Down Cake, 376–77
dressings, 113, 118–20, 323–34, 332–34
  Aunt Peggy's Italian, 119
  Avocado, 41
  Balsamic Vinaigrette, 333
  Buttermilk, 120
  Creamy Roquefort Dip, 22
  Greek Salad, 334
  Honey, 224
  Honey Mustard, 119–20
  Lime Vinaigrette, 332
  Poppy Seed, 119
  Roasted Red Pepper Vinaigrette, 333
  Sweet-and-Sour, 35, 118
  Warm Brie Salad, 332
Duck Burgundy, 78–79
dumplings:
  Chicken and, 76–77
  Chicken with Drop Dumplin's, 273–74
  Collard Green Wontons, xix
  Dumplings (recipe), 73
  Spiced Beef with Dumplin's, 252–53
  Turnip Greens with Cornmeal
    Dumplings, 85
Dutch Apple Pancakes, Oven-Baked, 344
Dutch Bread, 108–9
Duxelles-Stuffed Tenderloin, 256–57

E

Eastwood, Clint, 100
Easy Caramel Icing, 378
Easy Herb Rolls, 314–15
Easy Hollandaise, 329
Easy Homemade Blender Mayonnaise, 327
Easy Rolls, 104
Easy Shrimp Bake, 243–44
Easy Yeast Rolls, 311
egg(s):
  Artichoke Frittata, 192
  Asparagus Casserole, 303–4
  Broccoli Soufflé, 90
  Caviar Mold, 201
  Caviar Spread, 196

French Toast Stuffed with Bananas and
  Walnuts, 342–43
Jamie's Chicken Salad, 35
and Lemon Sauce, 117
Mini Onion Quiches, 13
Pickled Beets and, 220
Potato-Egg Salad, 38
Sunday Morning Casserole, 253
Zucchini Custard Bake, 99
eggplant:
  Bo's Eggplant Supreme, 306
  Casserole, 89
Elizabeth on 37th, recipes from, 358–60
  Blueberry Raspberry Pecan Crisp,
    359–60
  Fried Grits Cakes with Sausage, 358
  Shrimp Bel Vedere, 359
English Trifle, 405–6
Esther's Dill Coleslaw, 40
Eye-of-Round Roast, Perfect, 252
Eye-of-Round Steak, Party, 198

F
Fancy Green Beans, 283
Farmer's Pork Chops, 64–65
feta cheese:
  Cheese-Stuffed Mushrooms, 14
  Herbed Stuffed Chicken Breasts, 73–74
  Roasted Beet Salad, 42
  and Tomato Salad, 219
  Watermelon Salad, 347
Fettuccine Chicken Salad, 222–23
Fiery Cajun Shrimp, 245
fig(s):
  Strawberry Fig Preserves, 121
Filet Mignon, Perfect Char-Grilled, 270
Fillet of Sole Paprika, 53
fish and shellfish, 43, 47–57, 231, 235–48
  Baked Flounder, 362
  Baked Shrimp-Crab Salad, 246–47
  Barbara's Mussels, 246
  Battered Fried Shrimp, 237–38
  Beaufort Shrimp Pie, 239
  Best Crab Casserole, 244
  Black Pepper Shrimp, 47–48
  Can't-Miss Red Snapper, 243
  Caviar Spread, 196
  Crab Bisque, 211
  Crab Cakes with Lemon Dill Sauce,
    349–50
  Deviled Seafood Casserole, 51

Easy Shrimp Bake, 243–44
Egg and Lemon Sauce, 117
Egg Caviar Mold, 201
Fiery Cajun Shrimp, 245
Fillet of Sole Paprika, 53
Ginger Shrimp, 244–45
Grilled Red Pepper Scallops, 238
Grouper Fromage, 241–42
Hot Crab Canapé, 12
Hot Crab Dip, 187
Jelly Roll's Crab Fried Rice, 286
The Lady & Sons Crab Stew, 210–11
The Lady's Bouillabaisse, 240
Lemon Butter for Fish, 118
Lemon Mackerel, 54–55
Lemon Shrimp Cocktail Sauce, 117
Low Country Boil, 47
Lucile Wright's Oyster Bisque, 365
Marinated Shrimp and Artichoke Hearts,
  228–29
Mushroom-Stuffed Baked Red Snapper,
  51–52
Nootsie's Chesapeake Bay Crab Cakes,
  248
Oriental Marinade, 115
Oysters in the Patty Shell, 15
Oyster Stew, 28
Red Snapper Stuffed with Crabmeat, 56
Savannah Crab Cakes, 48–49
Savory Salmon, 48
Scallops Charleston, 50
She Crab Soup, 27
Shore Is Good Seafood Dip, 190
Shrimp and Artichoke Bake, 56–57
Shrimp and Grits, xvii–xviii
Shrimp and Grits with Marinara Sauce,
  236–37
Shrimp and Mushroom Casserole, 55
Shrimp and Rice Croquettes with Aioli,
  235
Shrimp and Scallop Fraîche, 52
Shrimp Bel Vedere, 359
Shrimp Bisque, 29
Shrimp Butter, 18
Shrimp Gravy, 237
Shrimp Gumbo Casserole, 54
Shrimp Marinade, 115–16
Shrimp Mold, 193–94
Shrimp or Lobster Bisque, 32
Shrimp with Rice, 53
Smoked Oyster Cheese Balls, 200

fish and shellfish: (*cont'd*)
  Southern Shrimp Salad, 36
  Spicy Shrimp and Pasta Casserole, 49–50
  Spinach and Shrimp Dip, 188–89
  Stewed Salmon, 239
  Tangy Marinated Shrimp, 195–96
  Trey's Baked Grouper Parmigiano, 241
  Tuna Burgers, 247
  Venison Wellington with Oyster Pâté,
      261–63
  Wayne's Award-Winning Maryland Crab
      Soup, 214–15
  Wild Rice and Oyster Casserole, 242
Five-Minute Fudge, 161
Flan, Mexican, 406
Flounder, Baked, 362
Foolproof Standing Rib Roast, 63
Fourth-Generation Blackberry Jam Cake,
    375–76
Fowler, Damon Lee, recipes from, 345–47
  Asparagus with Leeks and New Potatoes,
      346–47
  Turnips Stuffed with Winter Greens,
      345–46
  Watermelon Salad, 347
French bread:
  Cheesy, 320
  Stuffed, 201
French Coconut Pie, 144–45
French Toast Stuffed with Bananas and
    Walnuts, 342–43
Fresh Cabbage and Sweet Sausages, 366
Fresh Corn Scallop, 94
Fricasé de Pollo, 276
Fried Apple Pies, 399
Fried Chicken, Southern, 68
Fried Chicken with Pecan-Honey Glaze,
    Gussie's, 340–41
Fried Green Tomatoes, 91
Fried Green Tomatoes with Dijon Pepper
    Dippin' Sauce, 295–96
Fried Grits Cakes with Sausage, 358
Fried Rice, Jelly Roll's Crab, 286
Fried Shrimp, Battered, 237–38
Fried Spare Ribs, 256
Fried Veal, 251–52
Frittata, Artichoke, 192
fritters:
  Okra, 297
  Pear, 106
Frozen Waldorf Salad, Golda's, 218–19

fruit(s):
  Bowl, 226
  Coconut White Fruit Cake, 388–89
  Salad with Honey Dressing, 224
  see also specific fruits
fudge:
  Double-Dutch Chocolate Fudge Upside-
      Down Cake, 376–77
  Five-Minute, 161
  Hot Fudge Sauce, 131
  Old-Fashioned Fudge Pie, 400
  Old-Time Chocolate, 160–61
  Tunnel of Fudge Cake, 139
Fudgie Scotch Ring, 157

G
garlic:
  Butter, 108
  Cheese Spread, 21
  Oven-Roasted Red Potatoes with
      Rosemary and, 287
Gastonian, recipes from, 352–54
  Pesto Cheese Blossom, 353–54
  Strawberry Soup, 353
  Traditional Raisin Scones, 352
Georgia Cracker Salad, 36
Georgia Spiced Pecans, 195
Georgia Sugared Peanuts, 11
Giblet Gravy, 71
gingerbread:
  Pumpkin Gingerbread Trifle, 401
Ginger Shrimp, 244–45
Gingersnap Pear Salad, 220
Glaze, Chocolate, 143
Glazed Honey Bars, 415
Glazed Spice Bars, 413
goat cheese:
  Warm Apple and Goat Cheese Salad, 227
Golda's Frozen Waldorf Salad, 218–19
Goodies, 154
Gooey Butter Cakes, 133–34
Gorilla Bread, 319
Grandgirl's Fresh Apple Cake from
    Georgia, 389
Grandmama Hiers's Carrot Cake, 138–39
Grand Marnier, Snow Peas with, 294
Grandma's Iced Georgia Squares, 156–57
Grandmother Paul's Red Velvet Cake,
    134–35
Grandmother Paul's Sour Cream Pound
    Cake, 133

Granite Steps Inn, recipes from, 342–44
  French Toast Stuffed with Bananas and
    Walnuts, 342–43
  Lemon-Pecan Sunburst Coffee Cake,
    343–44
  Oven-Baked Dutch Apple Pancakes, 344
grape(s):
  Golda's Frozen Waldorf Salad, 218–19
  Hawaiian Chicken Salad, 217
  Walnut Praline Brie with Fruit, 163
gravies:
  Giblet, 71
  Shrimp, 237
Greek Salad Dressing, 334
green(s):
  Collard, 88–89
  Collard Green Wontons, xix
  Green Muffins, 316
  Steak and, 65–66
  Susan's Caldo Soup, 210
  Turnip Greens with Cornmeal
    Dumplings, 85
  Turnips Stuffed with Winter Greens,
    345–46
  see also spinach
green bean(s):
  Casserole, 305
  Chicken and Rice Casserole, 75–76
  Fancy, 283
  with Onions, 341
Green Muffins, 316
Green Rice Casserole, 289
Green Tomato Cake, 374–75
Grilled Chicken, Basil, 274
Grilled Chicken Sauce, Savory, 117–18
Grilled Filet Mignon, Perfect, 270
Grilled Peanut Butter Ham, Ron's, 249
Grilled Red Pepper Scallops, 238
Grilling Sauce, Daddy's Tangy, 115
grits:
  Baked, 83
  Fried Grits Cakes with Sausage, 358
  Sausage and, 67
  Shrimp and, xvii–xviii
  Shrimp and Grits with Marinara Sauce,
    236–37
  Tomato, 287–88
grouper:
  Fromage, 241–42
  The Lady's Bouillabaisse, 240
  Trey's Baked Grouper Parmigiano, 241

Gruyère cheese:
  Scallops Charleston, 50
Guacamole-Spinach Dip, Quick, 21
gumbo:
  Savannah, 279–80
  Shrimp Gumbo Casserole, 54
Gussie's Fried Chicken with Pecan-Honey
    Glaze, 340–41

H
haddock:
  Deviled Seafood Casserole, 51
Half-Baked Potato, 301
Half-Million-Dollar Pie, 398–99
ham:
  Devilish Cheese Logs, 194–95
  Potato and Ham Soup, 211
  Ron's Grilled Peanut Butter, 249
Hash Brown Potato Casserole, 303
Hawaiian Chicken Salad, 217
hearts of palm:
  Spinach, Strawberry, and Hearts of Palm
    Salad, 221
Heavenly Banana Delight, 408
helpful hints, 167–68, 181–83
herb(s):
  "Boursin Cheese," 197
  Corn Bread, 110
  Easy Herb Rolls, 314–15
  Herb-Baked Chicken, 77–78
  Herbed Cheese-and-Cracker Bits, 197
  Herbed Cream Cheese Round, 20
  Herbed Stuffed Chicken Breasts, 73–74
Hidden Kisses, 411
Hoecakes, 105
hollandaise:
  Easy, 329
  Lemon Hollandaise Sauce, 367
Homemade Dried Onion Soup Mix,
    216–17
honey:
  Butter, 122
  Fruit Salad with Honey Dressing, 224
  Game Hens, 74
  Glazed Honey Bars, 415
  Gussie's Fried Chicken with Pecan-
    Honey Glaze, 340–41
  Mustard Dressing, 119–20
Hoppin' John, 98
Horseradish Cream, 58
Hot Asparagus Dip, 12

Hot Crab Canapé, 12
Hot Crab Dip, 187
Hot Fudge Sauce, 131
Hot Savannah Chicken Salad Casserole,
   270–71
House Seasoning, 325
Hummingbird Cake, 381–82
Hurry-Up Chicken Pot Pie, 271–72
Hush Puppies, 318

I
Italian Chicken Sticks, 189
Italian Dressing, Aunt Peggy's, 119
Italian Love Cake, 388
Italian Potatoes, 300
Italian Roasted Red Peppers, 19

J
Jack cheese:
   Salsa Chicken Salad, 199
   see also Monterey Jack cheese
Jamie's Chicken Salad, 35
jellies, jams, and preserves, 113, 120–22
   Fourth-Generation Blackberry Jam Cake,
      375–76
   Mint Julep Jelly, 120–21
   Pepper Jelly, 121–22
   Port Wine Jelly, 121
   Strawberry Cheese Ring, 22
   Strawberry Fig Preserves, 121
   Thumb Print Cookies, 155–56
Jelly Roll's Crab Fried Rice, 286
Jezebel Sauce, 330
Johnny Harris Restaurant, recipes from,
   361–63
   Baked Flounder, 362
   Pasta Puttanesca Sauce, 363
   Steak au Poivre, 361–62

K
Kahlúa:
   Brenda's Kahlúa Brownies, 413
Key Lime Pie, 397–98

L
Lady & Sons Beef Vegetable Soup, The,
   205–6
Lady & Sons Crab Stew, The, 210–11
Lady & Sons Onion-Cheese Bread, The,
   313
Lady & Sons Pot Roast, The, 257–59

Lady & Sons Smoked Boston Butt Roast,
   The, 255–56
Lady Brownies, 157–58
ladyfingers:
   Savannah "Tiramisu," 165
Lady Lock Cookies, 152–53
Lady's Barbecue Sauce, The, 116
Lady's Bouillabaisse, The, 240
Lady's Cheesy Mac, The, 86
Lady's Chicken Noodle Soup, The, 30–31
Lady's Coleslaw, The, 37
Lady's Oven-Roasted Ribs, The, 66
Lady's Pork Stew, The, 264
Lady's Warm Potato Salad, The, 38
Landers, Anne, 352
leek(s):
   Asparagus with Leeks and New Potatoes,
      346–47
lemon(s):
   Bars, 414–15
   Butter for Fish, 118
   Butter for Steak, 118
   Dill Sauce, 350
   Egg and Lemon Sauce, 117
   Hollandaise Sauce, 367
   Mackerel, 54–55
   Meringue Pie, 149–50, 396
   Old-Time Lemon "Cheesecake,"
      139–40
   Pecan Sunburst Coffee Cake, 343–44
   Shrimp Cocktail Sauce, 117
lentil(s):
   Sausage and Lentil Soup, 31–32
lettuce:
   BLT Soup, 213
lime(s):
   Key Lime Pie, 397–98
   Luscious Lime Cheesecake, 132–33
   Vinaigrette, 332
Lisa's Southern Pecan Pie, 393
Lobster Bisque, 32
Low Country Boil, 47
Low Country Cookies, 155
Low-Fat Peach Cake, 129–30
Lucile Wright's Oyster Bisque, 365
Lucile Wright's Tomato Sandwiches, 364
Luscious Lime Cheesecake, 132–33

M
macadamia nut(s):
   Sugar-and-Nut Glazed Brie, 190

macaroni:
  The Lady's Cheesy Mac, 86
  Wayne's Beef Macaroni and Cheese, 263
macaroons:
  Savannah "Tiramisu," 165
Mackerel, Lemon, 54–55
Magical Peanut Butter Cookies, 412–13
main courses, 43–79, 231–80
  see also beef; chicken; fish and shellfish;
    pork; poultry; sausage(s); veal
Mama's Chess Pie, 149
Mama's Pound Cake, 131
marinades:
  Chicken or Shrimp, 115–16
  Oriental, 115
Marinara Sauce, Shrimp and Grits with,
    236–37
Marinated Asparagus Salad, 222
Marinated Cornish Hens, 77
Marinated Shrimp, Tangy, 195–96
Marinated Shrimp and Artichoke Hearts,
    228–29
Marsala Sauce, Quail with, 272–73
marshmallow(s):
  Five-Minute Fudge, 161
  Golda's Frozen Waldorf Salad, 218–19
  Mississippi Mud Cake, 383
  Pecan Clusters, 160
Mashed Potato Bake, 299
mashed potatoes:
  Crème Fraîche, 296
  Mashed Potatoes (recipe), 93
  with Sautéed Mushrooms, 98
mayonnaise:
  Aioli, 235
  Easy Homemade Blender, 327
meat, 44, 57–67, 232–33, 248–70
  see also beef; pork; sausage(s); veal
meat loaf:
  Barbecue, 269–70
  Basic, 58–59
  Cheeseburger Meat Loaf and Sauce,
    62
meringue:
  Chocolate Cream Pie, 394–95
  Lemon Meringue Pie, 149–50, 396
  Topping, 165
Mexican Chicken, 271
Mexican Flan, 406
Mexican Layered Dip, 198–99
Michele's Chicken Noodle Soup, 208–9

Milky Way Cake, 377
Million-Dollar Pie, 150–51
Mini Handle Sandwiches, xviii–xix
Mini Onion Quiches, 13
Mini Pecan Pies, 146
Mint Julep Jelly, 120–21
Mississippi Mud Cake, 383
Mrs. Sullivan's Benne Wafers, 350–51
Mrs. Wilkes' Boarding House, recipes from,
    355–57
  Baked Bean Casserole, 356
  Beef Stew Casserole, 356–57
  Mrs. Wilkes' Boarding House–Style
    Biscuits, 355–56
  Mixed Vegetable Casserole, 293
Mocha Sauce, 331
molds:
  Cranberry Salad, 39
  Egg Caviar, 201
  Pesto Cheese Blossom, 353–54
  Shrimp, 193–94
  Strawberry, 162, 226
Monterey Jack cheese:
  Baked Grits, 83
  Bobby's Pimento Cheese, 23
  Grouper Fromage, 241–42
  Spinach and Shrimp Dip, 188–89
  Sunday Morning Casserole, 253
Mosaic Chicken Terrine, 348–49
Mother's Rolls, 107
mozzarella cheese:
  Chicken Georgia, 73
  Tomato Pie, 95
muffins:
  Apple Raisin, 318
  Blackberry, 314
  Cheese, 310–11
  Corny Corn, 320–21
  Crunchy Peanut Butter, 312
  Green, 316
  Orange Blossoms, 384
mushroom(s):
  Canapés, 191
  Cheese-Stuffed, 14
  Cheesy Broccoli Bake, 83
  Cherry Tomato and Mushroom Salad,
    227–28
  Chicken Breasts in Sour Cream Sauce,
    78
  Chicken Georgia, 73
  Cloud Soup, 213–14

mushroom(s): (*cont'd*)
  Cornucopia Salad, 41
  Duxelles-Stuffed Tenderloin, 256–57
  Green Bean Casserole, 305
  Marinated Cornish Hens, 77
  Mashed Potatoes with Sautéed
    Mushrooms, 98
  Mushroom-Stuffed Baked Red Snapper,
    51–52
  Rice Casserole, 291
  Sauce, 328
  Sausage-Rice Casserole, 61
  Scallops Charleston, 50
  Shrimp and Mushroom Casserole, 55
  Steak Diane, 269
  Steakside, 86
mussels:
  Barbara's, 246
  The Lady's Bouillabaisse, 240
mustard:
  Dijon Pepper Dippin' Sauce, 295–96
  Honey Mustard Dressing, 119–20
  Turnips in Dijon Sauce, 289
My Mother's Congealed Salad, 224–25

N
Nancy's Coleslaw, 217
Nesbit, Martha Giddens, recipes from,
    348–51
  Crab Cakes with Lemon Dill Sauce,
    349–50
  Mrs. Sullivan's Benne Wafers, 350–51
  Mosaic Chicken Terrine, 348–49
noodle(s):
  Casserole, 300
  Cheese, 299
  Chicken Boudine, 276
  Chinese Salad, 219–20
  The Lady's Chicken Noodle Soup,
    30–31
  Michele's Chicken Noodle Soup, 208–9
  see also pasta
nut(s):
  Almond Sour Cream Cake, xxi–xxii
  Aunt Glennis's Blonde Brownies, 159
  Auntie's Peanut Sauce, 329
  Banana Nut Bread, 103
  Banana Nut Cake, xx–xxi
  Blueberry Raspberry Pecan Crisp,
    359–60
  Butter Fingers, 154

  Caramel-Nut Pound Cake, 381
  Chewy Pecan Cookies, 151
  Chocolate Almond Pie, 147–48
  Chocolate Chip Nut Cake, 132
  Chocolate Mound Brownies, 415–16
  Coconut White Fruit Cake, 388–89
  Cornucopia Salad, 41
  Corrie's Kentucky Pie, 145–46
  Cranberry Salad, 39
  French Toast Stuffed with Bananas and
    Walnuts, 342–43
  Fudgie Scotch Ring, 157
  Georgia Spiced Pecans, 195
  Georgia Sugared Peanuts, 11
  Golda's Frozen Waldorf Salad, 218–19
  Goodies, 154
  Grandgirl's Fresh Apple Cake from
    Georgia, 389
  Gussie's Fried Chicken with Pecan-
    Honey Glaze, 340–41
  Half-Million-Dollar Pie, 398–99
  Hidden Kisses, 411
  Hummingbird Cake, 381–82
  Lemon-Pecan Sunburst Coffee Cake,
    343–44
  Lisa's Southern Pecan Pie, 393
  Low Country Cookies, 155
  Mini Pecan Pies, 146
  Mississippi Mud Cake, 383
  Nutty Orange Coffee Cake, 319–20
  Orange Slice Cake, 386
  Orange Walnut Salad with Sweet-and-
    Sour Dressing, 34–35
  Pat's Almond Chicken Casserole, 277–78
  Pecan Chicken, 75
  Pecan Clusters, 160
  Pecan Cranberry Salad, 218
  Pecan Pudding Cake, 391–92
  Pecan-Stuffed Dates, 11
  Praline Pumpkin Pie, 146–47
  Sausage-Almond Rice, 298
  Shaver's Chocolate Pecan Pie, 398
  Sliced Nut Cookies, 153–54
  Strawberry Mold, 162, 226
  Sugar-and-Nut Glazed Brie, 190
  Sweet Potato Chips, 90
  Thanksgiving Pie, 148
  Volcano Cake, 386–87
  Walnut Praline Brie with Fruit, 163
  see also peanut butter
Nutty Orange Coffee Cake, 319–20

O

oat(s):
Apple Crisp, 395
Currant and Oat Scones, 309–10
Goodies, 154
Oatmeal Cookies, 410
okra:
Fritters, 297
Pickled Okra Sandwiches, 20
Savannah Gumbo, 279–80
Shrimp Gumbo Casserole, 54
Old-Fashioned Fudge Pie, 400
Old-Fashioned Rice Pudding, 401–2
Old-Fashioned Sweet Potato Pie, 396–97
Old-Time Beef Stew, 58
Old-Time Chocolate Fudge, 160–61
Old-Time Lemon "Cheesecake," 139–40
Old-Time Spoon Bread, 317
onion(s):
Green Beans with, 341
Homemade Dried Onion Soup Mix,
216–17
The Lady & Sons Onion-Cheese Bread,
313
Mini Onion Quiches, 13
Roasted, 304–5
Saturday Night Vidalia Onions, 285
Vidalia Onion Casserole, 291
Vidalia Onion Pie, 89–90
orange(s):
Blossoms, 384
mandarin
Fruit Bowl, 226
Fruit Salad with Honey Dressing,
224
Half-Million-Dollar Pie, 398–99
Hawaiian Chicken Salad, 217
Pig Pickin' Cake, 390
Nutty Orange Coffee Cake, 319–20
Savory Salmon, 48
Slice Cake, 386
Walnut Salad with Sweet-and-Sour
Dressing, 34–35
Oriental Chicken Salad, 37–38
Oriental Marinade, 115
Our Pear Cobbler, 400
Oven-Baked Dutch Apple Pancakes, 344
Oven-Fried Potato Wedges, 294
Oven-Roasted Red Potatoes with Rosemary
and Garlic, 287
Oven-Roasted Ribs, The Lady's, 66

oyster(s):
Lucile Wright's Oyster Bisque, 365
in the Patty Shell, 15
Smoked Oyster Cheese Balls, 200
Stew, 28
Venison Wellington with Oyster Pâté,
261–63
Wild Rice and Oyster Casserole, 242

P

pancakes:
Oven-Baked Dutch Apple, 344
Vegetable, 302
paprika:
Chicken, 72–73
Fillet of Sole, 53
Parmesan cheese:
Artichoke and Spinach Dip, 18
Bacon Wraps, 17
Cheese-Stuffed Mushrooms, 14
Trey's Baked Grouper Parmigiano, 241
Party Eye-of-Round Steak, 198
pasta:
Baked Pasta Florentine, 254
Baked Spaghetti, 260
Fettuccine Chicken Salad, 222–23
The Lady's Cheesy Mac, 86
Puttanesca Sauce, 363
Spicy Shrimp and Pasta Casserole, 49–50
Szechuan Chicken with Angelhair Pasta,
279
Wayne's Beef Macaroni and Cheese, 263
see also noodle(s)
pastry:
Brie en Croûte #1, 15–16
Brie en Croûte #2, 16
Oysters in the Patty Shell, 15
Sour Cream, 263
for Two-Crust Pie, 151
Venison Wellington with Oyster Pâté,
261–63
see also pies
Pat's Almond Chicken Casserole, 277–78
Pattypan Summer Squash Casserole, 97
peach(es):
Cobbler, 166
Low-Fat Peach Cake, 129–30
peanut(s):
Auntie's Peanut Sauce, 329
Georgia Sugared, 11
Sweet Potato Chips, 90

peanut butter:
  Balls, 160
  Bars, 158
  Bread, 110
  Buckeyes, 159
  Cake, 144
  Chocolate Sauce, 331
  Crunchy Peanut Butter Muffins, 312
  Goodies, 154
  Magical Peanut Butter Cookies, 412–13
  Pie, 393
  Ron's Grilled Peanut Butter Ham, 249
pear(s):
  Fritters, 106
  Gingersnap Pear Salad, 220
  Honey, 120
  Our Pear Cobbler, 400
  Pear-Licious Cake, 373
pecan(s):
  Aunt Glennis's Blonde Brownies, 159
  Banana Nut Cake, xx–xxi
  Blueberry Raspberry Pecan Crisp,
    359–60
  Caramel-Nut Pound Cake, 381
  Chewy Pecan Cookies, 151
  Chicken, 75
  Chocolate Mound Brownies, 415–16
  Clusters, 160
  Coconut White Fruit Cake, 388–89
  Corrie's Kentucky Pie, 145–46
  Cranberry Salad, 39, 218
  Georgia Spiced, 195
  Golda's Frozen Waldorf Salad, 218–19
  Goodies, 154
  Grandgirl's Fresh Apple Cake from
    Georgia, 389
  Gussie's Fried Chicken with Pecan-
    Honey Glaze, 340–41
  Half-Million-Dollar Pie, 398–99
  Hidden Kisses, 411
  Hummingbird Cake, 381–82
  Lemon-Pecan Sunburst Coffee Cake,
    343–44
  Lisa's Southern Pecan Pie, 393
  Low Country Cookies, 155
  Mini Pecan Pies, 146
  Nutty Orange Coffee Cake, 319–20
  Orange Slice Cake, 386
  Pecan-Stuffed Dates, 11
  Pie Squares, 414
  Praline Sauce, 380

  Pudding Cake, 391–92
  Ritz Cracker Pie, 395–96
  Shaver's Chocolate Pecan Pie, 398
  Sliced Nut Cookies, 153–54
  Strawberry Mold, 226
  Sugar-and-Nut Glazed Brie, 190
  Volcano Cake, 386–87
pepper(corns):
  Black Pepper Shrimp, 47–48
  Dijon Pepper Dippin' Sauce, 295–96
  Steak au Poivre, 361–62
pepper(s):
  Black-Eyed Pea Salad, 39
  Grilled Red Pepper Scallops, 238
  Italian Roasted Red, 19
  Jelly, 121–22
  Poblano Chicken Chowder, 206–7
  Roasted Red Pepper Soup, 28
  Roasted Red Pepper Vinaigrette, 333
  South Georgia "Caviar," 194
  Steak, 60, 261
  Stuffed Red Peppers, 254–55
Pepper Jelly, 121–22
Perfect Char-Grilled Filet Mignon, 270
Perfect Eye-of-Round Roast, 252
Pesto Cheese Blossom, 353–54
Pickled Beets and Eggs, 220
Pickled Okra Sandwiches, 20
pies:
  savory
    Beaufort Shrimp, 239
    Chicken Pot Pie, 68–69
    Hurry-Up Chicken Pot Pie, 271–72
    Mini Onion Quiches, 13
    Ron's Tybee Island Sausage, 268–69
    Tomato, 95
    Vidalia Onion, 89–90
  sweet, 123–24, 144–51, 370, 392–400
    Banana Cream, 150
    Blueberry Cream, 392
    Butterscotch, 145
    Cherry Cream Cheese, 394
    Chocolate Almond, 147–48
    Chocolate Chip, 147
    Chocolate Cream, 394–95
    Corrie's Kentucky, 145–46
    French Coconut, 144–45
    Fried Apple, 399
    Half-Million-Dollar, 398–99
    Key Lime, 397–98
    Lemon Meringue, 149–50, 396

Lisa's Southern Pecan, 393
Mama's Chess, 149
Million-Dollar, 150–51
Mini Pecan, 146
Old-Fashioned Fudge, 400
Old-Fashioned Sweet Potato, 396–97
Pastry for Two-Crust Pie, 151
Peanut Butter, 393
Praline Pumpkin, 146–47
Ritz Cracker, 395–96
Shaver's Chocolate Pecan, 398
Strawberry and Cream, 148
Thanksgiving, 148
Piggy Pudding, 67
Pig Pickin' Cake, 390
pimento(s):
Bobby's Pimento Cheese, 23
Cheese Tomato Bake, 304
Chicken and Rice Casserole, 75
South Georgia "Caviar," 194
pineapple:
Blueberry Salad, 221–22
Cake, 136–37
Casserole, 98–99
Cheese Bread, 110–11
Coconut White Fruit Cake, 388–89
Compote Clouds, 407
Cranberry Salad, 39
English Trifle, 405–6
Fritters, 106
Fruit Bowl, 226
Golda's Frozen Waldorf Salad, 218–19
Half-Million-Dollar Pie, 398–99
Hawaiian Chicken Salad, 217
Hummingbird Cake, 381–82
My Mother's Congealed Salad, 224–25
Pear Honey, 120
Pecan Pudding Cake, 391–92
Pig Pickin' Cake, 390
Punch Bowl Cake, 141
Sherry-Glazed Sweet Potatoes, 84
Strawberry Mold, 162, 226
Upside-Down Biscuits, 315
Pinto Beans, Crockpot, 298
Pirates' House, recipes from, 339–41
Plantation Skillet Cake, 309
plum(s):
Roast Pork with Plum Sauce, 259–60
Poblano Chicken Chowder, 206–7
Polite, Charles, 251
Polynesian Chicken Wings, 188

Popovers, 310
Poppy Seed Dressing, 119
pork:
Barbecue-Style Pork Chops, 59
Dixieland Pork Chops, 266–67
Farmer's Pork Chops, 64–65
Fried Spare Ribs, 256
The Lady & Sons Smoked Boston Butt
Roast, 255–56
The Lady's Oven-Roasted Ribs, 66
The Lady's Pork Stew, 264
Roast Pork with Plum Sauce, 259–60
Stuffed Red Peppers, 254–55
see also bacon; sausage(s)
Port Wine Jelly, 121
potato(es):
Asparagus with Leeks and New Potatoes,
346–47
Boursin Cheese, 91
Casserole, 96
Cottage, 302
Crunchy New Potatoes, 293
Egg Salad, 38
Farmer's Pork Chops, 64–65
Half-Baked, 301
and Ham Soup, 211
Hash Brown Potato Casserole, 303
Italian, 300
The Lady's Warm Potato Salad, 38
mashed
Crème Fraîche, 296
Mashed (recipe), 93
with Sautéed Mushrooms, 98
Mashed Potato Bake, 299
Oven-Fried Potato Wedges, 294
Oven-Roasted Red Potatoes with
Rosemary and Garlic, 287
Ring Tum Ditty, 340
Sunday Morning Casserole, 253
Susan's Caldo Soup, 210
Twice-Baked, 87
see also sweet potato(es)
pot pies:
Chicken, 68–69
Hurry-Up Chicken, 271–72
pot roast:
The Lady & Sons, 257–59
Pot Roast (recipe), 59–60
Pots de Crème, 367
poultry, 44–45, 68–79, 233, 270–80
Duck Burgundy, 78–79

poultry: (*cont'd*)
    Honey Game Hens, 74
    Marinated Cornish Hens, 77
    Quail with Marsala Sauce, 272–73
    see also chicken
pound cakes:
    Caramel-Nut, 381
    Chocolate, 141
    Chocolate Chip, 384–85
    Grandmother Paul's Sour Cream, 133
    Mama's, 131
    Red Velvet, 385
praline:
    Cheesecake with Praline Sauce, 380
    Pumpkin Pie, 146–47
    Walnut Praline Brie with Fruit, 163
preserves, *see* jellies, jams, and preserves
pretzel(s):
    Strawberry Pretzel Salad, 228
Prime Rib, Brandied, 248–49
Prince Charles' Calf's Liver, 251
puddings, *see* custards and puddings
pumpkin:
    Bread, 104
    Gingerbread Trifle, 401
    Praline Pumpkin Pie, 146–47
    Thanksgiving Pie, 148
Punch Bowl Cake, 141

Q
Quail with Marsala Sauce, 272–73
Quiches, Mini Onion, 13
Quick Guacamole-Spinach Dip, 21

R
raisin(s):
    Apple Raisin Muffins, 318
    Coconut White Fruit Cake, 388–89
    Cornucopia Salad, 41
    Traditional Raisin Scones, 352
raspberry:
    Blueberry Raspberry Pecan Crisp, 359–60
    Sauce, 330
red rice:
    Savannah, 88
    Spicy Tomato, 297
red snapper:
    Can't-Miss, 243
    Mushroom-Stuffed Baked, 51–52
    Stuffed with Crabmeat, 56

Red Velvet Cake, Grandmother Paul's, 134–35
Red Velvet Pound Cake, 385
Rib Roast, Foolproof Standing, 63
ribs:
    Barbecued Short Ribs, 266–67
    Fried Spare Ribs, 256
    The Lady's Oven-Roasted, 66
rice:
    Avocado Chicken Salad, 40–41
    Chicken and Rice Casserole, 75
    Chicken Bog, 274–75
    Chicken Casserole, 275
    Green Rice Casserole, 289
    Hoppin' John, 98
    Jelly Roll's Crab Fried, 286
    Mushroom Rice Casserole, 291
    Old-Fashioned Rice Pudding, 401–2
    Pudding, 164
    Sausage-Almond, 298
    Sausage-Rice Casserole, 61
    Sausage with Ravishing Rice, 266
    Savannah Red, 88
    Savory, 93
    Shrimp and Rice Croquettes with Aioli, 235
    Shrimp with, 53
    Southern Shrimp Salad, 36
    Spicy Tomato Red, 297
    Stuffed Red Peppers, 254–55
    Susan's Baked, 96
    see also wild rice
ricotta cheese:
    Italian Love Cake, 388
Ring Tum Ditty, 340
Ritz Cracker Pie, 395–96
Riz Biscuits, 313–14
Roasted Beet Salad, 42
Roasted Onions, 304–5
Roasted Red Peppers, Italian, 19
Roasted Red Pepper Soup, 28
Roasted Red Pepper Vinaigrette, 333
Roast Pork with Plum Sauce, 259–60
rolls:
    Easy, 104
    Easy Herb, 314–15
    Easy Yeast, 311
    Mother's, 107
Ron's Grilled Peanut Butter Ham, 249
Ron's Tybee Island Sausage Pie, 268–69

Roquefort:
Creamy Roquefort Dip, 22
rosemary:
Oven-Roasted Red Potatoes with
Rosemary and Garlic, 287
Rub, Southern Spice, 325
Rum Cake, 127–28
Rutabagas, 100

S
St. Paddy's Day Corned Beef and Cabbage,
265
salads, 25–26, 34–42, 204, 217–29
Avocado-Chicken, 40–41
Baked Shrimp-Crab, 246–47
Black-Eyed Pea, 39
Blueberry, 221–22
Broccoli, 42
Cherry Tomato and Mushroom, 227–28
Chinese, 219–20
Colo Cucumber, 223
Copper Pennies, 225
Cornucopia, 41
Cranberry, 39
Esther's Dill Coleslaw, 40
Feta Cheese and Tomato, 219
Fettuccine Chicken, 222–23
Fruit Bowl, 226
Fruit Salad with Honey Dressing, 224
Georgia Cracker, 36
Gingersnap Pear, 220
Golda's Frozen Waldorf, 218–19
Hawaiian Chicken, 217
Hot Savannah Chicken Salad Casserole,
270–71
Jamie's Chicken, 35
The Lady's Coleslaw, 37
The Lady's Warm Potato, 38
Marinated Asparagus, 222
Marinated Shrimp and Artichoke Hearts,
228–29
My Mother's Congealed, 224–25
Nancy's Coleslaw, 217
Orange Walnut Salad with Sweet-and-
Sour Dressing, 34–35
Oriental Chicken, 37–38
Pecan Cranberry, 218
Pickled Beets and Eggs, 220
Potato-Egg, 38
Roasted Beet, 42
Salsa Chicken, 199

Southern Shrimp, 36
Spinach, Strawberry, and Hearts of Palm,
221
Strawberry Mold, 162, 226
Strawberry Pretzel, 228
Thanksgiving Apple, 223–24
Warm Apple and Goat Cheese, 227
Watermelon, 347
see also dressings
salmon:
Savory, 48
Stewed, 239
salsa:
Black Bean, 23
Chicken Salad, 199
Mexican Layered Dip, 198–99
Spicy Shrimp and Pasta Casserole, 49–50
sandwiches:
Lucile Wright's Tomato, 364
Mini Handle, xviii–xix
Pickled Okra, 20
Saturday Night Vidalia Onions, 285
sauces, 113, 115–18, 323, 327–31
savory
Aioli, 235
Auntie's Peanut, 329
Berry Steak, 327
Daddy's Tangy Grilling, 115
Dijon Pepper Dippin', 295–96
Easy Hollandaise, 329
Easy Homemade Blender Mayonnaise,
327
Egg and Lemon, 117
Giblet Gravy, 71
Horseradish Cream, 58
Jezebel, 330
The Lady's Barbecue, 116
Lemon Butter for Fish, 118
Lemon Butter for Steak, 118
Lemon Dill, 350
Lemon Hollandaise, 367
Lemon Shrimp Cocktail, 117
Marinara, 236–37
Mushroom, 328
Pasta Puttanesca, 363
Plum, 259–60
Savory Grilled Chicken, 117–18
Spicy Barbecue, 116
Sweet-and-Sour, 326
Tarragon Butter, 328
Tartar, 49

sauces: savory (*cont'd*)
   Wayne's Cranberry, 326
   White, 65, 327
  sweet
   Caramel, 162
   Hot Fudge, 131
   Mocha, 331
   Peanut Butter Chocolate, 331
   Praline, 380
   Raspberry, 330
  see also dressings
Saucy Chicken and Asparagus Bake, 278
sausage(s):
  Almond Rice, 298
  Balls, 13
  Chicken Bog, 274–75
  Confederate Bean Soup, 33
  Fresh Cabbage and Sweet Sausages, 366
  Fried Grits Cakes with, 358
  and Grits, 67
  and Lentil Soup, 31–32
  Low Country Boil, 47
  Piggy Pudding, 67
  with Ravishing Rice, 266
  Rice Casserole, 61
  Ron's Tybee Island Sausage Pie, 268–69
  Savannah Gumbo, 279–80
  Savannah Red Rice, 88
  Sunday Morning Casserole, 253
  Susan's Caldo Soup, 210
  Texas-Style Chili, 268
Savannah Chocolate Cake with Hot Fudge
   Sauce, 130–31
Savannah Crab Cakes, 48–49
Savannah Gumbo, 279–80
Savannah Red Rice, 88
Savannah "Tiramisu," 165
Savory Grilled Chicken Sauce, 117–18
Savory Rice, 93
Savory Salmon, 48
scallop(s):
  Charleston, 50
  Deviled Seafood Casserole, 51
  Grilled Red Pepper, 238
  Shrimp and Scallop Fraîche, 52
scones:
  Currant and Oat, 309–10
  Traditional Raisin, 352
seafood, *see* fish and shellfish
Seasoning, House, 325
Senate Bean Soup, 212

sesame seeds:
  Mrs. Sullivan's Benne Wafers, 350–51
  Sesame Chicken Strips, 14–15
Shaver, Esther, 40
Shaver's Chocolate Pecan Pie, 398
She Crab Soup, 27
shellfish, *see* fish and shellfish
Sherried Avocado Bouillon, 30
Sherry-Glazed Sweet Potatoes, 84
Shore Is Good Seafood Dip, 190
shortcakes:
  Chocolate Strawberry, 129
  Strawberry Cream, 404
Short Ribs, Barbecued, 266–67
shrimp:
  and Artichoke Bake, 56–57
  Baked Shrimp-Crab Salad, 246–47
  Battered Fried, 237–38
  Beaufort Shrimp Pie, 239
  Bel Vedere, 359
  Bisque, 29, 32
  Black Pepper, 47–48
  Butter, 18
  Deviled Seafood Casserole, 51
  Easy Shrimp Bake, 243–44
  Fiery Cajun, 245
  Ginger, 244–45
  Gravy, 237
  and Grits, xvii–xviii
  and Grits with Marinara Sauce, 236–37
  Gumbo Casserole, 54
  The Lady's Bouillabaisse, 240
  Lemon Shrimp Cocktail Sauce, 117
  Low Country Boil, 47
  Marinade, 115–16
  Marinated Shrimp and Artichoke Hearts,
   228–29
  Mold, 193–94
  and Mushroom Casserole, 55
  with Rice, 53
  and Rice Croquettes with Aioli, 235
  and Scallop Fraîche, 52
  Shore Is Good Seafood Dip, 190
  Southern Shrimp Salad, 36
  Spicy Shrimp and Pasta Casserole, 49–50
  Spinach and Shrimp Dip, 188–89
  Tangy Marinated, 195–96
side dishes, 81–100, 281–306
  Asparagus Casserole, 303–4
  Asparagus with Leeks and New Potatoes,
   346–47

Baked Apples, 161–62
Baked Bean Casserole, 356
Baked Grits, 83
Baked Wild Rice, 306
Bo's Eggplant Supreme, 306
Boursin Cheese Potatoes, 91
Broccoli Casserole, 95
Broccoli Soufflé, 90
Cheese Noodles, 299
Cheesy Broccoli Bake, 83
Collard Greens, 88–89
Corn Casserole, 286
Corn Chive Pudding, 301
Cottage Potatoes, 302
Creamed Corn, 97
Crème Fraîche Mashed Potatoes, 296
Crockpot Pinto Beans, 298
Crunchy New Potatoes, 293
Curry-Crusted Bananas, 292–93
Eggplant Casserole, 89
Fancy Green Beans, 283
Fresh Corn Scallop, 94
Fried Green Tomatoes, 91
Fried Green Tomatoes with Dijon Pepper
    Dippin' Sauce, 295–96
Green Bean Casserole, 305
Green Beans with Onions, 341
Green Rice Casserole, 289
Half-Baked Potato, 301
Hash Brown Potato Casserole, 303
Hoppin' John, 98
Italian Potatoes, 300
Jelly Roll's Crab Fried Rice, 286
The Lady's Cheesy Mac, 86
Mashed Potato Bake, 299
Mashed Potatoes, 93
Mashed Potatoes with Sautéed
    Mushrooms, 98
Mixed Vegetable Casserole, 293
Mushroom Rice Casserole, 291
Noodle Casserole, 300
Okra Fritters, 297
Oven-Fried Potato Wedges, 294
Oven-Roasted Red Potatoes with
    Rosemary and Garlic, 287
Pattypan Summer Squash Casserole, 97
Pimento Cheese Tomato Bake, 304
Pineapple Casserole, 98–99
Potato Casserole, 96
Roasted Onions, 304–5
Rutabagas, 100

Saturday Night Vidalia Onions, 285
Sausage-Almond Rice, 298
Savannah Red Rice, 88
Savory Rice, 93
Sherry-Glazed Sweet Potatoes, 84
Snow Peas with Grand Marnier, 294
Southern Baked Beans, 92
Southern-Style Black-Eyed Peas, 284
Spicy Tomato Red Rice, 297
Squash Casserole, 84, 290
Steakside Mushrooms, 86
Susan's Baked Rice, 96
Sweet Potato Bake, 94
Sweet Potato Balls, 290
Sweet Potato Casserole, 283–84
Sweet Potato Chips, 90
Sweet Potato Yams, 288–89
Sweet Stewed Tomatoes, 292
Swiss Broccoli Casserole, 288
Tomato Casserole, 284–85
Tomato Grits, 287–88
Tomato Pie, 95
Turnip Greens with Cornmeal
    Dumplings, 85
Turnips in Dijon Sauce, 289
Turnips Stuffed with Winter Greens,
    345–46
Twice-Baked Potatoes, 87
Vegetable Pancakes, 302
Vidalia Onion Casserole, 291
Vidalia Onion Pie, 89–90
Watermelon Salad, 347
Zucchini and Corn Casserole, 92
Zucchini Custard Bake, 99
see also bread(s)
Skor candy bars:
    Better Than Sex? Yes!, 140
Sliced Nut Cookies, 153–54
Smoked Oyster Cheese Balls, 200
snapper, *see* red snapper
Snickerdoodles, 152
snow pea(s):
    with Grand Marnier, 294
    Oriental Chicken Salad, 37–38
sole:
    Fillet of Sole Paprika, 53
Soufflé, Broccoli, 90
soups, 25, 27–34, 203, 205–17
    Bean and Bacon, 215
    BLT, 213
    Chef Jack's Corn Chowder, 209

soups: (*cont'd*)
Chilled Zucchini, 212
Confederate Bean, 33
Crab Bisque, 211
Cream of Artichoke, 33
Creamy Cheddar, 31
Dian's Black Bean, 207
Homemade Dried Onion Soup Mix, 216–17
The Lady & Sons Beef Vegetable, 205–6
The Lady's Chicken Noodle, 30–31
Lucile Wright's Oyster Bisque, 365
Michele's Chicken Noodle, 208–9
Mushroom Cloud, 213–14
Poblano Chicken Chowder, 206–7
Potato and Ham, 211
Roasted Red Pepper, 28
Sausage and Lentil, 31–32
Senate Bean, 212
She Crab, 27
Sherried Avocado Bouillon, 30
Shrimp Bisque, 29
Shrimp or Lobster Bisque, 32
Strawberry, 353
Susan's Caldo, 210
Taco, 216
Tomato Dill, 34
Vegetable Cheese, 208
Wayne's Award-Winning Maryland Crab, 214–15
see also stews
sour cream:
Almond Sour Cream Cake, xxi–xxii
Butter Biscuits, 316
Caramel Cake, 378
Chicken Breasts in Sour Cream Sauce, 78
Grandmother Paul's Sour Cream Pound Cake, 133
Pastry, 263
Southern Baked Beans, 92
Southern Corn Bread Stuffing, 70–71
Southern Fried Chicken, 68
Southern Pecan Pie, Lisa's, 393
Southern Shrimp Salad, 36
Southern Spice Rub, 325
Southern-Style Black-Eyed Peas, 284
Southern Tea Cakes, 153
South Georgia "Caviar," 194
South of the Border Mason-Dixon Dip, 17
Southwestern Dip, 19–20
Spaghetti, Baked, 260

Spare Ribs, Fried, 256
Sparks, Donna Panoz, 342
spice(s):
Glazed Spice Bars, 413
House Seasoning, 325
Sliced Nut Cookies, 153–54
Southern Spice Rub, 325
Spiced Beef with Dumplin's, 252–53
Spiced Pecans, Georgia, 195
Spicy Barbecue Sauce, 116
Spicy Shrimp and Pasta Casserole, 49–50
Spicy Tomato Red Rice, 297
spinach:
Artichoke and Spinach Dip, 18
Cheese-Stuffed Mushrooms, 14
Chicken Florentine, 277
Orange Walnut Salad with Sweet-and-Sour Dressing, 34–35
Quick Guacamole-Spinach Dip, 21
Shrimp and Artichoke Bake, 56–57
and Shrimp Dip, 188–89
Strawberry, and Hearts of Palm Salad, 221
Veal and Creamed Spinach, 62–63
Spoon Bread, Old-Time, 317
spreads:
Baked Cheese, 187
"Boursin Cheese," 197
Caviar, 196
Egg Caviar Mold, 201
Garlic Cheese, 21
Herbed Cream Cheese Round, 20
Shrimp Butter, 18
Strawberry Cheese Ring, 22
see also dips
squash:
Casserole, 84, 290
Chilled Zucchini Soup, 212
Pattypan Summer Squash Casserole, 97
Praline Pumpkin Pie, 146–47
Pumpkin Bread, 104
Pumpkin Gingerbread Trifle, 401
Thanksgiving Pie, 148
Vegetable Pancakes, 302
Zucchini and Corn Casserole, 92
Zucchini Bread, 103
Zucchini Custard Bake, 99
steak:
Berry Steak Sauce, 327
Bubba's Country-Fried Venison, 250
Diane, 269

and Greens, 65–66
Party Eye-of-Round, 198
Pepper, 60, 261
Perfect Char-Grilled Filet Mignon, 270
Steak au Poivre, 361–62
Swiss, 64
Steakside Mushrooms, 86
Steele, Laura, 352
Stewed Salmon, 239
Stewed Tomatoes, Sweet, 292
stews:
Beef Stew Casserole, 356–57
Chicken Brunswick, 69–70
The Lady & Sons Crab, 210–11
The Lady's Bouillabaisse, 240
The Lady's Pork, 264
Old-Time Beef, 58
Oyster, 28
Texas-Style Chili, 268
White Bean Chili, 29
see also soups
Stone, Molly, xxi
strawberry(ies):
Cheese Ring, 22
Chocolate Strawberry Shortcake, 129
and Cream Pie, 148
Cream Shortcake, 404
English Trifle, 405–6
Fig Preserves, 121
Mold, 162, 226
Pretzel Salad, 228
Punch Bowl Cake, 141
Savory Salmon, 48
Soup, 353
Spinach, Strawberry, and Hearts of Palm
Salad, 221
Stroganoff, Beef, 61–62
Stuffed French Bread, 201
Stuffed Red Peppers, 254–55
Stuffing, Southern Corn Bread, 70–71
sugar:
Brown Sugar Cookies, 411
Cookies, 409–10
Sugar-and-Nut Glazed Brie, 190
Sugared Peanuts, Georgia, 11
Sunday Morning Casserole, 253
Susan's Baked Rice, 96
Susan's Caldo Soup, 210
Swedish Countess Cookies, 412
Sweet-and-Sour Dressing, 35, 118
Sweet-and-Sour Sauce, 326

sweet potato(es):
Bake, 94
Balls, 290
Biscuits, 317
Casserole, 283–84
Chips, 90
Old-Fashioned Sweet Potato Pie, 396–97
Sherry-Glazed, 84
Yams, 288–89
Sweet Stewed Tomatoes, 292
Swiss Broccoli Casserole, 288
Swiss cheese:
Mini Onion Quiches, 13
Swiss Broccoli Casserole, 288
Swiss Steak, 64
Szechuan Chicken with Angelhair Pasta,
279

T
Taco Soup, 216
Tangy Grilling Sauce, Daddy's, 115
Tangy Marinated Shrimp, 195–96
Tarragon Butter, 328
Tartar Sauce, 49
tenderloin:
Bourbon Beef, 57–58
Duxelles-Stuffed, 256–57
Terrine, Mosaic Chicken, 348–49
Terry, Elizabeth, 358
Texas Sheet Cake, 379
Texas-Style Chili, 268
Thanksgiving Apple Salad, 223–24
Thanksgiving Pie, 148
Thumb Print Cookies, 155–56
"Tiramisu," Savannah, 165
tomato(es):
Black Bean Salsa, 23
BLT Soup, 213
Broccoli Salad, 42
Canapés, 191
Casserole, 284–85
Cherry Tomato and Mushroom Salad,
227–28
Dill Soup, 34
Feta Cheese and Tomato Salad, 219
Fried Green, 91
Fried Green Tomatoes with Dijon Pepper
Dippin' Sauce, 295–96
Georgia Cracker Salad, 36
Green Tomato Cake, 374–75
Grits, 287–88

tomato(es): (*cont'd*)
Lucile Wright's Tomato Sandwiches, 364
Marinara Sauce, 236–37
Pasta Puttanesca Sauce, 363
Pie, 95
Pimento Cheese Tomato Bake, 304
Savannah Red Rice, 88
South Georgia "Caviar," 194
Spicy Tomato Red Rice, 297
Sweet Stewed, 292
Taco Soup, 216
Torte, Chocolate, 374
tortillas:
Mexican Chicken, 271
Traditional Raisin Scones, 352
Traub, Herb, and the Pirates' House,
recipes from, 339–41
Green Beans with Onions, 341
Gussie's Fried Chicken with Pecan-
Honey Glaze, 340–41
Ring Tum Ditty, 340
Trey's Baked Grouper Parmigiano, 241
trifles:
Chocolate, 404–5
English, 405–6
Pumpkin Gingerbread, 401
Tuna Burgers, 247
Tunnel of Fudge Cake, 139
turnip greens:
with Cornmeal Dumplings, 85
Green Muffins, 316
turnips:
in Dijon Sauce, 289
Stuffed with Winter Greens, 345–46
Turtle Cheesecake, 390–91
Twice-Baked Potatoes, 87
Tybee Island Sausage Pie, Ron's, 268–69

U

Upside-Down Biscuits, Pineapple, 315
Upside-Down Cake, Double-Dutch
Chocolate Fudge, 376–77

V

veal:
and Creamed Spinach, 62–63
Fried, 251–52
vegetable(s), 81–100, 281–306
Cheese Soup, 208
The Lady & Sons Beef Vegetable Soup,
205–6

Mixed Vegetable Casserole, 293
Pancakes, 302
see also side dishes; *specific vegetables*
Velveeta cheese:
Vegetable Cheese Soup, 208
venison:
Bubba's Country-Fried Venison Steak,
250
Wellington with Oyster Pâté, 261–63
Vidalia onion(s):
Casserole, 291
Pie, 89–90
Roasted, 304–5
Saturday Night, 285
vinaigrettes:
Balsamic, 333
Lime, 332
Roasted Red Pepper, 333
Volcano Cake, 386–87

W

Wafers, Mrs. Sullivan's Benne, 350–51
Waldorf Salad, Golda's Frozen, 218–19
walnut(s):
Aunt Glennis's Blonde Brownies, 159
French Toast Stuffed with Bananas and,
342–43
Fudgie Scotch Ring, 157
Golda's Frozen Waldorf Salad, 218–19
Gorilla Bread, 319
Mississippi Mud Cake, 383
Orange Walnut Salad with Sweet-and-
Sour Dressing, 34–35
Praline Brie with Fruit, 163
Volcano Cake, 386–87
Warm Apple and Goat Cheese Salad, 227
Warm Brie Salad Dressing, 332
Warm Potato Salad, The Lady's, 38
water chestnuts:
Cheesy Broccoli Bake, 83
Chicken and Rice Casserole, 75
Cornucopia Salad, 41
Marinated Shrimp and Artichoke Hearts,
228–29
Mixed Vegetable Casserole, 293
Mushroom-Stuffed Baked Red Snapper,
51–52
Oriental Chicken Salad, 37–38
Salsa Chicken Salad, 199
Snow Peas with Grand Marnier, 294
Watermelon Salad, 347

Wayne's Award-Winning Maryland Crab
    Soup, 214–15
Wayne's Beef Macaroni and Cheese, 263
Wayne's Cranberry Sauce, 326
weights and measures, 417
White Bean Chili, 29
White Sauce, 65, 327
wild rice:
    Baked, 306
    Chicken and Rice Casserole, 75
    Chicken and Wild Rice Casserole, 280
    and Oyster Casserole, 242
    Sausage-Rice Casserole, 61
    Shrimp with Rice, 53
Wilkes, Mrs. Sema, 355
wine:
    Burgundy Beef Roast, 60–61
    Chicken in Wine Sauce, 72
    Duck Burgundy, 78–79
    Port Wine Jelly, 121
    Quail with Marsala Sauce, 272–73

Sherried Avocado Bouillon, 30
Sherry-Glazed Sweet Potatoes, 84
Wontons, Collard Green, xix
Wright, Lucile, recipes from, 364–65
    Lucile Wright's Oyster Bisque, 365
    Lucile Wright's Tomato Sandwiches, 364

Y
Yams, Sweet Potato, 288–89
Yeast Rolls, Easy, 311
yellow squash:
    Squash Casserole, 290

Z
Zesty Cheese Straws, 200–201
zucchini:
    Bread, 103
    Chilled Zucchini Soup, 212
    and Corn Casserole, 92
    Custard Bake, 99
    Vegetable Pancakes, 302

PAULA H. DEEN was born and raised in Albany, Georgia. She later moved to Savannah, where she and her two sons, Bobby and Jamie, started the Bag Lady catering company. The business took off and evolved into The Lady & Sons Restaurant, which is located in Savannah's historic district and specializes in Southern cooking. Paula is the host of Food Network's *Paula's Home Cooking* and is a regular guest on QVC, where her cookbooks are one of the network's biggest sellers. Her recent books include *The Lady & Sons Just Desserts* and *Paula Deen & Friends*.

ABOUT THE TYPE

This book was set in Galliard, a typeface designed by Matthew Carter for the Merganthaler Linotype Company in 1978. Galliard is based on the sixteenth-century typefaces of Robert Granjon.